Development Strategies, Identities, and Conflict in Asia

POLITICS, ECONOMICS, AND INCLUSIVE DEVELOPMENT

Series Editors
William Ascher, Claremont McKenna College
John M. Heffron, Soka University of America
Natalia Mirovitskaya, Duke University

The *Politics, Economics, and Inclusive Development* series examines the challenges and progress in promoting humanistic development. The complex tasks of simultaneously pursuing economic growth, broad participation and equity, democratic peace, and sustainability require scholarship that merges in-depth analysis of the many factors that influence development outcomes with contextually rich experiences. The single- or multiauthored monographs use an interdisciplinary methodology to explore diverse experiences of individual nations, world regions, or the entire global system in their quest for more democratic, technically sound, and sustainable development. The publications from the *Politics, Economics, and Inclusive Development* series will be valuable to students, scholars, policymakers, and international development practitioners.

Economic Development Strategies and the Evolution of Violence in Latin America
    Edited by William Ascher and Natalia Mirovitskaya

Development Strategies, Identities, and Conflict in Asia
    Edited by William Ascher and Natalia Mirovitskaya

Development Strategies, Identities, and Conflict in Asia

Edited by
William Ascher and Natalia Mirovitskaya

Prepared under the auspices of the
Pacific Basin Research Center.
Soka University of America

First published in 2013 by
PALGRAVE MACMILLAN®
in the United States—a division of St. Martin's Press LLC,
175 Fifth Avenue, New York, NY 10010.

Where this book is distributed in the UK, Europe and the rest of the world ,
this is by Palgrave Macmillan, a division of Macmillan Publishers Limited,
registered in England, company number 785998, of Houndmills,
Basingstoke, Hampshire RG21 6XS.

Palgrave Macmillan is the global academic imprint of the above companies
and has companies and representatives throughout the world.

Palgrave® and Macmillan® are registered trademarks in the United States,
the United Kingdom, Europe and other countries.

ISBN: 978–1–137–33175–5

Library of Congress Cataloging-in-Publication Data

Development strategies, identities, and conflict in Asia / edited by
William Ascher and Natalia S. Mirovitskaya.
       pages cm.—(Politics, economics, and inclusive development)
    "Prepared under the auspices of the Pacific Basin Research Center,
Soka University of America."
    Includes bibliographical references and index.
    ISBN 978–1–137–33175–5 (hardback)
    1. Asia—Economic policy. 2. Economic development—Asia.
3. Violence—Economic aspects—Asia. 4. Ethnic conflict—Economic
aspects—Asia. 5. Social conflict—Economic aspects—Asia. I. Ascher,
William, editor of compilation. II. Mirovitskaia, N. S. (Nataliia Sergeevna),
editor of compilation.

HC412.D475 2013
338.95—dc23   2012049570

A catalogue record of the book is available from the British Library.

Design by Newgen Imaging Systems (P) Ltd., Chennai, India.

First edition: June 2013

10 9 8 7 6 5 4 3 2 1

To the memory of Sheila Ascher Glassman, mother, and compassionate teacher of thousands of needy students—WA

With gratitude to Gail Osherenko and Oran Young, who in the winter of 1989 came to my office in Moscow and changed my world—NM

Contents

Illustrations

Figures

Tables

Preface and Acknowledgments

This is the second volume to come out of our multicountry research project on Economic Development Strategies to Avert Collective Violence, begun in 2009 under the auspices of the Pacific Basin Research Center of Soka University of America. The goal of the project is to determine which development strategies and specific policies create conditions that reduce the likelihood of intergroup violence. To accomplish this, we have commissioned country case studies by experts on development and conflict in Africa, Asia, and Latin America. The first volume, *Economic Development Strategies and the Evolution of Violence in Latin America*, was published by Palgrave Macmillan in 2012. The present volume, with Asian country case studies and overview chapters covering the broad range of Asian subregions, also intends to outline considerations that can guide policymakers, development practitioners, and civil society leaders in conflict-sensitive development.

The project's focus on development strategies should not be taken as a reductive effort to account for violence or peace solely on governmental development efforts. In any country, development efforts are embedded within a much more complicated matrix of social and political conditions, and levels of confrontation and violence reflect these conditions as well as external shocks ranging from natural disasters to global economic distress. Rather, our focus on development efforts simply reflects the fact that governments, if aware of the risks and opportunities that broad strategies and specific policies hold for intergroup violence, have the potential to introduce *conflict-sensitive* development initiatives, which would proactively contribute to reducing violence and strengthening postconflict rehabilitation and reconstruction. Little can be done about the fact that Hindus and Muslims have a bitter history of conflict, or that Kurds in Turkey and Tajiks in Uzbekistan speak differently than the rest of the population languages. Yet governments can select projects that are less likely to set one group against another, they can facilitate new economic roles that undermine negative stereotypes of conflicting groups and enhance societal cohesion, and they can "expand the pie" to provide various stakeholders with incentives for intergroup reconciliation and cooperation.

The focus on development strategies is not restricted to narrowly economic aspects. When a government allocates a portion of the national budget to education, the "development implications" encompass issues ranging from the balance of spending on primary, secondary, and higher education—with drastic consequences for the distribution of income if underfunded primary education leaves a portion of the population without needed skills—to the languages of instruction. When a development strategy emphasizes a massive program of regional development, population movements into the targeted areas may have profound impacts on intergroup relations. Delivery of such basic services as health, social protection, and infrastructure can improve state-society and intergroup relations; yet poor design and implementation may exacerbate societal fragility and intergroup discord.

Earlier versions of contributions to this volume were presented at workshops at Soka University of America (May 2010 and November 2011) and at Duke University (October 2010). We are grateful for insights and comments from all the participants of these workshops. We again wish to express our gratitude to Soka University of America for financial and administrative support, and for the fine work of Dr. John M. Heffron, Professor of History at Soka and Associate Director of the PBRC, ably assisted by Jason Tran, Jacqueline Mills, and Dawn Minette, in organizing workshops and overseeing the administration required to put together a collected volume such as this. We also appreciate the efforts of the Duke Center for International Development, especially those of Jonathan Abels, for arranging talks and workshop sessions that contributed to shaping the chapters in this volume. Valuable research assistance was provided by Claremont McKenna College students—Heather Beck, Nathan Bengtsson, Molly Doyle, Jennifer Good, Isabel Harbaugh, Shanna Hoversten, Sofia Jamal, Daniel Maxwell, Catherine Raney, Nicholas Rowe, Carlton Rueb, Laura Spann, and Jennifer Zavaleta, as well as Ariana Ascher and Kaitlyn Tsai.

At various stages of this project, the editors received helpful suggestions and insightful comments from David Chick, Ekhson Holmuhamedov, Srinivas Katikithala, Maureen Lempke, Michael Lofchie, Raisa Anatolievna Mirovitskaya, Aseema Sinha, and Jenny Taw. We would also like to acknowledge the highly efficient assistance provided to us by Sara Doskow at Palgrave Macmillan.

Contributors

Ananthi Al Ramiah is an assistant professor of social sciences at Yale-NUS College in Singapore. With a doctorate in psychology from Oxford University, her research focuses on the social psychology of intergroup contact and intergroup conflict, and the psychological impact of affirmative action policies on beneficiaries and nonbeneficiaries.

Mikhail Alexseev is a professor of political science at San Diego State University. His research focuses on migration, ethnopolitical conflict, and post-Soviet Russia. He is the principal investigator of an international research project on migration and ethnoreligious violence in the Russian Federation.

Lorraine V. Aragon is a professor of anthropology at the University of North Carolina at Chapel Hill. A cultural anthropologist with interests in state institutions related to intergroup relations, cultural expression, and law, her research focuses on religious and ethnic differences in Southeast Asia, especially in Indonesia.

William Ascher is the Donald C. McKenna Professor of Government and Economics at Claremont McKenna College, and serves as the director of the Pacific Basin Research Center at Soka University of America. His research is on political economy of developing countries.

G. Shabbir Cheema is Director, Asia Pacific Governance and Democracy Initiative, and Senior Fellow at the East-West Center, Honolulu, Hawaii. He served as the Director of the Governance Division of the UN Development Programme and Program Director of the UN Department of Economic and Social Affairs. His research focuses on governance reform and democracy in Asia and the Pacific.

Ebru Erdem-Akcay is a professor in the Political Science Department at the University of California, Riverside. Her research focuses on identity politics (ethnic, religious, and gender identities), conflict, and politics of Muslim societies, particularly in Central Asia and Turkey.

Edward M. Feasel is Professor of Economics at Soka University of America, where he also serves as Dean of the Faculty. His research focuses on economic outcomes and societal values, regional economic issues, economic growth, and effects of monetary and fiscal policy. In addition to research on the United States, he has examined growth patterns in Northeast and Southeast Asia.

Sumit Ganguly holds the Rabindranath Tagore Chair in Indian Cultures and Civilizations, and is a Professor of Political Science at Indiana University in Bloomington, where he also serves as Director of the Center on American and Global Security. His research focuses on the domestic politics of South Asian nations and South Asian international security.

Natalia Mirovitskaya is a Senior Researcher and Lecturing Fellow, Duke Center for International Development. She has published extensively on sustainable development, environmental security, and peace-building. She has led and participated in numerous national and international research projects and has taught in several countries.

Jennifer Oetken is a visiting faculty member at the George Washington University, as she completes her doctorate in political science at Indiana University on insurgency in India. Previously she served as deputy director of the South Asia Program at the Carnegie Endowment. Her research focuses on insurgency, internal security, and South Asia.

Thillainathan Ramasamy is an adjunct professor of the Department of Economics at the University of Malaya. With a doctorate in economics from the London School of Economics, he has served in both government and private sector roles in economic policy, corporate leadership, and banking. His research interests range from domestic economic development to global financial reform.

CHAPTER 1

War, Peace, and Many Shades in Between: Asia in the New Millennium

William Ascher and Natalia Mirovitskaya

"Asia is rich in people, rich in culture and rich in resources. It is also rich in trouble."[1]

The cradle of world's oldest civilizations and major religions, Asia has seen and is still experiencing all variations and consequences of armed violence[2]—from the devastation of international and civil wars, to brutal repressions by militarized regimes; from long-lasting insurgencies and separatist struggles, to explosions of religious and communal violence and terrorism. Its extreme diversity and rich dynamics of economic and political development make Asia a perfect setting to explore the multiple pathways that connect economic development to intergroup relations. This chapter sets the stage for this inquiry. It begins with a brief summary of the current status, major trends, and evolving nature of intergroup violence in the region. We also identify major challenges for conflict-sensitive development and some new threats that may undermine human security in the region. We conclude the chapter by introducing the case studies selected for this volume and their major findings. The next chapter presents an assessment of the variety and evolution of development strategies as they were designed and implemented within different countries.

The Research Project

The main focus of the research project is on the multiple linkages between government choices—development strategies and policies and the institutional changes to promote such strategies—and the likelihood of intergroup violence or cooperation. Understanding constructive and destructive pathways is essential for designing conflict-sensitive development approaches. The pathways linking economic strategies and policies to the likelihood of violence are located within four broad dimensions: *predispositions, opportunities, incitement*, and *deterrence*. We assume that violence is more likely if people are primed (predisposed) for hostility against other group(s) or the state, which may favor such other group(s), or at least be perceived as allied with them. The concrete opportunity to engage in hostilities and remain in confrontation will determine the likelihood that predispositions will ignite overt outbreaks of violence (riots, pogroms, or rebellion,) or sustain its perpetuation (insurgency, civil war). Thus violence strongly depends upon political, economic, and social opportunities of potentially conflicting groups, as well as on the degree of their radicalization, organization, and acceptance of violence as legitimate or necessary behavior. Triggering events, including leaders' actions, incite overt intergroup violence (and may contribute to escalation), *unless* specific deterrence mechanisms override these other factors.

Development initiatives may affect these mechanisms via various pathways—from the initial stage when development initiatives are considered, to the selection of particular combinations of policies and institutional changes, to implementation and subsequent impacts on groups' economic roles, resources, and relative power, as interpreted by various actors. Asian development experiences provide ample opportunities to explore these connections.

Can Asian policymakers find development strategies that minimize violence while still overseeing healthy economic improvement? Some Asian nations have been surprisingly peaceful—in contrast with earlier predictions—while still progressing impressively in economic terms: Malaysia, following an anti-Chinese massacre in 1969; South Korea, as it successfully transitioned to democracy. The relative peace of economically advanced countries—Japan, Taiwan, Hong Kong, Singapore—gives more hope. However, other nations, earlier thought to be promising in terms of peaceful growth, have foundered badly in both respects; Sri Lanka is probably the most extreme case. While economic structures and development strategies are certainly not the exclusive drivers of peace and prosperity, they are often prominent factors alongside of domestic political and social causes and international interactions. The cases presented in this volume demonstrate that economic policy initiatives often antagonize groups against the government, and against other groups seen as allied with the government. In other cases, the policies, or their consequences, have threatened particular groups to the point that their members became desperate enough, or simply angry enough, to initiate aggressive actions. Some policies put groups into confrontation, such as competition over property rights. In other cases, modernization policies that reconfigured group economic roles have reinforced negative stereotypes (i.e., perceptions of exploitative Chinese agricultural merchants in Indonesia or Sinhalese businessmen in Sri Lanka). Other initiatives bring people from different ethnic and religious groups into close proximity, magnifying the likelihood of clashes. Yet other policies propel individuals into the role of violence provocateurs, by denying them better opportunities or exposing them to radicalized education.

A broad review of Asia's conflicts reveals illuminating surprises. First, East Asia[3] has thus far reversed the patterns of large-scale violence that plagued the region prior to the 1980s. Tønnesson (2009, 111), referring to both international and intrastate conflict, observes that "since 1979, East Asia has been surprisingly peaceful." The Human Security Report (2011, 45) judges that in terms of violence, "over the past three decades, East Asia has undergone an extraordinary transformation. From 1946 to the end of the 1970s, it was the most war-wracked region in the world."

Second, despite fears of imminent carnage, the several million Russians remaining in the former Soviet republics of Central Asia (Kazakhstan, Kyrgyzstan, Tajikistan, Turkmenistan, and Uzbekistan)[4], have suffered remarkably little violence by the majority populations. However, violence toward other Asian and North Caucasian minority groups in all five republics has sometimes been acute, while Central Asian and North Caucasian migrants remain targets of extreme xenophobia and racial violence in Russia. Meantime, in Russia's North Caucasus regions, anti-Russian violence against both government forces and civilians has been persistently high, as Mikhail Alexseev's contribution to this volume demonstrates.

Third, in East and South Asia the most explosive current conflicts do not reflect the resentment against governments for *neglecting* the least developed areas within countries, but rather they reflect the clashes that emerge from efforts to *develop* those areas.[5] This important motif demonstrates the convergence of resettlement, natural resource, and regional development strategies.

Fourth, although it is plausible that poverty would engender resentment and increase the desperation in struggles for wealth, in some of the poorest Asian countries violence has been more likely in wealthier areas.[6] It is unclear whether this reflects urbanization that shifts poverty and resentment to cities, whether wealthier areas bring potentially antagonistic groups into proximity, or the capacity to mobilize violence is greater in wealthier areas.

Fifth, the liberalization reforms that brought acute disruption all over Latin America and in many African countries have generally been enacted with far less turmoil in Asia. Much of Asia's general success in economic growth is owed to the elimination of inefficient state interventions.

Sixth, despite the widespread preference of elites for education and health care that benefit their own strata (through budgetary emphasis on higher education and curative medicine), several East Asian nations have had extraordinary success in educating children from low-income families and improving the population's overall health status. Japan, South Korea, Taiwan, Singapore, and Malaysia owe much of their economic productivity and societal stability to social-service investments targeting the poor, and to increasing economic mobility.

These counterintuitive patterns demonstrate the need to get past the conventional wisdom and unexamined assumptions about the links between economic development strategies and intergroup conflict.

The Scope and Location of Violence in Asia

Assessing violence trends is fraught with underreporting, inconsistent definitions, and deliberate manipulation by official or unofficial information sources. Various databases present conflicting evidence.[7] Some sources indicate that although violence patterns have changed substantially through the past decades, the region in general is still one of the world's most conflict-prone. In 2011, out of 388 conflicts observed globally and judged as warranting inclusion in the Heidelberg Institute for International Conflict Research dataset (2012), nearly a third occurred in Asia and Oceania.[8] In addition to wars in Iraq, Afghanistan, and Pakistan, and violence in the context of the Arab Spring, the intensity of internal violence increased in 2011 in Turkey, Iran, Thailand, Cambodia, and Myanmar.

One approach to assess broad violence patterns is to use World Health Organization (WHO) data on deaths from intentional injuries and war, compiled from government figures.[9] For the first decade of the new millennium, WHO has figures for 2002, 2004, and 2008, displayed in Table 1.1.

Apart from the countries engaged in international wars (Afghanistan and Iraq) and straightforward civil wars (Nepal and Sri Lanka), most countries have quite similar figures for the three years, lending confidence in the results, although this does not address underreporting across different countries. For example, the 2008 recorded rate for Indonesia is 10.2 deaths per 100,000 people from intentional injury and war (World Health Organization

Table 1.1 Violence Rates in Asia, 2002, 2004, 2008

	2002	2004	2008	Avg.
Arab Asia				
Bahrain	1.1	1.2	0	1.5
Iraq	10.5	210	160.5	200.5
Jordan	3.0	7	6.8	8.9
Kuwait	2.5	1.4	1.1	2.9
Lebanon	8.3	7.9	9.2	13.9
Oman	2.1	2.1	2.1	3.5
Qatar	1.1	1	0.6	1.6
Saudi Arabia	3.0	3.9	2.8	5.5
Syria	2.7	2.6	2.4	4.3
UAE	1.0	0.5	0.5	1.1
Yemen	2.2	4.9	9.9	8.0
Average				22.9
w/o Iraq				5.1
Central Asia-FSU				
Kazakhstan	19.7	16.2	17.4	29.7
Kyrgyzstan	8.9	8.6	6.7	13.9
Tajikistan	15.8	3.5	0.1	12.9
Turkmenistan	10.2	8.8	11.5	16.5
Uzbekistan	3.8	3.7	3.5	6.2
Average				15.8

	2002	2004	2008	Avg.
East Asia-South				
Brunei	1.4	1.1	0.2	1.7
Cambodia	18.2	19.4	20.9	32.1
Indonesia	13.3	10.2	8.5	18.5
Laos	6.7	6.5	4.5	10.3
Malaysia	8.7	9.4	2.2	12.8
Myanmar	25.5	25	10.8	37.3
Papua New Guinea	15.6	15.2	13	24.9
Philippines	24.6	23.3	22.2	39.3
Singapore	0.8	1.3	0.8	1.7
Thailand	10.4	8	11.2	16.0
Viet Nam	4.2	3.8	1.5	5.9
Average				18.2
South Asia				
Bangladesh	7.6	7.9	7.7	12.9
Bhutan	4.4	4.3	4	7.1
India	6.0	6	4.9	9.6
Nepal	19.8	34.5	8.9	39.2
Pakistan	7.0	6.9	10.2	12.7
Sri Lanka	12.9	12	167.9	72.6
Average				25.7
w/o Sri Lanka				16.3
w/o Nepal & Sri Lanka				10.6

Continued

Table 1.1 Continued

	2002	2004	2008	Avg.		2002	2004	2008	Avg.
East Asia-North					**West Asia**				
China	3.0	2.1	1.6	3.9	Afghanistan	29.7	9.9	54.3	44.5
Japan	0.6	0.5	0.5	0.9	Armenia	3.8	3.3	4.4	6.2
N. Korea	19.5	19.2	15.4	30.9	Azerbaijan	3.0	2.9	1.8	4.5
Mongolia	3.5	3.2	3.9	5.8	Georgia	4.7	4.7	15.8	11.5
S. Korea	2.0	2.3	2.2	3.6	Iran	3.9	2.5	1.4	4.7
Average				9.0	Israel	7.4	6.5	5.8	11.2
					Turkey	3.6	2.9	3.8	5.6
					Average				12.6
					w/o Afghanistan				7.3

Source: World Health Organization, *Global Burden of Disease 2008.*

2009). Yet Varshney (2010, 6), reviewing more intensive analyses of riots, pogroms, and lynchings, argues that "the scale of ethnocommunal violence in Indonesia does appear to be enormous." The underreporting often occurs in rural areas where state presence is low. A World Bank (2010, 1) assessment of Indonesian violence in just six provinces concluded that

> high levels of routine violent conflict...have resulted in 2,000 violent conflict incidents on average per year since 2006, in areas accounting for only 4 percent of Indonesia's population. During 2006–2008, these conflicts led to over 600 deaths, 6,000 injuries, and the destruction of more than 1,900 buildings.

Individual country rates can be supplemented by comparisons provided by the Geneva Declaration Secretariat. These subregional rates demonstrate that despite the reputation of all Asian subregions for notoriously violent cases—Iraq in Arab Asia, Chechnya within the Russian Federation, Cambodia and Vietnam in East Asia, Sri Lanka in South Asia, and Afghanistan in Western Asia—the levels of *recorded* fatalities in the first decade of the 2000s were relatively low compared to the developing regions of Africa and Latin America. For the 2004–2009 period, Central America's fatalities (29 deaths from violence per 100,000 population), Southern Africa (27), the Caribbean (22.5), Middle Africa (19), and South America (18) were far higher than in South Asia (10), West Asia (7.5), Central Asia (6.5), Northeast Asia (5.5), and Southeast Asia (4). Only West Africa (9) was lower than the highest Asian subregion.[10]

However, peace in many parts of Asia is fragile. Conflicts may remain dormant for years and suddenly flare-up (e.g., the 2012 Armenian-Azerbaijan clash over Nagorno-Karabakh); they may be chronic and deteriorating over a long period, or erupt in unexpected ways. Many Asian conflicts have been protracted and although as of 2012 most are of low intensity and are localized in specific geographical areas (e.g., Mindanao in the Philippines), some are spreading (e.g., Pakistan). After a respite from violence in the first decade of this century, major violence flared in the Ferghana Valley, as more than 400 people were killed in Kyrgyz-Uzbek riots in southern Kyrgyzstan, and roughly 100,000 Uzbek residents fled to Uzbekistan. According to the International Crisis Group (2012b), the ultranationalist Kyrgyz government leaders in southern Kyrgyzstan have been provoking anti-Uzbek sentiment for both political and economic objectives:

> Uzbeks are subject to illegal detentions and abuse by security forces and have been forced out of public life ... Uzbeks are increasingly withdrawing

into themselves. They say they are marginalised by the Kyrgyz majority, forced out of public life and the professions; most Uzbek-language
media have been closed; and prominent nationalists often refer to them
as a diaspora, emphasising their separate and subordinate status . . . While
Uzbeks are far from embracing violence and have no acknowledged leaders, their conversations are turning to retribution, or failing that a final
lashing out at their perceived oppressors.

According to Kyrgyzstan's acting president, the violence was far worse,
with nearly 2,000 people killed (Harding 2010). If true, the death rate from
that episode alone would account for a rate of 36 fatalities per 100,000.

The new decade has also seen violence associated with the "Arab Spring,"
leading to major casualties in both Arab Asian and North African nations.
North African conflicts were mercifully short, but the Syrian conflict,
already spilling over into Lebanon, promises to be long and extremely
bloody. The confrontation in Bahrain remains unresolved; in Kuwait, one
hundred thousand stateless people ("Bidun"), including many in the military, have begun to agitate for more rights.

The Nature of Violence in Asia

The *nature* of Asian violence is broadly distinctive in four respects: (1) confrontations based on religious divisions have been far more violent, leading to both extremist movements and communal riots; (2) conflicts remain
more acutely ideological than in other regions; (3) clan and tribal distinctions are also potent bases for intergroup violence; and (4) nativist reactions
against the arrival of outsiders into rural areas have led to chronic violence,
sometimes escalating into insurrections.

Sectarian Conflict

Sectarian violence has been widespread. In South Asia, Hindu-Muslim violence still erupts periodically; in Sri Lanka, Sinhalese Buddhism and Tamil
Hinduism reinforce the ethnic differences. Muslim-Christian violence
(especially on Indonesia's Outer Islands) is endemic. In the Asian Middle
East, highly publicized state and communal violence pits Sunni against
Shia. Islam, far from being a unifying force, long ago fractured into highly
antagonistic sects. Several Arab governments are dominated by minority sects: Syria's Alawite regime and Bahrain's Sunni regime demonstrate
how the risk of a minority losing control increases its desperation to cling
to power. Economic discrimination against majorities has led to protests

frequently met with strong repression, igniting a cycle of bombings, assassinations, and further repression. Other Middle Eastern conflicts entail repression of Baha'is (in Iran especially) and clashes between Muslims and Yazidis (especially in Iraq). As many as a third of Turkey's Kurds are adherents of Yazdânism—a relevant factor in the Kurdish desire for independence. In Southeast Asia, religious antagonism continues to play a major role in Muslim separatist movements in predominantly Christian Philippines and Buddhist Thailand.

The Persistence of Ideological Polarization

More than other world regions, Asia is still riven by sharp ideological conflicts. North Korea's Communist regime and extreme leftist movements (e.g., Maoists in Nepal and India) contrast sharply with the withering of extreme Latin American leftist and rightist movements of the 1960s and 1970s. The more pervasive ideological polarization in Asia involves the clashes of radical Islam against secularism, other religions, or sects. This is clearly more ideologically based than the conventional sectarian conflicts that reflect the confluence of religious and ethnic identifications.

Clan and Tribal Divisions

However, religious or ideological differences are not the only bases of intergroup conflict. Clan or tribal rivalries are particularly important in the Middle East, Central Asia, and the Caucasus. In some monarchic countries, such as Bahrain, Kuwait, Oman, and the Emirates, clans constitute the "ruling families," based on lineage rather than religion or other externally discernible differences. This leaves other clans with the incentive either to contest rule or to struggle against other clans for resources or government favor. Glinkina and Rosenberg (2003, 517)—writing before the recent Kyrgyz-Uzbek conflict—noted that "ethnic-confessional nationalism is not currently the dominant form of social political identification in the region, but rather narrower sub-ethnic relational identity groups, which may unite for a common purpose or may compete for resources in a set of complex interactions."

Nativist Reactions to Incursions

Violence in Asia has been characterized by a greater incidence of so-called sons of the soil conflicts, in which rural residents react against incursions by outsiders. Fearon and Laitin (2011, 201) calculate that 41 percent of post-WWII Asian civil wars arise out of such clashes, particularly in economically backward areas. This greatly exceeds the 15 percent world average—only Eastern Europe comes close at 38.5 percent, with Latin America at 0, North Africa and the Middle East at 9.5 percent, and sub-Saharan Africa at 11 percent.

The Perhaps Surprisingly Low Levels of Intergroup Violence

Although intergroup violence has been distressingly high in some Asian countries, some cases are illuminating because of rather surprisingly *low* levels of violence along certain dimensions.

First, East Asia has experienced a marked decline in *organized* large-scale armed conflict since 1979 (Svensson and Lindgren 2011). For Northeast Asia, democratic Japan and South Korea have enjoyed the absence of insurgencies. The high level of repression and militarization in North Korea has presumably stifled antigovernment conflict. In China, although an unknown level of violence is occurring over property confiscations, and sporadic clashes erupt between Muslim Uighurs and Hans moving into western China, the Chinese government has faced very little organized disturbance.[11]

Southeast Asia, among the world's most violent subregions through the 1970s, has experienced a remarkable decline in organized violence. Simon Frasier University's Human Security Report (2009/2010, 45) argues that "in explaining the reduction in the number of civil conflicts in Southeast Asia, we cite both the ending of Chinese support for the communist insurgencies in the subregion and the security implications of the unparalleled period of economic growth the region has experienced since the 1950s."[12] Unarmed protests, sometimes leading to looting and burning, have become the modal form of reactions against government actions and policies in East Asia. Yet the potential for large-scale organized violence remains fairly high in the Philippines if clashes that pit the Muslims on Mindanao against the government and the now-majority Christian settlers re-escalate. The risk of large-scale organized violence is also substantial in Thailand, from the southern Malay-Muslims or from the poorer north if the military again ousts a pro-north populist government.

Comparatively Low Levels of Gang and Other Criminal Violence

In general, Asian countries have markedly less gang and other criminal violence[13] than either Latin America or Africa. The Asian homicide rate, perhaps the best (though still imperfect) indicator of such violence, at 3.1 per 100,000 in the mid-2000s, was far lower than those of other regions.[14] This pattern continues into this decade. The *Global Homicide Report 2011* noted "that the [2010] homicide rate in Africa and the Americas (at 17 and 16 per 100,000 population, respectively) is more than double the global average (6.9 per 100,000), whereas in Asia, Europe and Oceania (between 3 and 4 per 100,000) it is roughly half" (UN Office on Drugs and Crime 2011, 9).

However, the relatively low aggregate violence levels masks vigilantism in rural, and even some urban, areas of South and Southeast Asia. Welsh (2008; 2009) documents rampant extrajudicial lynchings in rural Indonesia; vigilantism is also prevalent in both rural and urban Mindanao in the Philippines (Schiavo-Campo and Judd 2005, 6; Alston 2009). Sundar (2010, 113) notes that in 2008, just as India's president and Supreme Court chief justice were exchanging accusations of responsibility for the rise in "mob justice," the home minister asserted that "people should take steps for self protection."

The more benign interpretation for vigilantism is that the state's presence is inadequate to administer justice. Eilenberg (2011, 238) asserts: "vigilantism...refers to the taking of or advocating the taking of the law into one's own hands...in the face of the apparent failure of state authorities to deal effectively with criminal matters." Yet this may be a pretext to assault members of other groups, and vigilantism reflects a quite different state failure. Referring to largely rural Indonesia, Welsh (2008, 474) argues: "The evidence suggests that the main factor contributing to increased levels of violence was the implementation of the decentralization policy of 1999. When the policy took effect, there were sharp spikes in local mobbing, due in part to the power vacuum in law enforcement/local bureaucratic institutions as well as the opportunity to carry out revenge." Welsh (2008, 484) also found that "mobbing" reflected conflicts over water rights:

> For example, in Karangasem in northeastern Bali, there are four villages that have high concentrations of keroyokan [mob beatings] over the ten-year period 1995–2004. In total, 122 people were killed through keroyokan in eighty-four incidents. The overwhelming majority of these cases (94 percent) involved local custom and contestation between villages over water rights, leading to a cycle of revenge between villages. Interviews in these villages reveal that leaders did not oppose the practice of keroyokan, and in fact encouraged the practice.

Similarly, Louis (2007) argues that in India's Bihar state the practice of lynching is a mechanism of maintaining the dominance of higher-caste communities over the *dalits* (untouchables). Senechal de la Roche (1996, 114) makes the same point for South Asia in general.

The comparatively low level of street violence may also reflect relatively low levels of urbanization—which has been accelerating in the last decade. Observers from countries as diverse as India, Pakistan, China, Vietnam, and Cambodia report that rapid and poorly managed urbanization has contributed to the increase of urban crime and drug-related violence (Asian Development Bank 2007). Sahni (2012, 13) reports that urban settlements in India are increasingly characterized by ghettoization and "concentration of poverty and de-concentration of opportunity," giving rise to escalating crime and urban terrorism.

Lack of Violence between Russian and Native Populations in Central Asia

Aside from the flare-up of violence against Russians in Tajikistan in the immediate aftermath of the break up of the Soviet Union (Shogren 1990), the predictions of *chronic* violence between "Westerners"—especially Russians—and the majority populations did not materialize, despite the resentments periodically expressed by local nationalist media against prior "Russification" and the initially superior economic and educational status of the Westerners. One might expect political mobilization of the Russian population upon change to its less advantaged status in the Central Asian republics. In similar situations of displaced groups—overturned, pushed aside, and humiliated by others who earlier regarded them as inferior—especially sharp resentment is often observed (Williams 2003, 138). However, few Russians have contested their declining status through political action; instead, by 2003 roughly 4 million had emigrated,[15] out of fear of conflict and apprehensions about repressive political systems; discomfort of living as a minority; poor job opportunities due to general decline of the economies; poor mastery of indigenous languages as governments root out Russian in official and educational interactions; or direct discrimination (Radnitz 2006). Policy discrimination against Russians may have served as the outlet for resentment against them by the non-Russian populations, without a need for physical aggression. Yet another explanation is that people officially labeled as "Russians" remaining in the Central Asian republics stayed largely out of politics and found economic niches (i.e., "ethnic businesses"). Most importantly, the very possibility of anti-Russian violence was prevented by large-scale labor migration of Kyrgyz, Tajiks, and Uzbeks to more prosperous and economically dynamic Russia. Economic pragmatism trumped nationalism as Central Asian governments saw the need to restrain anti-Russian actions. Russians remaining in Central Asia are certainly in an economically precarious situation. Peyrouse (2008, 5–6) notes that they "find themselves in a paradoxical position: a discriminated minority seeking to profit from a new rapprochement with Russia in which they are neither principal actors nor principal beneficiaries"). The Russian government has also made sure that "power" agencies of the former Soviet republics have been involved in training, joint exercises, and other collaborations with Russian agencies that have built informal relationships between Russian and Central Asian law enforcement bodies—an efficient mechanism for preventing anti-Russian violence. With the Russians leaving rather than actively protesting, and Central Asian labor migrants serving as "hostages" in Russia, the conflicts in Central Asia have emerged along other dimensions, pitting groups of Central Asian origin against one another. Thus conflicts in Kyrgyzstan, resulting in the overthrow of repressive presidents in 2005 and 2010, were based on factions and clan rivalries among the Kyrgyz (Temirkulov 2010); between ethnic Kyrgyz and Uzbeks in 2011 and 2012; and in Tajikistan in 2012 between the Pamiris and the central government.

Another particular Asian feature is the existence of non-warring groups and systems within otherwise conflict-prone countries: societies that have long avoided internal violence and external warfare. The anthropological literature[16] provides examples of non-warring societies, including several groups populating cross-border regions within South Indian states; the Buid living in the Mindoro Island highlands in the Philippines; and the Semai, Chewong, and Batek of Malaysia (Fry, Bonta, and Baszarkiewicz 2009; Dentan 2004; Fry 2012). Most of these groups are comparatively egalitarian tribes or nomadic bands, differing in social organization from more hierarchical and more aggressive neighboring groups (Fry 2012). Many of these groups are united in "peace systems"—sets of neighboring societies maintaining peaceful relations among themselves and often with outsiders as well, such as Central Peninsular Orang Asli societies of Malaysia (Fry 2006; Fry 2012). Some argue that these societies are characterized by an overarching social identity; close friendship and kinship bonds among subgroups; ecological, economic, or defensive interdependence; and nonwarring values[17] reinforced by symbols and ceremonies (Howard 2004), and higher-order systems of governance and conflict management[18] (Fry 2006; Fry 2012).

Contextual Differences

Spatial Differences

The nature of violence also depends on the spatial location of potentially antagonistic groups. Some Asian nations face the challenge that potentially contending groups live in proximity with one another, with economic relations involving microexchanges (e.g., the agricultural merchant purchasing the farmer's crop; the forest guard excluding people from the forest) that can personalize the resentments for perceived exploitation and bias. When groups live side by side, as is the case of Hindus and Muslims in many parts of India, or Shia and Sunni in Iraq, these resentments raise the risk of communal violence.

Other Asian nations have minorities living in regions where they are in a majority or close to it, or had been a majority prior to the influx of outsiders. Insofar as perceived economic discrimination against these minorities prevails (e.g., Muslims in Thailand and the Philippines, Tamils in Sri Lanka, or Baloch in Pakistan), members of disaffected minorities may launch separatist movements.

Occasions for intergroup violence may also arise when members of the same ethnic group live across international borders—common throughout Asian countries—due to their colonial past. Competition among local elites for control over people and resources prompts them to seek support across borders, enhancing economic resources for rebellions, and providing cross-border havens for insurrectionists.

Among former Soviet republics—Armenia, Azerbaijan, Georgia, and the five Central Asian republics—some confrontations involve the contested borders pitting Armenia against Azerbaijan over the Nagorno-Karabakh area, Georgia against Russia over Abkhazia and South Ossetia, and Kyrgyzstan against Uzbekistan over the Fergana Valley. These are both "interstate" and "intrastate" conflicts; they reflect ethnic contention: Russian-supported Abkhaz and Ossetians versus Georgians; Uzbeks versus Kyrgyz and Meskhetian Turks; ethnic Armenians of Nagorno-Karabakh backed by Armenia versus ethnic Azeri backed by Azerbaijan.

Perceptions of "Foreignness"

In some Asian countries, particular groups consider others as "foreign," no matter how many generations they may have resided within the country. Many ethnic Russians, other Slavs, and Germans in the Caucasus and Central Asia have descended from families that settled there in the nineteenth century and earlier. In Bahrain, where the ruling family came in with Sunni tribes to conquer the Shiites in the late eighteenth century, Shiites still consider themselves as the "real natives of the island" (Bahry 2000,132). In Southeast Asia (with the exception of Thailand) "overseas Chinese" populations have been in a continual state of vulnerability to the majority population. Similarly, many Sri Lankan Sinhalese see Tamils as foreign intruders from India's Tamil Nadu state.

The perception of "foreignness" can be even more convoluted for "repatriated" populations. The Oralman (ethnic Kazakh) diaspora deserves particular mention. Over the past two decades the Kazakh government repatriated over a million ethnic Kazakhs from other former Soviet republics, China, Mongolia, Afghanistan, Iran, and Turkey. Despite being ethnically Kazakh, many have encountered considerable hostility (UN Development Programme Kazakhstan 2006), although local communities had generally demonstrated tolerance to other newcomers in the nineteenth and twentieth centuries. Speaking neither Kazakh nor Russian (the working language in Kazakhstan), having adopted different cultural practices, and, often, having lower education attainment, many of these immigrants have faced problems with employment, access to land and training, acquisition of citizenship, and simply "fitting in." On several occasions, they have been attacked by local Kazakhs (UN High Commissioner for Refugees 2010, note 7). "Strangers amidst their own,"[19] the Oralmans consider themselves to be disadvantaged compared to both Kazakhs *and* Russians. This social and economic exclusion may have radicalized some of these groups. Some politicians and scholars claim that failures in Oralman repatriation scheme were responsible for deadly strikes in December 2011 in the oil town Zhanaozen; others link Oralmans to the new Islamist groups responsible for bombings and attacks on police in 2011 (Naumann 2012, 121).

"Indigenous" Peoples

An equally important phenomenon is the presence of "indigenous" populations whose residence in a particular area predates the dominant culture. Asia is home to the majority of the world's indigenous people in this sense. These "tribals" or "hill people" tend to live in the least economically developed areas, often subjected to incursions by outsiders attracted by the apparent wealth of forests or minerals, and by government efforts to promote economic activity in these areas. Throughout the region, the debate around indigenous people and the protection of their rights is caught up in legal complexities—including the very definition of indigenous status—and concerns that affording specific rights to them will undermine national unity (Clarke 2012, 33). In 2011, Bangladesh passed amendments to the constitution that replaced the term "adivasi" (indigenous) with "small ethnic groups," in effect denying the status of indigeneity—the act was strongly criticized by indigenous peoples and international community (Loy 2012; Clarke 2012). Though other countries of the region formally recognize indigenous rights, often existing legislation is unenforced (Cambodia), undermined by other legal acts (Philippines), or challenged by courts (Malaysia) (Clarke 2012; Girard 2012).

Encouragingly, an early draft of the Association of Southeast Asian Nations (ASEAN) Human Rights Declaration (January 2012) included a specific reference to the rights of indigenous peoples and ethnic groups, and the obligation on states to obtain their free and informed consent prior to starting certain development projects (Clarke 2012, 33). However, it remains to be seen whether such provisions will have practical effect.

Ethnic Minority Governments

For several Arab Asian countries, religious minorities came to power, gaining economic advantage through greater favor in economic policy or government employment. Their defense of these advantages has often prompted the government to resist democratization and to use coercion to stave off demands and agitation by other groups to redistribute benefits. The Assad regime in Syria has favored the minority Alawites (Faksh 1984, 141), previously an impoverished coastal minority; the Saddam Hussein regime in Iraq continued the strong favoritism for the minority Sunnis (Dawisha 2005, 726; 733).

The Challenges for Conflict-Sensitive Economic Development Strategies

To understand the dual challenge of securing peace and prosperity, we must recognize the extraordinary policy dilemmas that Asian leaders have had to face.

Complex, Easily Mobilizable Intergroup Differences

Almost all Asian nations have *potentially* acrimonious intergroup divisions that can be mobilized or exacerbated by economic policies seen to favor some groups over others. The mosaic of religious sects (as well as secularists), ethnolinguistic groups, regional groups and clans makes this potential particularly high for Asia, compared to more homogeneous regions. These distinctions are not always relevant for intergroup conflict, if people in different groups do not perceive favoritism or exploitation, yet so many economic policies are believed to favor one or more groups over the others.

Growing Income Disparities in Most Asian Nations

These divisions are especially likely to be acrimonious when major disparities in income and wealth among groups are perceived, often—but not always—driven by actual patterns of inequality. Although there are notable exceptions—Japan and South Korea being the most prominent—Asia as a whole has high and increasing income inequality.

Though gauging degrees of inequality is difficult, combining Gini indices developed by Solt (2012) and the World Bank data set (World Bank 2012a) robustly reveals higher levels of inequality in several countries of Southeast Asia (Cambodia, the Philippines, Thailand), Western Asia (Iran, Turkey, Lebanon, Qatar), and in Turkmenistan, China, and Hong Kong. In contrast, the nations reporting more equitable income distribution are post-Soviet countries of Central Asia (Kazakhstan, Kyrgyzstan, Tajikistan, and Uzbekistan) as well as Azerbaijan; Japan and South Korea in East Asia; and Indonesia and Laos in Southeast Asia.

Yet income disparities in more than half of Asian countries have been increasing. Of the 28 Asian countries assessed by a UN Children's Fund study (Ortiz and Cummins 2011) covering the period from 1990 to 2008, the largest increases in inequality occurred in Turkmenistan, Uzbekistan, and Kazakhstan in Central Asia; China, Hong Kong, Japan, and Taiwan in Northeast Asia; Papua New Guinea, Laos, and Singapore in Southeast Asia; Nepal, Bangladesh, and Sri Lanka in South Asia; and Armenia, Georgia, and Israel in West Asia.[20] In contrast, major reductions in income inequality occurred in Azerbaijan, Thailand, and Malaysia. The data on Arab Asia, though limited, reveal no major changes. Overall, these trends show a strong convergence: countries that had been the most equitable are becoming less so; some of the initially least equitable have experienced reduced inequality.

The risk of conflict due to group distinctiveness rises when ethnic, religious, and caste differences correspond to differences in economic roles, which in turn correspond to differences in opportunities, income, and wealth. Farmers, merchants, moneylenders, factory workers, fishers, herders, and so on, within a particular area are often ethnically distinctive (and still often of distinctive caste in India). Economic policies favoring the occupants of particular roles, therefore, will often increase intergroup tensions. Ethnic identifications can be heightened by the consequences of economic policies that differentiate the economic roles of different groups.

Widening Income Gaps across Regions

Within most Asian countries, economic development has increased regional disparities. Even when efforts are made to redress these disparities, the intrinsic economic attractiveness that drew investment to particular areas, and the infrastructure and clusters of related firms of already-developed areas, make regional development of backward areas an uphill battle unless the government provides extremely powerful incentives. China has had rare success in rural industrialization, bringing greater prosperity to previously economically impoverished areas, yet the regional disparities have grown nonetheless because of faster growth of other areas. An additional dilemma is that regional development strategies to redress these disparities may exacerbate intergroup relations, as outsiders are drawn into targeted areas (this is reviewed at greater length in the next chapter).

Transnational Groups, Nomads, and Shifting Cultivators

Formal boundaries on both the macro level (i.e., between nations or subnational units) and micro level (i.e., specific property-right boundaries) are often ineffective in limiting transitory population movements, and nevertheless arouse resentment from populations that regard these boundaries as artificial impositions upon livelihoods, extended family relations, and sense of nationhood. As Shabbir Cheema notes in this volume, the Baloch and others regularly cross the Afghanistan-Pakistan border for work and to meet with clan members. Such porous borders also facilitate attacks by individuals who can seek refuge across the border, as has been the case of the various borders separating Kurds of Iran, Iraq, Syria, and Turkey. Efforts to settle nomads, whether to enhance their education and economic status or to deter them from defying political boundaries, are often strongly resisted.

In addition to pastoralist nomads in desert and mountain areas (especially in West and Central Asia), shifting cultivators are still prevalent in the forests of Southeast Asia. As populations grow and permanent agriculture spreads, conflicts over property rights escalate. Because shifting (or "swidden") agriculture requires that the cultivators move from one location to another, the land on which they depend is often regarded by others as "empty" and therefore open to incursions.

Reliance on Nonrenewable or Depleting Renewable Resources

Roughly half of Asian nations rely heavily on natural resources beyond agriculture, most importantly hydrocarbons, hard minerals, and timber. Natural resource earnings can be a boon, especially when raw material prices are high, but dependence can seriously damage livelihoods and government budgets when international prices decline. While resource exploitation is by no means inevitably a "curse," distributional conflicts often arise over control of natural resource assets, the allocation of natural resource revenues, and the environmental impacts of extraction and processing.

All Central Asian republics are resource rich; more than a quarter of gross domestic product is contributed by net natural resource earnings in Kazakhstan, Kyrgyzstan, and Uzbekistan, and over 40 percent for Turkmenistan; the same as for Azerbaijan and Iran. For Arab Asia, oil and gas dependence are extraordinarily high for Iraq and Kuwait (roughly two-thirds of gross domestic product [GDP]) and over 50 percent for Saudi Arabia. Yet high levels of dependence are not inevitable for significant hydrocarbon exporters: only roughly a fifth of GDP comes from natural resource earnings for Bahrain and the United Arab Emirates, a quarter for Qatar, and a third for Oman (World Bank 2012c). These nations have been able to convert resource wealth into various combinations of infrastructure, savings instruments, and foreign investments more successfully than Saudi Arabia or Kuwait. This has not happened thus far for Central Asia.

For Southeast Asia, hydrocarbon and timber exports and domestic production provide a quarter of GDP of Indonesia, while the same combination in Malaysia has been reduced recently from nearly 20 percent to 10 percent. For Papua New Guinea, Southeast Asia's least developed nation, net natural resource revenues account for more than a third of GDP. For Southeast Asia's richest nation, Brunei, they account for over 40 percent (World Bank 2012c). According to Minority Rights Group International (2012), an unprecedented demand for natural resources across Southeast Asia is feeding ethnic conflict and forced displacement of minorities and indigenous peoples.

Forest-product revenues account for a much smaller GDP portion for the major Asian timber producers than fuel revenues provide for the hydrocarbon producers, yet forests are very important for reasons ranging from the livelihoods of low-income people living in or near the forests, to ecosystem integrity to limit soil erosion, flooding, dust storms, and localized climate change. Although timber is classified as renewable, forests are often "mined" when deforestation proceeds at a rate higher than replanting and natural regeneration. Pakistan and North Korea have been losing forest cover at over 2 percent annually, while Armenia, Cambodia, and Timor-Leste have been deforesting at over 1 percent per year, and Myanmar nearly so. Indonesia, which had an annual deforestation rate of 1.75 percent during the 1990s (only Brazil had a greater absolute loss of forest cover), has reduced the annual rate to 0.5 percent in 2000–2010. Malaysia's deforestation rate has also fallen to less than 0.5 per year (UN Food and Agriculture Organization 2010, 230–231). However, the extension of agriculture and aquaculture into forest areas, especially for lucrative export-oriented crops such as oil palm[21], fish, and shrimp, remains a serious policy challenge because of the livelihood loss or displacement of local people. An estimated 4.6 million hectares in Malaysia, and 9.4 million in Indonesia, have been swallowed by plantations (Girard 2012).

Reliance on Official Development Assistance and Other External Sources

One of most difficult challenges for policymakers is their low degree of control over foreign aid, such as official development assistance (ODA)[22], along with remittances and other transfers from the diaspora. Among Asian Arab nations, three rely on ODA as a significant portion of their gross national income (Yemen at 2 percent, Jordan at more than 3 percent, and Iraq at 4.5 percent according to 2009 figures provided by the Organization for Economic Co-operation and Development [2011, 62]). In Western Asia, Armenia and Georgia have been heavily dependent (at nearly 6 percent and 8.5 percent respectively); the same is true for two of the Central Asian republics, with Kyrgyzstan at over 7 percent and Tajikistan over 8 percent. Afghanistan in 2010 relied on official foreign assistance to the astonishing degree of 42 percent of gross national income.[23] Among South Asian nations, Nepal received ODA accounting for nearly 7 percent of gross national income. In Southeast Asia, Vietnam's ODA amounted to more than 4 percent of national income (with implications reviewed in Edward Feasel's chapter in this volume); Laos and Cambodia were even more dependent at over 7 percent. Aside from Afghanistan, Mongolia was the most dependent of all, at nearly 9.5 percent.[24]

The relevance of dependence on foreign assistance to intergroup conflict is complicated. The funds can assuage resentment and conflict by providing humanitarian assistance and productivity increases to otherwise disaffected or desperate populations. However, foreign aid may magnify the impacts of projects and programs, such as Indonesia's *transmigrasi* resettlement program, that trigger intergroup conflict. Recent evidence demonstrates how real and perceived imbalances in aid distribution within recipient countries have ignited resentment, and have reinforced preexisting intergroup hostility (CDA 2011). An additional challenge is ODA volatility, which is particularly detrimental to fragile states. For example, Pakistan, long a major ODA recipient, has often seen steep increases and abrupt cutoffs of aid. Rather than buffering the country against its internal instability, aid has seemingly reinforced its effects (Chandy 2011, 5). Moreover, development assistance often comes with economic policy "conditionalities" attached, which may not be able, or be permitted, to take into account the conflicts that may arise from their implementation. However, the model of "country ownership" now enshrined in the Paris Declaration on Aid Effectiveness brings additional challenges to countries where recipient governments have weak capacity and elites are more concerned with rent-seeking and clientelism (Chandy 2011, 6). In Pakistan, the implementation of US-funded "signature" infrastructure projects (mostly dams and other large infrastructure projects) has been consistently jeopardized by corrupt and dysfunctional local bureaucracies when "appropriated funds get stuck in the pipeline, with USAID [the US Agency for International Development] consequently coming under intense pressure from Congress to disburse large, unspent funds elsewhere, which risks greater waste" (International Crisis Group 2012a, 4). Many billions of ODA dollars spent in Pakistan by USAID and other donors have brought neither stability nor much love for the donors. Instead, by giving more power to the military to pursue projects, often not supported by local population, and more profits to the contractors connected with the ruling group, it aggravates preexisting tensions within this turbulent country.

Recently, development and security assistance provided by countries within the region has grown steeply. Saudi Arabia and Kuwait, along with Russia, continue as the main nontraditional donors aside from developed nations.[25] After the Arab Spring, the United Arab Emirates, Qatar, and regional bodies such as the Islamic Development Bank have taken a more prominent role in security and economic development assistance in the Persian Gulf region. In Asia at large, both China and India, though major aid recipients,[26] have significantly expanded their aid and declared their intentions to increase it even more.[27] Though these "needy donors" offer assistance without explicit conditionality, their aid is often packaged with trade, investment, and security arrangements,[28] including the safeguarding of burgeoning private and state investments in the recipient states, maintaining security of energy supply, and protecting the expanding expatriate communities (Wainwright 2011, 14). In addition, both India and China employ their own manpower in aid projects, which helps them to address the demographic problem of "bare branches"—excess young male population. China is the principal supplier of economic and military assistance to Myanmar, Cambodia, Laos, and North Korea, and has been providing assistance for infrastructure, agriculture, energy (particularly hydropower), and public works to an increasing number of other Asian countries. The bulk of India's aid goes to Afghanistan,[29] where India currently is the largest regional donor and fifth largest international donor; some assistance has been traditionally provided also to Nepal and Bhutan. These donors—as well as, on a smaller scale, Indonesia and Turkey—"are entering a terrain that has traditionally been dominated by OECD donors, but at a time when the latter's policy landscape is in flux" (Sherman et al. 2011, 4). All of these donors have high economic and political stakes in the region as well as their own "darlings" in the recipient countries, whether these are expatriate communities, related religious or ethnic groups, or favored businesses. Thus, despite assurances of neutrality and "win-win" partnerships, change in the geography, composition, and modality of development assistance will probably affect the balance of power among various groups in the recipient states.

Another factor with significant impacts on Asian development trends is remittances, largely the flow of funds from temporary migrant workers back to their home countries. In 2011, seven of the top ten remittance recipients were Asian countries: India, China, the Philippines, Bangladesh, Pakistan, Lebanon, and Vietnam.[30] Since 2000, remittances to India were about six times the net capital transfers from international capital markets and ODA (Kapur 2010, 18). Dependence on remittances is particularly high in Tajikistan, where remittances from migrants is estimated at $2.1 billion (World Bank 2011b), thus constituting 41 percent of its GDP. Other post-Soviet countries are also remittance-dependent: 15.4 percent of Kyrgyz GDP; 9.0 percent for Armenia; 6.4 percent for Georgia (World Bank 2011).[31] Other countries with high dependence on remittances are the small Pacific countries of Tonga and Samoa (27.7 percent and 22.3 percent respectively), Lebanon in West Asia (22.4 percent), Nepal in South Asia (22.9 percent), and the Philippines (13.3 percent) in Southeast Asia. Labor migration allows struggling economies to "export" unemployment and therefore trouble, as most of labor migrants are young, potentially politically volatile males. Remittances are typically more stable than other forms of external finance and in many cases are a critical pillar of family and sometimes even national finance. However, their role can be quite precarious as well, insofar as recipient countries become "hostages" of global market instability as well as destination countries' migration policies. For instance, as the 2008–2009 Russian financial crisis unfolded and the Russian government curbed labor migration, the remittances to Central Asia dropped across the board. Other challenges associated with high dependence on remittances are rent-seeking behavior of authorities, their tendency to relax fiscal discipline in anticipation of flows from abroad, and often their inability to use these resources efficiently.[32]

Yet another challenge is increasing intergroup inequality. International migration is concentrated in certain groups and regions. Large volumes of remittances produce income inequalities across regions, groups, and households. Large interstate variations in remittance receipts that have amplified interregional inequality are reported for India (Kapur 2010, 115); the distribution of remittances heightens the urban-rural divide and spatial inequality in Central Asia (Laruelle and Peyrouse 2012).

The impact of migration and diaspora formation on the development-conflict interface in the countries of exit is not limited by remittances. Several case studies of Kurdish, Tamil, and Sikh diasporas (Hoffman et al. 2009; Singh 2007) present the phenomenon of long-distance ethnic nationalism, when communities in exile (either voluntary or forced) support intergroup conflicts in their homelands by providing their former compatriots with economic opportunities, voice, media attention, and continuous incitement. These minority groups may have voted "with their feet" to leave the conflict behind them, but they carry the bloodied soil of homeland on their heels. They may still feel resentment against other group or government—amplified by indignities of immigration, which often strengthen group identity; frequently they also have more access to economic and political resources to support their cause but they do not have to face physical encounter in hostilities nor are they deterred by a threat of accountability. On the other hand, examples of Vietnamese-Swedish diaspora (Swain and Phan 2012) as well as Indian diaspora (Kapur 2010) portray the diaspora's potential contribution to peace and development processes in the exit countries. The important factors that define diasporas' inclination to support or to mitigate conflict are rarely explored or discussed; in particular, the connection between development policies and the circumstances of "exit," and the impact of differential rates of groups' emigration upon societal inequality. Exploring the case of India's diaspora, Kapur (2010) offers surprising observations. He argues that the distinctively elite characteristics of modern Indian immigration (exercising its "exit" strategy following the introduction of affirmative action policy) contributed to "social remittances"—transmission of development ideas from the countries of residence to the political economy of India[33] through both the influence of policymakers who were trained and worked abroad and the activities of diasporas.[34] The Chinese strategy of effectively utilizing economic, technological, and political resources of its large and successful overseas diaspora also exemplifies an important but rarely recognized approach.

Challenges Specific to the Transition of Former Soviet Republics

The former Soviet republics in Western and Central Asia have faced distinctive economic challenges, beginning with the economic collapse upon the disintegration of the Soviet Union. This led to virtually total disruption of preexisting trade, the withdrawal of subsidies from Moscow, and major armed conflicts involving Armenia, Azerbaijan, Georgia, and Tajikistan. While Uzbekistan suffered *only* a 20 percent contraction of GDP, the other republics declined by 40–60 percent (Dowling and Wignaraja 2006; Glinkina and Rosenberg 2003, 515). These nations were among those most challenged with the politically difficult tasks of dismantling the state-enterprise-dominated economy, which had been thoroughly controlled from Moscow (Henley and Assaf 1997, 261). This led to widespread unemployment, increasing rural poverty, and large labor migrations—both internal and external. Another consequence of the transition was extreme rise of social exclusion, particularly in Central Asia (UN Development Programme 2011a). Growing corruption, state involvement in the "shadow economy," and drug trade also marked the transition. Laruelle and Peyrouse (2012, 153) posit that with the exception of Kazakhstan, post-Soviet states "have a limited capacity to find a model of economic development capable of lifting them out of their post-Soviet pauperization." Their proximity to hotbeds of conflict in Afghanistan and Pakistan, the region's entry into drug trafficking, and increasing activity of radicalized Islamic groups present major challenges for peaceful development.

New Risks on the Horizon

The compelling economic policy dilemmas that Asian leaders have faced thus far are compounded by new economic, geopolitical, societal, and environmental risks. Recent surveys of major systemic risks (World Economic Forum 2011; 2012)[35] have identified several global threats: (1) currency volatility, asset-price collapse, and fiscal crises; (2) illicit trade, organized crime, corruption, and fragile states; (3) climate change challenging water security, food security, and threatening extreme energy price volatility; (4) the demographic conjunction of a large youth population facing chronic unemployment and the burdens of a growing proportion of retirees dependent upon already heavily indebted governments; (5) weak government capacity to address risks arising from emerging technologies, financial interdependence, resource depletion, and climate change, and (6) vulnerability to digital disruptions. For most Asian countries, the risk dimensions that prominently stand out as drivers of instability and potential violence are the interplay between fiscal imbalances and demographic trends; climate change concerns and associated risks to water, food, and energy security; weak government capacity to address the challenges of increasingly complex, interdependent, and volatile interactions with the global system; and the dangers of the illicit economy.

Youth "Crisis," Super-Aging and Other Demographic Challenges

The Arab Spring and other recent incidents of civil discontent signal the growing frustration among youth and their ability to mobilize rapidly through technological connectivity. Yet this "youth bulge" phenomenon and its potential to contribute to higher levels of violence is only one facet of demographic transition.

In general, the demographic transition of declining birth rates reflecting lower child mortality and urbanization has not yet reversed population growth in Asia: in 2010, the Asia Pacific population growth rate was at 1 percent, having declined from 1.5 percent in the early 1990s (UN Economic and Social Commission for Asia and the Pacific 2011, 1). However, demographic trends evolve differently across Asia. While Northeast Asia is growing at only 0.5 percent per year, South Asia and Southeast Asia are growing at 1.4 percent annually, and Western Asia and Central Asia at 1.8 percent (UN Food and Agriculture Organization 2010, 6). These diverging trends are paralleled by shifts in age structure: in 2010, the proportion of children (aged 0–14) in the total population in Northeast Asia, West Asia, and Central Asia was approximately 19 percent; while in Southeast Asia and South Asia the figures were 24 percent and 31 percent respectively (UN Economic and Social Commission for Asia and the Pacific 2011, 5). If large youth cohorts[36] can be employed productively, such an age structure becomes a demographic dividend. Yet in countries where rapid population growth is combined with lack of economic opportunities, inequality, and weak institutions, the potential for youth violence is very high. Henrik Urdal (2006, 623), using a broader and more sophisticated approach than prior studies[37] to assess the impact of a high proportion of youth, concludes that relatively large youth cohorts are associated with a significantly increased risk of domestic armed conflict, terrorism, and riots/violent demonstrations. While factors like level of development and regime type are found to be more important explanations of violence, the effect of youth bulges is not negligible (ibid.).

Urdal (2008, 609) also found, in a study of differences among 27 Indian states over the 1956–2002 period, that "young age structure is the only demographic factor that is statistically associated with increased risks of all three forms of political violence [domestic armed conflict, terrorism, and riots/violent demonstrations]." Not surprisingly, the regions with the largest shares of youth within the working-age population (the Middle East and Central Asia) fare worst in terms of youth unemployment and incidents of violence.

The risk of "youth bulge" violence is especially high for Tajikistan, as the "child bulge" of roughly 40 percent of the population will become a "youth bulge" over the coming decade. Sophie Roche (2010) argues that disaffected Tajik youth are susceptible to manipulation by "vanguard groups" intent on large-scale mobilization. The capacity of Asian economies to utilize the youth bulge constructively varies. Judging by the youth unemployment rate, Northeast Asian nations were most successful in meeting this challenge—most likely contributing to peaceful development. Even in 2011, in the aftermath of economic crisis, the youth (ages 15–24) unemployment rate in the subregion remained below 10 percent, though it was still 2.8 times higher than the adult rate (International Labour Office 2012, 15). However, further enjoyment of the "demographic dividend" requires the development of "21st century skills" among young people and policies that improve youth employment prospects.

Youth unemployment rates in other subregions range from 8.6 percent in South Asia to 25.7 per cent in the Middle East in 2008 (International Labour Office 2012, 14). Because population obviously "grows from the bottom," birth rates sufficient to maintain a large enough productive workforce are important for economic growth, and can help to offset the pressures to permit migration of workers from other countries, which poses its own risks of intergroup friction. Yet the "bulge" in the number of children puts extra pressure on education and other social services.

The Middle East situation is particularly troubling. The subregion stands out in terms of overall unemployment: youth unemployment has been very high for decades and exceeded 26.5 percent in 2011. The 4:1 ratio of youth-to-adult unemployment rates is also exceptionally high (International Labour Office 2012). High unemployment combines with other factors that "stall" youth transition into adulthood, such as the inability to afford housing, get access to credit, get married, or start a family. Djavad Salehi-Isfahani and Navtej Dhillon (2008) find that the root cause of this youth exclusion lies in the rigid institutions and social norms that mediate transitions from school to work and family formation through interconnected systems of education, labor, housing, and marriage. This stalled transition to adulthood, known as "waithood," fosters widespread frustration and discontent. Rapidly increasing populations of young people, growing up in extremely vulnerable circumstances, are posing urgent demographic challenges in Afghanistan, Pakistan, Central Asia, and some states of India.[38]

Reducing the youth bulge is partially amenable to economic policy. Successful pro-growth policies bringing prosperity tend to reduce family size; youth employment programs may reduce the likelihood that youth will be caught up in aggressive acts; investments in education and health tend to enhance employment possibilities.

On the other end of the population pyramid, the proportion of elderly (aged 65 and above) has been steadily increasing in Asia, having reached 9.5 percent in Northeast Asia and 10 percent in Central and Western Asia[39] (UN Economic and Social Commission for Asia and the Pacific 2011, 4), placing these subregions into the "aging societies" category. Fiscal stress rises as the ratio of workers to the elderly falls. Hong Kong, Japan, South Korea, and Taiwan have to bring in migrants to take care of rapidly aging populations, raising the potential for intergroup conflict.

The Asian countries with the fastest growing economies (India, China, and to some extent Indonesia, Vietnam, and Philippines) are facing demographic pressures on both sides. The impressive economic growth of these countries for the last decade has been underpinned by their ability to generate new jobs while also relocating young workers from low-productivity agricultural activities to high-productivity manufacturing and global services. However, according to UN projections, the portion of the population aged 65 or older will more than triple in China, India, and Indonesia between 2000 and 2050 (Stone 2010, 1559), creating a new set of development challenges in the absence of adequate financing solutions to serve the public health and social services sectors.

Climate Change, Natural Disasters, and Other Stresses due to Interactions between Humans and Nature

The risks posed by climate change for conflict-sensitive economic development are quite diverse. Since the Stern Report (Stern 2007), there has been an intense scientific debate on the climate-conflict link. Several studies and policy-relevant documents of international agencies (UN Development Programme 2011a; 2011b; Vivekananda 2011) suggest that climate-induced threats to food, water, and health will increase poverty, affect migration patterns, and potentially exacerbate conflict. Some scholars claim a direct connection between climate change and incidence of civil wars (Burkea et al. 2011), while others trace the Arab Spring to global warming (Johnstone and Mazo 2011). In their reviews of the literature, Bernauer, Bohmelt, and Koubi (2012), Gleditsch (2012), and Scheffran et al. (2012) conclude that evidence on climate-conflict connection is inconclusive, though under certain circumstances climate-related environmental change may indeed increase the risk of violence. Recently, scholars and policymakers have broadened their approach by focusing on multiple risks to the interaction between natural and social systems (Scheffran et al. 2012). In Asia, such risks include high vulnerability of agriculture to changes in temperature, precipitation, and storm intensity. An Asian Development Bank (2011, 189) assessment concludes that

> in the Asian subregion, Afghanistan, Bangladesh, Cambodia, India, the Lao People's Democratic Republic, Myanmar, and Nepal are the countries most vulnerable to climate change. Bhutan, the People's Republic of China (PRC), Pakistan, Thailand, Timor-Leste, Uzbekistan, and Viet Nam are significantly vulnerable. Smallholder farmers, forest dwellers, herders, and fishers who live in fragile areas with limited access to natural resources and adaptation capacity will be the most affected.

The impact on agriculture is closely connected to food insecurity, found to be linked to increased risk of democratic failure, protests and rioting, communal violence, and civil conflict (Arezki and Brückner 2011). Even small fluctuations in food prices can have detrimental effects where a high share of household budgets is spent on food, as in Central Asia.[40] In addition, increased agricultural vulnerability (droughts, storms, or floods) may reduce employment opportunities in this sector and possibly contribute to recruitment to violent organizations.

Desertification is another important challenge, calling for revised land use regulations and the possibility of population resettlement. Unchecked desertification not only undermines food security and incomes of affected farmers, but also triggers urbanization and the risks that overburdened cities present. Squires (2007, 1–2) reports:

> Out of a total land area of 4.3 billion hectares, Asia contains some 1.7 billion hectares of arid, semi-arid, and dry sub-humid land reaching from the Mediterranean coast to the shores of the Pacific. Degraded areas include expanding deserts in China, India, Iran, Mongolia and Pakistan, the sand dunes of Central Asia, the steeply eroded mountain slopes of Nepal, and the deforested and overgrazed highlands of the Lao People's Democratic Republic. Asia, in terms of the number of people affected by desertification and drought, is the most severely affected continent.

The third major policy challenge posed by global climate change is the sea-level rise. As the frequency and severity of floods increase, large population segments living in flood-prone areas become more vulnerable. Consequently, the cost of such extreme events is increasing for communities, infrastructure, and livelihoods, overtaxing government and community resources, undermining their resilience, contributing to massive migration and, in the absence of alternative employment, providing new recruits to violent groups. In addition to the reduction of farmland in low-lying areas, sea-level rise threatens major coastal cities. In terms of numbers of people likely to be directly exposed, 14 of the 20 most heavily impacted cities are Asian: Guangzhou, Ningbo, Shanghai, and Tian in China; Mumbai and Kolkata in India; Tokyo in Japan; Chittagong, Dhaka, and Khulna in Bangladesh; Rangoon in Myanmar; Bangkok in Thailand; and Haiphong and Ho Chi Minh City in Vietnam (Nicholls et al. 2008, 53–57). Except for Tokyo, regulating residence in these cities can pose huge problems with both legally sited residents and squatters.

Potential conflicts between flood victims and host communities are not limited to large cities. In the summer of 2008, 60,000 people had to be resettled in the Terai region of Nepal as the result of the worst flooding in five decades. The host communities, themselves struggling to survive, saw flood victims as competitors for scarce resources; newcomers' expectations of the provision of basic necessities were not met, either. Manipulation by political groups there has further fueled escalation of intergroup tension into hostilities (Vivekananda 2011, 8).

Another area of concern is the link between acute natural disasters and societal violence. Between 1950 and 2010 Asia experienced over 3,000 disasters judged to be significant by the Center for Research on Epidemiology of Disasters (2011), resulting in more than 5.6 million deaths (83 percent of the world total) and affecting 5.4 billion people (90 percent of the world total). Asian countries with very high disaster risk—the Philippines, Bangladesh, India, Timor-Leste, and Cambodia, to name just a few—are also more prone to violence.

There is a growing recognition that disasters and conflicts are integrally linked to the broader national development context (UN Development Programme 2011a). For instance, the UN Development Programme's (2011b, 52–57) analysis of Sri Lanka after the 2004 tsunami identifies several ways in which the international tsunami-related response intensified conflict. The installation of a buffer zone took people from their livelihoods, thereby increasing their vulnerability. In the resettlement process, groups moved inland to live among different populations, changing power dynamics and contributing to intergroup conflict. Disaster funding allowed both the government and the insurgent Liberation Tigers of Tamil Eelam (LTTE) to strengthen their military resources, through the rise in the value of Sri Lanka's rupee and the influx of aid-workers' money. The perceived inequality in the financing and focus of the response added legitimacy to the LTTE's violence. Similarly, poorly planned and managed resettlement of populations caused by volcanic eruptions and small-scale flooding in Papua New Guinea led to land use disputes. Perceptions of unfair distribution of humanitarian and recovery aid, and the lack of participatory approaches, also generated tensions between resettled populations and host communities (UN Development Programme 2011b, 49–51).

However, while the experiences of Nepal, Sri Lanka, and Indonesia demonstrate that disaster-blind conflict interventions (e.g., population resettlement into environmentally vulnerable locations such as flood plains) can reinforce disaster risks, a strong focus on internal conflict issues can reduce the attention given by international donors and national governments to disaster response and rehabilitation (UN Development Programme 2011b, 29; Vivekananda 2011, 8). An Overseas Development Institute study reported that between 1999 and 2004 at least 140 disasters occurred in contexts that were also experiencing conflict (Buchanan-Smith and Christoplos 2004). In their study of 167 countries between 1970 and 2007, Berrebi and Ostwald (2011) found a strong positive association between natural disasters and the subsequent incidence of terrorism and fatalities, particularly in poorer countries. The correlation between the tsunami and significant escalation of terrorism was noted by others (Le Billon and Waizenegger 2007), while some scholars posit that civil war is also more likely following quick-onset natural disasters, such as earthquakes, volcanic eruptions, floods, and cyclones (Brancati 2007; Nel and Righarts 2008). Other case studies confirm that conflicts and disasters contribute to each other (UN Development Programme 2011b), most strongly in countries with high levels of inequality and low economic growth. Bergholt and Lujala (2012) find, unsurprisingly, that natural disasters depress economic growth, but their cross-national statistical approach does not find a correlation between natural disasters and conflict; however, whether this is because of the measurement-error or omitted-variable problems of the approach is unclear.

Certainly not all aspects of the disaster-conflict relationship have been comprehensively examined. Several explanations for this association are plausible. Natural disasters can exacerbate preexisting societal cleavages, creating vulnerabilities that some conflict entrepreneurs might exploit. Poor infrastructure or unsafe construction can significantly increase disaster vulnerability, and governments often spend less on disaster prevention in politically weak or hostile areas (Cohen and Werker 2008). Disasters tend to disproportionately affect marginalized or disempowered groups (Bolin 2007; Cohen and Werker 2008; Mustafa 1998). Another challenge to identifying risks presented by climate change to societal stability and intergroup conflict is the importance of framing the debate and the patterns of organizing relief and development assistance to affected communities. Feitelson, Tamimi, and Rosenthal (2012) argue that framing climate change as a security issue influences the perceptions of the actors in conflict and may provoke militarized responses. This observation highlights the need for conflict-sensitive climate mitigation and adaptation efforts. However, mounting evidence shows that climate-related financing, policies, and programs have not adequately considered local conflict, and have contributed to serious unintended consequences in Aceh in Indonesia and in Sri Lanka (UN Development Programme 2011b, 25). Vivekananda (2011, 9) argues:

> Climate change impacts could incentivise or even compel elite groups to further tighten their grip on resources and/or manipulate adaptation funding to their own benefit through patronage and clientelism, with contracts for adaptation projects providing both legal and illicit

money-making opportunities...Ill-informed climate change adaptation policies and actions that do not take into account the broader socio-political and cultural contextual realities can unwittingly reinforce existing tensions, engendering greater poverty, inequality and conflict, rather than build resilience.

Organization of the Volume

Chapter 2 provides a broad overview of prevailing economic doctrines and the implications of various development strategies. The rest of the volume consists of case studies selected to demonstrate different combinations of development trajectories and patterns of intergroup violence. The cases help to understand why seemingly similar strategies and policies brought drastically different outcomes to various countries and many groups within these countries. Included in this selection are India and Pakistan, highly conflict-prone states of South Asia; Indonesia, Malaysia, and Vietnam representing diverse Southeast Asian approaches to development and intergroup conflict, and several cases from the post-Soviet region and West Asia.

Sumit Ganguly and Jennifer Oetken explore the connection between economic development policies and the role of tribal groups in the Naxalite Maoist insurgency. Beginning as a peasant revolt against West Bengal landlords, it was subsequently co-opted by Maoists capitalizing on threats that local people felt from incursions by outsiders, challenges to property rights, and other grievances. This ad hoc peasant rebellion turned into a "people's war" that spread to other areas in India. The extraordinary expansion of the Maoist insurgency is frequently cited as a consequence of development policies following economic liberalization. However, Ganguly and Oetken's analysis does not confirm this assumption. Their research reveals that it is insecurity over land rights, rather than new economic development policies, that continues to underpin the region's conflict. They show that even when the national government attempts to address legitimate grievances of the disadvantaged communities, the intended impact may be jeopardized at the state or local levels. They conclude that to curtail local support for the Maoist insurgency, the government needs to ensure wider community inclusion in development decision making. They also recommend redesign of compensation packages and integration of *adivasis* into the new labor market.

G. Shabbir Cheema's chapter on Pakistan, a nation severely affected by several violent conflicts at once, focuses on Balochistan—one of Pakistan's most ethnically diverse provinces. This highly volatile region is poorly suited for settled agriculture and has underdeveloped infrastructure. It has the weakest fiscal base and lowest growth among Pakistan's provinces, remaining the poorest region of the country. It is underrepresented in the federal government, and receives comparatively low levels of aid. Consequently, the local population has little trust in the government and its development initiatives. Yet Balochistan also possesses impressive mineral resource wealth and easy trade access to neighboring countries, and is therefore an important focus of national development strategies. The control and direction of the development process have been major points of contention between the central government and ethnic Baloch both under civilian and military regimes. Cheema's research identifies two main factors behind the long-standing violence in the province: how various development strategies led to an uneven and socially inequitable pattern of development, and the absence of sustained political institutions and mechanisms of equitable political participation.

Indonesia, another mix of ethnically, linguistically, and culturally diverse groups reluctantly brought together under colonialism, presents a different variant of the development-conflict nexus. Lorraine V. Aragon focuses on Central Sulawesi, where groups of long-standing residence have had to accommodate to the influx of outsiders of different culture, religion, and economic roles. She recounts how regional development, particularly the controversial transmigration program, contributed to dramatic changes in the demographic composition and distribution of economic and political power, resulting in the explosion of intergroup violence, large-scale displacement, and religious territorialization.

The resettlement scheme, a combination of "nation building" and demographic engineering for the socioeconomic goals of alleviating the poverty, unemployment, and landlessness of Indonesia's overcrowded "Inner Islands," was implemented in Central Sulawesi with little understanding of the region's resources, regarding the resettlement sites as "empty territory" appropriate for the migration of predominantly Muslim settlers. Resettlement and labor migration were accompanied by government incentives for mono-cropping, provoking land seizures and eroding environmental conditions and the economic status of native populations. Intensified religious tensions exploded in violence in 1998; jihadists rushed in to fight alongside Muslims, while Christians moved in to reinforce the Christians already present. However, the development policies did not have the same effect in all provinces; some development initiatives were more successful in meeting the needs and traditional institutions of local residents.

Malaysia, also a country of ethnoconfessional diversity, is often presented as a model of interethnic peace, which some scholars and development practitioners ascribe to the impact of carefully designed development strategies (Muscat 2002). While Malaysia has indeed transitioned into one of the most prosperous states in Southeast Asia, Ananthi Al Ramiah and Thillainathan

Ramasamy present a more tempered view of Malaysia's record in managing its development and multiethnic population. They trace several stages of post-independence development policies, highlighting successes leading to some degree of disassociation of race and economic function and the creation of a large and vibrant middle class. Preferential treatment for the Malay majority has elevated its group status and provided these "sons of the soil" with opportunities for economic advancement, reducing the tension with wealthier Malaysian Chinese and Indians. However, the authors argue that Malaysia's peace is coercive and fragile. Their field research reveals that affirmative action that quelled Malay resentment also hardened group identities and increased the sense of deprivation experienced by the Chinese and Indians. They conclude that Malaysia would benefit from greater social cohesion and economic progress with policies based on meritocratic rather than ethnic-based approaches.

Edward M. Feasel's chapter focuses on Vietnam, yet another model for achieving rapid economic development, with ODA playing an important role. He explores the impact on Vietnam's economic and political development resulting from foreign assistance provided by Japan, its top single donor. Feasel recounts the Japanese efforts to support free market-oriented reforms, the consequences for intergroup relations, and the Vietnamese government's management of these relations. Feasel posits that Japan's strategy is premised on the belief that infrastructure development will bring about prosperity and stability, in turn addressing the needs of disadvantaged groups. Yet the significant economic growth and poverty alleviation have been accompanied by increasing inequalities between rural and urban dwellers, and among various ethnoreligious and indigenous groups, leading to violence suppressed by government repression. Providing stability in turbulent times, from Feasel's perspective, may be the greatest contribution the Japan could make. However, he presents evidence that the Kinh majority benefits more from infrastructure improvements; therefore, development assistance may have contributed to growing interethnic inequality. Feasel argues that Japan could reshape its development assistance in a more conflict-sensitive manner and thereby influence the Vienamese government to improve its treatment of ethnic and religious minorities.

Ebru Erdem-Akcay's contribution explores the impact of economic development strategies upon social networks and authority structures of the politically mobilized Kurdish minority in Turkey and the nonmobilized Tajiks in Uzbekistan. She examines the links between regional development policies and the salience of ethnic identity and political mobilization of these minorities. The comparison is well justified: both are Iranic minorities politically dominated by Turkic peoples. Erdem-Akcay attributes the differing political salience of ethnic identity to development choices of the central governments. Although central governments are generally aware that development initiatives inevitably affect existing social and political structures, they may be unable or unwilling to manage sociopolitical changes accompanying such initiatives. Erdem-Akcay shows that the Turkish government's failure to appreciate the full extent of development-related changes contributed to the emergence of a potent and militant Kurdish political movement. In contrast, the Uzbek government has avoided development initiatives altogether for fear that resultant sociopolitical change would disrupt interethnic stability. Uzbekistan's case shows that a lack of development may maintain stability and prevent challenges to the state, though this circumstance stalls economic progress and poverty alleviation for all, and may be possible only under an authoritarian government. Erdem-Akcay suggests incorporation of ethnic political entrepreneurs into the broader political system and involving local actors in the design of development projects.

Finally, Mikhail Alexseev explores the flow of economic development budget support and the levels of insurgency in Russia's violent North Caucasus region. Despite substantial flows of Russia's development aid, violence in the region has increased. Alexseev compares two provinces, Dagestan and Kabardino-Balkaria (KBR)—the latter receives the least assistance and the slowest growing budget, but is the least violent among four ethnic provinces in the area. He demonstrates that the nature of insurgency (or the insurgent group's stakes in the outcome of local competition for power and resources), explains differential impacts of regional development assistance. Alexseev categorizes insurgencies as "local" (high personal stakes for residents) versus "itinerant"/"mobile-dispersed" (low personal stakes for local residents). Dagestan is experiencing community-centered violence; insurgents have a relationship with the community and violence is linked to local political and economic competition. The KBR, in contrast, is experiencing itinerant insurgency, where actors have little stake in the local competition for power and resources and are more focused on funding the network, such that when more aid is available the area sees a rise in insurgent activity. Alexseev suggests that more economic aid would be beneficial in areas experiencing community-centered violence, whereas areas experiencing itinerant insurgency would benefit more from improving the quality of law enforcement, security, and government institutions. He concludes that development assistance needs not only to target economic sectors with the greatest grievances, but also to improve the accountability and professionalism of local police and security forces to reduce arbitrary harassment of civilians (and hence social support for the insurgents), while more narrowly targeting the staging areas of itinerant insurgency leaders. Governments must credibly commit to long-term development assistance, especially in the context of "local" insurgencies where repeated cooperation is necessary to strengthen resource sharing.

Notes

1. US vice president Hubert Humphrey's Speech, April 23, 1966, Washington, DC.
2. Development practitioners understand armed violence as the use or threatened use of arms to inflict injury, death, or psychological harm (Organization for Economic Co-operation and Development 2009). This perspective broadens the approach beyond the traditional definition of armed conflict to include situations of violent crime and other types of social violence.
3. We use the following classification of Asian subregions: East Asia (China, Hong Kong, Japan, Mongolia, South Korea, and Taiwan), Southeast Asia (Brunei, Cambodia, Indonesia, Laos, Malaysia, Myanmar, Papua New Guinea, Philippines, Singapore, Thailand, and Vietnam), South Asia (Bangladesh, Bhutan, India, Nepal, Pakistan, and Sri Lanka), post-Soviet countries of Central Asia (Kazakhstan, Kyrgyzstan, Tajikistan, Turkmenistan, and Uzbekistan), and Caucasus (Armenia, Azerbaijan, and Georgia), West Asia (Afghanistan, Iran, Israel, Turkey, and Arab Asian countries).
4. In 1989, Russians made up nearly 20 percent of the total population of these 5 states: some 9.5 million individuals—from over 40 percent in Kazakhstan to 8 percent in Uzbekistan. Following the Soviet Union's collapse, more than 80 percent of the Russians in Tajikistan, two-thirds of those in Turkmenistan, half in Uzbekistan, and one-third in Kazakhstan and Kyrgyzstan left for another country (mainly Russia).
5. In 1998–2004, lagging South Asian regions had more than three times the number of internal conflicts per capita, compared with prosperous regions, and on average almost twice as many fatalities (Ghani and Iyer 2010).
6. This observation corresponds to the empirical analysis of local income inequality and locations of conflict outbreaks reported by Buhaug et al. (2011).
7. Trends in armed conflict are tracked by over 60 datasets maintained by international organizations and research groups for various purposes. Some datasets record only episodes of violence with direct government involvement; others also include incidents between nonstate factions, but not genocides or democides. Differences in epistemology affect methodology of data collection, which in turn affects possible conclusions. While reports produced by major datasets during the Cold War correlated rather tightly, for the last two decades differences among the recorded data are more pronounced.
8. Classifications of the world regions and definitions of what constitutes a violent conflict differ among most prominent academic and institutional databases, creating much confusion in the analyses of global trends in violence, especially intrastate or intergroup violence.
9. This is a limitation of this database.

10. These rates are from the Geneva Declaration on Armed Violence and Development (2011, 60). The rates for developed and transitional subregions were as follows: Western Europe (1.25); Southern Europe (2); Northern Europe (2.5); Oceania (3.5); North America (4); and Eastern Europe (4.75).

11. Some recent reports, however, reveal signs of increasing ferment in Chinese society. In 2011, the Chinese government called for accelerated development in minority areas, intensifying the majority Han migration to the western provinces and autonomous regions. Violent encounters between local minority groups and authorities were reported in 2011 in the Xinjiang Uighur and Ninghia Hui Autonomous Regions, in Inner Mongolia and Tibet (Perazzi 2012; Heidelberg Institute for International Conflict Research 2012).

12. The quantitative basis for this assessment is from the Human Security Report Project (Human Rights Watch 2011); UN Development Programme 2008; and UN Office on Drugs and Crime 2011; World Health Organization 2002; 2009.

13. Criminal violence and ethnic violence often converge, as criminal gangs frequently prey on victims of other groups.

14. The numbers for other regions are as follows: Africa (21.8 per 100,000), Americas (17.6 per 100,000), Europe (5.4 per 100,000), and Oceania (4.0 per 100,000) (UN Development Programme 2008, 11).

15. Until the early 2000s, Russian media in Kazakhstan periodically expressed concerns about the promotion of the Kazakh language and culture as well as a de facto affirmative action for ethnic Kazakhs within state service (Schatz 2010, 258). With large-scale emigration the demographic power of ethnic Russians diminished and articulation of grievances subsided.

16. Summaries on the characteristics of these peaceful societies can be found at http://www.peacefulsocieties.org. The website includes a description of over 20 peaceful societies around the world for which there is significant scholarly literature to support the claims of peacefulness.

17. Many such societies devalue competition, self-focus, interpersonal comparisons, and other ego-centered social behaviors that they feel might lead to violence. For instance, while some of the peaceful societies have political leaders, they tend to not glorify leadership. Very few people in the peaceful societies glorify individualism, ego-satisfaction, or material self-interest: they tend to cherish gentleness, nonaggression, and interpersonal harmony.

18. Peaceful societies use a wide range of mechanisms that devalue conflicts, foster toleration for individual differences, and maintain internal nonviolence. In particular, many groups use effective sanctions, such as ostracism, against deviant or aggressive behavior.

19. The title of a famous Russian movie "Svoi sredi chuzhikh, chuzhoi sredi svoikh" ("One's own among strangers, a stranger amidst one's own") reflects the widespread identity confusion of many people in the former Soviet Union.

20. The somewhat arbitrary cutoff for the designation of a "major" increase or decrease is a .03 change in the Gini index.

21. Although oil palms do provide tree cover, and the European Union has been considering reclassifying oil palm plantations as forest, these plantations are

not considered as such in the UN Food and Agriculture Organization's statistics, but rather as "other land with tree cover" (UN Food and Agriculture Organization 2010, 97).

22. ODA includes bilateral aid from individual governments and multilateral assistance from international organizations such as the World Bank, the Asian Development Bank, and other international financial institutions.

23. Because the OECD did not report the figure for Afghanistan, the percentage is taken from the World Bank 2012b.

24. The cutoff point for the above is 2 percent; much smaller countries, such as Bhutan and the Maldives are excluded. Afghanistan is not included in the OECD table.

25. The developed countries' foreign assistance is subject to coordinative efforts through the Development Assistance Committee, comprised of 17 Western European countries; the European Union as a member in itself; Canada and the United States; Australia and New Zealand; and Japan and South Korea.

26. In 2009, the outflows of development aid from China were estimated between 1.5 and 25.1 billion dollars; India's aid flows were estimated between 0.5 and 2.2 billion dollars (calculated from OECD DAC database). Meantime, in 1995–2009, India was the fourth largest recipient of ODA in the world.

27. In April 2011, China released its first Foreign Aid White Paper, reiterating its position that its international engagement should be thought of as mutual assistance between two developing countries. The paper described the rapid growth of China's foreign aid levels by nearly 30 percent each year in 2004–2009 and proclaimed the intention to expand assistance to other developing countries to "foster local personnel and technical forces, build infrastructure, and develop and use domestic resources, so as to lay a foundation for future development and embarkation on the road to self-reliance and independent development." (Information Office of the State Council 2011).

28. In fact, the Chinese aid strategy explicitly states the concept of "equality, mutual benefit, and win-win" between China and the recipient state, and stresses that both should benefit economically from their trade, aid, and investment relationship. In addition, Chinese aid, like that of most bilateral donors, is tied, requiring around half of the services and materials for each project to come from China (Wainwright 2011, 15).

29. India has provided Afghanistan with some $2 billion since 2001; it trains Afghan civil servants in India, supports small business development, and provides medical treatment and education (Sidhu 2011).

30. In 2010, India topped the list of recipients with $55.0 billion, China was close second with $51.0 billion, followed by Philippines ($21.3 billion), Bangladesh ($11.1 billion), Pakistan ($9.4 billion), Lebanon ($8.2 billion), and Vietnam ($7.2 billion) (World Bank 2011b).

31. Assessments differ. The Central Bank of Russia (2011) reports much higher remittances from Russia to Central Asia, estimating that Tajikistan gets 49 percent of its GDP from remittances, Kyrgyzstan between 27 and 29 percent, and Uzbekistan between 10 and 13 percent.

32. For instance, in Tajikistan, according to the 2007 household survey data, remittances compensate more than 80 percent of poor households' consumption in rural areas and 50 percent in urban areas (State Statistical Agency of Tajikistan 2009). While remittances do contribute to household "survival" and poverty reduction, these financial flows do not go through official banking routes and are practically never invested; their contribution to national economic growth/development is minimal.

33. As we will see in chapter 2, liberalization policies in India are less connected with recipes from the international financial institutions than in other countries. In fact, they were designed and implemented by Indian economists who had studied and worked abroad (Kapur 2010, 149).

34. Kapur claims that the Telugu Association of North America and US-based Telugu professionals were instrumental in shaping economic policies in Andhra Pradesh (2010, 152–153).

35. *Global Risks* assessments is an initiative launched by The World Economic Forum's Risk Response Network (RRN) to provide private and public sector leaders with an independent vision of major systemic risks. These assessments are based on the insights of experts chosen across stakeholder groups and regions and include the perception of risk likelihood, risk impact, and risk interconnections from 2010 to 2020. See World Economic Forum 2012.

36. "Youth" defined here are of ages 15–24 (UN Economic and Social Commission for Asia and the Pacific 2011, 120).

37. Urdal's study included smaller-scale violence than the civil war analyses that dominated the literature, and his data cover "internal armed conflict" from 1950 to 2000, and "terrorism and rioting" for 1984 to 1995.

38. As much as 63 percent of India's population growth in the first quarter of this century is expected to happen in the most undeveloped states, which are most prone to social disturbance. Meantime, South India has completed the demographic transition and currently has very low population growth rates and an increasing age profile. See Sahni 2012.

39. The UN Economic and Social Commission for Asia and the Pacific regional nomenclature differs from that used in this book and other sources; the designations above have been adapted from the UNESCAP regional divisions of "East and Northeast Asia" and "North and Central Asia."

40. According to World Bank information, in Uzbekistan and Tajikistan almost 80 percent of household income is devoted to food, in Kyrgyzstan the figure is 58 percent, and in Kazakhstan it is 42 percent, making these countries particularly vulnerable to market fluctuations.

References

Alston, Philip. 2009, April. *Report of the Special Rapporteur on extrajudicial, summary or arbitrary executions: Addendum follow-up to country recommendations—Philippines.* New York: UN Human Rights Council.

Arezki, R., and M. Brückner. 2011. Food prices and political instability. *IMF Working Paper* WP/11/62. Washington, DC.

Asian Development Bank. 2007. *The rising tide of violence in Asia's cities*. Manila: Asian Development Bank

———. 2011. *Food for all: Investing in food security in Asia and the Pacific—issues, innovations, and practices*. Manila: Asian Development Bank.

Bahry, Louay. 2000. The socioeconomic foundations of the Shiite opposition in Bahrain. *Mediterranean Quarterly*, 11 (3): 129–143.

Bergholt, Drago, and Paivi Lujala. 2012. Climate-related natural disasters, economic growth, and armed civil conflict. *Journal of Peace Research*, 49 (1): 147–162.

Bernauer, Thomas, Tobias Bohmelt, and Vally Koubi. 2012. Environmental changes and violent conflict. *Environmental Research Letters*, 7: 1–8.

Berrebi Claude, and Jordan Ostwald. 2011. Earthquakes, hurricanes, and terrorism: Do natural disasters incite terror? RAND Labor and Population working paper 876. Santa Monica, CA: RAND Corporation.

Bolin, B. 2007. Race, class, ethnicity, and disaster vulnerability. In *Handbook of disaster research,* edited by H. Rodríguez, E. L. Quarantelli, and R. R. Dynes, 113–129. New York: Springer.

Brancati, D. 2007. Political aftershocks: The impact of earthquakes on intrastate conflict. *Journal of Conflict Resolution*, 51 (5): 715–743.

Buchanan-Smith, Margie, and Ian Christoplos. 2004. *Natural disasters and complex emergencies.* London: ODI. Retrieved from http://www.odihpn.org/humanitarian -exchange-magazine/issue-27/natural-disasters-amid-complex-political-emergencies

Buhaug, Halward, Kristian Skrede Gleditsch, Helge Holterman, Gudrun Ostby, and Andreas Foro Tollefsen. 2011. It's the local economy, stupid! Geographical wealth dispersion and conflict outbreak location. *Journal of Peace Research,* 55 (5): 814–840.

Burkea, Marshall, Edward Miguel, Shanker Satyanath, John Dykemad, and David Lobelle. 2011. Climate robustly linked to African civil war. Response to Buhaug. *Proceedings of the National Academy of Sciences*.

CDA (CDA Collaborative Learning Projects, Inc.). 2011. *Local perceptions of international engagement in fragile states and situations.* Cambridge, MA: CDA Collaborative Learning Projects, Inc.

Center for Research on Epidemiology of Disasters. 2011. EM-DAT: The OFDA/ CRED Emergency Disaster Database. Universite Catholique de Louvain, Louvain, Belgium. Retrieved from http://www.emdat.be. Accessed July 20, 2012.

Chandy, Laurence. 2011. *Ten years of fragile states: What have we learned?* Washington, DC: The Brookings Institution.

Clarke, Carla. 2012, Strategies of resistance: Testing the limits of the law. In *State of the world's minorities and indigenous peoples 2012,* edited by Beth Walker, 23–35. London: Minority Rights Group International.

Cohen, C., and E. D. Werker. 2008. The political economy of natural disasters. *Journal of Conflict Resolution,* 52 (6): 795–819.

Dawisha, Adeed. 2005. The prospects for democracy in Iraq: Challenges and opportunities. *Third World Quarterly*, 26 (4–5): 723–737.

Dentan, R. K. 2004. Cautious, alert, polite and elusive: The Semai of Central Peninsular Malaysia. In *Keeping the peace: Conflict resolution and peaceful societies around the world,* edited by Geoffrey Kemp and Douglas Fry, 167–185. New York: Routledge.

Dowling, Malcolm, and Ganeshan Wignaraja. 2006. Central Asia after fifteen years of transition: Growth, regional cooperation, and policy choices. *Asia-Pacific Development Journal,* 13 (2): 113–144.

Eilenberg. Michael. 2011. Flouting the law: Vigilante justice and regional autonomy on the Indonesian border. *Austrian Journal of South-East Asian Studies*, 4 (2): 237–253.

Faksh, Mahmud A. 1984. The Alawi community of Syria: A new dominant political force. *Middle Eastern Studies,* 20 (2): 133–153.

Fearon, James, and David Laitin. 2011. Sons of the soil, migrants, and civil war. *World Development,* 39 (2): 199–211.

Feitelson, Eran, Abdelrahman Tamimi, and Gad Rosenthal. 2012. Climate change and security in the Israeli–Palestinian context. *Journal of Peace Research,* 49 (1): 241–257.

Fry, Douglas. 2006. *The human potential for peace.* New York: Oxford University Press.
———. 2012, May 18. Life without war. *Science,* 336: 879–884.

Fry, Douglas, Bruce Bonta, and Karolina Baszarkiewicz. 2009. Learning from extant cultures of peace. In *Handbook on building cultures of peace,* edited by Jorge de Rivera, 11–26. New York: Springer Science.

Geneva Declaration on Armed Violence and Development. 2011. Global burden of armed violence. Retrieved from http://www.genevadeclaration.org/measurability/global-burden-of-armed-violence/global-burden-of-armed-violence-2011.html. Accessed May 20, 2012.

Ghani, Ejaz, and Lakshmi Iyer. 2010. Conflict and development—lessons from South Asia. *Economic Premise.* Retrieved from www.worldbank.org/economicpremise. Accessed September 31, 2012

Girard, Nicole. 2012. South East Asia. In *State of the world's minorities and indigenous peoples 2012,* edited by Beth Walker, 143–159. London: Minority Rights Group International.

Gleditsch, Nils Petter. 2012. Whither the weather? Climate change and conflict. *Journal of Peace Research*, 49 (1): 3–9.

Glinkina, Svetlana, and Dorothy Rosenberg. 2003. The socioeconomic roots of conflict in the Caucasus. *Journal of International Development,* 15: 513–524.

Harding, Luke. 2010, June 18. Kyrgyzstan death toll could be 2,000, warns leader. *The Guardian.* Retrieved from http://www.guardian.co.uk/world/2010/jun/18/kyrgyzstan-death-toll-2000-leader. Accessed May 24, 2012.

Heidelberg Institute for International Conflict Research. 2012. *Conflict barometer.* Retrieved from http://www.hiik.de/en/konfliktbarometer/index.html. Accessed July 26, 2012.

Henley, John, and George Assaf. 1997. Restructuring large scale state enterprises at the end of the Russian supply chain: The challenge for technical assistance and investment in the Central Asian republics. *Journal for East European*

Management Studies, 2 (3): 259–286. Retrieved from http://rhverlag.de/Archiv
/JEEMS_3_1997.pdf#page=31. Accessed June 9, 2012.

Hoffman, Bruce, William Rosenau, Andrew J. Curiel, and Doron Zimmermann,
eds. 2007. *The radicalization of diasporas and terrorism*. A joint conference by the
RAND Corporation and the Center for Security Studies, ETH Zurich.

Howard, A. 2004. Restraint and ritual apology: The Rotumans of South Pacific. In
Keeping the peace: Conflict resolution and peaceful societies around the world, edited
by Geoffrey Kemp and Douglas Fry, 33–53. New York: Routledge.

Human Rights Watch. 2011. *Human security report 2009/2010*. New York: Oxford
University Press.

Information Office of the State Council. People's Republic of China. 2011, April.
China's foreign aid. White paper. Beijing. Retrieved from http://english.gov.cn
/official/2011–04/21/content_1849913.htm. Accessed July 24, 2012.

International Crisis Group. 2012a, June 27. *Aid and conflict in Pakistan*. Crisis
Group Asia Report N°227.

———. 2012b, March 29. Kyrgyzstan: Widening ethnic divisions in the South.
Retrieved from http://www.crisisgroup.org/en/regions/asia/central-asia/kyrgyzs
tan/222-kyrgyzstan-widening-ethnic-divisions-in-the-south.aspx

International Labour Office. 2012. *Global employment trends 2012*. Geneva: ILO.

Johnstone, Sarah, and Jeffrey Mazo. 2011. Global Warming and the Arab Spring.
Survival, 53 (2): 11–17.

Kapur, Devesh. 2010. *Diaspora, development, and democracy*. Princeton, NJ: Princeton
University Press.

Laruelle, Marlene, and Sebastien Peyrouse. 2012. The challenges of human security
and development in Central Asia. In *The security-development nexus*, edited by
Ramses Amer, Ashok Swain, and Joakim Ojendal. London: Anthem Press.

Le Billon, P., and A. Waizenegger. 2007. Peace in the wake of disaster? Secessionist
conflicts and the 2004 Indian Ocean tsunami. *Transactions—Institute of British
Geographers*, 32 (3): 411–427.

Louis, Prakash. 2007, November 3. Lynchings in Bihar: Reassertion of dominant
castes. *Economic and Political Weekly*, 44: 26–28.

Loy, Irvin. 2012. South Asia. In *State of the world's minorities and indigenous peoples 2012*, edited by Beth Walker, 131–143. London: Minority Rights Group
International.

Minority Rights Group International. 2012. *State of the world's minorities and indigenous peoples 2012*, edited by Beth Walker. London: Minority Rights Group
International.

Muscat, Robert J. 2002. *Investing in peace: How development aid can prevent or promote conflict*. New York: M. E. Sharpe.

Mustafa, D. 1998. Structural causes of vulnerability to flood hazard in Pakistan.
Economic Geography, 74 (3): 289–305.

Naumann, Matthew. 2012. Central Asia. In *State of the world's minorities and indigenous peoples 2012*, edited by Beth Walker, 120–130. London: Minority Rights
Group International.

Nel, Philip, and Marjolein Righarts. 2008. Natural disasters and the risk of violent civil conflict. *International Studies Quarterly,* 52: 159–185.

Nicholls, R. J., S. Hanson, C. Herweijer, N. Patmore, S. Hallegatte, J. Corfee-Morlot, J. Château, and R. Muir-Wood. 2008. Ranking port cities with high exposure and vulnerability to climate extremes: Exposure estimates. OECD Environment Working Paper No. 1. Paris: Organisation for Economic Cooperation and Development. Retrieved from http://www.aia.org/aiaucmp/groups/aia/documents/pdf/aias076737.pdf. Accessed June 8, 2012.

Organization for Economic Co-operation and Development, Development Cooperation Directorate. 2011. *Statistics on resource flows to developing countries.* Paris: Organization for Economic Cooperation and Development. Retrieved from http://www.oecd.org/dataoecd/53/43/47137659.pdf. Accessed June 7, 2012.

Ortiz, Isabel, and Matthew Cummins. 2011, April. *Global inequality: Beyond the bottom billion: A rapid review of income distribution in 141 countries.* New York: United Nations Children's Fund.

Perazzi, Marusca. 2012. East Asia. In *State of the world's minorities and indigenous peoples 2012,* edited by Beth Walker, 159–167. London: Minority Rights Group International.

Peyrouse, Sébastien. 2008. The Russian minority in Central Asia: Migration, politics, and language. Occasional Paper 297. Washington, DC: Woodrow Wilson International Center for Scholars.

Radnitz, Scott. 2006. Weighing the political and economic motivations for migration in post-soviet Space: The case of Uzbekistan. *Europe-Asia Studies,* 58 (5): 653–677.

Roche, Sophie. 2010. From youth bulge to conflict: The case of Tajikistan. *East Asian Survey,* 29 (4): 405–419.

Salehi-Isfahani, Djavad, and Navtej Dhillon. 2008. *Stalled youth transitions in the Middle East: A framework for policy reform.* The Middle East Youth Initiative Working Paper Number 8, Wolfensohn School of Government / Dubai School of Government. Retrieved from http://www.shababinclusion.org/content/document/detail/1166/

Sahni, Ajai. 2012. *India's internal security challenges.* NBR Special Report 13.

Schatz, Edward. 2010. Proactive policymaking and Leninism's long shadow in Central Asia. In *Multi-nation states in Asia*, edited by Jacques Bertrand and André Laliberté, 244–262. Cambridge: Cambridge University Press.

Scheffran, Jürgen, Michael Brzoska, Jasmin Kominek, Michael Link, and Janpeter Schilling. 2012, May 18. Climate change and violent conflict. *Science,* 336: 869–871.

Schiavo-Campo, Salvatore, and Mary Judd. 2005. The Mindanao conflict in the Philippines: Roots, costs, and potential peace dividend. Washington, DC: World Bank Conflict Prevention & Reconstruction Paper No. 24, February.

Senechal de la Roche, Roberta. 1996. Violence as social control. *Sociological Forum,* 11 (1): 97–128.

Sherman, Jake, Megan M. Gleason, W. P. S. Sidhu, and Bruce Jones. 2011. Introduction and overview of the new actors and new debates. In *Engagement on development and security: New actors, new debates,* edited by Jake Sherman, Megan M. Gleason, W.P.S. Sidhu, and Bruce Jones, 1–13. New York: New York University Center on International Cooperation.

Shogren, Elizabeth. 1990, August 5. Thousands flee anti-Russian rage: Soviet Union: Surging nationalism in two republics breeds brutality against those who speak a different tongue. *Los Angeles Times.*

Sidhu, W. P. S. 2011. India's evolving role in development and security in states at risk. In *Engagement on development and security: New actors, new debates,* edited by Jake Sherman, Megan M. Gleason, W. P. S. Sidhu, and Bruce Jones, 23–30. New York: New York University Center on International Cooperation.

Singh, Pritam, 2007. The political economy of the cycles of violence and non-violence in the Sikh struggle for identity and political power: Implications for Indian federalism. *Third World Quarterly,* 28 (3): 555–570.

Solt, Frederick. 2012. Frederick Solt Dataverse: Research on the political & social consequence of economic inequality. Retrieved from http://dvn.iq.harvard.edu /dvn/dv/fsolt. Accessed June 2, 2012.

Squires, Victor. 2007. Assessment of progress on mitigating and reversing desertification and land degradation processes, and implications for land management in the changing context of the ESCAP region with special reference to the Asia Pacific countries. Bangkok: UN Economic and Social Commission for Asia and the Pacific. Retrieved from http://www.un.org/esa/sustdev/csd/csd16/rim/escap _desert.pdf. Accessed June 8, 2012.

State Statistical Agency of Tajikistan. 2009. *Tajikistan, living standards measurement survey 2007.* Survey report, Dushanbe: The State Statistical Agency of Tajikistan.

Stern, Nicholas. 2007. *The economics of climate change: The Stern Review.* Cambridge: Cambridge University Press.

Stone, Richard. 2010. Asia's looming social challenge: Coping with the elder boom. *Science,* 330: 1599

Sundar, Nandani. 2010. Vigilantism, culpability and moral dilemmas. *Critique of Anthropology,* 30: 113–121.

Svensson, Isak, and Mathilda Lindgren 2011. From bombs to banners? The decline of wars and the rise of unarmed uprisings in East Asia. *Security Dialogue,* 42: 219–237.

Swain, Ashok, and Nhi Phan. 2012. Diaspora's role in peace building: The case of the Vietnamese-Swedish diaspora. In *The security-development nexus,* edited by Ramses Amer, Ashok Swain, and Joakim Ojendal, 161–182. London: Anthem Press.

Szayna, Thomas. 2003. Potential for ethnic conflict in the Caspian region. In *Faultlines of Conflict in Central Asia and the South Caucasus: Implications for the U.S. Army,* edited by Olga Oliker and Thomas S. Szayna, 145–183. Santa Monica, CA: RAND Corporation.

Temirkulov, Azamat. 2010. Kyrgyz "revolutions" in 2005 and 2010: Comparative analysis of mass mobilization. *Nationalities Papers,* 38 (5): 589–600.

Tønnesson, Stein. 2009. What is it that best explains the East Asian peace since 1979? A call for a research agenda. *Asian Perspective,* 33 (1): 111–136.

UN Development Programme. 2008. *Armed violence in Asia and the Pacific: An overview of the causes, costs and consequences.* Geneva.

———. 2011a. *Beyond transition.* New York: United Nations Development Programme.

———. 2011b. *Disaster-conflict interface: Comparative experiences.* New York: Bureau for Crisis Prevention and Recovery. United Nations Development Programme.

UN Development Programme Kazakhstan. 2006. *Status of Oralmans in Kazakhstan: Overview.* Almaty: United Nations Development Programme.

UN Economic and Social Commission for Asia and the Pacific. 2011. *Statistical yearbook for Asia and the Pacific.* Bangkok.

UN Food and Agriculture Organization. 2010. *Global forest resources assessment 2010.* FAO Forestry Paper 163. Rome: UN Food and Agriculture Organization.

UN High Commissioner for Refugees. Refworld. 2010. 2009 country reports of human rights practices—Kazakhstan.

UN Office on Drugs and Crime. 2011. *Global homicide report 2011.* Vienna: United Nations.

Urdal, Henrik. 2006. A clash of generations? Youth bulges and political violence. *International Studies Quarterly,* 50: 607–629.

———. 2008. Population, resources, and political violence: A subnational study of India, 1956–2002. *The Journal of Conflict Resolution,* 52 (4): 590–617.

Varshney, Ashutosh. 2010. Analyzing collective violence in Indonesia: An overview. In *Collective violence in Indonesia,* edited by Ashutosh Varshney, 1–18. Boulder, CO: Lynne Rienner Publishers.

Vivekananda, Janani. 2011. *Practice note: Conflict-sensitive responses to climate change in South Asia.* Brussels: Initiative for Peacebuilding.

Wainwright, Elsina. 2011. China's growing role in fragile and conflict-affected states. In *Engagement on Development and Security: New Actors, new Debates,* edited by Jake Sherman, Megan M. Gleason, W. P. S. Sidhu, and Bruce Jonespp, 14–22. New York: New York University Center on International Cooperation.

Welsh, Bridget. 2008. Local and national: Keroyokan mobbing in Indonesia. *Journal of East Asian Studies,* 8 (3): 473–504.

———. 2009. Local and national: Lynch mobs in Indonesia. In *Collective violence in Indonesia,* edited by Ashutosh Varshney, 119–144. Boulder, CO: Lynne Rienner Publishers.

Williams, Robin M. Jr. 2003. *The wars within: Peoples and states in conflict.* Ithaca, NY: Cornell University Press.

World Bank. 2010. New patterns of violence in Indonesia: Preliminary evidence from six "high conflict" provinces, Understanding Conflict Dynamics and Impacts in Indonesia Working Paper, Conflict and Development Program. Retrieved from http://reliefweb.int/sites/reliefweb.int/files/resources/6DBA70EB56B017918525 782C007CDFAD-Full_Report.pdf. Accessed June 18, 2012.

———. 2011a. *The changing wealth of nations: Measuring sustainable development in the new millennium.* Washington, DC: World Bank.

———. 2011b. *Migration and remittances factbook 2011.* Washington: The World Bank Group.

————. 2012a. World Bank Databank: Gini index. Retrieved from http://data.world
bank.org/indicator/SI.POV.GINI. Accessed June 2, 2012.

————. 2012b. World Bank Databank: Net Development Assistance. Retrieved
from http://search.worldbank.org/data?qterm=NET%20DEVELOPMENT%20
ASSISTANCE&language=EN. Accessed June 7, 2012.

————. 2012c. World Bank Databank: Total Natural Resource Rents % of Gross
Domestic Product. Retrieved from http://data.worldbank.org/indicator/NY.GDP
.TOTL.RT.ZS. Accessed June 8, 2012.

World Economic Forum. 2011. *The global risks 2011 report.* Geneva.

————. 2012. *The global risks 2012 report.* Geneva.

World Health Organization. 2002. *World report on violence and health.* Geneva:
World Health Organization.

————. 2009. Disease and injury country estimates: Burden of disease. Retrieved
from http://www.who.int/healthinfo/global_burden_disease/estimates_country
/en/index.html. Accessed May 21, 2012.

CHAPTER 2

The Nexus of Economic Strategies and Intergroup Conflict in Asia

William Ascher and Natalia Mirovitskaya

Since independence, Asia has grown more than twice as fast as the rest of the world, with stunning changes in economic approaches and structures in most countries. The transitions included experimentation with several economic doctrines and many development strategies. In the 1950s and 1960s, structural transition away from agriculture was pursued through import-substitution industrialization (ISI); by the mid-1980s most Asian countries had embraced an export-oriented growth model, accompanied by market-based economic reforms, though often partly reversed or applied in ways to maintain state control. The Asian financial crisis of the late 1990s, which plunged most regional economies into deep recession, led to yet another shift in economic development strategies. And alternative development models, including the Chinese approach, have emerged. The specific strategies and policies to implement these doctrines were different in scale, timing, and resultant economic performances of Asian subregions and individual countries. Their impacts on conflict varied greatly as well. Some of key differences are presented in this chapter.

Economic Doctrines

Patterns of economic, political, and social development in Asia were heavily affected by the region's colonial heritage.[1] Colonization left most countries with "lopsided" economic structures: except for Singapore and Hong Kong, all countries were agricultural economies exporting low-value primary products and importing high-value manufactures (Tan 2003). This reality was widely interpreted as too problematic to tolerate.

State-Directed Development

The post-WWII doctrines reflected statist approaches prominent in the pre-WWII period and heavily state-directed mobilization of resources among belligerents and their colonies. Following WWII, this inertia was reinforced by the perceived imperative for strong government leadership for "nation building." The economic conditions included a scarcity of mobilizable savings for voluntary investment, due to poverty and because existing wealth was held in gold and other nonproductive forms. Investment opportunities were generally not as compelling for foreign direct investment (FDI) as were opportunities in recovering Europe. Many national leaders believed that the state had to take the leading role in promoting new development models, to mobilize domestic capital and overcome the limited capital and timidity of private investors. State-directed investment capital could be generated through taxation, utilization of natural resources, and eventually through international borrowing.

Channeling capital could take two forms. State enterprises held the attraction (and danger) that they could be directed to serve other than purely economic purposes. The government could also channel capital to private firms in particular industries. This had the attraction (and danger) that government planners could select the industries and firms regarded as more productive—or the firms owned by favored industrialists. In South Korea, under General Park Chung-hee, state-generated capital was channeled to relatively efficient firms (Ascher and Overholt 1983, 202); in the Philippines under Ferdinand Marcos it was unproductive "crony capitalism" (Kang 2002).

This statist doctrine is not intrinsically wedded to a particular inward- or outward-looking orientation. The commonality was that governments heavily directed capital, rather than allowing market signals to steer investment. Many governments adopted the most direct form of state involvement, placing state enterprises over large portions of the economy. Communist nations (China, North Korea, and Vietnam) were naturally dominated by state enterprises; as were the Soviet republics. Yet so, too, were India and many other Asian countries.

Import-Substitution Industrialization

The allure of manufacturing-based industrialization was powerful in the early post-WWII period. Some nations (China, India, Indonesia, Iran, Pakistan, and Turkey) had large enough populations to foster optimism toward inward-looking development. Other nations, with much smaller populations, also fell under the thrall of ISI. Governments supported nascent industries through low-interest loans and subsidies, and protected them from foreign competition through tariffs, quotas, licensing, and exchange controls, prompting reciprocal measures by potential trading partners.

Manufacturing was greatly favored over agriculture, on the premise that agricultural productivity was constrained by limits of arable land and the lack of payoff from technology. Low food prices could keep the cost of living for industrial workers low enough to permit lower industrial wages to enhance manufacturing profits. Rural poverty and unchecked urbanization from this "bias against agriculture" (Bautista and Valdes 1993) still presents a huge socioeconomic and political burden on many countries. ISI generally favored light industry, with some success in establishing consumer goods industries, such as textiles, leather, and pharmaceuticals (Dwyer 1990, 210). Some countries lessened their dependence on traditional economic activities, and generated wealth for further domestic investment. Some governments were even able to launch heavy industry (e.g., India's "Mahalanobis strategy," emphasizing steel, machine tools, cement, and chemicals).

However, fledgling industries were generally constrained by small domestic markets and poor resource bases. Economic controls stifled private sector expansion, bringing in inefficiency, rent-seeking, and political patronage. In Sri Lanka, for instance, the public sector expanded over industry, agriculture, trade, and banking, managed by inefficient state enterprises, with losses covered by government transfers. Sri Lanka's "welfare democracy" roused expectations of upward social mobility, yet the country faced increasing economic stagnation, unemployment, trade imbalances, consumer goods shortages, and, unsurprisingly, political dissatisfaction (Abeyratne 2002, 15). Some scholars trace the Tamil separatism and the Sinhala youth uprising to this combination of "welfare democracy" and economic stagnation (Abeyratne 1998; Abeyratne 2002).[2]

In fact, the real challenges of ISI have always been both economic and political. The expansion of the domestic market needed to implement ISI implied a redistribution of wealth and power (Black 1999, 95); recognition of this challenge mobilized threatened elites to seek new development strategies. Some governments responded by shifting to export-led growth, while others (Indonesia's Suharto, Iran's Shah Pahlavi, Fiji's Colonel Rabuka)—by redistributing assets and income from the bottom up.

The Shift to an Export Orientation

In Northeast and Southeast Asia, the unsuccessful inward-looking orientation of several countries (Indonesia, Malaysia, South Korea, Singapore, and

Taiwan) was abandoned earlier than in other Asian subregions, in favor of an outward-looking manufactured-exports strategy (Daly 2011, 11), following the Japanese example. Competitive export industries were built eclectically, to find niches in the world economy dominated by more advanced countries. Thus, in mid-1950s South Korea developed a large-scale export industry based on wigs (Petri 2012, 50); more impressive industries such as shipbuilding and steel followed.

Resources for these initiatives came from domestic savings and FDI, though Japan and South Korea were less welcoming to foreign investment (Daly 2011, 12). China, relying on its huge labor force and huge trade surpluses, began the transition in 1978, along with crucial market-liberalization reforms. India shifted to an export-oriented approach in the early 1990s.

Liberalization Trends

Daly (2011, 12) emphasizes that this largely successful outward-looking development strategy, much admired beyond the subregion, depended also on "the maintenance of macroeconomic stability; reliance on a functioning market system to allocate resources; and committed, capable, and credible governments." The first two criteria call for "liberalization" of economic policy, requiring fiscal, monetary, pricing, and banking policy reform; the elimination of regulatory, legal, and paperwork impediments to doing business; fair and nondistorting tax systems; the reduction of regulatory and bureaucratic obstacles to international trade; and either privatization or restructuring of state enterprises. Gauging the complex liberalization trends must rely on broad summary measures. Combining assessments by the World Bank Group and the Fraser Institute captures most of the relevant dimensions. The World Bank Group (2012) assesses ten dimensions of "ease of doing business" globally in the face of bureaucratic and regulatory requirements, delays, and so on. One dimension is the important (but somewhat limited) measure of the ease of trading across borders.[3] The Fraser Institute's "Economic Freedom of the World" assessment, though less current (2009) and more limited in-country coverage, uses broader elements in scoring nations on liberalization.[4] The World Bank Group rankings correlate with the broader "Economic Freedom of the World" rankings at 0.77 for the 32 Asian countries covered by both. The trade openness measures are less similar: the correlation is only 0.55, accounting for 30 percent of the variation. Table 2.1 displays the overall 2011 "Doing Business" rankings of Asian nations among the assessments of 183 countries (column 2). It also displays the percentage of convergence to the highest possible score over the 2006–2011 period (column 3), indicating the

Table 2.1 Economic Liberalization Levels and Trends

[1]	[2] World Bank "Ease of doing business" rank (out of 183)	[3] "Ease of doing business": % of narrowing "distance to the frontier" 2006–2011	[4] "Economic Freedom" rank 2009 (out of 141)	[5] World Bank Trading across borders rank	[6] "Economic Freedom" Freedom to trade internationally	[7] "Economic Freedom" Private sector share of enterprises & investment
Singapore	1	1.5	2	1	1	7
Hong Kong	2	5.5	1	2	2	10
Korea, Rep.	8	6.5	30	4	40	8
Saudi Arabia	12	16	..	18	..	..
Georgia	16	28	27	54	24	8
Thailand	17	7	65	17	16	6
Malaysia	18	6	78	29	29	0
Japan	20	0.5	22	16	114	10
Taiwan	25	4.5	26	23	28	7
United Arab Emirates	33	6	14	5	11	2
Israel	34	2	83	10	45	4
Qatar	36	..	..	57	..	..
Bahrain	38	..	11	49	..	4
Kazakhstan	47	11	56	176	95	4
Oman	49	4.5	28	47	37	0
Armenia	55	7.5	43	104	79	6
Azerbaijan	66	13	84	170	80	2

Continued

Table 2.1 Continued

[1]	[2] World Bank "Ease of doing business" rank (out of 183)	[3] "Ease of doing business": % of narrowing "distance to the frontier" 2006–2011	[4] "Economic Freedom" rank 2009 (out of 141)	[5] World Bank Trading across borders rank	[6] "Economic Freedom" Freedom to trade internationally	[7] "Economic Freedom" Private sector share of enterprises & investment
Kuwait	67	2.5	47	112	100	7
Kyrgyzstan	70	16	70	171	68	4
Turkey	71	4	75	80	83	7
Mongolia	86	1.5	36	159	19	10
Sri Lanka	89	2	107	53	121	6
China	91	14	92	60	30	0
Jordan	96	7.5	62	58	32	0
Vietnam	98	5	88	68	43	4
Yemen	99	11.5	..	118	..	..
Papua New Guinea	101	2.5	61	99	12	8
Pakistan	105	2	114	75	116	4
Nepal	107	2.5	129	162	124	4
Russia	120	10	81	160	111	10
Bangladesh	122	4.5	103	115	118	4
Indonesia	129	7.5	84	39	65	7

West Bank and Gaza	131	2.5	:	114	:	:
India	132	10	94	109	76	4
Syria	134	9.5	121	122	113	2
Philippines	136	1	89	51	74	6
Cambodia	138	8	:	120	:	:
Bhutan	142	6	:	169	:	:
Iran	144	4	105	138	134	4
Tajikistan	147	12	:	177	:	:
Afghanistan	160	7	:	179	:	:
Iraq	164	:	:	180	:	:
Lao PDR	165	7	:	168	:	:
Uzbekistan	166	5.5	:	183	:	:
Timor-Leste	168	:	:	89	:	:
Myanmar	:	:	140	:	141	4

extent of recent liberalization. Column 4 displays the overall "Economic Freedom" rankings among 141 countries; Columns 5 and 6 present the World Bank Group's trade-openness rankings and the "Economic Freedom" assessment. Column 7 is the "Economic Freedom" assessment, from zero to ten, of private sector dominance vis-à-vis the government's own enterprises and investment (Gwartney, Lawson, and Hall 2011, 5).

Table 2.1 conveys the very high level of liberalization of Northeast Asian nations (Hong Kong, South Korea, Japan, and Taiwan). The obvious exception is China, yet China has been moving strongly toward greater liberalization. All but China also rank very high on ease of trading, yet by the broader "Economic Freedom" criteria, Japan is quite protectionist, South Korea is less open than its export-promotion orientation might imply, and China is far more open in this respect.

The second striking pattern is the high liberalization rankings and openness of oil exporting nations (Saudi Arabia, the United Arab Emirates, Qatar, Bahrain, and Oman), with the exception of Kuwait. These countries are assured of export markets even with their import restrictions. Of other Arab Asian nations, the most telling ranking is Syria's—extremely low rankings in both openness and general liberalization may reflect protection of Assad-supporters' businesses.

Iran maintains a highly regulated economy with numerous impediments to private business. It went from one of the most free trade-oriented countries in the 1970s to one of the least by 1980. Whether this reflects economic sanctions, reactions to sanctions, or ideology, is difficult to say.

South Asian nations, except for Sri Lanka, also exhibit little overall liberalization, though India has significantly higher ease of doing business since 2006. India's trade liberalization has lagged behind its transition to an export orientation in the 1990s. Sri Lanka and Pakistan are relatively open compared to other South Asian nations.

Southeast Asia shows the greatest variation. Singapore has one of the world's most liberalized economies, and, like other city states, is highly open to international trade. Thailand and Malaysia are both highly liberalized and open, while the other Southeast Asian nations rank low on both dimensions. However, Papua New Guinea, Indonesia, the Philippines, and Thailand have become more open according to the broader "Economic Freedom" assessment. There is a discrepancy between the macroeconomic aspects of trade openness and the impediments to conducting trade. Sally and Sen (2011, 574) observe that "Southeast Asia fits the developing-world pattern of fast trade-and-FDI liberalization through the 1980s and first half of the 1990s, followed by a slowdown of momentum after the Asian crisis," but they note that "with the exception of Singapore, government enthusiasm for further liberalization declined markedly." Myanmar has long been among the least open nations, and as of 2009 ranked as the absolute lowest.

For West and Central Asia, the European Bank for Reconstruction and Development (EBRD) (2010) has assessed liberalization in the former Soviet republics, Turkey, and Mongolia. It gives Armenia, Azerbaijan, Georgia, Kyrgyzstan, Mongolia, and Turkey the highest possible score for movement toward more liberalized trade policies. However, "Doing Business" rankings show that trade-related business still faces severe impediments in Azerbaijan, Kyrgyzstan, and Mongolia, which may reflect regulations and bureaucratic processes facilitating rent-seeking or favoritism. For the other Central Asian republics, Kazakhstan has liberalized recently, but not in trade openness, and Tajikistan, Uzbekistan, and Turkmenistan[5] are far less open.

The "Economic Freedom" assessment, going back to 1970 for many countries, shows an overall liberalization trend, but also oscillation between liberalizing efforts and illiberal policies. We can conclude that liberalization has been highly contested, as its impacts—positive or negative—affect different groups. And the churning itself often triggers confrontations among presumed winners and losers.

Trade Liberalization. One might think that the most obvious aspect of liberalization to promote an export orientation is greater trade openness. However, openness often threatens owners and workers in sectors vulnerable to imports. It is not surprising that despite the lip service paid to trade openness, trade reform has a mixed record and the degree of trade openness has fluctuated over time.

"Harmonization" with Other Economies within Trade Pacts. Free trade pacts call for some degree of economic policy harmonization. Ishida and Fukunaga (2012, 1–2) note the "critical roles of domestic regulatory reform" required to create a "consolidated region wide free trade framework" for Southeast Asia. Harmonization may secure gains through greater trade, but it frequently entails eliminating the subsidies, regulations, and exemptions that favor particular groups.

Trade pacts have proliferated throughout Asia. Hufbauer and Schott (2007, 41) reported 17 trade agreements in East and South Asia prior to 2000, and 37 concluded between 2000 and 2007. Among postcommunist countries, Armenia, Georgia, and Mongolia have joined only one regional trading arrangement, but each of the Central Asian republics has joined between three and five such arrangements (Pomfret 2009, 55). Turkey has a trade agreement with the European Union, in addition to other agreements. The Pan-Arab Free Trade Area mandates zero tariffs among Arab nations of Asia and North Africa, and many of these countries have trade agreements well beyond the Arab region (Hoekman and Zarrouk 2009).

Privatization. Controversies over the extent, nature, and beneficiaries of state-enterprise privatization are so contentious that it deserves separate attention. Privatization has two modes: selling off state-owned enterprises, and contracting with the private sector to build, operate, and (in some cases) own new developments, particularly in large-scale infrastructure. The promise of privatization—not always realized—is providing revenues by selling the assets, reducing budgetary drains by shedding money-losing state enterprises, greater investment to upgrade facilities and services, greater operational efficiency, greater economic efficiency as prices reflect competition, and reducing opportunities for state corruption. Opposition to privatization varies across sectors. Privatization of manufacturing or service raises concerns over employment, as private firms are often more prone to shed labor. Privatization of services raises concerns over coverage, as private companies may not find it profitable to provide service to more remote areas, and competitive pricing may not be affordable to low-income people. Privatization of natural resources and certain major industries raises concerns over private (and often foreign) ownership of "strategic industries" and the economy's "commanding heights." A huge concern for natural resource–dependent nations is that international firms frequently reduce investment or extraction when other areas are more attractive or international prices fall. From a political perspective, "economic nationalism" and "resource nationalism" often have high political resonance as populist stances.

The pace of privatization reflects the contestation that reemerged after what many had thought was a consensus in favor of privatization. Nellis (2012, 2) wryly notes his own erroneous 2001 presumption that "privatization has swept the field and won the day." However, this consensus was never complete. In that same year, the influential economist Dwight Perkins noted that "there are a number of highly efficient state enterprises in Asia" (Perkins 2001, 267–268). Yet Perkins then emphasized the crucial importance of state-enterprise autonomy and commitment to profit: "Stringent conditions were needed to achieve success with these state firms...All enjoyed a high degree of autonomy. Management's performance was judged mainly or even solely on its ability to generate long-term profits for the company" (Perkins 2001, 268).

For Asia, Chinese privatization has dominated in terms of both number of transactions and their value. Yet even by 2009, Chinese state enterprises still accounted for a third of industrial production and 30 percent of gross domestic product and total workforce (Nellis 2012, 7; 10). While some Asian nations launched their first significant privatizations toward the very end of the twentieth century (India, Iran, Saudi Arabia, Syria, and Vietnam), Tajikistan,[6] Turkmenistan, and North Korea have not engaged in significant privatization at all (Nellis 2012, 1; 9). Malaysia, following one of Asia's most ambitious privatization programs, later renationalized sewer, transit, airline, and automotive enterprises (Tan 2007, 4). Vigorous efforts are ongoing to renationalize Indonesian and Malaysian water systems; South Korean governments vacillate in privatizing and nationalizing the banking system; Kazakhstan recently recaptured partial state control of oil and mining.

Except for China, the scores of private sector prevalence (column 7 of Table 2.1) show East Asian nations as highly private-sector-oriented. South Asian nations of Bangladesh, India, Nepal, and Pakistan score fairly low, consistent with overall low levels of liberalization.

The two Central Asian republics in the set, Kazakhstan and Kyrgyzstan, are relatively state-enterprise-dominated; various sources (Henley and Assaf 1997; Dowling and Wignaraja 2006, 127–128; Nellis 2012) confirm that other Central Asian economies remain dominated by state enterprises. This contrasts sharply with the former Soviet republics of Armenia and Georgia.

Except for Kuwait, Arab countries (oil rich or not) score low to very low. In Western Asia, Turkey has a relatively large private sector, whereas the Iranian and Israeli economies are relatively state-dominated. Papua New Guinea and Indonesia have rather high private sector dominance; Vietnam is still quite state-dominated, though Malaysia much more so. The remarkably high Russian score reflects the possibility of coexistence between an ostensibly privatized economy and indirect state control. Russia's low rankings on general liberalization and ease of doing business reflect the levers that the Russian government uses to influence private sector operations.

In essence, two different state-enterprise doctrines have been common. The cases cited by Perkins reflect the doctrine of insulating state enterprises from the demands to serve political or social goals. The public provision of social services should be provided by line agencies with more direct links to accountable officials. The other doctrine, manifested frequently in Indonesia, India, Arab Asia, and many other countries, casts state enterprises as more general-purpose government entities, to set prices or deploy revenues to serve noncommercial objectives, whether to provide employment, make goods or services more affordable, gain political support, promote migration, and so on.

The "Flock of Geese" with Asiatic values, the China Model, and Other Unorthodox Development Doctrines

These complex trends reflect important doctrinal conflicts between East and West. While export-led growth in Asia started with East Asian countries launching the production of labor-intensive products to then move into more skill- and capital-intensive industries, they left the labor-intensive manufacturing opportunities to other Asian states.[7] The similar trajectories of export-oriented trade regimes of "advanced Asia" reflect the "Flying Geese" model.[8] Coined to illustrate how less-developed countries can catch up with more developed countries by adopting the technologies of the latter, this paradigm involves importing a particular product, developing its internal market, and, through policy interventions, forcing domestic production to expand into the external market. The "Flying Geese" process adopted by the "ASEAN-5" (Indonesia, Malaysia, Philippines, Thailand, and Vietnam) and by China and India, followed similar combinations of trade, foreign investment, aid, and technology-transfer policies of more advanced nations. The more advanced nations pursued stronger regional integration through their corresponding policies, to try to sustain their own "flight" (Naya 2002; Dowling and Valenzuela 2010).

However, the "Flying Geese" model was just one among many explanations of the economic success. The *East Asian Miracle* report (World Bank 1993) credited East Asia's success to neoliberal development strategies and human capital development. In contrast, some Asian political leaders de-emphasized economic policy and structures, positing the "Asian values" thesis that the capacity for sustained economic growth was inherent in Asian culture: hard work, education, respect for authority, and—in contrast to Western liberal democracy—the priority of national, community, and family interests above those of the individual, as well as social harmony and stability over individual rights (Kingsbury 2008).[9] Others questioned neoliberalism as responsible for the "Asian miracle" by noting the high degree of state intervention,[10] controls on foreign investment, targeted infrastructure investments, and policy flexibility (ISI alongside export promotion; regulations, subsidies, and rigorous taxation along with liberalization). Others (Li 2002; Rigg 2003; Petri 2012) cite significant differences in the design and implementation of economic development strategies even among the four "Asian Tigers." Japan and South Korea used interventionist industrial policies and relied on domestic and licensed technologies while Hong Kong and Singapore pursued market approaches and relied on foreign investment. Some repressed labor costs; others imposed restrictions on capital markets. All these measures contributed to power differentials among production firms, labor, investors, and consumers, and occasionally stirred public discontent. While high exposure to international competition is a common denominator for most Asian countries, the degree of trade openness, private foreign investment, and market orientation in general differed substantially among countries and across time.

The "advanced" Asian countries were also much more ethnically and culturally homogenous than most of Asia,[11] while religious differences were rather subdued. Intergroup rivalry was largely limited to class conflicts kept under control by government through means ranging from repression to bargaining. For the "Asian Cubs" (Indonesia, the Philippines, Malaysia, and Thailand), modernization exacerbated at least some crosscutting cleavages and therefore was more politically controversial and socially turbulent (see the chapters by Aragon and Al Ramiah and Ramasamy in this volume).

Just as the Asian Development Bank (1997, 121–128) made its ill-timed prediction that in 30 years many Asian countries would match the West in economic development and living standards, the 1997 Asian financial crisis revealed the vulnerability of East Asian economies to the global financial and trade regime. Although East Asia was able to reemerge as a dynamic economic region, the crisis cast doubt over the foundations of the "Asian miracle."

The quest for new development paradigms highlighted the reform strategies of China and India, which were previously regarded as economic "losers." Their economic ascent has occurred despite their deviations from standard policy prescriptions. The "China model" has been particularly prominent, representing a gradualist reform strategy as distinct from the "shock therapy" prescribed by the international financial institutions (Huang 2008; Yong 2008).

Since 1978, China, following its own development path, has achieved dynamic economic performance, dramatically reduced the extent of poverty, and weathered the Great Recession much better than most of the world. Yet China is experiencing deteriorating income distribution, increased urban-rural divides, and spatial inequalities, though not to the extent to provoke overt organized internal violence. The economic success has been achieved despite the absence of private property rights or a market-based banking system, in defiance of orthodox prescriptions.

India's takeoff since 1991 has quadrupled its per capita GDP[12]. While India's growth has not matched China's 22-fold increase since 1991, India's growth defies the conventional wisdom that high economic growth in democracies is severely constrained by interest groups' power to block policy reforms required for rapid economic expansion. India's development trajectory has differed from China's; certainly the success is closely correlated with the pro-market policy reforms of "stabilization, liberalization and privatization." However, detailed analysis (Joshi and Little 1997; Nayyar 2008; Roland 2011) reveals that India's economic strategy has also deviated from standard development prescriptions, as its rankings on liberalization dimensions have indicated above. Despite some pro-business reforms, the Indian government retained management control of key enterprises. Though a World Trade Organization member (as is China), India remains a relatively closed economy protected by tariffs and other trade barriers. And, though on the path toward financial liberalization, the government still has a higher degree of control over financial market and capital movements than most other Asian economies. Unlike China, however, India has a long tradition of "mixed" economy with well-developed market-supporting institutions.

However, one cannot argue that India's deviations from orthodox prescriptions have succeeded in attending to the broader social dimensions of development. Drèze and Sen (2011) note that whereas in 1990 India had higher life expectancy than Bangladesh, Bhutan, and Nepal, these nations have exceeded India's current life expectancy; Pakistan and Sri Lanka, which started out higher in 1990, are still higher despite lower economic growth. India's 1990 infant mortality rate was lower than all other South Asian countries but Sri Lanka, but currently only Pakistan has a higher rate. India's female literacy rate for young women (15–24) was higher than those of Bangladesh and Nepal, but now their rates are higher.[13] All other South Asian nations have higher infant immunization rates and lower proportions of underweight children (though data are missing for Pakistan) than India.

While neither China nor India can be categorized as an epitome of societal peace and stability, their growth can be considered an "against all the odds" phenomenon, which makes their experiences extremely valuable. Roland (2011, 165) attributes their economic success to "the combination of bottom-up with top-down reforms, the use of experiments, the coexistence of the state and the market, compensation of reform losers, a gradual reform approach, the use of transitional institutions, and creation of competition," though one can certainly question whether most losers have been compensated. Both countries have experimented (special economic zones [SEZ] for foreign trade and investment policies in India; pilot enterprises in China) before launching large-scale economic changes. India's political system also allowed extensive stakeholder consultations. The gradual approach gave policymakers in both countries opportunities to refine their initiatives, create buy-ins for reforms, and find ways to compensate some reform losers. Dual-track liberalization and the introduction of the Township-Village Enterprises in China, and the partial privatizations in both countries, are examples of buy-ins and compensatory mechanisms (Roland 2011, 166). Both China and India deviated from standard privatization prescriptions, opting for coexistence of state and private enterprises. However, both ventured to develop the private sector, to create competition between states and provinces and between the state and nonstate sectors, forcing state enterprises to reform and find new economic niches.

Some common factors link the nonorthodox development approaches of China and India to the development strategies of the Asian Tigers:

- a strong and multifaceted state role, ranging from state-owned enterprises to oversight of private companies within strategic industries;
- export-led growth based on evolving comparative advantages (Lin 2011);
- manipulation of the supply, prices, and access to inputs ("factor market repression"), to support export-led growth, and periodic economic and financial rebalancing of development distortions created by factor repression;
- policy flexibility through market-oriented and nonmarket policy mechanisms;
- some compensation for development losers; and
- mechanisms to suppress opposition to reforms.

Links between Development Strategies and the Likelihood of Conflict

To evaluate the impact of economic development strategies systematically, it is useful to summarize the possible dynamics associated with each broad category of strategies. These categories are as follows:

- explicit redistribution, targeting assets or future earnings of particular groups;
- macroeconomic policy changes, including fiscal, monetary, and pricing policies, and restructuring banking, labor markets, and the state sector;
- sectoral promotion, favoring particular types of industrialization, agriculture, physical infrastructure, or social services;
- regional development, allocating more government resources or favorable policies to particular areas of the country;
- population resettlement and other forms of demographic engineering;
- natural resource policies, affecting both the nature and extent of resource extraction and the disposition of resource revenues.

Explicit Redistribution

In Asia, the most significant explicitly redistributive policies are confiscations of existing assets, affirmative action policies, and direct transfers of cash, goods, or services to the poor. By definition, these policies make it clear who the winners and losers are, although losers often have exaggerated perceptions of harm, and winners often discount the advantages as compensation for past disfavor.

Outright Confiscation. The most obvious redistribution begins with direct asset expropriation. Turkmenistan has a negative reputation for "capriciously" expropriating both domestically owned assets (especially from out-of-power officials) and foreign investors (Olcott 2006, 211). Yet direct expropriation need not be complete: Malaysia's pro-Malay policies in the early 1970s required Malaysian Chinese to "sell" company shares at a 30 percent discount. Policy-induced expropriations run the gamut from extremely high taxes or fines, to discriminatory regulations levied against particular populations or activities. An even more corrosive dynamic is provocation by the government, or by nongovernmental violence entrepreneurs, to induce expulsion or physical attacks. Demonized groups face additional stereotyping and physical jeopardy as well as economic loss. A chilling example was the state's confiscation of $58 billion of Indonesian-Chinese assets following President Suharto's ouster in 1998; anti-Chinese agitation also cost them 2,000 deaths and the burning and looting of 5,000 businesses and homes (Chua 2004, 1244).

Affirmative Action. Some analysts applaud affirmative action for reducing "horizontal inequalities," presuming that reducing income gaps reduces the violence potential (Stewart, Brown, and Langer 2007). This premise downplays the backlash that affirmative action programs often have been, and, in some contexts underestimate the costs of perpetuating sharp ethnic distinctions.

One distinctive affirmative-action scenario entails favored treatment of a nondominant economically disadvantaged minority, requiring the sufferance of the more affluent majority. India is the most prominent example, as upon independence the very low-income *dalits* ("untouchables") and the isolated *adivasi* ("tribals") were accorded special access to education, jobs, and economic opportunities. These policies were effective in raising the economic levels of these groups (Desai and Kulkarni 2008). However, in 1989, the government enacted a highly controversial expansion of affirmative action to include "Other Backward Castes" (OBCs),[14] constituting roughly 30 percent of the population, qualifying well over half the total population for favored treatment. Considerable disruption, ranging from demonstrations to self-immolation, resulted from clashes over university admission, accusations of corruption in eligibility certification, and the dilution of benefits through the extension to the OBCs. The affirmative action programs have, contrary to the hopes of India's founders, accentuated caste identity.

The second scenario, most prominently represented by Malaysia and Sri Lanka, entails an economically backward majority achieving favored treatment through its power over policy, rationalized on the grounds of equity and poverty alleviation, and invoking the unfairness of colonial administrations in favoring minorities. The majority but less prosperous Malays have enjoyed favored economic and educational status since independence, which became stronger through the "New Economic Policy" (NEP), following the 1969 anti-Chinese riots. The riots, causing nearly two hundred deaths, reflected resentment against Chinese economic dominance, a belief that the British had favored the Chinese, and fears that "outsiders" were undermining Malay culture.[15] Jomo and Hui (2003, 444) argue that "while the NEP probably eliminated some ethnic Malay resentment of Chinese economic success by accelerating the advance of Malay middle class and business interests, it may well also have generated even greater Malay expectations of their rights, entitlements and privileges under the Malaysian sun, thus inadvertently fuelling inter-ethnic resentment at the same time."

The combination of economic growth and affirmative action have, in fact, elevated the Malays' employment status, diversity of economic roles, educational access, and incomes—reducing their poverty dramatically. Because of economic growth, the economic situation of the Chinese (roughly a quarter of the population) and East Indians (roughly 8 percent of the population) have also improved, though the Malays' national income share has increased (Al Ramiah and Ramasamy, this volume). Compared to dire predictions of the 1970s, violence has been remarkably low. Unsurprisingly, the case has received highly divergent judgments—astonishing success, due to Malay advances, rising incomes for all, and low levels of violence;[16] or egregious discrimination perpetuating ethnic separation (Jomo 2004), undermining the faith of Chinese Malaysians, many of whom desire to emigrate (Al Ramiah and Ramasamy, this volume). Economic dynamism seems to be eroding, prompting the government to gradually weaken affirmative action provisions.

Sri Lanka's affirmative action, in granting greater access to the majority Sinhalese to higher education and government jobs, has been a major rationale for Tamil separatism. Overt university-admission quotas have been a blatant aspect of the program, but the Sinhalese language requirement for government employment, rationalized as nation-building, is equally provocative. Ironically, it is unclear how much the Sinhalese could have benefited from it,[17] even if the civil war had not ravaged the economy.

This experience highlights the potential of language policy to redistribute income opportunities, through educational or government-employment measures. It is particularly attractive to postcolonial ethnic-majority governments, to marginalize minority groups that had no need or opportunity to gain fluency in the majority indigenous language, and particularly groups originating in the colonial center (e.g., Russians in Central Asia).

More generally, a fine line separates pro-majority affirmative action that reduces animosity through judicious elevation of an economically backward majority, and affirmative action provoking a backlash or even separatist efforts. Malaysian political parties have been interethnic even if the economic advantage was reluctantly ceded to the Malays (Muscat 2002, 74–82). Sheth (2004, 33) argues that in

> the countries where the [affirmative action] policy was explicitly conceived as a means of removing persistent conditions of structural exclusion that caused injustice and deprivation to people of certain communities and regions and was administered by ethnoneutral and *democratic* state, it has enormously contributed to making the society more inclusive, even equitous. On the other hand, in countries where the policy was adopted and implemented by an ethno-majoritarian state (democratic or otherwise), even for the good reason of uplifting and accommodating the deprived and backward communities within the country, it almost invariably ended up as an instrument for appeasing the ethno-religious majority and discrimination of the minorities.

Direct Transfers to the Poor. One of the most direct means of addressing poverty and resentment against policies that seem threatening to low-income groups is to transfer assets to eligible families. Eligibility is based on need, and often on the willingness to engage in activities expected to enhance the family's human capital. Conditional cash transfers (CCTs) have become the most promising social-safety-net mechanism to alleviate poverty, enhance human capital, and preempt disruption during policy reform.[18] Adopted widely since the 1990s, CCTs require recipients to adhere to such conditions as keeping their children in school and providing them regular health care. Other conditions may include work on public infrastructure and training-program attendance. Typical programs in middle-income developing countries entail roughly $20 monthly payments, targeting the poorest population quintile. The potential enhancement of the children's productivity can reduce resistance from the non-poor, insofar as they appreciate the contribution to the economy's long-term productivity.

Indonesia CCTs in the early 2000s helped to cushion the poor when fuel prices were liberalized; the budgetary savings also permitted the government to increase social service spending (Grosh et al. 2008, 52; Widianto 2007; World Bank 2008a). In Turkey, the 2000 agricultural pricing liberalization, a "signal achievement" according to the World Bank's Independent Evaluation Group, saved $4 billion in government expenditure on agricultural subsidies and lowered food prices (World Bank 2006, 21). Cash transfers for small-scale farmers were important for enacting the reform. The Turkish government enacted a "Social Risk Mitigation Program" for the poorest 6 percent of Turkish families during the 2001 economic crisis that prompted the withdrawal of children from school and threatened their nutrition (World Bank 2008b). The program led to over a million children re-entering school by the end of 2001, and ultimately increased primary-school enrollment (Commission of the European Communities 2007, 19).

CCTs do face pitfalls. In Syria, the antagonism toward a 2008 elimination of fuel subsidies was not mitigated despite a transfer program. A UN Development Programme (2011, 82) report noted:

> In order to soften the impact of the increase on key economic sectors and the poor, the government planned to set up an export support fund, a social aid fund, an agricultural support fund and an industrial support fund to channel back 50% of the savings generated . . . The promised compensatory measures proved hard to establish and difficult to manage. Citizens were victims of wrangling between sector ministries and finance. The process of building and operating those new mechanisms was slow, over politicized and tactical rather than strategic.

The case demonstrates that programs that are not mounted quickly and fairly may fail to assuage the economic pain resulting from the accompanying reform. These programs also require bureaucratic infrastructure, and may arouse conflict if some groups believe they are unfairly excluded. In Indonesia, the distribution of safety net benefits has varied enormously from one locale to another.

A World Bank (2005, 9–10) analysis of Indonesian safety net services reports:

> Despite the existing eligibility list, in reality village officials had almost complete authority to determine how the rice would be distributed within their villages . . . Virtually all aspects of distribution—generation of eligibility lists, the amount of rice each household was allowed to buy, the price of the rice—varied dramatically from village to village . . . In some areas, the rice was well-targeted to poor families; in others, the rice was simply divided equally among recipients . . . [I]n some areas local decision-makers felt pressure from communities to change the distribution of rice from the designated "eligible" households, which were

deemed equally deserving, to the entire community. In other areas, it was simply announced that cheap rice was available for sale, and whoever could afford to buy it was allowed to do so...Regarding the "health card" program...one of the reason[s] for mis-targeting...resulted from lack of community involvement in targeting at [the] village level, as [the] village and the head of [the] local community health center were dominating the determination of beneficiaries.

This was not only because rules established at the center were poorly communicated, but also because local-level norms and politics prompted local authorities and community activists to set their own eligibility criteria, sometimes excluding qualified recipients in favor of others.

Macroeconomic Policy Changes

In contrast to the transparency of explicit redistributive policies, the huge gamut of macroeconomic policy changes has affected livelihoods in complex ways, with impacts that are difficult for people to identify and understand: manipulations of interest rates and exchange rates, arcane tax rules, licenses awarded by public administrators, and so on. This can aid farsighted policies to fly under the radar without arousing contention over short-term costs. Yet often the negative perceptions of macroeconomic policy reform, insofar as changes are noticed, are significantly exaggerated.

Although the bulk of Asian countries have experienced some macroeconomic liberalization since the 1970s, the typical pattern is not at all linear. As long as nonliberal policies remain or are reinstituted, the context is ripe for another contentious battle over raising prices to stem budget deficits, dismantling state enterprises, opening trade, relaxing strangling regulations, and so on. The backlash comes both from groups feeling threatened by liberalization, and reactions to the corruption believed to accompany liberalization, particularly privatizations transferring assets to government cronies or foreigners.

Understanding the connections between these changes and the likelihood of intergroup conflict requires distinguishing between highly publicized and low-key launchings, between policy design and implementation, and between short-term and long-term impacts. Strategies devised out of long-term considerations, emulation of other nations' successes, or tutelage from trusted experts, avoid association with the austerity programs that often create so much pain and opposition. The Indian government undertook liberalization in 1980 with relatively little involvement of trading partners and international organizations and, in fact, earlier than is widely believed (Mattoo and Subramanian 2008; Nayak, Chakravarti, and Rajib 2005, 11). Although in 1990–1991 (the standard dating of the liberalization initiative) the Indian government was working with the International Monetary Fund and the World Bank to overcome a critical lack of foreign reserves, there were no huge confrontations; parliamentary debates received only the standard degree of attention. Ahmed and Varshney (2008, 36) report that

> in a survey of mass political attitudes in India conducted in 1996, only 19 percent of the electorate reported any knowledge of economic reforms, even though reforms had been in existence since July 1991 ... In contrast, close to three fourths of the electorate, urban and rural, literate and illiterate, rich and poor, were aware of the 1992 mosque demolition in Ayodhya; 80 percent expressed clear opinions of whether the country should have a uniform civil code or religiously prescribed and separate laws for marriage, divorce, and property inheritance; and 87 percent took a stand on the caste-based affirmative action.

However, by 2004, awareness of the reforms was widespread—Ahmed and Varshney (2008, 37) report that over 85 percent had "clear judgments" on the reforms—largely negative.

When governments engage in highly visible structural adjustment programs involving loud confrontations with international organizations and intertwined with austerity programs, short-term impacts are typically very contentious. Contention is also more likely when liberalization is launched through highly publicized trade pacts, such as the US-Korean Trade Agreement (Wainwright and Kim 2008). Nevertheless, sometimes structural adjustment must be conducted in an atmosphere of high attention and high risk of polarization. In such cases, the potential of cash transfers to enact "adjustment with a human face" ought to be seriously considered.

Regarding long-term impacts, liberalization will jeopardize the livelihoods of those in roles vulnerable to competition or loss of subsidies. In some countries, relatively homogeneous roles held by particular groups increase the likelihood that they would see themselves as singled out for economic deprivation; longer-term fortunes of these groups may decline, reducing their economic standing and power. For example, Hadiz (2004, 60) argues that the radicalization of some indigenous Indonesian merchants resulted from their drawn-out economic decline upon the much earlier opening of the Indonesian economy to foreign and Indonesian-Chinese competition.

Price Liberalization. Allowing prices to reach market levels has been particularly contentious. Most prominently, fuel-price liberalization not only increases expenditures on the fuels per se, but also the costs of bus fares, electricity, and other amenities, leaving governments reluctant to engage in the reform, even if the economic disadvantages are extreme. For Syria, a UN Development Programme (2011, 82) report notes:

> Syria was forced to reduce fuel subsidies in 2008, due to their rising cost which...reached US$ 7 billion...The rising gap between local and international prices increased smuggling to...almost 15 per cent of Syria's total consumption. Artificially low prices caused excess demand and encouraged energy-intensive manufacturing...that would eventually have to close when prices could no longer be subsidized. The subsidies were also inequitable, with the top 10 per cent of income earners benefitting 52 times more in absolute terms than the lowest 10 per cent of the population...The government had to pay the price of not having dealt with the issue in a planned manner by being forced to increase heating diesel prices by 260 per cent on June 1st 2008.

If Syria had not subsidized fuel, the need to abruptly remove the subsidies resulting in huge increases in energy and transport costs would not have been necessary in the first place.

Thus despite the potential pitfalls of liberalization, strong arguments can be leveled against the illiberal policies that macroeconomic reform would address. The *lack* of liberalization led to some of the most acute conflicts in Asia. The 1979 Iranian Revolution received decisive early support from the *bazaaris* chafing under the economic dominance by the Shah's conglomerate of more than two hundred firms (Rakel 2008). In Central Asia, the inter-clan struggles, whether traditional or emerging, are strongly rooted in the competition for special economic privileges, as is true of the sectarian clashes in Bahrain and Syria.

More generally, although it is difficult to trace explicitly, prosperity unleashed by liberalization can reduce the incidence of violence. Despite all the diatribes against liberalization, few could dispute that the more liberal economies across Asia have had the greatest success in *aggregate* economic growth. The record of pervasive economic growth across most of Asia during the past two decades of more neoclassical liberal policies is indisputable. As Table 2.2 demonstrates, the former Soviet republics recovered in the last decade from the collapse of the Soviet economic system. The Chinese and Indian successes are well-known, yet the bulk of Asian nations have had respectable average annual growth rates, especially considering the three major global downturns during this 20-year period (1990–1993, 2001–2003, and 2008–2009) (International Monetary Fund 2009, 2–3).

Table 2.2 Economic Growth Rates and Per Capita Gross Domestic Product in Asia, 1991 to 2011

	Real GDP Growth				Real GDP Growth		
	1991–2001	2001–2011	2001 GDP/ capita*		1991–2001	2001–2011	2001 GDP/ capita*
Arab Asia				**FSU Western Asia**			
Bahrain (2008)**	4.6%	5.1%	25,799	Armenia	-1.7%	9.5%	$5,463
Iraq	6.2%	0.7%	$3,562	Azerbaijan	-4.2%	12.9%	$9,936
Jordan	5.5%	5.6%	$5,749	Georgia	-6.7%	6.0%	$5,074
Kuwait (2007)	9.9%	5.3%	$57,657	**FSU Central Asia**			
Lebanon	4.2%	3.8%	$14,069				
Oman (2009)	4.8%	4.3%	$26,791	Kazakhstan	-1.2%	7.3%	$12,169
Qatar	7.2%	8.7%	$80,944	Kyrgyzstan	-2.7%	3.7%	$2,239
Saudi Arabia	1.3%	3.0%	$22,713	Tajikistan	-8.1%	6.9%	$2,163
Syria	5.1%	3.6%	$5,285	Turkmenistan	-1.5%	7.3%	$8,274
UAE	5.2%	5.6%	$47,213	Uzbekistan	0.3%	5.3%	$3,106
Yemen	5.3%	3.1%	$2,653	**South Asia**			
East Asia (North)				Bangladesh	5.0%	4.6%	$1,659
China	7.8%	7.5%	$7,599	Bhutan	6.0%	9.0%	$5,328
Hong Kong	4.8%	4.3%	$46,502	India	6.1%	6.0%	$3,425
Japan	0.9%	1.0%	$33,733	Nepal	4.6%	2.6%	$1,199
Mongolia	0.5%	0.6%	$4,036	Pakistan	3.5%	3.8%	$2,688
South Korea	5.6%	3.5%	$29,101	Sri Lanka	4.6%	4.0%	$5,078
Taiwan	5.4%	2.5%	$36,300***				

Table 2.2 Continued

East Asia (South)

	Real GDP Growth		
	1991–2001	2001–2011	2001 GDP/capita*
Brunei (2009)	0.8%	2.5%	$49,935
Cambodia	5.4%	9.5%	$2,194
Indonesia	3.9%	4.1%	$4,325
Laos	5.7%	5.4%	$2,551
Malaysia	6.1%	3.9%	$14,731
Myanmar	8.4%	9.2%	$1,950
Papua New Guinea	4.5%	4.5%	$2,472
Philippines	3.3%	3.8%	$3,969
Singapore	6.8%	3.6%	$57,932
Thailand	3.8%	3.8%	$8,554
Vietnam	7.7%	6.0%	$3,205

Western Asia

	Real GDP Growth		
	1991–2001	2001–2011	2001 GDP/capita*
Afghanistan	3.1%	7.7%	$1,207
Iran (2009)	3.7%	4.1%	$11,570
Israel	4.8%	2.6%	$28,573
Turkey	2.7%	3.5%	$15,687

*Gross domestic product in 2010 international purchasing power parity dollars.

**Parenthetical dates refer to the gross domestic product figure if 2010 data are not available.

***Because the World Bank does not recognize Taiwan, this GDP per capita figure is taken from the CIA World Factbook (US Central Intelligence Agency 2012).

Source: Authors' calculations based on data from International Monetary Fund 2012, Tables A2 and A4; Groningen Growth and Development Centre 2010.

The strong economic growth eventually generated by liberalization means that there are more periods of robust growth. Bohlken and Sergenti (2010) found that for India, Hindu-Muslim riots are less frequent when the economy is growing. Expectations of continued prosperity, if only violence can be curbed, increase the incentive to form intergroup alliances against violence entrepreneurs. Varshney (2002) notes the lower levels of riots in cities where Hindu-Muslim associations comprised largely of businesspeople work to quell incitements that threaten to trigger riots.

Restructuring the State Sector. Continued reliance on state enterprises in the majority of Asian countries is significant in terms of the potential for favoring particular regions or groups over others. Conflicts over the actions of these enterprises sometimes arise as they push into regions where residents feel the threats to their property rights and economic viability by entities with the force of government behind them. They may also arise when price subsidies that state enterprises had been required to offer are suddenly removed, provoking food riots, bus-fare riots, and so on, or when redundant employees are shed. However, irrespective of the virtues of dismantling inefficient and corrupt state enterprises, the privatization process itself often generates opportunities and perceptions of corruption, resentments, and group rivalries. When, as in the former Soviet republics (Kaufmann and Siegelbaum 1997), state assets are yielded to a few favored businesspeople, resentments are likely to arise against the government and the winners and the groups to which they are seen to belong

Sectoral promotion

Restoration of the Agricultural Priority. How soon and how thoroughly the bias in favor of industry over agriculture was redressed has far-ranging implications. James, Naya, and Meier (1989, 158–167) note that since the mid-1960s (far earlier than in Latin America or much of sub-Saharan Africa) governments of East and South Asia strongly reduced the bias against agriculture, through infrastructure, institutional reform, and liberalization. Agro-exports become more profitable; farmers obtain higher profits when food price ceilings are eliminated. Agricultural promotion obviously can increase food supply, with the potential to reduce the incidence of food riots and demonstrations, which during 2007–2008 alone were experienced in Bangladesh, Cambodia, India, Jordan, North Korea, the Philippines, Thailand, and Yemen (Hendrix, Haggard, and Magaloni 2009, 2). Food price liberalization can have opposite effects, depending on the security of supply. Free market prices are vulnerable to supply shortages, the core problem of the global 2007–2008 food crisis. However, when governments depress food prices through subsidies financed through the budget, budget deficits may reach the point where the government is compelled to allow prices to rise sharply.

Agricultural promotion—if successful—increases the potential marketable surplus from small farms.[19] Along with infrastructure promotion, this expands agricultural marketing beyond local exchange. This may increase farmers' incomes, but also would increase the role of agricultural middlemen. Often the dependence on these middlemen has been a major source of contention, especially where farmers and merchants are of different ethnicities. The most widespread impact has been in Southeast Asia, where agricultural merchants are predominantly the overseas Chinese.

Rural Industrialization. Enhancing rural incomes often requires increasing nonfarm incomes. Otsuka and Yamano (2006, i), assessing labor opportunities in Bangladesh, India, the Philippines, and Thailand, conclude that "the reliance on agricultural labor markets alone will not reduce poverty to a significant extent, in view of the declining share of agricultural wage income in Asia." Arguably the most promising potential for nonfarm rural income is rural industrialization, with the combined goals of providing employment, enhancing profits due to lower rural wages, making the transition from agriculture to manufacturing, and deconcentrating industry away from overpopulated, polluted cities. In enhancing rural incomes, rural industrialization may give rural people a greater stake in cooperating with others. Rigg (2003, 228) notes that rural industrialization may also substitute for land reform, which often risks high conflict levels. Heavily advocated by development experts (Rigg 2003, 226–231), rural industrialization has several variants: general manufacturing (typically relocated from urban areas), expansion of traditional rural manufacturing (e.g., silk production and weaving), agro-industry (e.g., food and fiber processing), and heavy natural resource processing (e.g., sawmills and metal refining). Some variants emphasize supporting community initiative and control (Parnwell 1994). Economic success in establishing sustainable industries in rural areas has been impressive in Japan, South Korea, and China; it has been moderately successful in Thailand and Indonesia. However, the impacts on rural incomes and the creation of cooperative links have been mixed. Rigg (2002) points out that because new operations may attract outsiders who displace the local people, rural industrialization may share the general risk facing regional development:

> In both Thailand and Indonesia... researchers have noted the extent to which local people are "displaced" from accessible rural areas to more remote places. Enticed by the rising value of their land, especially if it is

located near a transit corridor, but unable to benefit from the process of rural industrialization that is occurring around them, they sell their land. The proceeds are then used either to buy a larger parcel of land in a more remote location ... or "squandered" on luxuries ... If this process is widespread, then "rural industrialization" should perhaps be reformulated as "industrial extension and rural displacement." (Rigg 2002, 229)

However, prior or simultaneous educational improvement of the local population would make them more competitive for employment opportunities, as demonstrated in Japan, South Korea, and Taiwan.

Rural industrialization in India had a peculiar relationship with the Mahalanobis heavy-industry import-substitution strategy. Gandhian philosophy called for cottage industries to provide light manufactures (such as textiles) that in other countries were the mainstay of ISI. Rural cottage industries received subsidies and protection from internal competition (Saith 2001, 90–91). Yet as Indian liberalization proceeded, rural-based industries lost to competition from cheaper, preferable urban-produced or imported goods (Saith 2000).

In Turkey, rural industrialization was pursued through the establishment of new towns. The record is not encouraging (Marin 2005, 498); as in many other countries, rural residents have resisted relocating to the new towns to take on employment.

Resource-based Industrialization. An important variant of the export-oriented strategy is "resource-based industrialization": promoting raw-material processing, adding greater value to the exported products. Resource-based industries can utilize petroleum (refining, petrochemicals, plastics), hard minerals (smelting, finished metal products), timber (sawn lumber, furniture), and crops (bulk processing, prepared foods). If industrialization *per se* is an objective, reliance on the country's own raw materials is frequently seen—though often incorrectly—as an advantage. "Downstream" processing is often also seen as creating employment, buffering against low raw-product world-market prices, and improving both entrepreneurial and technical skills. To induce resource-based industrialization, governments may subsidize these industries or restrict the export of raw materials. Timber export restrictions are common; the government can also invoke conservation. Log-export quotas or bans have been enacted in Cambodia, China, Indonesia, Malaysia, Papua New Guinea, the Philippines, Thailand, and Vietnam (Resosudarmo and Yusuf 2006, 2). The subsidy strategy risks creating inefficient, unsustainable firms. The export-restriction approach risks losing potentially greater revenues from exporting the raw material, especially if domestic processing is inefficient. Gillis (1988, 88) calculated that

Indonesian "plywood exports worth $109 per cubic meter of processed logs cost $133; a cubic meter of logs that could be exported for $100 produced only $89 in sawn timber from the local sawmills, and a $20 loss in export taxes." Either approach risks creating so much demand as to lead to excessive resource depletion, as has been the case of timber supply for sawmills.

Mixed Record in the Social Sectors. Social-sector investment has varied widely throughout Asia. Even acknowledging that delivering health, education, and other social services is more difficult and expensive for nations with populations living in remote areas, the differences are striking in their consequences.

For education, given the scarcity of comparative data on government expenditures, the best indirect indicator of the state's investment in education is the secondary-school gross enrollment rate.[20] Table 2.3 reveals that the oil-rich Arab nations have quite high secondary-school enrollments, as do Jordan and Lebanon, with the other Arab nations considerably lower. South Asia has relatively low enrollment rates, with the exception of Sri Lanka, long distinctive for its social-sector emphasis. These outcomes largely reflect the investment in education, although compared to the rest of Asia, Sri Lanka seems to be able to do more with less.

The success of the "East Asian miracle" countries is reflected in high secondary-school enrollments, with Japan, South Korea, and Taiwan, all at very high levels of investment and enrollment. However, one indication of other East Asian nations' failure to gain developed-nation status is that among Southeast Asian countries, only the Philippines exceeds 80 percent in secondary-school enrollment. However, Indonesia has made remarkable progress: the reported secondary-school enrollment rate currently exceeds 75 percent, up from 50 percent in 1995 and 60 percent in 2005. What makes such a rapid increase credible is that spending on education, even discounting for inflation, more than doubled between 2001 and 2009 (World Bank 2009, 19–20). Malaysia's low level is puzzling, in light of high education spending; this reflects and reinforces the cultural and economic gulf between the Malays and the better-educated Chinese and Indians.

China has achieved a secondary-school enrollment rate of over 80 percent, compared to barely 50 percent in 1995. This is a telling contrast with India, where roughly a third of secondary-school-aged children are not enrolled. The enrollment rates of the former Soviet republics (and Mongolia, formerly under Soviet tutelage) reflect the prior advances of the Soviet system, although Kyrgyz enrollments have been declining.[21] Pomfret (2009, 49) notes that all Central Asian republics "have maintained the relatively high social indicators of the Soviet Union, with life expectancies of 66–70 years and almost universal literacy, although there are concerns about

Table 2.3 Education and Health Expenditures and Indicators

	Government per student expenditure on primary education PPP$	Government per student expenditure on secondary education PPP$	Gross secondary school enrollment percent	Total per capita expenditure on health US$	General government per capita expenditure on health	Under-5 mortality rate per 1000
	2008, 2009, or 2010	2008, 2009, or 2010	2009 or 2010	2010	US$ 2010 [and % of total budget 2009]	live births 2010
Afghanistan	..	..	46	38	$4 [38%]	149
Armenia	928	1495	92	133	54 [6.4]	20
Azerbaijan	..	..	85	332	67 [4.2]	46
Bahrain	..	187	103[1]	864	634 [11.4]	10
Bangladesh	134	1509	51	23	8 [7.4]	48
Bhutan	343	1509	70	108	94 [10.5]	56
Cambodia	149	150	46	45	17 [10.5]	51
China	..	..	81	221	118 [12.1]	18
Georgia	730	764	86	272	64 [6.9]	22
Hong Kong	6094	7411	83	..	..	..
India	300	548	63	54	16 [3.6]	63
Indonesia	443	501	77	114	55 [7.8]	35
Iran	1727	2394	91	317	127 [10.5]	26
Iraq	..	..	48[2]	247	200 [9.0]	39
Israel	5382	5641	102	2183	234 [10.4]	5
Japan	7213	7481	102	4065	3355 [18.4]	3
Jordan	627	806	87	357	242 [18.6]	22

Continued

Table 2.3 Continued

	Government per student expenditure on primary education PPP$	Government per student expenditure on secondary education PPP$	Gross secondary school enrollment percent	Total per capita expenditure on health US$	General government per capita expenditure on health	Under-5 mortality rate per 1000
	2008, 2009, or 2010	2008, 2009, or 2010	2009 or 2010	2010	US$ 2010 [and % of total budget 2009]	live births 2010
Kazakhstan	..	..	97	393	233 [11.4]	33
Korea, Dem. Rep.	..	..	..	..	..	..
Korea, Rep.	5223	6240	97	1439	848 [12.4]	5
Kuwait	5292	7227	101[1]	1223	983 [6.9]	11
Kyrgyzstan	..	..	84	53	30 [10.7]	38
Laos	..	..	47	46	15 [5.9]	54
Lebanon	..	..	81	651	255 [9.5]	22
Malaysia	2042	1776	68	368	204 [9.2]	6
Mongolia	571	731	89	120	66 [8.0]	32
Myanmar	..	..	54	17	2 [1.0]	..
Nepal	196	137	44[1]	30	10 [7.9]	50
Oman	3428	3923	100	574	460 [6.2]	9
Pakistan	..	..	34	22	8 [3.6]	87
Papua New Guinea	..	..	20[2]	49	35 [8.1]	61
Philippines	305	309	85	77	27 [7.6]	29

Country						
Qatar	8699	9242	94	1489	1153 [5.5]	8
Saudi Arabia	4178	4162	101	680	427 [7.0]	18
Singapore	5860	8920	..	1733	629 [8.0]	3
Sri Lanka	373	..	87[3]	70	31 [5.8]	17
Syria	863	733	72	97	44 [5.6]	16
Tajikistan	..	432	87	49	13 [6.1]	63
Thailand	1928	1321	77	179	134 [12.7]	13
Timor-Leste	..	..	56	57	32 [4.7]	55
Turkey	..	..	78	678	510 [12.8]	13
Turkmenistan	..	..	..	106	63 [9.9]	56
United Arab Emirates	2807	3873	92[1]	1450	1078 [8.8]	7
Uzbekistan	..	..	105	82	39 [8.5]	52
Vietnam	551	483	77	83	31 [7.8]	23
Yemen	..	..	44	63	15 [4.3]	77

[1] 2006 latest figure.
[2] 2000 latest figure.
[3] 2004 latest figure.

Sources: UNESCO *Global Education Digest* 2011; UNESCO Institute for Statistics data base; World Health Organization data base; World Bank data base.

declining educational and health standards." Except for Kazakhstan, education spending and enrollments declined when the Soviet Union dissolved—in Armenia and Georgia the general government expenditures for education fell by two-thirds in the second half of the 1990s compared to the pre-1992 levels; for Azerbaijan they declined by half (Glinkina and Rosenberg 2003, 515). The recovery has been remarkable.

The relationships between education and the likelihood of violence are obviously complicated and heavily influenced by both context and instructional content. Insofar as the state is expected to meet educational aspirations, the expansion of educational opportunities can reduce disappointment and antagonism. The greater incomes of workers employed at levels commensurate with higher education can deter risking confrontations with the government or other groups. Yet mismatches between educational attainment and the levels of available jobs can also generate dissatisfaction, and more education often brings greater capacity to mobilize against the government or other groups. Weak state-educational coverage provides space for religious schools; some *madrasas* have contributed to the radicalization of Muslim youth. However, the content of state-provided education can itself be radicalizing, or students may reject what they regard as overly secular state educational content.

Government investment in health care shows similarly wide variation, though a good part of this variation is defined by the balance between government and nongovernment spending. Central Asian republics, except Tajikistan, devote fairly large proportions of government spending on health care. In contrast, the governments of the former Soviet republics of Azerbaijan, Armenia, and Georgia spend smaller proportions of their budgets on health care. Referring to these low levels, for both education and health care, Glinkina and Rosenberg (2003, 514–516) argue that disruptions in these countries arise from the violation of the "social contract" of state social protection. They contend that this perception results from a redistributive policy to withdraw benefits from the general population for the benefit of those with "political connections."

Social protection is amply provided by governments of wealthier Northeast Asian and Western Asian countries (Israel, Japan, South Korea, and Turkey). This contrasts starkly with the low proportions for South Asian countries, even though one might expect that governments of much wealthier nations would not need to spend such a proportion of their budgets to meet health needs. Except for Bhutan, South Asian governments do not prioritize health-care spending; even Sri Lanka is at only 5.8 percent, down from 7 percent in 2000. The governments of the poorest Southeast Asian countries contribute the least to health care, although the Cambodian government spends over a tenth of its budget on health care. The government of Myanmar—an ostensibly socialist country—spends an astonishingly low 1 percent.

The Arab nations show a fairly wide range of support for health care, whether oil rich or not. The Jordanian government devotes a remarkable percent of general expenditures, and Lebanon spends at roughly the same 10 percent level as the Central Asian republics. The governments of oil-rich Bahrain, Kuwait, Qatar, and the United Arab Emirates spend a lot on health care, even if the proportions of total government spending are middling. The absolute and proportionate levels for Saudi Arabia and Oman seem surprisingly low. While the per capita amounts for the oil-rich nations (even excluding Saudi Arabia and Oman) average around $1,000 in purchasing power parity terms, this is far less than the $2,500 average for Organization for Economic Co-operation and Development (OECD) countries, even though the per capita incomes of Arab oil exporters are comparable to the OECD countries. It may be that citizens of the oil-rich nations receive enough direct remuneration to be able to purchase health care, leaving the stateless families and foreign workers with minimal state support.

For Southeast Asia, the Thai government provides the largest proportion of the general budget, at 12.7 percent, up from less than 10 percent in 2000; Malaysia, with roughly the same 8 percent proportion of the general budget covering health care as Indonesia or the Philippines, provides a much higher absolute amount. However, the proportion of the Indonesian budget devoted to health care increased dramatically from 2000 to 2010. Although the Singaporean government's health-care allocation is not a very high proportion of the budget compared to other wealthy Asian nations, private spending on health care brings the total amount to comparable levels of the wealthy countries, with the exception of Japan's much higher total.

Regional Development Strategies

As mentioned in Chapter 1, many Asian countries have strong spatial disparities in development; in some cases, these disparities have sharpened in the last two decades, contributing to intergroup tension and violence. Thus, liberalization-led economic growth in India has intensified spatial inequalities between urban and rural areas, and between its more prosperous and industrialized Southern states and the impoverished Northeast. Growing disparities are also striking in China; Kanbur and Zhang (2006) find it to be consistent with the economic development strategies: the heavy-industry development strategy was largely responsible for urban-rural gaps in the pre-reform period, while liberalization plays a key role in the rapid increase of inland-coastal disparity. In Central Asia, spatial and regional income differences have widened in the move to a market economy and large-scale labor migration (Anderson and Pomfret 2006), prompting observers to report increasing security threats (Laruelle and Peyrouse 2012) and perils of increasing mobilization (Schatz 2010). Unprecedented positive macroeconomic performance of Turkey after 2001 has yet to bring benefits to Eastern Anatolia and other underdeveloped and conflict-ridden Turkish provinces.

Growing regional disparities have prompted regional development strategies targeted to poorer areas, but this focus may be at odds with maximizing economic growth. Regional development strategies are based on the assumption that every area has a combination of assets (natural resources, physical factors, financial, human and social assets) that carry some potential for furthering development.[22] Regional development practices of most Asian countries have been "trial and error" policy experiments in pursuit of various goals. Policymakers have targeted, explicitly or implicitly, more advanced regions, economically backward regions, resource-abundant regions,[23] frontier regions, and borderlands. The rationales as well as policy tools to pursue regional development have differed around the region, but they are rarely limited to economic objectives.

The strategy of devoting even greater resources to more advanced regions is typically defended on the grounds of regional competitive advantage, assuming that the infrastructure, business clusters, appropriately skilled labor, and proximity to domestic markets simply make economic activities more productive. For example, despite incentives to lure manufacturing into less populated areas of northern Thailand to "deconcentrate" industry away from the congested and polluted Bangkok area, Bangkok continues to grow faster. Pansuwan and Routray (2011, 40) conclude that "the very high level of industrial development pattern is still scattered around the [Bangkok Metropolitan Region] because of its comparative advantages. Interestingly, almost all provinces falling within the very low industrial development level are located in the northeastern and northern regions of the country mainly due to lack of physical and human as well as capital resources." Yet even if favoring already-developed areas is not an explicit strategy, these areas may be more attractive because of government subsidies such as cheap power and water available in regions with more developed infrastructure.

In contrast, arguments invoked to justify favoring less-developed regions include the potential to take advantage of as-yet-untapped potential, as well as doing more to alleviate poverty. The argument is that with apparently abundant land, natural resources, less costly labor, and new capital, less-developed regions can outstrip more developed regions. Another rationale is to deconcentrate industrial production away from overcrowded metropolitan areas, reducing environmental stress and stemming urbanization.

Of course, shifting population and pollution to economically backward areas puts greater pressure on the infrastructure and the environment; the question is whether the area's growth will generate sufficient resources and willingness to address these stresses. An additional source of contention arises from the need to provide more energy and transport infrastructure to the backward area, when this displaces local people to make way of hydroelectric dams, highways, or other infrastructure.[24]

The goals and practices of regional development change along with policymakers' ideologies, their visions of what constitutes "development," and the resources at hand. Thus regional development strategies in Communist-bloc countries were designed and implemented by central governments pursuing not only economic but also ideological and geopolitical considerations. The Soviet legacy of regional development is important for understanding the situation in Russia and the other former Soviet republics. Soviet economic development was pursued through Five Year Plans with objectives to ensure rapid industrialization, diminish regional disparities, and develop strategically secure locations for development hubs ("territorial-industrial complexes," or TPKs). In early periods (1928–1975), Soviet regional development reflected the principle of interregional equalization, entailing centralized planning of state investment in almost all sectors of the economy and its even spatial distribution. Budget allocations, along with forced migration under Stalin and later economic incentives to stimulate migration,[25] ensured interregional labor and capacity redistribution among many regions of the vast Soviet empire. The pursuit of interregional equalization contributed to the creation of TPKs in frontier areas of Siberia, the Far North, the Far East, and Central Asia; quite often at the expense of traditional livelihoods of the indigenous population.[26]

Equalization of regional economic conditions, however, came at the expense of economic efficiency and eventually became too onerous for the federal budget. In the mid-1970s, the central government shifted investments to more economically advanced regions of European Russia and resource-abundant areas of Siberia and the Far East (KPSS 1978)—much to the chagrin of the Central Asian and Caucasus republics. Still, subsidization of the regional economies of Central Asia and the Caucasus from the federal budget continued until the Soviet collapse. The end of Moscow's support and the massive exodus of Russian professionals delivered a final blow to the industries created in these republics.

China under Mao Zedong first followed the Soviet Union in pursuing the strategic trinity of industrialization, poverty reduction, and security.

Different political-economic periods (The Great Leap Forward, the Cultural Revolution, the 1970s rural reform and the post-1978 Opening) carried clear regional development imperatives. The First Five Year Plan (1953–1957) emphasized the relocation of heavy industry away from coastal provinces for fear of invasion of US-supported armed forces from the sea; the massive construction of military-industrial complexes in western China, popularly referred to as "Third Front industries," followed in the 1960s (Demurger et al. 2002). Later, with concerns about the Soviet threat from the western flank, the development of coastal provinces again became a priority. However, the regional development mechanism was no longer mainly through budget allocations, but rather through market-oriented preferential policies. SEZs were intended to reduce China's overreliance on heavy manufacturing and to boost economic growth in regions then seen as "backward" (Ge 1999). Economic success of these initiatives also led to a rapid increase in the coastal versus inland disparity and to yet further reorientation of the government regional strategy: in the 2000s, another "Go West" campaign, with the explicit goal of reducing regional disparities and bringing economic development to the impoverished western provinces was initiated. The fact that most of these provinces are rich in natural resources and inhabited by minorities allowed critics to classify this as "internal colonization" (Girard et al. 2012, 160); many observers have reported increased tension between minority groups and government-supported Han settlers.

When Asian governments focus significantly increased resources on a particular region, the consequences for intergroup cooperation or conflict can cut both ways, depending on perceptions of motives and vulnerabilities. We might expect that greater efforts by the Iranian government to develop the economically backward Khuzestan would reduce Khuzestani Arabs' resentment about gaining little from the oil extracted from the province, yet any development strategy is likely to arouse the Arabs' suspicions that their numerical dominance in the province would be threatened by a flood of non-Arabs. A parallel situation holds for Indonesia's Aceh region, except that the greater autonomy of the region may give greater control of job opportunities and terms of investment to the Acehnese.

One clearly successful pacification through regional development, though short-lived, was in southern Thailand in the 1980s and 1990s, where the combination of strong, government-led development in the heavily Muslim provinces, along with the fact that the Muslims still enjoyed a majority in that region[27], led to a reduction in conflict. Croissant (2007, 2–3) reports:

General Prem's government (1980–88) supported Muslim cultural rights and religious freedoms, offered the insurgents a general amnesty, and implemented an economic development plan...The transition to democracy offered the Malay-Muslims new opportunities for political participation including the emergence of political parties...Finally, in the 1990s, the democratic government of Prime Minister Chuan Leekpai (Democratic Party) formulated a National Security Policy for the Southern Border Provinces, based on a "development as security" approach...these developments contributed significantly to the decline of Muslim insurgency.

The improved relations lasted until the Thaksin Shinawatra government (2001–2006), with its main support coming from the predominantly Buddhist northern regions, became far more aggressive vis-à-vis the Muslims.

The partial success of improved relations through regional development in Thailand is contrasted by the conflict on Mindanao in the southern Philippines, where the Muslim "Moros" have been engaged in violent confrontations with the government and the Christian population since before the country's independence. Resentment over low incomes and public services is exacerbated by the fact that the Moros have become a minority among settlers from other islands. Ewing (2009, 15–16) notes that only 5 of the island's 24 provinces have Moro majorities—and these five provinces are among the poorest in Southeast Asia. He argues that Moro "minoritization" and the appropriation of Mindanao's more economically productive areas by outsiders have inflamed the conflict and have blocked a stable peace despite significant governance decentralization for the majority Muslim areas. Although the majority Muslim provinces came under the Autonomous Region of Muslim Mindanao in 1989, providing considerable autonomy, armed conflict continued, and, despite various peace initiatives and pacts since then, a stable peace is by no means assured.

The most widespread conflict triggered by regional development initiatives is in India, where the combination of aggressive state industrialization and mineral extraction in the economically backward eastern states has rekindled a broad Maoist insurgency. As Ganguly and Oetken (this volume) point out, whatever the intentions of the federal and state governments, the influx of outsiders and the threats to property rights made some of the *adivasis* highly susceptible to mobilization by antigovernment ideologues.

The challenge to conflict-sensitive regional development initiatives is particularly great in borderlands that straddle international borders. The territorial legacy of colonialism, partition, and boundary superimposition in many Asian countries is exemplified in such places as Federally Administered Tribal Areas (FATA) in Pakistan and its counterpart on the Afghan side of the border; Central Asia's Fergana Valley; the Kurdish homeland straddling

Iraq, Turkey, and Iran; and Israel and Palestinian territories. Many border-lands are heavily militarized and policed, creating security dilemmas on both sides of the border. Their inhabitants also have cross-border societal ties with many transnational actors and often host profitable, though not necessarily legal, transborder economies.[28] Jonathan Goodhand (2008, 240) argues that "borderlands are central to the dimensions of war and peace, yet they tend to be peripheral to policy discourse and practice."

Regional development strategies applied in Asian borderlands include major infusions of resources along with migration and resettlement of the ethnic majority (e.g., China and Indonesia); the development of trans-boundary cooperation (e.g., cooperative projects for the Greater Mekong Subregion by Burma, Cambodia, Laos, Thailand, Vietnam, and China's Yunnan Province and Guangxi Autonomous Zone) (Cronin 2011). The cre-ation of cross-border peace parks has been attempted in several locations.

In some borderlands, regional authorities defy the central government. For instance, while many Russian policymakers voice concerns about the "Yellow threat" in Siberia and the Far East and weakened economic ties between these regions and central Russia, Siberian regional authorities and the Siberian population, seem to embrace economic opportunities offered by China. By 2007, Chinese investments in Siberia and the Far East already exceeded those by the Russian federal government by a factor of four (Naumov 2007). Meantime, tourism and transborder trade flourish on both sides of the border, with unexpected consequences: Russian Buriats on the Russian side have reportedly restored kin relations with the Buriat diaspora communities in Inner Mongolia (China) and the eastern provinces of Mongolia to create transborder trade groups. Local perceptions of the needs of borderland development may be at odds with the central government's strategy, which may consider transborder interaction as an economic and political threat. Depending on circumstances and the deftness of policies, borderlands may become flashpoints for intergroup conflict or an opportu-nity for peaceful development.

Population Resettlement

As mentioned in Chapter 1, many Asian policymakers face challenges related to age and gender shifts as well as differential growth among ethnic and reli-gious groups. Several development strategies have been employed to address these issues, including variations of "demographic engineering." One prom-inent strategy is straightforward population resettlement. Virtually all eco-nomic development strategies may induce people to relocate; a distinctive set of development strategies entails deliberate promotion of long-distance resettlement, beyond simple displacement to make way for infrastructure projects.[29] Inducements include offering land at low or no cost, subsidizing firms willing to expand into targeted areas, creating growth poles to attract labor and investors, expanding infrastructure to expedite migration, and defraying migration costs. However, coercion has also been used, ranging from Soviet forced resettlement of various ethnicities to Central Asia and the Asian territories of Russia, to the expulsion of people of particular groups to make way for others to move in voluntarily or not.

The major Asian resettlement strategies have had mixed motivations: to develop the targeted regions, enhance growth on the premise that the productivity of targeted regions can be unleashed through the activity of new settlers, and relieve population pressures of the areas of origin. Political motivations are often present, to shift the population balance among different groups in order to strengthen government control over the targeted area or the area of origin.

In China, nomads have been systematically relocated into settled communities as part of "ecological migration" policy. Since 2005, 50,000 Tibetans have been relocated from Qinghai Province into unfamiliar urban areas; some observers point out that the locations of recent self-immolations largely correspond to areas of intensive resettlement. The relocation is justified by the government by the need to preserve fragile ecosystems of the National Reserve. However, in 2011 the boundaries of the reserve were redrawn to allow for large-scale gold mining (Girard et al. 2012, 164).

The most prominent resettlement programs have focused on moving populations to the least developed but seemingly potentially productive areas. Forested areas in India and Southeast Asia have been the most common site for resettlement, out of a combination of low initial population density and the often mistaken presumption that forestlands are fertile for intensive agriculture. It is telling that the three Asian cases featured in the International Labour Office evaluation of resettlement programs (Oberoi 1988a) were Indonesia, Malaysia, and the Philippines, targeting rural areas with little sedentary cultivation (and, in the Philippine case, moving Christians into predominantly Muslim areas).

The potential conflicts arising from resettlement programs parallel those of regional development programs, and may be more acute. While regional development initiatives attract outsiders as investment and job opportunities beckon, resettlement brings in people with no guarantee of employment, and often little preparation to secure it. Therefore clashes with preexisting residents over jobs, land, and natural resources have been common in all these cases.[30] As Fearon and Laitin (2011, 199) argue, governments often intervene in favor of the migrants, and frequently are "indiscriminate in retribution and repression against members of the indigenous group." This is unsurprising in situations of government sponsorship of either regional development programs that induce migration or direct resettlement programs. The problems are particularly severe for shifting cultivators, inasmuch as property assignments to the newcomers rarely recognize the need of shifting cultivators to rotate their cultivated areas from one place to another (Fox et al. 2009).

Yet resettlement programs may stimulate higher incomes overall in the target areas, and may reduce conflict in the area of origin by reducing congestion. For Indonesia's *transmigrasi* resettlement program, Oberoi (1988b, 9) notes that "the removal of between 300,000 and 400,000 people a year during the period 1979–84 must have done something to relieve the population pressure and consequent social problems in some of the poorest areas of Java."

Natural Resource Exploitation

The presence of exportable natural resources has been both a bane and a boon for Asian nations. For some countries, sound resource exploitation has fueled general prosperity that presumably has dampened discontent. For example, the exploitation of oil and timber augmented Malaysia's growth, raising the incomes of all major groups, and in all likelihood kept the government's redistribution of income shares from the Malaysian Chinese to the indigenous Malays from unleashing more open conflict.

Obviously, natural resource exploitation is intimately related to the regional development and population resettlement strategies. One rationale to focus on a particular region is the potential of more intensive resource extraction. Logging is widely viewed as having the double advantage of providing timber revenues and opening up land for crops or grazing—though the suitability for either may be greatly exaggerated. Regions with hard minerals and hydrocarbons may seem ideal for downstream resource-based industrialization, given the proximity of supply.

The controversies over the control and benefits of resource extraction depend on how groups claim to be "more indigenous" to the country or to the resource-extractive region. Among the significant hydrocarbon-export-dependent countries (Arab states of Bahrain, Iraq, Kuwait, Oman, Qatar, Saudi Arabia, Syria, and the United Arab Emirates; Central Asian republics of Kazakhstan and Turkmenistan; West Asian nations of Azerbaijan and Iran; Southeast Asian nations of Brunei, Indonesia, and Malaysia), all but Iraq have one clearly dominant group. And all but Bahrain, Iraq, and Syria have a politically dominant group claiming to be the essential "nation" of that country. Unsurprisingly, Iraq and Bahrain, though on very different scales, have experienced intergroup struggles based in part on the distribution of oil-based wealth. The Bahraini government has been granting citizenship to foreigners, but only to Sunni; this is presumed to increase the proportion of the politically dominant but numerically minority Sunni population (Partrick 2009).

For the other Arab oil exporters, the dominant group has invoked its claim of "native" status to exclude other groups from equitable wealth sharing. In Kuwait, families whose male ancestor failed to register during a brief registration period in 1959 just prior to independence, or could not demonstrate continuous residence since 1920, have been denied citizenship with few exceptions; unsurprisingly, the illiterate nomads had a very low registration rate. Most families arriving later have also been denied citizenship. Together, these stateless "Bidun" number roughly 100,000. A similar situation holds in the United Arab Emirates, with a comparable Bidun population (Fattah 2008). Bidun numbers in Saudi Arabia are unknown, but may be considerably greater than in other Gulf countries, given the overall size of the Saudi population, availability of jobs, and ease of entry into Saudi Arabia to pilgrims who decide to remain (Aldeeb Abu-Sahlieh 1995). While Qatari "citizens" are entitled to socioeconomic benefits, two-thirds of them, whose families cannot trace continuous residence to 1920, lack voting rights. All of these citizenship policies have straightforward distributional implications, and are obvious sources of discontent. In Iran, where ethnic Persians hold only a slim population majority, the disaffected Arab population lives in the southwest region, with the largest oil fields and refineries. Wood (2006) notes that "Khuzestan province is Iran's oil pump and the home of its Arab minority. Iran extracts the oil and leaves Arab areas economically unimproved. Seeking independence, several Arab groups have bombed government offices. Tehran frequently accuses the British military in nearby Basra of fomenting rebellion." Whether the Arabs in this province are a majority is hotly debated; their numbers are estimated to range from "500,000 to 3 million" (Straker 2011, 348), in a province of roughly 4.3 million people. The publication of a document purported to be a secret government blueprint for expelling Arabs into other regions, and enticing non-Arabs to settle in Khuzestan, incited demonstrations in 2005, leading to the deaths of "scores of Iranian Arabs" and hundreds of injuries (Amnesty International 2006).

Sporadic attacks against the Iranian government and ethnic Persians have also been conducted by Kurds, Baloch, and Azeris. However, one crucial factor that keeps Iran from massive interethnic conflict (as in Iraq) is that Azeris, who constitute as much as a third of the population, are both Shiite and prosperous (Wood 2006).

Kazakhstan also has an oil-rich region with a substantial minority population that does not receive significantly greater oil-revenue benefits than other areas. Pomfret (2006, 15) notes that in the expansion of oil production, "the petroleum-producing regions of Atyrau and Mangistau only increased their combined share of GDP from 9.0 percent to 9.5 percent, implying that although Kazakhstan's growth was fueled by the hydrocarbon sector the real beneficiaries were in the commercial capital rather than near the oil fields. This pattern appears to have continued during the post-1999 oil boom." Writing in 2008, Najman et al. (2008, 113) noted that "in the midst of an oil boom, being located in the oil-producing western region is not associated with higher living standards, and indeed the relative position of households in those regions was worse than in 1996."

In Syria, a much smaller country, regional distribution is not at issue. Rather, the politically dominant Alawite minority benefits from oil revenues, which, in financing the expansion of the bureaucracy, has provided favorable opportunities for the Alawites. (Haddad 2005, 2).

In contrast, Indonesia and Malaysia have demonstrated rather effective strategies for ameliorating distributive battles over resource benefits. Significant proportions of the hydrocarbon reserves are in regions where the local majority is a minority in the country as a whole. In Indonesia, revenue collection from hydrocarbons, hard minerals, and timber are controlled by the central government. Under Suharto, the central government kept control over the revenue *distribution* as well. In Aceh, the oil-rich but impoverished northernmost region of Sumatra, a major separatist movement emerged in the late 1970s out of discontent with the oil-revenue distribution. In the post-Suharto era, budgetary decentralization has given provinces and districts greater shares of natural resource revenues, with additional favoritism to resource-producing areas. This revenue reallocation, supplemented by granting Aceh a special semiautonomous status, contributed to a peace agreement between the Indonesian government and the separatists.[31]

In the Malaysian case, Malaysia's Sabah and Sarawak states on Borneo have both hydrocarbon and timber wealth, and are economically backward compared to most of the rest of the country. Ross (2006) notes:

In the 1960s and 1970s, Sabah and Sarawak were high-risk areas for a separatist rebellion: they were part of a country that, at the time, was relatively poor; their terrain is mountainous; they are separated from West Malaysia by water; most of their populations are ethnically and linguistically distinct from the peoples of West Malaysia; they had markedly different colonial histories from West Malaysia; and they only joined the

Malaysian Federation in 1963, six years after the rest of the country had gained independence. Moreover, Sabah and Sarawak's natural resource wealth gave both of them an economic incentive to secede: they have both been major timber exporters, and about half of Malaysia's petroleum exports come from off the shores of the two states, even though the state governments get only a five percent petroleum royalty.

The Malaysian government's solution was to divide the royalty proceeds: the federal central government controls oil revenues; the states control timber revenues. Although a policy of restricting log exports has restricted timber revenues, the state-level funds (the Sabah Foundation and the Sarawak Foundation) have been able to distribute considerable benefits to limit both resentment against the governments and intergroup hostilities.

Conclusions

Asian governments have employed a huge range of development strategies since WWII, with far-reaching effects on the dynamism of each country and the levels of contention or cooperation among different groups. Understanding the evolution of economic doctrines and broad strategies helps to put the levels and nature of violence into perspective, but we also find that the specific policies and implementation approaches to pursuing strategies are crucial for success in pursuing peaceful development. The following chapters provide much more detailed analysis of these dynamics in enlightening cases.

Notes

1. With the exception of Japan and Thailand, all countries of Asia had been either colonized by imperial powers, or subjugated by them.
2. Other analysts argue that the civil war was mainly due to trade liberalization, sweeping away agriculture in the North, adversely affecting the Tamil farmers, and damaging ethnic relations (Gunasinghe 1984) and causing widened inequality among groups and regions (Dunham and Jayasuriya 2000).
3. The other dimensions are the ease of starting a business, getting electricity, enforcing contracts, protecting investors, dealing with construction permits, registering property, resolving insolvency, paying taxes, and obtaining credit.
4. The assessments cover multiple dimensions of the size of government; the legal structure and security of property rights; access to sound money; freedom to trade internationally; and regulation of credit, labor, and business.
5. Neither the "Doing Business" nor "Economic Freedom" rankings include Turkmenistan; the judgment is based on the EBRD 2010 assessment.

6. The World Bank (2011) however, gives a different assessment of Tajikistan's privatization.

7. ASEAN-5 (Indonesia, Malaysia, Philippines, Thailand, and Vietnam), China and India.

8. Coined by Akamatsu (1962)

9. Singapore's prime minister Lee Kuan Yew and Malaysia's prime minister Mahathir Mohammad were the most ardent "Asian values" advocates. The formal articulation was in the 1993 Bangkok Declaration on Human Rights (Kingsbury 2008)

10. Economically progressive policies were often undertaken by authoritarian and, in some countries, socially elitist governments

11. Taiwan presented an interesting semi-exception, with intergroup differences between the native Taiwanese and the government dominated by the refugees from the mainland

12. World Bank Databank. This is in the most meaningful metric: gross national income in international purchasing power parity terms, which incorporates the different costs of purchased items from one country to another.

13. The rates for 1990 are not available for Bhutan.

14. The list of 3,428 non-*dalit* (i.e., not untouchable) "communities," predominantly of the fourth and lowest caste grouping was drawn up by the Mandal Commission in 1979–1980 under the previous Janata administration. See Gang, Sen, and Yun 2010.

15. For pro-affirmative action treatment of the policies and consequences, see Abdullah 1997 and Muscat 2002. Al Ramiah and Ramasamy in this volume provide a more balanced assessment.

16. Muscat (2002, 74–82)argues that despite partial expropriation, cronyism, and dissatisfaction with educational bias, the Chinese fared better than they would have without the economic accommodations; that the preferential treatment of Malays was likely to diminish as their status improved; and that Malaysian politics featured interethnic coalitions rather than polarized single-ethnic parties.

17. De Silva 1997 recounts the limitations of the policies and their effects.

18. The most comprehensive single treatment of conditional cash transfer programs is Grosh et al. (2008).

19. The reason why this is not inevitably the case is that the additional yield may be consumed by the farmer's family.

20. The gross rate is the total secondary enrollment (irrespective of age), as a percentage of the population of the official secondary education age. The net rate is the proportion of the population within the official secondary education age cohort who are enrolled. That measure does not account for people who are older when they enroll later, perhaps because of disruptions, displacements, and so on. In most cases, the levels and trends of the two measures are quite similar.

21. No data are reported for Turkmenistan.

22. The OECD (2001) defined such asset combinations as "territorial capital," distinct from that of other areas and, which may have the potential to generate a higher return for specific kinds of investments better-suited to the area.

23. The strategy of developing resource-abundant regions will be addressed later in this chapter.
24. See Fernholz 2010.
25. Development incentives used to entice labor migration to particular regions included job placements for college graduates, wage controls, housing provision, and other employment-assistance measures.
26. Most native populations (at least in the Far North and Far East) could not oppose the authoritarian regime's top-down socialist development. However, frontier regions and societies are not necessarily economically backward, though often "unruly" in the eyes of the center. Russia's southern frontiers, settled by Cossacks with their own system of governance, had been prosperous agricultural regions. These regions experienced the greatest wave of peasant uprisings against collectivization—later suppressed by extreme state violence.
27. According to the 2000 census, roughly three-quarters of the population in the "Deep South" provinces of Yala, Pattani, and Narathiwat are Muslims.
28. When heroin crosses the Afghan-Iranian border the price increases fourfold (Goodhand 2008, 235)
29. Long-distance resettlement is also distinct from c relocation efforts to remove people from conservation-protection areas, areas to be flooded due to new dams, or "villagization" that concentrates formerly dispersed populations. Conflict potential nevertheless is high in both categories.
30. In addition to the cases in Oberoi's volume, see Ganguly and Oetken in this volume, and Fox et al. 2009 on the impact on swidden agriculturalists.
31. See Bertrand (2004, 202) on the decentralization; Miller (2008) for details on the insurrection and the government's responses.

References

Abdullah, Firdaus. 1997. Affirmative action policy in Malaysia: To restructure society, to eradicate poverty. *Ethnic Studies Report,* 15 (2): 189–221.
Abeyratne, Sirimal. 1998. *Economic change and political conflict in developing countries with special reference to Sri Lanka.* Amsterdam: VU University Press
———. 2002. Economic roots of political conflict: The case of Sri Lanka. Working paper.
Ahmed, Sadik, and Ashutosh Varshney. 2008. *Battles half won: The political economy of India's growth and economic policy since independence.* Washington, DC: World Bank.
Akamatsu, Kaname. 1962. A historical pattern of economic growth in developing countries. *The Developing Economies* (Tokyo), 1: 3–25.
Aldeeb Abu-Sahlieh, Sami. 1995. The Islamic conception of migration: Past, present and future. Retrieved from http://www.sami-aldeeb.com/articles/view.php?id=206. Accessed May 29, 2012.
Amnesty International. 2006, April 19. Iran: Need for restraint as anniversary of unrest in Khuzestan approaches. Retrieved from http://www.amnesty.org.au/news/comments/407/. Accessed May 30, 2012.

Anderson, Kathryn, and Richard Pomfret. Spatial inequality and development in Central Asia. In *Spatial disparities in human development: Perspectives from Asia*, edited by R. Kanbur, A. J. Venables, and G Wan, 233–269. Tokyo: United Nations Press.

Ascher, William, and William H. Overholt. 1983. *Strategic planning and forecasting: Political risk and economic opportunity.* New York: John Wiley.

Asian Development Bank. 1997. *Emerging Asia: Changes and challenges.* Manila: Asian Development Bank.

Bautista, Romeo, and Alberto Valdes, eds. 1993. *The bias against agriculture: Trade and macroeconomic policies in developing countries.* San Francisco: ICS Press.

Bertrand, Jacques. 2004. *Nationalism and ethnic conflict in Indonesia.* Cambridge: Cambridge University Press.

Black, Ian. 1999. *Development in theory and practice: Paradigms and paradoxes* (2nd ed.). Boulder, CO: Westview Press.

Bohlken, Anjali, and Ernest Sergenti. 2010. Economic growth and ethnic violence: An empirical investigation of Hindu–Muslim riots in India. *Journal of Peace Research,* 47 (5): 589–600.

Chua, Amy. 2004. Sixth annual grotius lecture: World on fire. Faculty Scholarship Series. Paper 429. Retrieved from http://digitalcommons.law.yale.edu/fss_papers /429. Accessed May 27, 2012.

Commission of the European Communities. 2007. *Turkey 2007 progress report.* Commission Staff Working Document, Brussels.

Croissant, Aurel. 2007. Muslim insurgency, political violence, and democracy in Thailand. *Terrorism and Political Violence,* 19: 1–18.

Cronin, Richard. 2011. The environment and development: Greater Mekong sub-region dynamics considered. In *The borderlands of Southeast Asia: Geopolitics, terrorism, and globalization,* edited by James Clad, Sean McDonald, and Bruce Vaughn, 157–186. Washington, DC: National Defense University Press.

Daly, Michael. 2011, September 14. Evolution of Asia's outward-looking economic policies: Some lessons from trade policy reviews. Geneva: World Trade Organization Economic Research and Statistics Division Staff Working Paper ERSD-2011–12.

De Silva, K. M. 1997. Affirmative action policies: The Sri Lankan experience. *Ethnic Studies Report,* 15 (2): 245–287.

Demurger, Sylvie, Jeffrey Sachs, Wing Thye Woo, Shuming Bao, Gene Chang. 2002. The relative contributions of location and preferential policies in China's regional development: Being in the right place and having the right incentives. *China Economic Review,* 13 (2002): 444–465.

Desai, Sonalde, and Veena Kulkarni. 2008. Changing educational inequalities in India in the context of affirmative action. *Demography,* 45 (2): 245–270.

Dowling, Malcolm, and Rebecca Valenzuela. 2010. *Economic development in Asia.* Singapore: Cengage.

Dowling, Malcolm, and Ganeshan Wignaraja. 2006. Central Asia after fifteen years of transition: Growth, regional cooperation, and policy choices. *Asia-Pacific Development Journal,* 13 (2): 113–144.

Drèze, Jean, and Amartya Sen. 2011, November 14. Putting growth in its place. *Outlook*: 50–59.

Dunham, D., and S. Jayasuriya. 2000. Equity, growth and insurrection: Liberalization and the welfare debate in contemporary Sri Lanka. *Oxford Development Studies*, 28 (1): 97–110.

Dwyer, Denis, ed. 1990. *Southeast Asian development: Geographical perspectives*. New York: Longman.

EBRD (European Bank for Reconstruction and Development). 2010. Retrieved from http://www.ebrd.com/downloads/research/economics/macrodata/sci.xls. Accessed June 12, 2012.

Ewing, J. Jackson. 2009. Converging peril: Climate change and conflict in the Southern Philippines. Singapore: RSS Working Paper, S. Rajaratnam School of International Studies.

Fattah, Zainab. 2008, March 30. U.A.E. denies 100,000 residents access to riches from oil boom. *Bloomberg News*. Retrieved from http://www.bloomberg.com/apps/news?pid=newsarchive&sid=a_ciA0lSxo0Q&refer=home. Accessed May 28, 2012.

Fearon, James, and David Laitin. 2011. Sons of the soil, migrants, and civil war. *World Development*, 39 (2): 199–211.

Fernholz, Rosemary. 2010. Infrastructure and inclusive development through "free, prior, and informed consent" of indigenous people. In *Physical infrastructure development: Balancing the growth, equity, and environmental imperatives*, edited by William Ascher and Corinne Krupp, 225–258. New York: Palgrave Macmillan.

Fox, Jefferson, Yayoi Fujita, Dimbasb Ngidang, Nancy Peluso, Lesley Potter, Niken Sakuntaladwi, Janet Sturgeon, and David Thomas. 2009. Policy, political-economy, and swidden in Southeast Asia. *Human Ecology*, 37 (3): 305–322.

Gang, Ira, Kunal Sen, and Myeong-Su Yun. 2010. Caste, affirmative action and discrimination in India, Manchester, United Kingdom: Chronic Poverty Research Centre, Ten Years of War against Poverty Conference Paper.

Ge, Wei. 1999. Special economic zones and the opening of the Chinese economy: Some lessons for economic liberalization. *World Development*, 27 (7): 1267–1285.

Gillis, Malcolm. 1988. Indonesia: Public policies, resource management, and the tropical forest. In *Public policies and the misuse of forest resources*, edited by Robert Repetto and Malcolm Gillis, 43–114. New York: Cambridge University Press.

Girard, Nicole, Irwin Loy, Matthew Naumann, Marusca Perazzi, and Jacqui Zalceberg. 2012. Asia and Oceania. In *State of the world's minorities and indigenous peoples 2012*, edited by Beth Walker, 118–171. London: Minority Rights Group International.

Glinkina, Svetlana, and Dorothy Rosenberg. 2003. The socioeconomic roots of conflict in the Caucasus. *Journal of International Development*, 15: 513–524.

Goodhand, Jonathan. 2008. War, peace and the palace in between: Why borderlands are central. In *Whose peace? Critical perspectives on the political economy of peacebuilding*, edited by Michael Pugh, Neil Cooper, and Mandy Turner, 225–244. New York: Palgrave Macmillan.

Grosh, Margaret, Carlo del Ninno, Emil Tesliuc, and Azedine Ouerghi. 2008. *For protection and promotion: The design and implementation of effective safety nets.* Washington, DC: Work Bank.

Gunasinghe, N. 1984, January 7, 14, and 21. Open economy and its impact on ethnic relations in Sri Lanka. *Lanka Guardian*, cited in Abeyratne 2002.

Gwartney, James, Robert Lawson, and Joshua Hall. 2011. *Economic freedom of the world: 2010 annual report*; data set supporting the report. Retrieved from http://www.freetheworld.com/2011/2011/Dataset.xls. Accessed May 30, 2012.

Haddad, Bassam. 2005, March. Left to its domestic devices: How the Syrian regime boxed itself in. Instituto Real Instituto Elcano de Estudios Internationales y Estratégias, Working Paper 43/2005.

Hadiz, Vedi. 2004. The rise of neo-third worldism? The Indonesian trajectory and the consolidation of illiberal democracy. *Third World Quarterly,* 25 (1): 55–71.

Hendrix, Cullen, Stephan Haggard, and Beatriz Magaloni. 2009, February. Grievance and opportunity: Food prices, political regime, and protest. Paper presented at the International Studies Association Meeting, New York. Retrieved from http://www.kent.ac.uk/brussels/conference/documents/Food_prices-protests.magahaggahendrix_isa.pdf. Accessed June 18, 2012.

Henley, John, and George Assaf. 1997. Restructuring large scale state enterprises at the end of the Russian supply chain: The challenge for technical assistance and investment in the Central Asian republics. *Journal for East European Management Studies,* 2 (3): 259–286. Retrieved from http://rhverlag.de/Archiv/JEEMS_3_1997.pdf#page=31. Accessed June 9, 2012.

Hoekman, Bernard, and Jamel Zarrouk. 2009. Changes in cross-border trade costs in the Pan-Arab Free Trade Area, 2001–2008. World Bank Policy Research Working Paper 5031, August. Washington, DC: World Bank

Huang, Yasheng. 2008. *Capitalism with Chinese characteristics: Entrepreneurship and the state.* Cambridge: Cambridge University Press.

Hufbauer, Gary, and Jeffrey Schott. 2007. Fitting Asia-Pacific agreements into the WTO system. Peterson Institute for International Economics Working Paper. Washington, DC: Peterson Institute for International Economics. Retrieved from http://www.iie.com/publications/papers/hufbauer1107.pdf. Accessed June 6, 2012.

International Monetary Fund. 2009. *World Economic Outlook Update.* Washington, DC: International Monetary Fund, January. Retrieved from http://www.imf.org/external/pubs/ft/weo/2009/update/01/pdf/0109.pdf. Accessed May 16, 2012.

Ishida, Hikari, and Yoshifumi Fukunaga. 2012. Liberalization of trade in services: Toward a harmonized ASEAN ++ FTA, Economic Research Institute for ASEAN and East Asia Policy Brief. Retrieved from http://www.eria.org/pdf/ERIA-PB-2012–02.pdf. Accessed June 7, 2012.

James, William E., Seiji Naya, and Gerald M. Meier. 1989. *Asian development: Economic success and policy lessons.* Madison: University of Wisconsin Press.

Jomo, K. S. 2004. The New Economic Policy and interethnic relations in Malaysia, United Nations Research Institute for Social Development; Identities, Conflict and Cohesion Programme Paper 7.

Jomo, K. S., and Wee Chong Hui. 2003. The political economy of Malaysian feder-alism: Economic development, public policy and conflict containment. *Journal of International Development,* 15: 441–456.

Joshi, Vijay, and I. M. D. Little. 1997. *India's economic reforms 1991–2001.* New York: Oxford University Press.

Kanbur, Ravi, and Xiaobo Zhang. 2006. Fifty years of regional inequality in China. In *Spatial disparities in human development: Perspectives from Asia,* edited by Ravi Kanbur, Anthony Venables, and Guanghua Wan, 89–114. Tokyo: United Nations University Press.

Kang, David. 2002. *Crony capitalism: Corruption and development in South Korea and the Philippines.* Cambridge: Cambridge University Press.

Kaufmann, Daniel, and Paul Siegelbaum. 1997. Privatization and corruption in transition economies. *Journal of International Affairs,* 50 (2): 419–458.

Kingsbury, Damien. 2008. Universalism and exceptionalism in Asia. In *Human rights in Asia: A reassessment of the Asian Values debate,* edited by Leena Avonius and Damien Kingsbury, 19–40. New York: Palgrave Macmillan.

KPSS. 1978. Osnovnye napravleniya razvitiya narodnogo khoziaistva SSSR na 1976–1980 gody (Main directions for the development of people's economy of the USSR for 1976–1980s). *KPSS v rezolyutsiyakh I resheniyakh,* 175–257. Moscow, Politizdat.

Laruelle, Marlène, and Sébastien Peyrouse. 2012. The challenges of human secu-rity and development in Central Asia. In *The security-development nexus: Peace, conflict, and development,* edited by Ramses Amer, Ashok Swain, and Joakim Öjandal., 137–160. London: Anthem Press.

Li, Kui-Wai. 2002. *Capitalist development and economism in East Asia: The rise of Hong Kong, Singapore, Taiwan and South Korea.* London: Routledge.

Lin, Justin Yifu. 2011. *Demystifying the Chinese economy.* New York: Cambridge University Press.

Marin, Mehmet. 2005. A retrospective view of the Turkish rural urban develop-ment policies and the case of the village towns. *Urban Policy and Research,* 23 (4): 497–518.

Mattoo, Aaditya, and Arvind Subramanian. 2008. India and Bretton Woods II. *Economic and Political Weekly,* 43 (45): 62–70.

Miller, Michelle. 2008. *Rebellion and reform in Indonesia: Jakarta's security and autonomy policies in Aceh.* London: Routledge.

Muscat, Robert J. 2002. *Investing in peace: How development aid can prevent or pro-mote conflict.* New York: M. E. Sharpe.

Najman, Boris, Richard Pomfret, Gaël Raballand, and Patricia Sourdin. 2008. Redistribution of oil revenue in Kazakhstan. In *The economics and politics of oil in the Caspian Basin: The redistribution of oil revenues in Azerbaijan and Central Asia,* edited by Boris Najman, Richard Pomfret, and Gaël Raballand, 111–131. Oxford: Routledge.

Naumov, Igor. 2007, December 17. Line of departure. *Nezavisimaya Gazeta.*

Naya, Seiji. 2002. *The Asian development experience.* Hong Kong: Asian Development Bank.

Nayak, Amar, Kalyan Chakravarti, and Prabina Rajib. 2005. Globalization process in India: A historical perspective since independence, 1947. *South Asian Journal of Management,* 12 (1): 7–22.

Nayyar, Deepak. 2008. *Liberalization and development.* New Delhi: Oxford University Press.

Nellis, John. 2012, January. The international experience with privatization: Its rapid rise, partial fall and uncertain future. Calgary: University of Calgary School of Public Policy Research Paper No. 12–13.

Oberoi, A. S. 1988a. *Land settlement policies and population redistribution in developing countries.* New York: Praeger.

———. 1988b. Overview of settlement policies. In *Land settlement policies and population redistribution in developing countries,* edited by A. S. Oberoi, 7–47. New York: Praeger.

OECD (Organization for Economic Co-operation and Development). 2001. *Territorial Outlook 2001.* Paris: Organization for Economic Cooperation and Development.

Olcott, Martha. 2006. International gas trade in Central Asia: Turkmenistan, Iran, Russia, and Afghanistan. In *Natural gas and geopolitics from 1970 to 2040,* edited by David G. Victor, Amy M. Jaffe, and Mark H. Hayes, 202–233. New York: Cambridge University Press.

Otsuka, Keijiro, and Takashi Yamano. 2006. The role of rural labor markets in poverty reduction: Evidence from Asia and East Africa, FASID Discussion Paper Series on International Development Strategies No. 2006–12–007. Retrieved from http://fasid.or.jp/daigakuin/fa_gr/kyojyu/pdf/discussion/2006–12–007.pdf. Accessed May 28, 2012.

Pansuwan, Apisek, and Jayant Routry. 2011. Policies and pattern of industrial development in Thailand. *GeoJournal,* 76: 25–46.

Parnwell, Michael. 1994. Rural industrialisation and sustainable development in Thailand. *Thai Environment Institute Quarterly Environment Journal,* 1 (2): 24–39.

Partrick, Neil. 2009, February 9. The Shia factor in Gulf politics. *JIME News Report.* Retrieved from http://jime.ieej.or.jp/htm/english/2009/0209.htm. Accessed May 29, 2012.

Perkins, Dwight. 2001. Industrial and financial policy in China and Vietnam: A new model or a replay of the East Asian experience? In *Rethinking the East Asian economic miracle,* edited by Joseph Stiglitz and Shahid Yusuf, 247–294. New York: Oxford University Press.

Petri, Peter. 2012. Asia and the world economy in 2030: Economic growth, integration, and governance. In *Strategic Asia 2010–11: Asia's rising power and America's continued purpose,* edited by Ashley Tellis, Andrew Marble, and Travis Tanner, 47–77. Seattle: National Bureau of Asian Research.

Pomfret, Richard. 2006. *Central Asian economies since independence.* Princeton, NJ: Princeton University Press.

———. 2009. Regional integration in Central Asia. *Economic Change and Restructuring,* 42: 47–68.

Rakel, Eva Patricia. 2008. *Power, Islam, and political elite in Iran: A study on the Iranian political elite from Khomeini to Ahmadinejad.* Leiden: Brill.

Resosudarmo, Budy, and Arief Yusuf. 2006. Is the log export ban effective? Revisiting the issues through the case of Indonesia. *Asian Economic Papers,* 5 (2): 75–104.

Rigg, Jonathan. 2003. *South East Asia: The human landscape of modernization and development.* London: Routledge.

Roland, Christian. 2011. Successfully catching up: Non-orthodox economic and governance reforms in India and China. In *Good governance in the 21st century,* edited by Joachim Ahrens, Rolf Caspers, and Janina Weingarth, 145–174. Cheltenham, UK: Edward Elgar.

Ross, Michael. 2006. Mineral wealth and equitable development. Background Paper for the World Development Report 2006. Washington, DC: World Bank. Retrieved from http://siteresources.worldbank.org/INTWDR2006/Resources /477383–1118673432908/Mineral_Wealth_and_Equitable_Development.pdf. Accessed June 20, 2012.

Saith, Ashwani. 2000, June. *Rural industrialization in India: Some policy perspectives.* New Delhi: SAATILO.

———. 2001. From village artisans to industrial clusters: Agendas and policy gaps in Indian rural industrialization. *Journal of Agrarian Change,* 1 (1): 81–123.

Sally, Razeen, and Rahul Sen. 2011. Trade policies in Southeast Asia in the wider Asian perspective. *World Economy,* 34 (4): 568–601.

Schatz. Edward. 2010. Leninism's long shadow in Central Asia. In *Multination states in Asia: Accommodation or resistance,* edited by Jacques Bertrand and Andre Laliberte, 244–262. Cambridge: Cambridge University Press.

Sheth, D. L. 2004. Caste, ethnicity and exclusion in South Asia: The role of affirmative action policies in building inclusive societies. United Nations Development Programme Occasional Paper 2004/13. Retrieved from http://hdr.undp.org/en /reports/global/hdr2004/papers/HDR2004_DL_Sheth.pdf. Accessed June 15, 2012.

Stewart, Frances, Graham Brown, and Arnim Langer. 2007. Policies towards horizontal inequalities, Oxford University Centre for Research on Inequality, Human Security, and Ethnicity, Working Paper 42. Retrieved from http://economics .ouls.ox.ac.uk/12998/1/workingpaper42.pdf. Accessed June 15, 2012.

Straker, Jason. 2011. Between two masters: Khuzestan, Southern Iraq, and dualities of state making in the Arab/Persian Gulf. *The Arab World Geographer / Le Géographe du monde arabe,* 14 (4): 336–361.

Tan, Gerald. 2003. *Asian development: An introduction to economic, social and political change in Asia.* London: Eastern Universities Press.

Tan, Jeff. 2007. *Privatization in Malaysia: Regulation, rent-seeking and policy failure.* London: Routledge.

UN Development Programme. 2011. *Arab Development Challenges Report 2011: Towards the developmental state in the Arab region.* Retrieved from http://www .undp.org/content/undp/en/home/librarypage/hdr/arab-development-chal lenges-report-2011/. Accessed June 1, 2012.

Varshney, Ashutosh. 2002. *Civic life and ethnic conflict: Hindus and Muslims in India.* New Haven, CT: Yale University Press.

Wainwright, Joel, and Sook-Jin Kim. 2008. Battles in Seattle *redux*: Transnational resistance to a neoliberal trade agreement. *Antipode,* 40 (4): 513–534.

Widianto, Bambang. 2007, October. Are budget support and cash transfer effective means of social protection? Asian Development Bank Forum on Inclusive Growth and Poverty Reduction in the New Asia and Pacific. Manila. Retrieved from http://www.adb.org/Documents/Events/2007/Inclusive-Growth-Poverty-Reduction/papers.asp. Accessed June 12, 2011.

Wood, Graeme. 2006. Iran: A minority report: Mapping the rise of discontent. *Atlantic Monthly,* 298 (5): December.

World Bank. 1993. *The East Asian miracle: Economic growth and public policy.* New York: Oxford University Press.

———. 2005, December. *Protecting the vulnerable: The design and implementation of effective safety nets: The case of a post-crisis country: Indonesia.* Washington, DC: World Bank.

———. 2006. *The World Bank in Turkey: 1993–2004: An IEG country assistance evaluation.* Washington, DC: World Bank.

———. 2008a, January 30. Report No: ICR0000903 Implementation Completion and Results Report (IBRD-47610) on a Series of Credit and Loans in the Amount Of SDR47.4 Million ($ 70 Million Equivalent) in Credit and $1.830 Billion in Loans to the Republic of Indonesia for Development Policy Loans I-IV. Washington, DC: World Bank.

———. 2008b, June 26. Implementation Completion and Results Report (AID-54459 IBRD-46380 JPN-26884 JPN-55800) on a Loan in the Amount of US$500 Million to the Republic of Turkey for a Social Risk Mitigation Project. Washington, DC: World Bank.

———. 2009, August. *Towards 2015—spending for Indonesia's development: Shaping the prospects of a middle-income country.* Washington, DC: World Bank.

———. 2011. *Republic of Tajikistan, country economic memorandum: Tajikistan's quest for growth: Stimulating private investment.* Washington, DC: World Bank.

World Bank Group. 2012. Doing business 2012: Doing business in a more transparent world. Retrieved from http://www.doingbusiness.org/reports/global-reports/doing-business-2012/. Accessed August 10, 2012.

Yong, Wang. 2008. Domestic demand and continued reform: China's search for a new model. *Global Asia,* 3 (4): 24–28.

CHAPTER 3

Tribal Participation in India's Maoist Insurgency: Examining the Role of Economic Development Policies

Sumit Ganguly and Jennifer Oetken

Introduction

For over four decades, revolutionary Maoist groups have been at war with the government of India. The insurgency began as a tribal uprising in 1967 in Naxalbari, West Bengal. "Naxalites," or extremist ideologues, utilized Maoist tactics to overthrow the government, began mobilizing *adivasis* (tribals) and peasants in pockets of eastern India. While the Naxalite movement was virtually eliminated by the early 1970s, it was quickly revived in the central plains of Bihar and Andhra Pradesh's North Telengana region. New Maoist organizations—the Communist Party of India (Marxist-Leninist) (CPI [M-L]) People's War, CPI (M-L) Party Unity, and Maoist Communist Centre (MCC)—mobilized *dalits* (untouchables) and lower-caste Hindus against perceived upper-caste landlord exploitation. Frequently, Maoists launched violent attacks against their political and economic enemies.

After 2000, the *adivasi*-inhabited area of Orissa, Jharkhand, and Chhattisgarh's Dandakarayna forests emerged as the new epicenter of India's Maoist insurgency. Maoist groups had mobilized *adivasis* against land alienation and displacement, exploitation by traders and moneylenders, and frequent abuse and harassment from forest officials. By the mid-2000s, violence in the tribal areas escalated to unprecedented levels and casualties indicated that *adivasis* not only provided the new Maoist organization, CPI

(Maoist), with ground level support, but were also frequently caught in the cross fire.

This chapter seeks to explain how India's *adivasi* populations have become the predominant "foot soldiers" as well as victims in India's contemporary Maoist insurgency. Government officials, journalists, activists, academics, and the Maoists alike most frequently cite extreme socioeconomic "backwardness," alienation from forest lands, and rampant exploitation as drivers of *adivasi* involvement with Maoist violence. However, the policies that lie at the root of *adivasi* mobilization have been underexamined. This chapter specifically investigates the connection between economic development policies, both in India's postindependence and the economic reform eras, and the role of *adivasis* in the Maoist insurgency. Given the great variation in economic development patterns within India's tribal areas, this chapter focuses on Maoist conflict in the Dandakarayna forests in Chhattisgarh's Bastar region. Between 2002 and 2009 there were roughly 1,600 recorded fatalities associated with the Maoist conflict, primarily located in the Bastar region. Approximately one-third of the fatalities were civilian deaths, indicating that *adivasis* have also become the victims in Maoist violence.

The first section of the chapter provides an introduction to the history of India's Maoist insurgency, with special reference to *adivasi* involvement. The second section discusses the role of India's postindependence policies regarding forest and land use rights for initial *adivasi* mobilization for the Maoist movement in the Bastar region. The third section provides a critical examination of the connection between Chhattisgarh's new economic development policies in the era of economic reform and the recent escalation of Maoist violence. The chapter finds that between the 1980s and 1990s, Maoist organizations mobilized mass support for the movement around *adivasi* grievances stemming from forest and land use polices. However, there is little connection between Chhattisgarh's new economic development policies and the escalation of the Maoist insurgency in the 2000s. Increased violence appears to be a consequence of Maoist groups and state counterinsurgency operations clashing over territorial control of the Bastar region. Moreover, *adivasi* support for the movement appears to be largely based on their earlier mobilization, as opposed to the impact of new economic development policies.

Adivasi Participation in India's Maoist Insurgency

Approximately 70 million of India's 85 million "Scheduled Tribes" currently live in the country's central and eastern states. While there are over five hundred distinct tribal communities within India, the tribals of Andhra

Pradesh, Chhattisgarh, Jharkhand, Madhya Pradesh, Maharashtra, and Orissa are commonly referred to as *adivasi*.[1] Common cultural, political, and economic characteristics unify *adivasis* as a social group, and these characteristics are largely shaped by their traditional habitat in the hills and forests of these states. The livelihoods of *adivasis* are still heavily dependent on forest land and resources, and many *adivasis* also engage in "primitive" agricultural cultivation given limited access to modern technology.

Soon after independence, India's first national government incorporated the Fifth Schedule into the constitution, to protect and promote the social, cultural, economic, and political interests of the tribal populations. Verrier Elwin, a British anthropologist and advisor to the national leadership of the Congress party, argued that tribal areas needed a separate system of administration to prevent land dispossession by nontribal settlers, bondage to moneylenders, and restricted access to forests (Guha 1996, 2379). Given that tribal communities live in contiguous areas, unlike other minority groups, it was convenient to designate administrative districts with predominant tribal populations as Scheduled Tribal areas. In addition to the Fifth Schedule, Article 46 of the constitution requires the state to "promote with special care the educational and economic interests of the weaker sections of society and in particular, of the Scheduled Castes and Scheduled Tribes and shall protect them from social injustice and all forms of exploitation" (NCST 2010, 2).

Six decades later, India's indigenous tribal communities are the most socioeconomically "backward" and vulnerable group in the country. The majority of *adivasis* live in insolated, rural areas with limited access to schools, hospitals, electricity, and roads. According to the 2001 census, the literacy rate for Scheduled Tribes was 47 percent, as compared to the national average of 65.3 percent. Granted, this was a remarkable improvement from the 1991 literacy rates for Scheduled Tribes, which was just under 30 percent (NCST 2010, 4). Tribals also have disproportionately high dropout rates in primary and middle school, which has directly translated into a higher percentage of Scheduled Tribes living below the poverty line. According to estimates for 1999–2000, 46 percent of tribals living in rural areas live below the poverty line (ibid.).

Given the failure of the national and state governments to protect and develop tribal communities, as set out in the constitution, it is not surprising that Maoist organizations have been able to rival the state for *adivasi* allegiance. The following sections provide the historical background of India's Maoist insurgency between 1967 and 1998, with specific reference to *adivasi* participation. The recent expansion of the Maoist insurgency into India's tribal heartland is also discussed.

Adivasi Involvement in the Onset of the Maoist Insurgency

Adivasis have been always been entwined with India's Maoist movement. The origin of India's contemporary Maoist movement traces back to a 1967 Santhal tribal uprising in the Naxalbari area in West Bengal.[2] Local tribal leader Jangal Santhal, with organizational support from local CPI (Marxist) leaders, Charu Mazumdar and Kanu Sanyal, mobilized the *adivasis* in armed struggles against landlord exploitation and evictions. On May 25, 1967, the West Bengal police, as directed by the CPI (Marxist)-led state government, were sent in to suppress the movement and fired into a crowd, killing 11 villagers. Realizing that radical land and political reforms could not come through peaceful and parliamentary politics, a radical faction broke from the CPI (Marxist) and soon founded CPI (Marxist-Leninist), one of the original predecessors of CPI (Maoist).

During the same period, a similar uprising was underway in a tribal area in Andhra Pradesh's Srikakulam district. The uprising began as a local tribal movement for better wages, cessation of forest official harassment, and the right to harvest wastelands. In 1968, the movement joined, and adopted the Maoist tactics, of CPI (Marxist-Leninist) after two landlords were acquitted for the murder of two tribals. A separate militant Communist organization was also mobilizing tribals against landlord and forest official exploitation in the forested tribal areas of the North Telegana region of Andhra Pradesh.[3]

Limited Role of *Adivasis* in the Remobilization of the Maoist Insurgency

State-led counterinsurgency operations in the early 1970s, followed by the National State of Emergency in 1975, nearly eliminated the Maoist insurgency by decapitating its leadership and by severely repressing tribal supporters. Between 1978 and 1998, several Maoist groups successfully remobilized the movement, most notably in Andhra Pradesh and central Bihar. While Maoist groups did make inroads in some tribal areas during this period, India's *adivasi* populations played a fairly limited role in the insurgency during this period. In both areas, the Maoist groups worked primarily with sharecroppers and agricultural laborers of low-caste origin, mobilizing them against upper-caste moneylenders and landlords.

In Bihar, the predominant Maoist organizations, CPI (M-L) Party Unity and MCC had limited involvement with tribal mobilization. Both groups were primarily based in the central districts of Bihar, where they mobilized *dalit* (untouchable) and low-caste struggles against upper-caste landlords to end abuse and monopolization of land. They staged boycotts against bonded labor, demanded minimum wages, and protested the social oppression of *dalits*. During the late 1970s and 1980s, landowners organized *senas* (private militias) to counter Naxalite groups. Most of the Maoist-related violence in the 1990s in Bihar is attributed to the massacres of *dalits* and low castes by land owning upper-caste *senas*, as well as retaliatory Maoist massacres of upper-caste landlords and their families (Louis 2002).

In Andhra Pradesh the predominant Maoist organization, CPI (M-L) People's War, launched its activities in the North Telegana districts of Warangal, Khamman, Adilabad, and Karimnagar. While the first three districts do have significant tribal populations, CPI (M-L) People's War party efforts were not focused on mobilizing the tribals as they had been during the onset of the insurgency. In addition to working with low-caste and tribal peasants to fight for land redistribution and minimum wages for farm labor, People's War also adopted a broad based mobilization strategy. Mass front organizations, such as the Radical Students Union and Radical Youth League, were set up by People's War to raise widespread awareness of political oppression and mobilize aggrieved communities.

Expansion of the Maoist Insurgency to Tribal Areas

Since 2000, India's *adivasis* have become increasingly entwined with the Maoist insurgency, as the Maoist organizations thrust their activities into the central and eastern forested regions of Chhattisgarh, Orissa, and Jharkhand. Between 2002 and 2008, Chhattisgarh and Jharkhand, the states with the largest *adivasi* populations witnessed the greatest levels of violence (see Table 3.1). While tribals make up a substantial portion of Orissa's population, Naxalite violence did not escalate to the same levels of violence as Chhattisgarh and Jharkhand. However, Maoist influence and violence significantly increased during this period. Whereas in 2002 there were only 11 Maoist-related fatalities, there were 101 in 2008 (SATP 2010a).

The expansion of the Maoist insurgency into the tribal areas of these states was due to two important developments. First, beginning in 1998, Maoist organizations engaged in a series of mergers, allowing them to consolidate their territory, cadres, and resources. In 1998, People's War of Andhra Pradesh and Party Unity of Bihar merged to form CPI (M-L) People's War Group (PWG). In 2004, PWG merged with MCC, operating in both Bihar and the new state of Jharkhand, merged into CPI (Maoist)

However, the consolidation of the Maoist groups, and the expansion of the movement into India's tribal heartland, was largely motivated by increased state repression against PWG in its traditional strongholds in North Telengana. Following the October 2003 assassination attempt on

Table 3.1 Most Severely Affected States by Maoist Violence

State	Fatalities in Maoist Violence 2002–2008	Percent Tribal Population
Andhra Pradesh	656	6.6
Bihar	697	0.9
Chhattisgarh	1379	31.8
Jharkhand	1050	26.3
Maharashtra	217	8.9
Orissa	175	22.1
West Bengal	56	5.5

Source: SATP 2010a

Chief Minister Chandrababu Naidu, the state government launched an extensive counterinsurgency campaign in the region. Maoist violence that had plagued Andhra Pradesh since the early 1990s, substantially subsided in 2006 following successful counterinsurgency operations conducted by an elite state-run special forces squad, the Greyhounds. However, Andhra Pradesh's counterinsurgency successes largely translated into increased Maoist activities in other states as CPI (Maoist) cadres were forced to retreat to Chhattisgarh and Orissa's bordering forest areas (Sahni 2007b).

Maoist expansion into central India's tribal regions was clearly motivated by the hilly geography and dense forests that provide a strategic advantage for guerrilla warfare. According to the CPI (Maoist) Party Program:

> These regions have strategic importance for the Indian revolution from the military viewpoint due to their favorable terrain that facilitates the establishment of base areas...Proper tactics have to be adopted to ensure the eradication of [imperialist and comprador bureaucratic bourgeoisie] influence on the *adivasi* masses...while at the same time proper tactics have to be adopted so that a strong unity within the toiling adivasis people can be achieved...(CPI [Maoist] undated, 71)

While the actual number of *adivasis* active in the Maoist movement is difficult to ascertain, the Maoists have acquired substantial support among the *adivasi* community. While the CPI (Maoist) leadership largely consists of college-educated people from the lower-middle class, *adivasis* fill the local-level ranks in the party and militia (Guha 2009, 181; ICI 2006, 11). Mass organizations have mobilized possibly hundreds of thousands of *adivasi* supporters. Many journalists, academics, activists, and NGOs attribute the escalation and expansion of the Maoist insurgency in India's tribal areas to new development programs in India's era of economic liberalization. To drive economic growth, states are increasing mining and industrial projects in mineral and resource rich areas inhabited by tribals. Consequently, land alienation, displacement, and loss of employment are driving *adivasis* to support Maoist organizations. Arundhati Roy writes:

> Over the past five years or so, the governments of Chhattisgarh, Jharkhand, Orissa, and West Bengal have signed hundreds of MoUs [Memorandum of Understandings] with corporate houses, worth several billion dollars, all of them secret, for steel plants, sponge-iron factories, power plants, aluminum refineries, dams and mines. In order for the MoUs to translate into real money, tribal people must be moved. Therefore, this war. (*Outlook India* March 28, 2010)

However, explanations about recent economic development strategies overlook the fact that Maoists were mobilizing *adivasi* support prior to the onset of India's economic reforms, and the economic development policies underlying *adivasi* grievances. The next two parts of the chapter look at the connection between economic development policies and the Maoist conflict in Chhattisgarh's Bastar region, an area of India that has been most severely affected by Maoist violence. While the third part of the chapter specifically investigates the connection between the violence and the state's new development initiatives in the era of economic reform, the second part takes a step back to examine the initial Maoist mobilization of *adivasis* and the role of older economic development policies.

Maoist Mobilization in Chhattisgarh's Dandakarayna Forests

Between 1980 and 1998, Andhra Pradesh's PWG started working with *adivasis* in the Bastar region of the Dandakarayna forests. Unlike other tribal areas where Maoist groups had made inroads in the late 1960s, this was the Bastar region's first exposure to Maoist activities. In 1980, the PWG sent a few armed squads in the Dandakarayna forests to establish a rear base for the guerrilla movement in North Telegana. The long-term perspective was to develop it into a base area for the extension of the Maoist movement (CPI [M-L] 1999, 200). Since India's independence this area has been subject to political and administrative reorganization on a number of occasions. Until 2000, this area was under the administration of a single Bastar district in the undivided state of Madhya Pradesh. In 1998, Bastar was separated into two districts, Dantewada (south Bastar) and Bastar (north Bastar). A year later the northern section of Bastar district was reorganized as Kanker district.

In 2000, Chhattisgarh was granted separate statehood, which included the Bastar region.

The Bastar region of Chhattisgarh is one of India's most remote and underdeveloped areas. Compared to many tribal forest areas in India, Bastar's Dandakarayna forests were minimally impacted by the forest and mining industries during British colonialism. Much of the land features undulating hills, 50 percent of which is covered by dense deciduous forests. Scheduled Tribes make up 79 percent of Dantewada district's population, 66 percent in Bastar district, and 56 percent in Kanker district (GoI 2010). Given that the area is predominately inhabited by *adivasis*, the Fifth Schedule largely preempted development activities in postindependence.[4] In 1991 only 13 percent of inhabited villages in the Bastar district were connected by paved roads. This is significantly lower than the state average for Madhya Pradesh, which was 22 percent (GoI 1991). The region currently has only one rail line that runs through half of southern Bastar district. Parts of the region, such as the Abhujmar hills in western Bastar, have never been surveyed by the Indian government.

Chhattisgarh's Bastar region is socioeconomically underdeveloped and has extremely low human development indicators, a common feature among *adivasi* communities. In 2001, 90 percent of Bastar's population and 93 percent of Dantewada's population lived in rural areas. Over 80 percent of the rural inhabitants are *adivasi*, while the rest are nontribal traders, low-level officials, teachers, and health workers who have immigrated to the area (PUDR 2006, 5). While many *adivasis* depend on agricultural cultivation for household subsistence and income, only 2 percent of the cultivated lands are irrigated.

Adivasis also have very limited access to health and medical services. In Dantewada, for instance, 1,161 villages in the district's 1,220 villages have no medical facility (PUDR 2006, 6). Dantewada is one of India's least literate districts with a 30 percent literacy rate. Bastar's literacy rate of 45 percent is closer to the national average for Scheduled Tribes of 47 percent (GoI 2010). In Chhattisgarh, only 26 percent of the Scheduled Tribes finish primary school and only 9 percent matriculate from a secondary school (GoI 2010). These figures are certainly much lower for *adivasis* living in the state's more isolated southern districts. Low rates of education, even at the primary level, are directly linked to the high rates of poverty in Bastar as it precludes tribals from securing income that is not derived from cultivation, wage labor, and the collection of forest produce.

Given the extremely isolated and underdeveloped nature of the Bastar region, it is not surprising that the PWG was able to establish its presence among the *advisasi* communities. Any assistance, whether it was Maoist cadres digging small ponds for irrigation, providing medical or educational services, or assisting with agricultural production, was welcomed by people so neglected by the state. However, Maoist mobilization of *adivasis* into militant activities and organizations was secured in response to the tribal exploitation and abuse stemming from the national forestry policies put in place in the Bastar region. Before turning to these policies, the PWG movement in Bastar is briefly discussed.

Initial Maoist Activity in the Dandakarayna Forests, 1980–1998

The PWG first entered the Dandakarayna forests in 1980, and in 1982 officially set up a Forest Liaison Committee to guide the Dandakarayna movement. Two mass front organizations were initially built to mobilize the support of the tribals—the Dandakaranya Adivasi Mazdoor Kisan Sangh (DAMKS), a tribal peasant organization, and Krantikari Adivasi Mahila Sanghatan (KAMS), a tribal women's organization. Local-level resistance organizations were also organized to settle village disputes and increase social awareness. In 1987, the PWG set up a separate forest committee consisting of five members at the Forest Party Conference (*30 Years of Naxalbari* 2003, 70).

After 1990, People's War activities in the Dandakarayna forests became significantly more militarized. This is most likely the result of increased police repression by both the state government, and in some areas, paramilitary force deployment by the central government's Ministry of Home Affairs. By 1993, the party declared Dandakaranya to be a "primary level" guerrilla zone, an area where revolutionaries and ruling classes are contending for power. As such, the movement was reorganized into separate political and military wings to more effectively resist increasing repression and escalate militancy.

Maoist political organizations primarily consisted of *Gram Rajya* (village government) committees formed under the leadership of a party member. The *Gram Rajyas* committees were responsible for overseeing three types of local organizations. Development organizations, such as cooperative societies that provided loans and village development committees that utilized government schemes for the benefit of the village and organized development projects for the village. Administrative organizations, such as the *panchayat* committee, arbitrated village disputes and administered a "people's court" to settle problems and issue punishments. Village defense squads were also formed to provide local armed support for the PWG's activities and committees.

The military arm of People's War was given a well-defined, hierarchical military command, consisting of a central guerrilla squad that covered a squad area of 50–60 villages. Two or three local guerrilla squads with seven members, called *dalams*, would be responsible for the villages in this squad area (*30 Years of Naxalbari* 2003, 57). Each *dalam* in Bastar had 20–25 armed men; the *dalam* commander had an AK-47 rifle and the others were armed with smaller caliber rifles and guns. The *dalams* were also highly trained in guerrilla war tactics and laying road mines (Shukla 1999, 154).

By 1999, the PWG estimated that 60,000 tribals participated in their mass front organizations, including the DAKMS, KAMS, and also Adivasi Bal Sangha and Chetana Natya Mandali (CPI [Maoist], Chhattisgarh State Committee 2006, 80). According to police sources, 2,034 out of 3,880 villages in southern Bastar alone were under Maoist influence. It was also reported 8 *dalams* were extremely active in the Dandakarayna forests in the Bastar region of Madhya Pradesh (Shukla 1999, 148).

Violence associated with the PWG during the 1980s was considerably low. Police estimated that there were 170 Maoists in the *dalams* that had been involved in a number of violent incidents. The *dalams* frequently engaged in gun snatching, burning trucks and buses, as well as beating up forest officials. Between 1980 and 1989 there were 37 incidents where the Madhya Pradesh Special Armed Forces and People's War *dalams* exchanged fire. There were seven recorded instances of murder in which suspected police informers or village middlemen were killed. Overall, there were around 30 fatalities including police personnel, Maoists, and tribals (PUCL 1989, 15–23). Although limited data is available on this time period, levels of Maoist violence did not appear to substantially escalate between 1990 and 1998. Between 1991 and 1995, there were 32 encounters between the Maoists and police. Statistics for Maoist violence in Madhya Pradesh show that around 100 police officers, 70 informers, and 40 Maoists have been killed, the majority of which were in the Bastar region (Shukla 1999, 165–169)

National and State Forestry Policies and Maoist Mobilization in the Bastar Region

During the 1980s and the 1990s, the PWG mobilized, recruited, and gained the support of *adivasis* in Bastar primarily due to grievances arising from national and state policies regarding tribal forest and land use rights. For most *adivasis* the national forestry department was the only interaction they had with the government. The Madhya Pradesh government was virtually absent in Bastar, as most development activities percolated through the local administration, which effectively siphoned off all the funds before it could reach the tribal communities (Ganguly and Chaudhary 2003, 2986). In that the lives of tribals were so intricately connected to the forests, national and state forestry programs exerted significant influence on the existence of Bastar's *adivasi* communities. Given that interactions with the forestry department were characterized by restrictive policies, exploitation, and harassment, the Maoists largely directed their efforts toward mobilizing the *adivasis* against the forest officials who enforced, and the contractors who manipulated the forestry policies.

The livelihoods of Bastar's *adivasis* are almost entirely dependent on agricultural cultivation and the collection of forest produce. Most *adivasis* in Bastar own small landholdings, where they cultivate rice and other minor crops, such as maize, pulses, and vegetables. Agriculture production is largely subsistence as rain-fed cultivation produces small crops, but the surplus that is sold in the market significantly contributes to the *adivasis* yearly income. Due to the low productivity of the land, the collection and sale of forest produce is a major source of income. Nationalized forest produce, such as timber and *tendu* leaves used to roll tobacco, are sold through various channels to state-sponsored agencies. Other nontimber forest produce, such as mahua flowers, mango seeds, and tamarind, are sold in weekly *haats* (markets). Furthermore, *adivasis* depend on forest land for grazing cattle, wood for tools and fuel, fishing, hunting, medicines, and materials for making huts.

Under British colonialism, unlike many tribal forest areas in India, the Bastar region of the Dandakarayna forests was minimally impacted by forestry. The British brought Bastar under state administration relatively late in 1896, and commercial forestry only began in 1907, thereby limiting forest degradation and tribal displacement during the colonial period. After independence much of this land came under the National Forestry Policy, 1952, which was essentially a reincarnation of the British India Forest Act, 1878. In the interest of "national security" the first Indian government adopted the British forestry principles to ensure "forest conservation" and "industrialization." In effect, these policies placed heavy restrictions on *adivasi* forest rights. Under the National Forestry Policy, 55 percent of Bastar's forests were classified as "Reserved," 30 percent as "Protected," and 15 percent as "Other" (PUCL 1989, 6). According to the forestry policy, reserved forests were prohibited areas that unless specified by the government, *adivasis* were not permitted to use for any purpose, commercial or household. Protected forests included forests on hill slopes, watersheds, riverbanks or other vulnerable areas, where certain activities were restricted. The Forest (Conservation) Act of 1980 placed even more severe restrictions on *adivasi* use of forests by making it illegal to encroach or use any lands where a personal claim could not be established. Forest officials were given the authority to evict anyone living within the reserved forests.

People's War mobilized *adivasi* support for the Maoist movement around three key areas regarding forest land and forest produce rights. These included exploitation of tribal forest produce and wage labor, restricted land use rights, and abuse and harassment by forest officials and contractors.

Exploitation by Forests Officials, Contractors, and Traders

One of the most serious forms of exploitation occurred under the *malik makhbuja* system that forced *adivasis* to sell timber to contractors at extremely low rates. After independence, *adivasi* communities were assigned ownership of the trees in their allotted Scheduled Tribal areas. Accordingly, *adivasis* were permitted to cut timber to be sold in the market. Lacking the technology and equipment required to lumber forests, *adivasis* had to hire contractors to purchase, fell, log, and transport the trees. A *malik makhbuja* system emerged as contractors would purchase timber trees from *adivasis* for 5 to 10 cents a tree, and then sell it in the open market for $5 to $7 (Joshi 1976, 1785). This system was facilitated with the cooperation of forest officials, whose authorization was required for the sale of trees. Their permission was frequently purchased through small bribes, and even without the consent of the tribals. Despite a series of policy measures enacted to protect tribals from contractors, prevent unauthorized cutting, and give authorities the power to prosecute exploitative traders, the *malik makhbooja* system flourished until the late 1990s when the Supreme Court banned all tree cutting in the state.

One of the earliest issues taken up by Maoist organizations was the exploitation of *adivasis* by the forest department and contractors. *Dalams* of the PWG not only attacked contractor vehicles, but on some occasions killed contractors who refused to end their exploitative trading practices. The group's village committees also frequently held *jan adalat* or "people's courts" to try traders, contractors, and forest officers who had engaged in tribal exploitation (Shukla 1999, 148).

Another important issue taken up by the PWG was the exploitative prices paid to *adivasis* for tendu leaves. In the summer season, many *adivasis* in Bastar engage in *tendu* leaf collection, which accounts for a third of their annual income. For two decades, *adivasis* had received three to eight paise as wages for a bundle of fifty leaves.[5] The Maoist organizations mobilized yearly struggles, strikes, and attacks on contractors until the rates have steadily increased to 17 paise by 1984 and 80 paise by 1993. According to the PWG, one of the biggest gains the movement achieved was in the *tendu* leaf collection struggles (*30 Years of Naxalbari* 2003, 64–65).

Given the meager earnings from agricultural cultivation and forest produce, most *adivasis* also work as wage laborers in the winter months. Most work for the state's large commercial forestry industry, while others are wage laborers for construction work. The exploitation of *adivasis* by forest and labor contractors is common practice. In some instances laborers were paid as little as 21 cents a day. Nontribal settlers also received higher daily wages, though the difference was only about nine cents (PUCL 1989, 12–13). On a number of occasions, DAKMS organized laborers to strike for an increase in wages.

Land Restrictions for Agricultural Cultivation

Dependence on agricultural cultivation for subsistence and as a source of income, in addition to the low productivity of the land, put major pressure on *adivasis* to expand their area of cultivation. The PWG employed three main tactics to relieve local tensions associated with land restrictions. First, many *adivasis* encroached on notified national forest land, without actual forest cover, as well as forest covered land. Slash and burn methods were typically used to encroach on forest lands, which was strictly prohibited by national and state forestry laws. In the 1980s and 1990s, the PWG mobilized *adivasis* to cultivate land unused forest lands without forest cover. Initially, the party also encouraged *adivasis* to clear forest trees to increase areas of cultivation; however, the party later put a ban on this practice to stop forest degradation (*30 Years of Naxalbari* 2003, 68).

Second, people also frequently lacked *patta* (ownership papers) on the forest lands brought under cultivation, and on all cultivated land in forest villages. Maoist-backed mass organizations, such a DAKMS, would chase away forest and revenue officials looking to prosecute suspected encroachers. The Maoists also attacked forest check posts to remove forest officials (PUDR 2006, 11). Finally, Maoist organizations sought to address the inequity of land ownership by distributing the larger holdings of tribal families to those without land. Frequently the land belonged to the tribal headman or political leader (ibid.).

Abuse and Harassment by Forest Officials and Police Personnel

Many human rights organizations have documented abuse and harassment committed by forest officials or police personnel as well as traders and moneylenders operating illegally in the forests. Frequently *adivasis* would collect forest produce or graze cattle in reserved forests, where such activities were prohibited. Forest officials used the National Forest Act, 1927, and later the 1980 Forest Conservation Act, to intimidate and harass *adivisis*. Under these laws any use or encroachment on reserved forests was punishable by a fine or imprisonment. However, more often than not, corrupt officials would bribe *adivasis* for cash, liquor, and meat. The Human Rights Forum found that Maoists have stopped harassment by forest and police officials. According to their report, "The harassment used to take the form of threats of being booked in criminal cases for cutting trees or grazing cattle in the forests . . . The threat of violence by the Maoists or the people with the support of Maoists has put an end to this to a large extent." (HRF 2006, 9)

Recall that 1980 and 1998, the PWG actively mobilized *adivasi* support for the Maoist movement, primarily against grievances emerging from national forestry and land use policies. In many parts of the Bastar region, harassment of *adivasis* by forest officials and exploitation by traders ceased, wages for forest produce had substantially increased, and *adivasis* acquired more land either through redistribution or encroachment. The success of Maoist agitations and attacks surrounding these policies buttressed the *adivasi* base of support as well.

The Maoist Insurgency and New Economic Development in the Bastar Region

During the initial period of Maoist mobilization in the Bastar region, levels of violence were relatively low. However, between 2002 and 2009 the Maoist movement escalated into a full-scale insurgency with nearly 1,600 recorded fatalities including Maoists, security forces, and civilians. Yearly fatalities substantially increased from 55 in 2002 to 126 in 2005, but in 2006 and 2007 there were more than recorded 700 deaths (Table 3.2). The dramatic increase in violence during these two years was primarily the result of a state-sponsored anti-Maoist campaign, called *Salwa Judum*.

In 2005, a Congress Party MLA from Dantewada, Mahendra Karma, organized a Maoist opposition group to go into villages and threatened villagers to identify Maoists and Maoist supporters. If *Salwa Judum* was resisted, the members would loot and burn the village, in addition abusing, raping, and even killing *adivasi* villagers. The *Salwa Judum* campaign gained momentum as Chhattisgarh's chief minister, Raman Singh, authorized the vigilante group to conduct raids on the villages with the support of state and central government security forces. Many villages were cleared to isolate the Maoists and the villagers were forcibly relocated into roadside

Table 3.2 Fatalities in Chhattisgarh's Maoist Conflict

	Insurgents	Security Forces	Civilians	Total
2002	–	–	–	55
2003	8	30	44	82
2004	15	8	75	98
2005	26	48	26	126
2006	117	55	189	361
2007	73	182	95	350
2008	66	67	35	168
2009	137	121	87	345
Total	**442**	**511**	**551**	**1585**

Source: 2002–2004 data: SATP 2010b; 2005–2009 data: SATP 2010a.

settlement camps. The state government also authorized the appointment of 3,500 Special Police Officers to reinforce the anti-Maoist campaign, most of which were local *adivasis* from the same district (ICI 2006). Until the end of January 2006, there were 43,740 internally displaced persons living in relief camps (ACHR 2006, 3). While official estimates vary, 268 civilians were killed in the first year of violence (ICI 2006, 28). In retaliation, the Maoists have targeted and killed more 248 *Salwa Judum* activists (SATP 2010b).

Following the termination of the *Salwa Judum* campaign in early 2007, violence associated with the Maoist conflict in Chhattisgarh substantially decreased in 2008 with only 168 recorded fatalities. However, violence reescalated in 2009 with 345 fatalities.

Many journalists, activists, and human rights organizations have implicated Chhattisgarh's new industrial development as the driver behind the escalation of Maoist violence as well as increased *adivasi* support for the Maoists. The Asian Centre for Human Rights (ACHR) notes:

> The Chhattisgarh government has reportedly signed Memorandum of Understandings for an investment of Rs. 17,000 crores (US$ 3.8 billion) in Bastar region for the proposed Tata and Essar Steel plants...The industrial houses have been responsible for pushing the Adivasis towards the Naxalites. (2006, 47)

The implied connection is that *adivasi* land and livelihoods are under attack by state-led development projects, thus driving *adivasis* to support the Maoists and provoking increasing Maoist violence against the state and new industry. However, despite these frequent assertions, there has been little systematic analysis of how Chhattisgarh's new development initiatives have fueled the Maoist insurgency. The next section gives an overview of Chhattisgarh's new economic development policies and its industrialization initiatives.

Chhattisgarh's Development Initiatives in the Era of Economic Reform

At the same time that the Maoist violence was escalating, the newly formed state of Chhattisgarh launched new economic development initiatives for the Bastar region. In November 2000, Chhattisgarh was granted separate statehood from Madhya Pradesh, primarily on the basis of its distinct history and sociocultural regional identity. Political movements during the 1990s also mobilized around the idea that a separate state was necessary for the socioeconomic development of this lagging region of Madhya Pradesh. Chhattisgarh emerged as one of India's poorest and economically undeveloped states. In 2000–2001, Chhattisgarh's per capita income was Rs. 9,922 versus the India's per capita income of Rs. 16,555 (Directorate of Economics and Statistics, 2010). Chhattisgarh's growth rate of 4.37 percent significantly lagged behind the Indian growth rate of 8.01 (ibid.).

According to the Chhattisgarh government's 2004–2009 New Industrial Policy, the expansion of natural resource-based industrial production is a priority area for the state's rapid economic growth (GoC 2010). Chhattisgarh's abundant mineral resources are clearly a central feature in the state's new economic development policy. Chhattisgarh has 28 major minerals, including 16 percent of India's coal reserves and 10 percent of the iron ore reserves (CSE publication, 2008). Chhattisgarh's new industrialization polices have been emboldend by India's 1991 economic reforms that liberalized the mining sector and devolved considerable authority to grant mining leases and licenses to the state governments.

Another important objective of the industrial policy is to ensure that industries are also set up in the state's industrially backward areas to ensure regionally balanced growth in the state (GoC 2010). Bastar and Dantewada are among the most mineral rich districts in Chhattisgarh; however, until the 2000s the region's mining and mineral- based industries have been undeveloped, with the exception of an iron ore mine. According to the industrial policy a key strategy that the government is undertaking to increase industrialization is to ensure quality roads, developed land, water resources, and power to private investors (GoC 2010). To this end, the Bastar Development Authority was established in 2003 to develop the region's infrastructure critical to industrialization.

Efforts to develop natural resources in the Bastar and Dantewada have gained momentum. In 2005, the National Mining Development Corporation initiated a new steel plant at Nagarnar village in Bastar district. The state government-led by Chief Minister Raman Singh government has also signed Memorandums of Understanding with the two industrial houses, Tata and Essar, to set up steel plants on land leased by the government. Essar has also received a contract to build a pipeline, capable of transporting 8 million tons of iron ore slurry per year to the Visakhapatum port in Andhra Pradesh. This is another indicator of state plans for intensifying mining in the region. To facilitate regional development a new Dalli-Rajhara-Raoghat-Jagdalpur railway line is being built in the Bastar-Dantewada region.

Maoist Drive to Establish a "Liberated" Zone

Since the early 2000s, CPI (Maoist) has undertaken a major campaign against any and all development projects. A prominent theme in their propaganda is to warn that mining projects will not bring development to *adivasi* communities but rather alienate them from their land and livelihoods. One *People's March* (2007, 8) article states:

> The pattern of so-called development being pursued by the reactionary ruling classes...is to plunder the mineral and forest wealth in the name of developing the industries, displacing local adivasi communities, snatch their rights over the forests, convert them into cheap laborers for the big business and imperialist ventures.

As part of their antidevelopment campaign, Maoists in Chhattisgarh's Bastar region have frequently attacked mining industries, as well as the construction of roads and rail lines. Since 2006, CPI (Maoist) has regularly attacked development companies and projects in Bastar and Dantewada.

However, the overall escalation in the Chhattisgarh's Maoist insurgency appears to be more the result of Maoist organizations rivaling the state for territorial control of the Bastar region, as opposed to actual conflict over new development initiatives. In the years between 1998 and 2004, PWG and CPI (Maoist) set out to establish Dandakaranya as a primary guerrilla zone. After the merger of PWG with Party Unity, the merged party announced the establishment of two guerrilla zones in India; one in North Telengana and the other in the Dandakaranya forests, called the "Dandakarayna Special Zone" (CPI [M-L] 1999, 297–308). Nihar Nayak writes that "Bastar is, in fact, emerging as a 'Base Area' for the unification of the Maoist movement and direction of operations across multiple state boundaries" (2003).

The 2004 merger of PWG and MCC to form CPI (Maoist) reinforced the strategic importance of the Dandakarayna forests in Chhattisgarh as a key guerrilla zone.

Starting in the early 2000s, it is clear that the Maoists were engaged in a major armed struggle against the state and local governments for territorial control of the Bastar region. A People's Liberation Guerrilla Army was established with local guerrilla squads and military *dalams* (village militias) to more effectively carry out armed attacks. In the Dandakarayna Special Zone, local officials have estimated that there are 70 local guerrilla squads and 30 military *dalams*. (Kujur 2006). State police sources have also estimated that the Maoists in Chhattisgarh have over 5,000 armed cadre equipped with sophisticated assault weapons in the local guerrilla squads and 20,000 *dalam* member armed with guns, rifles, as well as bows and arrows (Sahni 2007b).

The Maoist party organization was also restructured to more effectively establish parallel governments at the local level. In the Dandakarayna Special Zone, the *Gram Rajya* (village) committees were converted to Revolutionary Peasant Committees. These committees are responsible for administering the *jan adalats* (people's courts), collecting taxes, overseeing a number of subcommittees involved with community development and administration. In addition to the *dawai* (medical committee) and educational subcommittees, the *vikaas* committee was established to work with *adivasis* on cooperative agriculture and the Jangal Bachao committee oversaw forest maintenance and surveillance. The Chetana Natya Manch committee continued to organize cultural performances. According to a CPI (Maoist) spokesperson for zone, the party cadres are entirely local and the party leadership was largely from Andhra Pradesh with few *adivasi* representatives. However, local *adivasis* were beginning to be incorporated into regional committees and take on leadership roles (ICI 2006, 11).

In a number of ways, the Maoists are working to cripple the government in the Bastar region. Both the PWG and the CPI (Maoist) have launched numerous attacks on Chhattisgarh police and security forces, resulting in hundreds of security personnel fatalities as well as extensive damage to police equipment and infrastructure. Numerous local officials and politicians, including *adivasi sarpanches* (local-level political leaders) designated and tribal village headmen, have been killed or driven out of the region by Maoist organizations. In 2003, the Maoists organized a violent boycott of the State Assembly elections.

The degree to which the Maoists have been successful in setting up parallel governments varies considerably across the Bastar region. According an interview with a CPI (Maoist) spokesperson, the party has been able to set up 1,000 Revolutionary Peasant Committees and 70 percent of these are in the Dantewara district (ICI 2006, 11). In a number of areas, Maoist front organizations such as DAKMS are the new authority in village administration, which are secretly supported by the Revolutionary Peasant Committees (HRF 2006, 13). In other locations, CPI (Maoist) claims that they have completely eliminated local government and administration, and have set up *janatan sarkars* or "people's government" (*People's March* 2007, 12). Various reports have substantiated that the Maoists have "liberated" the Abujhmar hills in Bastar district, which serves as the Maoist base of both political and military operations (Cherian 2005).

Beginning in 2003, very soon after the Maoists began to more forcefully establish their presence, the Chhattisgarh state, with the assistance of central paramilitary forces launched a sustained counterinsurgency campaign against the Maoists in the Bastar region. The state-sponsored *Salwa Judum* campaign was just one of the state's attempts to repress the Maoists. There is a good deal of speculation that Chhattisgarh's counterinsurgency operations, including the *Salwa Judum* campaign, was driven by government interests to clear the Bastar region of the Maoists and their *adivasi* supporters to make way for mining and mineral-based industries.[6] However, there is no evidence to support these claims. A Human Rights Forum field investigation maintains that the *Salwa Judum* was a counterinsurgency strategy, not a strategy to secure the forest lands (2006, 30).

Moreover, the initial mobilization of the anti-Maoist *Salwa Judum* is largely a consequence of grievances caused by Maoist attacks on nontribal traders and contractors regarding land and forest produce. Human rights groups have found that in addition to Mahendra Karma, the *Salwa Judum* was led by local elites adversely affected by Maoist redistribution of land as well as traders and contractors whose profits have declined due to Maoist efforts to increase *adivasi* wages for *tendu* leaf collection and selling forest produce. The Maoist opposition movement was also led by some *adivasi* village leaders whose lands had been taken or who were forced out of their villages (PUDR 2006, 15).

For the most part, the escalation of the Maoist insurgency between 2002 and 2009 is a consequence of CPI (Maoist) militants clashing with the state's counterinsurgency operations for territorial control of the Bastar region. To a very limited extent the violence can be associated with the state's new economic development initiatives.

Maoist Violence and Adivasis Caught in the Crossfire. During the 1980s and 1990s there was a clear connection between policies on tribal forest and land use rights and *adivasi* support from Maoist organizations. However, in the most recent phase of the insurgency the same nexus does not yet exist between the state government's new economic development polices and *adivasi* support for the Maoists. While the primary interest of CPI (Maoist) in the Bastar region is to secure the region as their guerrilla base, CPI (Maoist) documents reveal that the organization is actively working to mobilize *adivasis* around its antidevelopment campaign. For instance, their Party Program states that

> the Party should organize *Adivasis* with the slogans, *"Right over the forest belongs to people and Adivasis," "Political Autonomy to the Adivasi territories"* and transform the territory as exploitation-free territory i.e. "red land," "don't be divided, be united," "unite the real friends against the real enemies," "right over all the resources including water, forest etc," "right for protecting their own culture and development," and draw up a specific plan for work among them to mobilize them against economic, political, social and cultural oppression by imperialism, CBB and feudalism. (CPI [Maoist] undated, 71)

Since the Chhattisgarh government launched new development initiatives, a number of local-level *adivasi* resistance movements have formed in response to the land acquisition process. Protests first erupted in the Nagarnar village after the National Mineral Development Corporation (NMDC) identified 4,452 hectares of land belonging to four villages in the Bastar district. The *adivasis* make up 80 percent of the population, 90 percent of which own land. According to the 1996 Panchayat (Extension to the Scheduled Areas) Act, the *gram sabha*, the village or hamlet-level governing body, is to be consulted before starting the land acquisition process. The consent of the *gram sabha* regarding the land transfer and compensation must also be given. In one instance, after the *gram sabhas* rejected the proposed project, the district collector told the NMDC and state officials that the *gram sabhas* had consented, and the land acquisition process proceeded.[7] On October 2001, activists protesting the project were apprehended and shot at by the police and 45 people were injured. Most of the villagers were then forced to accept the compensation checks.

Similar agitations have occurred at the other proposed sites for industrial projects in the Lohandiguda region of Bastar district and Dantewada district after *gram sabhas* have been coerced into selling their land, or their decisions simply disregarded by the government. However, it is difficult to discern the degree to which CPI (Maoist) was even involved in these protest movements as there is little documentation of Maoist involvement.

The fact is that Chhattisgarh's new development initiatives have currently impacted very few *adivasis* in the Bastar region, partially due to both the Maoist presence and state failure. Maoist organizations built a tremendous base of *adivasi* support around the state policies regarding forest and land use rights, and these issues continue to motivate their participation in Maoists activities and support for the Maoists. State development initiatives, in any respect, are far off and grievances surrounding these policies are largely cosmetic. This was demonstrated by the DAKMS call for the strike and boycott against *tendu* leaf collection in 2005. That year the state government wanted to set up a system in which local cooperatives, as opposed to contractors, would purchase *tendu* leaves. However, this new policy reduced the wages from 90 to 45 paise per bundle.

While *adivasi* support remains strong, two new developments have emerged since the onset of the insurgency. First, there appears to be a growing contingent of *adivasis* who resent Maoist activities. One group includes former tribal leaders whose lands have been redistributed or who have been forced out of their communities by Maoist parties. Another group includes a disenchanted segment of *adivasis* who feel that they are exploited by the Maoist party and are socioeconomically worse off due to Maoist sabotage of development projects and strikes against *tendu* leaf collection.

A second important development is that *adivasis* are increasingly the victims of the Maoist insurgency. They are caught in the cross fire between the Maoist agenda to secure the Bastar region as a guerrilla zone and base of operations, and the state's counterinsurgency operations to flush out the Maoists.[8] This is demonstrated by the fact that over one-third of the fatalities in the conflict have been civilians (Table 3.2). *Adivasis* are frequently harassed, beaten, and even killed in counterinsurgency operations. The *Salwa Judum* campaign is perhaps one of the most extreme examples. The Human Rights Forum has estimated that in the aftermath of *Salwa Judum*, 70,000–100,000 people were displaced, including those forcibly relocated to resettlement camps as well as those that fled across the border to Andhra Pradesh or the interior jungles of Dantewada to escape the violence (2006, 4). The most recent counterinsurgency campaign in Chhattisgarh, called "Operation Green Hunt," had led to further displacement and violence against *adivasis* in the Bastar region.

CPI (Maoist) attacks against *adivasis* are dramatically increasing, particularly against those who do not follow Maoist dictates or who are known or suspected police informers. The Maoists have attacked farmers who have agreed to sell their land for development projects. In 2007, over 40 Maoists raided Bhansi village and killed two farmers for selling land to Essar Steel and warned other residents not to give up their land (SATP, 2007). The party is increasingly convinced that civilians are acting as police informers and brutally kill them to discourage cooperation with the state. However, this is partially a consequence of the state government "privatizing" its counterinsurgency operations, as was first seen in *Salwa Judum*. More recently the state government has enlisted *gram chowkidars* (village guards) to act as informers, who are required to submit a register of visitors to the village and incidents of theft and fraud (Singh 2010).

Conclusions

During the 2000s, the tribal areas of Chhattisgarh, Jharkhand, Maharashtra, and Orissa became the epicenter of India's Maoist insurgency. While Maoist organizations had been working with *adivasis* during the 1980s and 1990s, starting in 1998 the Maoist movement became increasing militant as the PWG and later CPI (Maoist) sought to establish guerrilla zones in these strategically important hilly and forested areas. The escalation of the Maoist insurgency during this period is frequently cited to be a consequence of new economic development policies, specifically the acquisition of land and displacement of tribals for mining and mineral-based industries. However, in the case of Chhattisgarh's Bastar region, the state government's new development initiatives have had a limited impact on the escalation of Maoist violence as well as increased *adivasi* support for the movement. Increased levels of violence are largely the result of Maoists clashing with state counterinsurgency operations for territorial control of the Bastar region. *Adivasi* participation in Maoist activities and support for the Maoists in the current phase is best explained by the initial mobilization of *adivasi* support around grievances stemming from national and state forest and land use policies. Moreover, forest and land use rights continue to motivate *adivasi* support for the Maoists, whereas thus far new development projects in the region have yet to impact the lives of a substantial number of *adivasis*.

If the Chhattisgarh government is to reduce *adivasi* support for Maoist organizations, new policies need to recognize *adivasi* rights to the land and forests that they have traditionally inhabited. While the Scheduled Tribes and Other Traditional Forest Dwellers (Recognition of Forest Rights) Act was passed in 2006, to grant legal rights of *adivasis* to their homes and lands in India's forest areas, and protect them from abuse, exploitation, and harassment, thus far, the Chhattisgarh government has coercively implemented the act, as opposed to working with local villages, and has made it exceedingly difficult for people and communities to establish their land claims.

Also, while Chhattisgarh's development programs in the Bastar region have yet to impact the lives of many *adivasis*, they certainly will in the near future. To ensure that these policies do not create new grievances that Maoists can use to mobilize *adivasi* support, the state needs to ensure that land for industrial projects and road is acquired democratically. Compensation and rehabilitation packages need to be designed to sustain the livelihoods as well as improve the lives of displaced *adivasis*. Finally, the state government needs to promote human development, particularly in the form of education, in order to integrate *adivasis* into the labor market that is created by new industry.

Notes

1. The other tribal communities live in India's northeastern states.
2. While nontribals also participated in the movement, Santhal tribals were the main participants in the uprising. Originally from southern Bihar (present-day Jharkhand), the Santhals were displaced from their lands and migrated to northern West Bengal to work in the tea gardens, forests, and mines. For more on the role of Santhals in the Naxalite insurgency see Duyker 1987.
3. For a detailed account of tribal involvement during the early years of the Maoist insurgency see Sinha 1989.
4. Interesting exceptions to Bastar's pattern of underdevelopment are Bengali refugee resettlement areas, set up under the Dandakaranya Development Authority in 1958. Small development zones, in Kanker and Bastar districts, include not only almost all of the region's irrigated land but also road connectivity to allow for improved market access. Unfortunately these development projects improved the livelihoods of very few local tribal inhabitants. See Farmer 1974.
5. Rs. 1 equals 100 paise and Rs. 53 equal roughly US$1.
6. For example, there were allegations that Tata was funding the *Salwa Judum* campaign so that the state government could clear these lands to sell to the Tata Iron and Steel Corporation.
7. The district collector is appointed by the Indian Central Government to govern a state district.
8. Nontribals in the Bastar region also fall victim to the conflict between the CPI (Maoist) and security forces. For example, in 2006, 13 civilians from the Bengali resettlement area in Kanker district were killed when their vehicle hit a landmine triggered by Maoists (*Express India* 2006).

References

30 Years of Naxalbari: An epic of heroic struggle and sacrifice. 2003. Delhi: New Vista Publications.

Asian Center for Human Rights (ACHR). 2006. *The Adivasis of Chhattisgarh: Victims of the Naxalite Movement and Salwa Judum Campaign*.

CSE (Centre for Science and Environment). 2008. *Sixth Citizens' Report: Rich Lands Poor People*, Center for Science and Environment.

Cherian, Saji. 2005. Chhattisgarh: Reality bites. *South Asia Intelligence Review Weekly Assessments and Briefings,* 3 (46). Retrieved from http://www.satp.org/sat porgtp/sair/Archives/3_46.htm#assessment1. Accessed May 1, 2010.

(CPI [Maoist]) Communist Party of India (Maoist). Undated. Party programme. *South Asia Terrorism Portal.* Retrieved from http://www.satp.org/satporgtp/countries /india/maoist/documents/papers/partyproram.htm. Accessed April 20, 2010.

(CPI [Maoist]) Communist Party of India (Maoist), Chhattisgarh State Committee. 2006, November. Salwa Judum: A "New Front" of "Hidden War": The inside story. Chhattisgarh State Committee Report.

(CPI [M-L]) Communist Party of India (Marxist-Leninist) (People's War). 1999. *Mao and people's war.* Utrecht: Vanguard Multi-Media Foundation. 123–213.

Directorate of Economics and Statistics, Chhattisgarh. 2010. Estimate of state domestic product of Chhattisgarh, 1993–94 to 2004–05. Retrieved from http:// www.descg.gov.in/File.aspx?category=State%20Income%20Division. Accessed on May 7, 2010.

Duyker, Edward. 1987. *Tribal guerrillas: The Santals of West Bengal and the Naxalite movement.* New Delhi: Oxford University Press.

Express India. 2006, March 25. "Maoists kill 13 in Chhattisgarh landmine blast." Retrieved from http://www.expressindia.com/news/fullstory.php?newsid=64927. Accessed July 25, 2010.

Farmer, B. H. 1974. *Agricultural colonization in India since independence.* London: Oxford University Press.

Ganguly, B. K., and Kalpana Chaudhary. 2003. Forest products of Bastar: A story of tribal exploitation. *Economic and Political Weekly,* 38 (38): 2985–2989.

(GoC) Government of Chhattisgarh. 2010. Industrial policy (2004–2009). Retrieved from http://cg.gov.in/govtpolicy/New%20Industrial%20Policy%20English .htm. Accessed May 5, 2010.

(GoI) Government of India. 1991. Census of India. Ministry of Home Affairs.

———. 2001. Census of India. Ministry of Home Affairs. Retrieved from http:// censusindia.gov.in/. Accessed April 15, 2010.

Guha, Ramachandra. September 1996. Savaging the civilised: Verrier Elwin and the tribal question in late colonial India. *Economic and Political Weekly,* 31 (35/37): 2375–2389.

———. 2009. Adivasis, Naxalites, and democracy. In *Challenges to Democracy in India,* edited by Rajesh M. Basrur, 167–188. New Delhi: Oxford University Press

HRF (Human Rights Forum). 2006, December. *Death, displacement & deprivation: The war in Dantewara: A report.* Hyderabad: Human Rights Forum Publication.

ICI (Independent Citizens' Initiative). 2006, July 20. *War in the heart of India: An enquiry into the ground situation in Dantewara District, Chhattisgarh.* New Delhi: Independent Citizens' Initiative.

Joshi, Ramsharan. 1976. Politics of timber trade. *Economic and Political Weekly,* 11 (46): 1785–1786.

Kujur, Rajat Kumar. 2006, June. Left extremism in India: Naxal movement in Chhattisgarh and Orissa. *Institute for Peace and Conflict Studies.* Special Report 25.

Louis, Prakash. 2002. *People Power: The Naxalite movement in Central Bihar*. Delhi: Wordsmith.

Nayak, Nihar. 2003. Chhattisgarh: Democracy vs. 'People's War. *South Asia Intelligence Review Weekly Assessments and Briefings*, 2 (20). Retrieved from http://www.satp.org/satporgtp/sair/Archives/2_20.htm. Accessed May 10, 2010.

NCST (National Commission on Scheduled Tribes). 2010. "Socio economic development." Retrieved from http://ncst.nic.in/writereaddata/mainlinkFile/File415.pdf. Accessed May 1, 2010.

People's March. 2007, July 3. Why the ruling classes want to continue their genocidal Salwa Judum campaign at any cost.

PUCL (People's Union for Civil Liberties). 1989. *Development and democracy*. New Delhi: People's Union for Civil Liberties.

PUDR (People's Union for Democratic Rights). 2006. *Where the state makes war on its own people*. New Delhi: PUDR.

Roy, Arundhati. 2010. Walking with the Comrades. *Outlook India*, March 29. Retrieved from http://www.outlookindia.com/article.aspx?264738

Sahni, Ajai. 2007a. Andhra Pradesh: The state advances, the Maoists retreat. *South Asia Intelligence Review Weekly Assessments and Briefings*, 6 (10). Retrieved from http://www.satp.org/satporgtp/sair/Archives/6_10.htm. Accessed April 12, 2010.

———. 2007b, July 16. So who's losing sleep over Chhattisgarh. *Outlook India*. Retrieved from http://www.outlookindia.com/article.aspx?235078. Accessed April 21, 2010.

Singh, Ajit Kumar. 2010, January 11. Chhattisgarh: Strategies of failure. *South Asia Intelligence Review Weekly Assessments and Briefings*, 8 (27). Retrieved from http://www.satp.org/satporgtp/sair/Archives/sair8/8_27.htm#assessment1. Accessed May 10, 2010.

Sinha, Shantha. 1989. *Maoists in Andhra Pradesh*. New Delhi: Gian Publishing House.

SATP (South Asian Terrorism Portal). 2010a. Fatalities in Left Wing Extremism. Retrieved from http://www.satp.org/satporgtp/countries/india/maoist/data_sheets/fatalitiesnaxal0.htm. Accessed May 5, 2010.

———. 2010b. Fatalities is Left Wing Extremism (Ministry of Home Affairs). Retrieved from http://www.satp.org/satporgtp/countries/india/maoist/data_sheets/fatalitiesnaxal ha.htm. Accessed May 5, 2010.

Shukla, H. L. 1999. *Chhattisgarh in making*. New Delhi: B. R. Publishing Corporation.

CHAPTER 4

Intrastate Conflicts and Development Strategies: The Baloch Insurgency in Pakistan

G. Shabbir Cheema

Introduction

Intrastate conflicts have been endemic in Pakistan since its independence in 1947. The most disastrous for the country was the civil war in former East Pakistan (now Bangladesh). The concentration of political power and government-initiated programs and investments in the western part of the country and the increasing regional disparities led to the alienation and resentment of the people in the eastern part. The triggers for the intrastate conflict were the unwillingness of the military regime to hand over power to the democratically elected leader from East Pakistan and long periods of military rule that deprived the country of democratic mechanisms to reconcile political and economic differences. Another long-simmering intrastate conflict in Pakistan is Balochistan—the largest province of the federation in area and the smallest in population. The demand of the local Baloch population for regional autonomy, their resentment at the slow pace of provincial economic development, the influx of people from other provinces, and the exploitation of the extensive natural resources of the province without equitable distribution of benefits have led to political and social tensions and the insurgency. Four waves of violent unrest took place during 1948, 1958–1959, 1962–1963, and 1973–1977. In early 2005, tensions in Balochistan again increased, with numerous clashes reported between security forces and the Baloch tribesmen.

The Pakistani experience suggests that there were two main determinants of the intrastate conflicts: (1) development strategies and approaches that led to uneven development and institutionalized exclusion of various groups and regions from benefits accruing from government-initiated programs, and (2) military-dominated governments in about half of Pakistan's 62-years history that deprived citizens of political mechanisms to express their grievances and resolve differences. Other causes include the feudal structures characterized by unequal patterns of land ownership, the manipulation of ideological and ethnic differences by politicians both at the national and regional levels for short-term political gains, and the failure of political leadership to provide the societal vision and mobilize citizens for the public good.

This chapter examines the impact of development strategies (independent variable) and democratic governance (intervening variable) on intrastate conflicts in Pakistan. After describing the main elements of development strategies and their impacts during various phases, the chapter discusses the evolution of the Baloch insurgency, the demand of regional autonomy, and the extent of economic and social disparities between Balochistan and other regions of the federation. Also examined are the government responses and insurgency management strategies and the recently introduced Balochistan Empowerment Package launched by the newly elected democratic government.

Pakistan's Development Strategies and Their Impact

Since independence, Pakistan's development strategies have undergone five phases: (1) centralized economic growth up to 1965, (2) increased state intervention in the national economy with populist approach in the 1970s, (3) rapid economic growth with greater intervention by the military in the 1980s, (4) the phase led by democratic governments from 1988 to 1999 and later the military-led Musharraf government that focused on policy package that is generally associated with the "Washington Consensus," and (5) development strategies followed by the newly elected democratic government in the context of political instability after the demise of the Musharraf regime and an alarming rise in terrorism and political violence (Hamid 2008, 47–52; European Commission 2006, 4–6)

During the 1950s and 1960s, the strategy was focused on the promotion of industrialization through import-substitution policies and central planning with leading role of government in the economy. The government established public enterprises in the manufacturing sector and subsequently sold many of these to the private sector. A system of multiple exchange rates was set up to encourage exports. Centralized planning was introduced with heavy investment in the western part of the country where the newly inde-pendent state had a relatively better developed infrastructure, seat of the federal government, and economic growth poles (Hamid 2008, 47–52).

The development strategies that followed in the 1950s and 1960s accel-erated economic growth leading to the worldwide recognition of Pakistan as one of the development "success" stories. The economic growth, however, was not equitably distributed among different constituent units of the fed-eration. There were pronounced differences in income levels, investments in infrastructure, economic opportunities, and access to basic social ser-vices between the western part of the country (West Pakistan) and the east-ern part (now Bangladesh). This led to political alienation and resentment on the part of the population in the eastern part. The military-dominated governments in the 1960s that deprived the citizens of the opportunities for political participation further increased alienation among the population of the poorer regions, especially in East Pakistan and the area that is now called "Balochistan." Political unrest in the late 1960s forced the military government to hold free elections, which resulted in the victories of the Awami League and the Pakistan Peoples Party in the eastern and western parts of the country, respectively. Unwillingness of the military to cede power to the Awami League, which had a majority in the Parliament, led to the civil war, intervention by India, and subsequently the independence of Bangladesh.

One of the lessons learned from the international experience in pro-moting pro-growth strategies in the 1950s and 1960s is that during the early years after independence such strategies worked more effectively in homogenous societies such as the Republic of Korea than in multiethnic and multilingual societies such as Pakistan. While there is no doubt about the efficiency of pro-growth strategies, heterogeneous societies are in greater need of democratic mechanisms for political bargaining during the initial years of political integration than homogeneous societies. The absence of balance between political development and economic development proved to be counterproductive to national integration in Pakistan.

The second phase of development strategies (1972–1977) was initi-ated by Zulfikar Ali Bhutto, the popularly elected leader after a decade of military-led governments. Major investments were made in megaproj-ects including steel mills, the Tarbella Dam, and the nuclear program. The private-sector-led growth strategy was reversed. The new strategy focused on heavy-industry-based industrialization led by the state. The Bhutto gov-ernment nationalized the engineering, cement, and chemical industries, as well as the oil refineries. Other industries that were nationalized included shipping, banking, life insurance, and power utilities. The government monopolized the export trade in rice and cotton, and initiated the public sector investment program in heavy industry (Hamid 2008, 47–52).

The above and related policies pursued by Bhutto led to the end of the first growth cycle of Pakistan, with an increase in fiscal and current account deficits. High level of government intervention in the economy including nationalization of selected industries led to the decrease in private investment. The decline in growth could also be attributed to the first oil crisis, the large-scale public investment program, and a large increase in the development expenditures including the expansion of investments in basic social services and heavy investment in large projects of national importance. The military expenditure was another drain on national resources. The dismissal of elected government of Balochistan increased political alienation and conflicts in the region, to be discussed in later section of the chapter.

The military-led government of Zia-ul-Haq, which came into power in 1977, reversed some of the populist policies pursued by the Zulfikar Bhutto government. Zia-ul-Haq denationalized some of the industries and liberalized trade. But he continued the public sector investment program, the state ownership of the banking sector, and restrictions on imports and zoning regulations for sugar mills.

The Zia-ul-Haq period was characterized by rapid economic growth due to a set of factors—large capital inflows from the United States, other Western countries, and international financial institutions following the Soviet invasion of Afghanistan, a sharp increase in workers remittances from the oil-rich Middle Eastern countries, and many years of bumper crops leading to increase in exports, especially of cotton and textiles. This phase of Pakistan's development, however, had many negative effects as well. It led to an inefficient and unbalanced industrial sector, consisting of state-owned industries producing steel, fertilizer, and cement. It contributed to a growing fiscal and current account deficit that was financed through domestic borrowing and inflow of foreign assistance. Heavy sanctions imposed on Pakistan by the United States in response to the continuation of the Pakistani nuclear program after the end of the Soviet invasion in Afghanistan led to the balance of payment crisis. This led to the end of the second cycle of economic growth (Hamid 2008, 47–52). During this period, the Baloch insurgency continued to simmer. However, the intensity of conflict was curtailed by Zia-ul-Haq because he forged an alliance with the Islamic political parties that were in power in Baluchistan

The fourth phase began in 1988. Democratic governments from 1988 to 1999 and later the military-led Musharraf government introduced various policy reforms. These governments implemented privatization, investment deregulation, trade liberalization, financial liberalization, and tax reforms. However, they failed to maintain adequate fiscal discipline and were at various points forced to implement stabilization programs.

During the Musharraf regime, growth levels were higher than during the earlier democratic governments led by Benazir Bhutto and Nawaz Sharif. However, growth began to slowdown after Musharraf's ouster from power. Pressures on the balance of payments, high inflation, and severe shortages of energy at an alarming scale demonstrated that the short-term growth during his regime was not sustainable. This could also be attributed to the period of political instability after the declaration of emergency by Musharraf, political unrest in the country, and mounting Taliban insurgency. As discussed in the later section of the chapter, the use of force to establish the authority of the government in Baloch-dominant areas of the province led to increased conflict between the Baloch nationalists and the central government.

The newly elected government in 2008 was faced with multitude of political and security challenges limiting its ability to cope with economic management and ensure investor confidence. According to the 2009 Economic Survey of Pakistan, the global economic slowdown, decreasing foreign direct investment, the security situation and an energy crisis severely affected Pakistan's economy (Government of Pakistan 2009, 1–4). The government resorted to multilateral and bilateral sources for its financing requirements, adding to its external debt. To support the stabilization program, the government entered into a 23-month standby loan agreement with the International Monetary Fund (IMF) to finance approximately 7.6 billion.

The July 2010 catastrophic floods in Pakistan have created an unprecedented humanitarian crisis in a nation already struggling with poverty, political instability, and violent militancy. The floods have left some 1,500 people dead, 4 million homeless, 8 million in urgent need of basic necessities, and over 20 million directly affected, including the loss of assets and income. The extent of damages to infrastructure and the economy are staggering. Half of Pakistan's cash crops, including cotton, sugar, and rice, have been wiped out. About 70 percent of bridges and roads in the affected areas have been destroyed. The losses have been estimated to be about $43 billion. (Cheema 2010, 12) Given the magnitude of this worst disaster in the world during the past 50 years, the state is going to face tremendous challenges in designing and implementing development strategies.

Over the past 60 years, many parts of the country have been transformed from rural to semi-industrial economy with increasing migration from rural to urban areas. Yet, various periods of growth have not benefitted equitably all provinces of the country, especially Balochistan. Karachi metropolitan region and major urban centers in Punjab led to the industrialization of Pakistan while most other parts of the country continue to be less developed (World Bank 2008).

The fiscal resource distribution among the four provinces of Pakistan has been one of the determinants of federal-provincial government tensions over the years and the intrastate conflict in Balochistan (Ahmed, Mustafa, and Khalid 2007, 11–16; Pakistan Institute for Peace Studies 2008, 179–185; World Bank 2008, 189–200). Most revenues were collected by the central government and then redistributed vertically between the federal and provincial governments and horizontally among the provinces. Population has been the sole distribution criterion adopted in all of the National Finance Commission (NFC) awards from the divisible pool. Other critical factors such as infrastructure, poverty level, revenue generation, and environment have not been criteria. Due to this lack of consensus between the federal and provincial governments, interim awards and grants benefiting larger provinces have been the norm. Another consequence of the present criterion is that the central government has been "overstretching" itself by expanding its activities to include road construction and rural development, which are the provincial subjects. In some of the recent awards by the NFC, provinces have been given more resources and development funds, which has encouraged fiscal decentralization. Despite being federally constituted, the NFC has not succeeded in providing rational and equity-oriented criteria for resource distribution.

The present government, however, recognizes the need to incorporate factors other than the population size into the criteria—including backwardness and development gaps, rural-urban disparities, natural resource endowment, poverty, population density, area, and environmental considerations. The recent NFC award announced in December 2009 is the first effective response to this issue in Pakistan's history. (Ali 2010, 1–4) Over the past 62 years, Pakistan's development strategies have largely been growth-oriented, with inadequate attention to the reduction of interregional disparities and the promotion of pro-poor growth. Even the pro-growth strategies, promoted by various military-led governments could not be sustained due to political instability following the demise of military regimes. Many factors have determined the unsustainable growth and continuing regional and intragroup economic and social disparities. According to Hussain (2008, 1–2), these include the following:

- an elite-based power structure, denying the majority of citizens adequate access to high-quality education, health facilities, land, the judicial system, and high wage end of the labor market;

- institutional constraints on the access to resources and decision making;
- patron-client relationships with the democratically elected governments for rent- seeking, which reduces incentives for enterprise, innovation, and savings;
- constraints on poor farmers, including higher prices on their inputs, lower prices on their outputs, and highly unequal land ownership.

But the most critical development challenge facing the country is unbalanced development among different regions of the country, especially backwardness of Balochistan. Disparities in income and access to services have led to political alienation and ongoing intrastate conflict among different groups in the province—the Baloch, Punjabis, Pashtun, and other groups. While the infusion of large-scale development funds is likely to increase income disparities in Baluchistan as has happened in other provinces, greater economic prosperity in Baluchistan would be conducive to the reduction of political alienation in the province, provided it is accompanied by participatory mechanisms to engage the Baloch communities in designing and implementing development projects.

As in the other developing countries, competition between those arguing for national integration through central actions and those demanding regional autonomy and identity on the basis of ethnicity has been pronounced throughout Pakistan's history. During early years of Pakistan, the centralizing forces held an upper hand, reflected in such major policies as the introduction of Urdu as the national language, the introduction of Five Year Plans designed and monitored by the federal government, and the merger of various provinces in the western part of the country to create one unit called "West Pakistan" with approximately the same population size as East Pakistan, the second unit of the federation. The 1973 Constitution recognized regional autonomy, but the military-led governments that followed continued the centralizing trend in political, economic, and administrative decision making in the country.

Experience suggests that ethnicity and regional disparities are interrelated determinants of intrastate conflicts in Pakistan. (Waseem 2000; Cohen 2005; Wirsing 2008) In addition, ineffective governance and absence of representative institutions over long periods of time have increased the perceptions of interregional disparities, and led to the absence of the political culture of tolerance and reluctance of different groups to forge compromises.

In the case of former East Pakistan (now Bangladesh), for example, attempts to impose Urdu as the single language of the country led to the language riots in 1952. West Pakistan's political and economic domination and low representation in military and civil service contributed to the political alienation of the Bengalis against the central government and civil war.

In Sindh, the native Sindhis opposed Punjabi settlers in rural areas and perceived threat to the Sindhi language from Mohajirs (refugees from India after Partition). They also pointed out inadequate access to services and income disparities vis-à-vis Punjabis and Muhajirs.

In Balochistan, the annexation of Balochistan states in 1948, the demand for political autonomy, and the dismissal of elected governments in 1973 and 1988 created alienation among the Baloch population, The case of the Baloch insurgency below shows the complexity of designing and implementing development strategies in the context of the regional disparities of income and access to services and the identification of the population with ethnicity. Impacts of some of these strategies on the resentment of the Baloch population are also examined.

Evolution of the Baloch Insurgency

Nationalism and quest for identity have been the predominant features of Baloch politics over the past one hundred years (Breseeg 2004; Barohi 2009; Naseer 2009). From the thirteenth to fifteenth century, Baloch population moved from smaller units of clans to tribes and "territorial differentiation" and started to assimilate other segments of ethnic groups including Iranians, Punjabis, Sindhis, and Pashtuns. Some scholars refer to Baloch today as a "transstate nation" in view of their presence in Pakistan, Iran, and border areas of Afghanistan (Breseeg 2004, 375–376). Baloch nationalism represents a combination of movements to oppose alien domination, gain self-rule in the homeland, and preserve cultural identity.

Though ethnicity constitutes key element of the Baloch nationalism, tribal rivalries have historically divided the Baloch national movements. This weakness has been used over the years by the central government in its policy of "divide and rule." Also there has been a contradiction between the movement's traditional leadership and the "relatively developed society it seeks to liberate" (Breseeg 2004, 377).

The Baloch are divided into two major groups—those who speak Balochi or its dialects, and a non-Balochi-speaking group including those from Sindh and Punjab and Brahuis of Eastern Balochistan. Though the two groups are different linguistically, they accept one another as Baloch with common ancestry partly because many of the Baloch leaders come from the second group. Historically, the characteristics that united all Baloch groups were their belief in common culture, their common history, and Sunni Islam. The most critical factor uniting these groups is the "tribal culture" as the basis of their social and economic organization. Grossly inadequate participation of the Baloch population in the national economy of Pakistan had further strengthened their perception of separateness from the other mainstream groups of the country, that is, Punjabis, Pashtuns, and Sindhis. Geography, including difficult mountain and desert terrains, enabled the Baloch population to protect their independence historically, which also strengthened their nationalism. Scarcity of water and harsh climate forced them into nomadic or seminomadic life styles. Breseeeg argues that Baloch nationalism is very different from the Punjabis and Persians because of two factors—a separate historical past in the region, and a different cultural and linguistic entity (Breseeg 2004, 381).

Before the British, the Baloch ruled not only Balochistan but also other parts of the region including parts of Sindh and Sistan (now in Iran). In the 1840s, the British started their occupation of Eastern Balochistan in order to protect their spheres of influence in Afghanistan and the Persian Gulf region. Tribal areas under "Sardars" (tribal chiefs) were given complete autonomy, with the "Sardar" acting as the feudal lord.

The British intervention in the region, especially in the beginning of the 1920s, led to the spread of the modern doctrine of nationalism among the Baloch. Because of internal divisions among the tribes and social class structures, the Baloch nationalist groups were fragmented, impeding the formation of unified positions among them. It also enabled governments to exploit their divisions and resort to the "divide and rule" policy. In 1928, the British facilitated Iran's incorporation of Western Balochistan to counter Soviet expansion, while in Pakistan they assisted the annexation of Eastern Balochistan to Pakistan. This division and the incorporation of the Baloch population in two states became the primary cause of intrastate conflict between the Baloch population and centralizing nationalist regimes in Iran and Pakistan. The Pahlavi Dynasty in Iran sought a modern, secular state under the Shah and crushed any revolt from Western Balochistan. Because of internal divisions and the social structures including the *Sardars*, the Baloch population could not be mobilized to challenge the central authority in Iran. Most revolts were tribal in nature and were suppressed by force. During the British period, the *Sardars* in Balochistan were given subsidies as well as complete control over internal tribal affairs. In return they agreed to give the British military access to Afghanistan and the control of the frontier.

The Baloch nationalist movement picked up momentum after the British decided to grant independence to India and Pakistan. In 1948, the Baloch nationalists were struggling for independence. However, the *Sardars* forged an alliance with the Muslim League led by Mohammed Ali Jinnah, the founder of Pakistan. Some have argued that "the reactionary tribal elite could not join the Khan (of Kalat State) who wanted to introduce modern institutions instead of protecting the tribal and feudal system" (Breseeg 2004, 387). From 1952 to 1955, Kalat and other states in Balochistan were given semiautonomous status as Balochistan States Union. With the declaration of West Pakistan as a single unit/province in 1955, this arrangement ceased to exist. When the one unit system was abolished after the independence of East Pakistan (now Bangladesh), former British Balochistan and the Balochistan States Union were merged into a separate province of Baluchistan.

The history of the Baloch insurgency after the independence of Pakistan centered on the federal government's policy to merge the Baloch identity into Pakistani identity (often with force), and the Baloch continued demand for greater autonomy, Baloch identity, and control of Balochistan's resources. In 1948, the Khan of Kalat and Mohammed Ali Jinnah, the governor general and founder of Pakistan, signed the Instrument of Accession, even though it was opposed by both houses of the Kalat state. The agreement promised full autonomy to the Baloch tribes on all subjects except defense, external affairs, and communication. The unwillingness of successive governments in Pakistan, after the death of Jinnah, to implement the agreement has been one of the main root causes of the Baloch insurgency.

As Table 4.1 shows, the Baloch insurgency has been simmering for the past 62 years, with periods of upsurge in violence and use of military force to suppress violence.

Though the Baloch insurgency is an old as the state of Pakistan, over the years significant changes have taken place both within the Balochistan and its external environment (Pakistan Institute for Peace Studies 2008; Wirsing 2008). First, there is an emerging Baloch middle class whose interests collided with more powerful and well-established Pashtuns. Over the years, the Baloch middle class increased its share in the transport sector. Modern intelligentsia replaced the traditional intelligentsia in the province. Urbanization increased the access of women to social services such as education and health. Second, one of the most significant changes has been the civil wars and political violence in Afghanistan over the past few decades, which led to the influx of refugees that brought many more Pashtuns to Balochistan affecting the demographic balance. Third, the influence of Islam-oriented parties expanded due to their alignment with the military-led governments in the central government. Finally, the federal government launched many development projects in Balochistan, which brought new groups of professionals from other regions of the country as well as provided more opportunities to the local population.

Table 4.1 Evolution of the Baloch Insurgency: Year and Key Events

Year	Key Event
1948	Pakistan's army invasion to suppress revolt in Kalat by Agha Abdul Karim, forcing him to take refuge in Afghanistan.
1955	The creation of One Unit leading to the merger of Balochistan with other provinces to form West Pakistan and the perceived by the nationalists loss of Baloch identity.
1960	Military action by central government to suppress uprising led by Nawab Nauroz Khan Zarakzai.
1970	The first general elections in 1970 leading to victory for the nationalists in the National and Provincial Assemblies; signing of the 1993 Constitutions by Ghaus Baksh Bizenjo, even though many of the Baloch tribes were not satisfied with the constitution; dismissal of the National Awami Party (NAP) government of Sardar Ataullah Mengal by Prime Minister Z. A. Bhutto after only nine months in office as they "crossed swords over the extent of provincial autonomy granted in the constitution."
1973	Dismissal of Baloch nationalist government in Balochistan by Bhutto charging the provincial government with lawlessness and collusion of Baluch separatists with foreign governments for the separation of Baloch and Pashtun territories.
1977	Zia-ul-Haq general amnesty for political prisoners. Some leaders went in exile.
1977–1988	General elections, the Baloch nationalists got together and formed the Balochistan National Alliance (BNA) led by Nawab Akbar Bugti; nationalists remained locked in struggle with Pakistan People's Party (PPP) government at the federal level; the democratic process provided a platform the nationalists; continued simmering of the grievances.
1999	Military coup led by General Musharraf; eventually a state of violent confrontation with the federal government; The issues: the construction of Gwadar port, rocket attack on Musharraf during his visit to Balochistan, a full-fledged military operation in the Baloch-dominated areas such as Dera Bugti.
2005–2008	Serious insurgency challenge to the writ of the government and subsequently more military operations in the region

Sources: Pakistan Institute for Peace Studies 2008; Naseer 2009; Barohi 2009.

The above changes in the society affected the context of the Baloch insurgency in several ways. First, they weakened the hold of the traditional *Sardars* on their "subjects." By 1993, for example, the Balochistan National Movement (BNP), a largely middle-class party, had won two national assembly and six provincial assembly seats. Second, while the *Sardars* continue to be the focal point for the Baloch insurgency because of strong perceptions of the Baloch population that the past development strategies had not equitably benefited the indigenous people, in practice, the tribal loyalties continue to play a "constantly diminishing role" in the political process in Balochistan (Breseeg 2004, 396).

Balochistan is facing multiple and overlapping insurgencies and conflicts—separatist, ethnic, and religious (Pakistan Institute for Peace Studies 2008, 135–150). The most serious insurgency has been led by nationalist groups in the Baloch-dominated areas in Balochistan as well as in Baloch areas of Sindh and Punjab. Between 2006 and 2007, over 1,700 terrorist attacks were carried out by nationalist insurgent groups (Table 4.2). Sectarian and pro-Taliban groups are active in Pashtun areas and also have influence in some of the other areas (Pakistan Institute for Peace Studies, 2008, 151–158). Pro-Taliban and Al-AQueda groups are present in the border areas with Afghanistan as well as in central Balochistan including Quetta, the largest city in the province. Recently Taliban and Al-AQueda who had been active in Federally Administered Tribal Areas (FATA) are extending their influence in Balochistan as well. Due to war in Afghanistan, 3.2 million Afghan refugees settled in Pakistan, out of which 26 percent settled in Balochistan. But the most serious insurgency that has challenged the writ of the government over the past few years has been led by the Baloch insurgents.

While the level of conflict has varied from one period to another over the past 62 years, the political autonomy for Balochistan has been the core demand of the Baloch nationalists since the establishment of Pakistan.

Table 4.2 Balochistan Terror Attacks 2007

District	Total Terror Incidents	Killed	Injured
Dera Bugti	102	47	223
Kech/Turbat/Mand	19	6	9
Sibi	19	5	11
Lasbela/Hub	23	37	73
Kohlu	82	14	32
Khuzdar	41	3	7
Quetta	102	65	152
Total Other Districts	148	44	58

Source: Pakistan Institute for Peace Studies 2008.

Demand for Provincial Autonomy

The 1973 Constitution was a landmark event because it was signed by some of the Baloch nationalist leaders and both the chief minister and the governor of Balochistan. However, the dismissal of the elected provincial government in 1973 by Zulfikar Bhutto reignited the demand for political autonomy. Other parties support the demands of nationalists but are unwilling to challenge the authority of the federal government to get their demands accepted.

In terms of their ideology, the political parties in Balochistan could be divided into three categories—Baloch nationalist parties, Pashtun nationalist parties, mainstream political parties with representation in all provinces of the country and religious parties. In 2008 elections, the two mainstream parties—Pakistan Muslim League (Nawaz) and Pakistan Peoples Party (PPP) Parliamentarians won majority of seats in both national and provincial assemblies, indicating weakening of the nationalist parties. Table 4.3 shows the ideologies, representation, and support base of various political parties in Balochistan in the 2002 and 2008 elections.

Over the years, the Baloch demand for autonomy has been affected by several contextual factors. (Breseeg 2004, 159–164; Pakistan Institute for Peace Studies 2008, 375–397). First, the military-led governments often used force to curtail the demand for autonomy and challenge the state authority, which further intensified conflict. Second, the goals of Pashtun nationalists are different than those of Baloch nationalists: the former want either more representation within Balochistan or the merger of the Pashtun-dominated areas with the Northwest Frontier Province (NWFP). Third, two parties have emerged with religious ideology and close alignment with the military. Fourth, the national-level parties—including the PPP and the Nawaz Muslim League—continue to gradually expand their representation in view of the expanding middle class and the urban and immigrant population in the province. Finally, the demographic structure of the province has changed with migration from the NWFP, Sindh, and the influx of Afghan refugees, considerably reducing the majority of the Baloch in the province.

The nationalist political parties and insurgent groups in Balochistan have been on the forefront of the demands for political autonomy and greater control over the provincial resources. Some of the nationalist insurgent groups now claim that they are struggling for the independence of Balochistan. Major insurgent groups active in different parts of Balochistan are Baloch Liberation Army (BLA), Balochistan Liberation Movement (BLM), Baloch Resistance Army (BRA), Baloch Liberation Front (BLF), Bugti Tigers, and the Baloch National Army (BNA). Most members of the insurgent groups are the most radical elements of the nationalist parties and have roots in earlier insurgencies.

Table 4.3 Ideologies and Representation of Political Parties in National and Provincial Assemblies

Party Name and Ideology	Representation in Parliaments (2002 and 2008 elections)		
	NA	Senate	PA
Jamhoori Watan Party (JWP) /	1	1	4
Nationalist	–	–	–
Balochistan National Party (BNP-Mengal group) /	1	1	2
Nationalist	–	–	–
Baloch Haq Tawwar (BHT) /	–	–	1
Nationalist	–	–	–
National Party (NP) / Nationalist	–	1	5
	–	–	1
Balochistan National Party (BNP Awami) /	–	1	3
Nationalist	1	1	5
Pakhtoonkhawa Milli Awami Party (PkMAP) /	1	2	4
Pushtoon	–	–	–
Jamiat Ulema-e-Islam (JUI-Fazal-ur-Rehman	6	6	13
group) / Religious	2	6	7
Jammat-e-Islami (JI) / Religious	–	–	–
Pakistan Muslim League (Nawaz	4	10	22
Sharif group) / Political	4	10	18
Pakistan People's Party	–	–	2
Parliamentarians (PPP) / Political	4	–	7

Source: Abstracted from Pakistan Institute for Peace Studies 2008.

Economic and Social Disparities

Balochistan is a resource rich region, with extremely low-density and multiethnic population. It covers about half of Pakistan's land area but has only one-twentieth of the country's population and a twenty-fifth of its economy. As per the 1998 census, the ethnic composition is 54.7 percent Baloch and 29.0 percent Pashtun. The Pashtun leaders, however, claim that the percentage of the Pashtun population is between 40 to 50 percent. In response, the Baloch state that these numbers include Afghan refugees who have received false documents. Balochistan is rich in natural and locational resources. It has two-thirds of the national coastline, which gives access to abundant fish resources. The province is well-suited for trade with Iran, Afghanistan, Central Asia, and the Persian Gulf states.

For the past four decades, Balochistan has been supporting Pakistan's industrialization by providing cheap natural gas to Pakistan's economic centers. It also has large deposits of coal, copper, lead, gold, and other minerals, which are important for the growth and development of the country. However, economic and social disparities between Balochistan and other federal units of Pakistan, especially the Punjab, continue to feed the Baloch discontentment and insurgency. A recent joint report by the World Bank, the Asian Development Bank, and the government of Balochistan concluded that series of factors had "destined Balochistan to the periphery of economic and institutional development" (World Bank 2008, 2).

Balochistan has the slowest growth record of any province in Pakistan, worst infrastructure, severe water shortages, and the weakest fiscal base. It has the highest incidence of poverty, lowest social indicators, and weak state institutions. It is the most backward region of Pakistan, far removed from various hubs of its economic activities. Balochistan provides 40 percent of the country's natural gas that enables the federal government to earn about Rs. 95 billion every year. However, it gets only Rs. 6 billion in return. The Baloch nationalists claim that the federal government buys gas from Balochistan at Rs. 27 per million cubic feet while the Punjab gets Rs. 280 and Sindh gets around Rs. 200. Sui gas was explored in 1953 in Balochistan. Yet, about 90 percent of the area of Balochistan is still without this facility.

Another grievance of the Baloch nationalists is about the distribution of resources from the federal divisible pool. The fact that the NFC awards have been based entirely on population basis had a negative effect on Balochistan. Table 4.4 shows the provincial share of NFC awards. The most recent 2009 NFC award attempts to resolve this issue.

There are glaring disparities in employment of the Baloch population (Pakistan Institute for Peace Studies 2008). While 50 percent of the laborers working in the gas companies in the province are local, only 3 percent are in the management cadre. In the Oil and Gas Development Corporation, which is managing the gas fields in Dera Bugti, only 12 of the 3000 employees are from Balochistan. Balochistan is underrepresented in the federal government agencies and departments, and many positions allocated to the province by the central government remain unfulfilled due to the nonavailability of qualified personnel from the Baloch population. The provincial government is usually short of cash, even though over the past few years the

Table 4.4 Provincial Share of National Finance Commission Awards

Province	Punjab	Sindh	NWFP	Balochistan
1970	56.50%	23.50%	15.50%	4.50%
1974	60.25%	22.50%	13.39%	3.86%
1990	57.88%	23.28%	13.54%	5.30%
1990*	1000	700	200	100
1996**	500	500	100	100

* Special Annual Grant to Provinces in Million Rupees.
** Matching Grants under 1996 Award in Million Rupees.
Source: National Human Development Report (UNDP 2003).

federal government has initiated about 40 megaprojects in the province. Yet, the Baloch generally perceive this as an incursion of outsiders to exploit their resources, with unanticipated and negative consequences for the Baloch population. For example, licenses given to foreign trawlers, including a 40-year fishing contract awarded to a Singaporean company, have negatively affected the livelihoods of the Baloch fishermen. The construction of the Gwadar port will lead to the relocation of some of the fishermen settlements. The persistent view among the Baloch is that programs initiated by the central government—such as the award of arable land—benefit the Punjabis and other immigrants more than the indigenous people (Pakistan Institute for Peace Studies, 2008, 9–11).

As compared to the other provinces of the federation, Balochistan's long-term growth performance has been the weakest. For example, from 1972/1973 to 2004/2005, its economy grew 2.7 times as compared to 3.6 times in Sindh and NWFP and 4.0 times in Punjab (World Bank 2008, 7). In 2004, Balochistan's per capita income level was $400, which was only two-thirds of Pakistan's level. The number of rural poor in Balochistan increased from 1.5 million people in 1998/1999 to 2.1 million in 2004/2005, though poverty levels declined in urban areas.

Public spending and budgetary resources in Balochistan have significantly increased over the past ten years. Compared to 1996, the per capita expenditure in the province increased by 40 percent in real terms to Rs. 5100 per capita in 2005/2006. Though public spending increased in all provinces, Balochistan continued to lead all provinces in expenditure in per capita terms, even though the Baloch nationalist parties do not recognize this fact in view of their political alienation. However, Balochistan continues to face challenges—public expenditure management, deficiencies in public financial management and procurement, and fiscal devolution to improve service delivery.

Wide gaps concerning social development between Balochistan and other provinces narrowed from 2001 to 2007 (World Bank 2008). Improved national economy during the Musharraf government increased the resource flow through the NFC award and increased central government investments such as the Gwadar Port, the expansion of the national highway network, and the Kachhi Canal Irrigation Project. Yet, in 2007, Balochistan scored the lowest among all provinces of Pakistan with regard to indicators for education, literacy, health, and water and sanitation. Only two in five children in the 5–9 age group were enrolled in primary school. Even though more resources through the national projects were channeled through the province, it did not lead to the reduction of trust deficit between the Baloch nationalists and the federal government because of a lack of consultation between the local population and the government in the process of designing and implementing the projects.

Balochistan has a labor scarce economy with little crop production, no industry except for near Karachi, and services that largely cater to local demands. However, other provinces of Pakistan have a labor abundant economy, with growth poles in intensive agriculture, manufacturing, banking, energy, and telecommunication. The remoteness and geographical diversity of Balochistan provides a development context that is different from other provinces.

Effective delivery of and access to services are essential to improve living standards of the population and expand economic opportunities. Yet, the geographical diversity and remoteness of Balochistan makes it more expensive vis-à-vis the densely populated areas. A World Bank Report suggested the following to cope with this situation (World Bank 2008). The public administration systems and processes at the district and local levels must be reformed—they are extremely weak and thus have not been able to ensure that basic education and health services reach the poor. In the educational sector, the government needs to build more public schools and improve school infrastructure and teacher qualifications. In the health sector, the need is to address the low utilization of public health services, lack of resources, inadequate coverage of essential services in remote areas, and the lack of skilled women. More than 46 percent of the households do not have electricity.

The feudal structure of Balochistan including the dominance of *Sardars* poses a serious challenge to socioeconomic changes in the province. One point of view is that the *Sardars* are not interested in the modernization and development of the masses, but want to exploit the tribal loyalties for their personal benefits. The other point is that the *Sardars* want both economic and social development of their respective areas as well as to maintain the

Baloch identity and tribal affiliation. In either case, one of the constraints facing the *Sardars* is their own internal disintegration and rivalries that often enable the federal government to divide them.

Government Response and Insurgency Management

To varying degrees, successive governments in Pakistan have used combinations of responses to cope with the rising Baloch insurgency—co-option of tribes to gain their loyalties, use of force especially when the government's legitimacy is challenged, sharing of revenues with the provincial government emanating from the exploitation of gas and other natural resources, and launch of the centrally planned socioeconomic development projects including megaprojects such as the port of Gwadar.

After independence, the federal government's strategy to control and enhance central power was to co-opt local *Sardars* and use force to subdue others who defied the central control. In some ways, the same process was followed in many postindependence developing countries as they tried to forge national integration out of ethnic, linguistic, and regional diversities.

During the military-led governments of the 1960s, the Baloch alienation continued to increase due to heavy use of force, the arrest of prominent Baloch dissidents, and the lack of effective participatory mechanisms to engage local leaders. The Baloch population also opposed the inclusion of three Pashtun-majority districts from the NWFP into Balochistan and separation of a few Baloch-majority areas from Balochistan into Punjab and Sindh. The demarcation of the new boundaries resulted in reduced Baloch majority in Balochistan.

The unanimous approval of the 1973 Constitution led by Zulfikar Ali Bhutto, was a landmark event in the political history of Pakistan. The National Awami Party (NAP) that included prominent Baloch leaders and had won the 1970 elections held in Balochistan agreed to endorse the constitution. However, the nationalist leaders believe that Bhutto as well as the successive leaders at the national level did not respect the democratic norms and principles of representative democracy. For example, Bhutto dissolved the NAP government in Balochistan, accusing the Baloch leaders of undermining the state in collaboration with foreign countries, that is, Soviet Union and India. But no proof of foreign involvement was provided. The banning of NAP in 1975 led to more proactive roles by the radical elements of the Baloch population, including the Balochistan People's Liberation Front, the BNA, and the Baloch Students Organization. With 80,000 troops, the military was able to restore the centralized control but at the cost of civilian lives and increasing Baloch alienation.

When General Zia came to power in 1977, he withdrew the army and released thousands of Baloch leaders and activists. At the same time, he made alliances with the Pashtun Islamic parties to counterbalance the power base of the Baloch nationalists and promote the military's agenda in Afghanistan in cooperation with the United States to defeat the Soviet Union. The result of that policy was that the Baloch nationalists had to deal with two adversaries—the dominant federal government and military-supported Pashtun Islamists.

During the democratic interlude in the 1990s, Balochistan witnessed alliances among three sets of political actors—those from the two predominant national political parties (PPP and Nawaz Muslim League), those from the Baloch nationalist parties; and those from Pashtun-based Islamic parties. During this period, various Baloch leaders assumed the positions of chief minister and governor and continued their demands for greater autonomy and share of the provincial natural resources. Because of these representative mechanisms, the situation in the province did not lead to conflict in the 1990s.

During the seven years of military-led governments under Musharraf (1999–2007), Baloch alienation increased and Baloch insurgents openly began to challenge the authority (writ) of the government in many parts of the province (International Crisis Group 2006). Three contextual factors define the response of the Musharraf regime to the Baloch insurgency—the geopolitics and energy security; the requirements of the economic growth strategies such as the need for external investments; and the initiation of megaprojects. After the *Sardars* openly challenged the authority of the central government by launching attacks against the civilian and military officials, Musharraf used force to suppress the challenge (Wirsing 2008; International Crisis Group 2006).

Over the years, the geostrategic importance of Balochistan has increased because of its location to the proximity to Afghanistan and land and air routes vital for trade and energy development (Wirsing 2008). With the improvement of relations between India and Pakistan, the feasibility of various proposals for energy pipelines were studied, including one from Iran to India through Pakistan.

Balochistan has also assumed greater military strategic importance. Gwadar Sea Port was considered by the security establishment in Pakistan as the best alternative naval base in case of a conflict with India. It was also considered of strategic importance to China because over 60 percent of Chinese oil imports pass through the nearby port of Hormuz. Chinese investments in Gwadar will give strategic depth to China, which is considered as a concern by India and to some extent by the United States.

However, heavy investments in megaprojects such as Gwadar further inflamed the local population because of the lack of adequate consultations with the local population and relocation of Baloch population from some of the coastal areas.

The responses of successive governments in Pakistan did not yield positive results vis-à-vis the social, economic, and political integration of the Baloch-dominated areas into Pakistan. The experience suggests that the resentment of the Baloch population against the central government emanates largely from three factors, namely, the continued backwardness of the region vis-à-vis other parts of the country, the exploitation of the region's natural resources for the benefit of other provinces, and the perception of local population that centrally initiated development projects benefit outsiders who have been migrating in large numbers to Balochistan over the past 62 years. Successive governments in Pakistan have failed to convince a large segment of Baloch population about the benefits that are accruing to the Baloch population as a result of the development projects supported by the central government. This lack of understanding on the part of the local population has been due to the feudal nature of the Baloch society and the absence of effective and democratic mechanisms for consultation between the government and the Baloch leadership at the regional and local levels. For example, during President Musharraf's regime, several megaprojects were initiated. Instead of gaining the support and goodwill of the local population, these increased the resentment of outsiders. Even when democratic institutions were introduced, the political leadership at the national level governed the region through "one person democracy," as was the case with the former prime minister Zulfikar Ali Bhutto, who dismissed the elected government in Balochistan.

Over the years, the trust deficit between the Baloch nationalists and the federal government has increased due to excessive use of force leading to political prisoners and "missing persons," population displacement due to conflict and some of the megaprojects, and dispute over royalties and the provision of gas and oil exploited from the province. The construction of more military cantonments, differences over megaprojects such as Gwadar Port construction, and poor structure and performance of security forces has worsened the conflict. Also the central government has continued to establish a highly centralized system of government that is in conflict with the aspirations of less populous federal units such as Balochistan.

Experience in Balochistan suggests that greater investments in Balochistan and the utilization of its resources are essential but not sufficient to promote peace, stability, and economic development in the province.

The most critical factor is the engagement of the nationalist political parties and groups in the decision making on issues affecting Balochistan. In this regard, the recently launched Balochistan Empowerment Package by the democratically elected government is the most comprehensive multifaceted set of actions to transform relationships between the Baloch leadership and the federal government.

The Balochistan Empowerment Package

The elected government that took over after the 2008 elections gave priority to resolve the issue of Balochistan. After coming to power, PPP apologized to the people of Balochistan for injustices done to them by past governments. A parliamentary committee was established to draw up the Balochistan Empowerment Package in consultation with all parties. The government launched the Aghaz-e-Haqooq-e-Balochistan (Balochistan Empowerment Package). It consists of a set of proposals to be discussed and approved by the joint sitting of the Parliament. After discussion in the Parliament, a resolution is to be passed approving the proposals on which there is an agreement. This is to be followed by enactment of laws by the federal Parliament.

The Balochistan Empowerment Package includes five categories of proposals (PILDAT 2009):

Constitutional Issues

The proposals in this field are (1) to increase the provincial autonomy through deletion of the concurrent list in the Fourth Schedule of the constitution; (2) to have the NFC revise the criteria for distributing the Baloch share of pooled taxes and resources among the Baloch provinces; and (3) implementation of the relevant articles of the constitution dealing with the work of the Council of Common Interest and National Economic Council and defining policies and principles to be followed in matter of electricity, natural gas, and broadcasting and telecasting.

Political Issues

The proposals related to political issues are (1) the release of political workers and the return of political exiles other than those charged with "heinous crimes or involved in acts of terrorism"; and (2) initiation of political dialogue with all stakeholders including those inside and outside the parliamentary system.

Administrative Issues

The main proposals related to administrative matters are the establishment of a Commission of Inquiry with respect of missing persons, judicial inquiries into the murder of certain Baloch leaders, and ceasing of all operations by the federal agencies except those related to fight against terrorism. Other recommendations include the replacement of the Pakistani Army by the Frontier Corps in the Sui area, stopping the construction of cantonments in the Sui and Kohlu area, authorizing the Frontier Corps to perform the law-and-order role under the supervision of the chief minister of Balochistan, and granting of a special quota of scholarships for Baloch students from the Higher Education Commission.

Economic Issues

The most significant components of the Balochistan Empowerment Package relate to the economic matters and include (1) a uniform price of gas throughout Pakistan for calculating the gas development surcharge; (2) the allocation for poverty to be in proportion to the percentage of people living below poverty line in each province; (3) greater shares of revenues and profits from gas exploration and production to be given to the provincial government and the concerned district government; and (4) supply of gas on priority basis to the residents of the district where gas fields are located.

There are specific recommendations about employment opportunities for Balochistan, including the creation of 5000 additional jobs for the province and the prescription of Balochistan quota in the rules for employment in government and its agencies.

There were several recommendations concerning megaprojects, including the consent and approval of the provincial government before initiating any new megaproject; special development packages for the districts of Sui and Kohlu; and the protection of local fishermen by keeping fishing trawlers out of a 33-kilometer zone along the coast. Other recommendations were to allocate Rs.1 billion by the federal government for the rehabilitation of internally displaced persons in Dera Bugti, to construct small dams in the province, appointment of local candidates for positions in the Gwadar Port, and greater control of Gwadar by the provincial government by appointing the Balochistan chief minister as the chairman of the Gwadar Development Authority.

The package also provides for monitoring mechanisms for the implementation of the recommendations, including oversight by the Parliamentary Committee on National Security and the Senate Standing Committee for the Establishment. The federal and provincial governments are required to present quarterly reports before both the houses of Parliament dealing with the status of implementation and certification from the federal minister of Inter-Provincial Coordination about the amount spent on the implementation of proposals.

The Balochistan Empowerment Package is a landmark document that aims to transform the federal government's relations with Balochistan. It is comprehensive and multifaceted. It is based on agreements among almost all of the political parties represented in the National Assembly. It presents a new model for the distribution of the divisible resources from the federal government. More importantly, it recognizes provincial autonomy as the core issue driving the Baloch insurgency.

As follow-up to the Balochistan Empowerment Package, in December 2009 the four provinces agreed on the historic seventh NFC award with the active support and participation of the federal government (Table 4.5). The provinces agreed on the distribution of financial resources allocated to them from the federal divisible pool on the basis of a four-point formula—population, backwardness (poverty), revenue (generation and collection having equal weight), and inverse population diversity, that is, create allocation for the population in remote areas. Weight given to population is

Table 4.5 NFC Award at a Glance: Vertical Distribution of Divisible Pool

	2010–2011	2011–2015
Federal share	44%	42.50%
Provincial Share	56%	57.50%

Horizontal Distribution

Province	7th NFC award	6th NFC award
Punjab	51.74%	53.1%
Sindh	24.55%	24.94%
NWFP	14.62%	14.88%
Balochistan	9.09%	7.17%

Weight allocated to four indicators for horizontal distribution

Population	82%
Poverty/Backwardness	10.3%
Revenue collection/generation	5.0%
Inverse Population Density	2.7%

Source: *Dawn* (daily newspaper), Islamabad, December 12, 2009.

82 percent in the horizontal distribution formula, backwardness 10.3 percent, revenue 5 percent, and inverse population density 2.7 percent.

The use of multiple criteria for the allocation of resources from the divisible pool has taken place for the first time in Pakistan's history. The willingness of Punjab, the largest and the most prosperous province of the federation, to share funds from the federal tax pool on multiple criteria will inevitably have positive impact on less populous provinces, especially Balochistan, which is the most backward and most sparsely populated. The three other provincial governments agreed to cut their shares in order to increase the share of Balochistan. Under the award, the share of Balochistan will increase from the existing 7.17 percent to 9.09 percent. The province will receive arrears of the gas development surcharge due since 2002. The NFC decided that the well-head price of gas would be equal in all provinces, which has been one of the demands of the Baloch nationalists.

The federal government also increased the share of provinces under the vertical distribution of funds from the divisible pool to 46 percent in the first year of award (2010–2011) and to 57.7 percent during the next four year of the award period. This was a significant increase because the share of provinces in the pool under the sixth NFC award was 47.5 percent. The federal government also agreed under the 7th award to reduce charges for the collection of taxes from 5 to 1 percent, which will increase the transfers from the divisible pool to the federating units.

Constraints

There are many limitations of the Balochistan Empowerment Package (PILDAT 2009). First, the recommendations on the constitutional issues need to be adopted by both houses of Parliament to be followed by the enactment of appropriate legislation by the federal and provincial legislatures. This will take time. For example, the deletion of the concurrent list in the Fourth Schedule has to be approved by the two-thirds majority in the National Assembly and the Senate. Also, about three-fourths of the provincial and district government expenditures are being met through resource transfers through the federal government. It will take time to ensure financial autonomy of the province.

Second, multi-stakeholder negotiations about political issues are hampered by the absence of the real opposition to the federal government from the present democratic parliamentary system and the unwillingness of some of the nationalist Baloch leaders to participate in negotiations till their demands are met. Even if negotiations with extra-parliamentary forces were to take place, the pending issue would be how to honor and implement the agreements with the forces outside the parliamentary system. In some cases, new elections at the provincial and district levels may have to take place.

Third, many of the recommendations about the administrative matters were also made by the Parliamentary Committee on Balochistan in 2005 under the Musharraf government. The perception of the Baloch nationalist leadership is that if earlier recommendations were not implemented, what is the guarantee that the new ones will be? Also, in view of Pakistan's War on Terror, it would be impossible for the federal government to limit the flexibility and options of its armed forces in the province.

Fourth, while the recommendations dealing with economic issues are the most significant and far-reaching, shrinking federal resources due to terrorism and intrastate conflicts in other parts of the country might impede the federal government from fulfilling its commitments.

Finally, the 2010 floods have set the country back many years, and billions would be needed to rebuild the infrastructure throughout Pakistan including in Balochistan.

Conclusion

The lack of sustained economic growth and the rising disparities among regions and groups in the context of ethnic tensions have been the root causes of intrastate conflicts in Pakistan since its independence in 1947. Short periods of economic growth have been interrupted by political instabilities and economic slowdown. Policies and programs designed centrally to reduce economic and social disparities among the units of the federation have not been effective, leading to the continued political alienation among smaller provinces. Though the Pakistani identity is strong among the citizens, centrifugal forces in smaller provinces such as Balochistan continue to identify with the ethnicity and the region. Unlike such countries as Malaysia, People's Republic of China, and South Korea where citizens have a stake in the expanding economies and all regions are growing despite expanding regional disparities, the absence of sustained economic growth in Pakistan has limited economic opportunities for all regions and has increased the sense of deprivation especially in the poorest regions of the country.

Ineffective governance and the frequent interventions by the military in the political process have made the situation worse, depriving the country of democratic mechanisms to reconcile differences among states in the federation. Though the military-led governments have facilitated short periods of economic growth, they have played havoc with the institutional infrastructure of the country, including the constitution and democratic institutions. Institutional weaknesses are the greatest constraints today on the state capacity for political reconciliation, economic management, and safety and security of citizens.

The simmering Baloch insurgency in Pakistan over the past six decades is a prime example of the failure of the central authority to recognize the Baloch quest for identity and regional autonomy, the lack of consultations with local leaders and the Baloch population in designing and implementing development programs, and inadequate investments to reduce poverty and improve access to social services in the most backward region of the country. The government response to the Baloch insurgency over the years has consisted of use of force to suppress insurgency, exploitation of the tribal loyalties and divisions within the Baloch society, initiation of development projects funded through the federal government including megaprojects such as Gwadar Sea Port, and investment in the exploitation of gas and natural resources of the province for Pakistan's industrialization.

The Balochistan Empowerment Package launched by the democratic government in 2009 is a landmark event in the federal-state relations. If enacted, it is likely to have profound impact on the Baloch insurgency because of its comprehensiveness in dealing with the core grievances of the Baloch population dealing with constitutional, political, and economic matters including the new NFC award, autonomy for Balochistan, and granting the province equitable share from its gas and other natural resources. However, the constraints on the implementation of the package are numerous—the catastrophic floods in 2010 that have devastated the economy and infrastructure of the country, continued violence and instability in neighboring Afghanistan, weaknesses of the present political order at the federal government level with weak political institutions, and the reluctance of some of the exiled leaders to accept the writ of the government and engage in political reconciliation. With Balochistan's new geostrategic position, the stakes are high, forcing the elected government to follow a new approach to the Baloch insurgency.

References

Ahmed, Iftikhar, Usman Mustafa, and Mahmood Khalid. 2007. *National Finance Commission Awards in Pakistan: A historical perspective*. Islamabad: Pakistan Institute of Development Economics.

Ali, Arshad. 2010. *National Finance Commission Award: A way forward*. Islamabad: Institute of Strategic Studies.

Barohi, Abdul Rahman. 2009. *Balochistan aur Pakistan* (Balochistan and Pakistan). Quetta: Pakistan Kalat Publishers.

Breseeg, Taj Mohammad. 2004. *Baloch nationalism: Its origin and development*. Karachi: Royal Book Company.

Cheema, G. Shabbir. 2010, July. U.S. response to Pakistan floods is an investment in trust. *East-West Center Wire*, 1–2.

Cohen, Stephen Philip. 2005. *The idea of Pakistan*. Lahore: Vanguard Books.

European Commission. 2006. *Pakistan country strategy paper*. Islamabad: European Commission.

Hamid, Naved. 2008, September. Rethinking Pakistan's development strategy. *The Lahore Journal of Economics*, Special Issue: 47–52.

Hussain, Akmal. 2008, February 28. Unstable growth & poverty in Pakistan. *Daily Dawn*.

International Crisis Group. 2006, September. Pakistan: The worsening conflict in Balochistan, *Asia Report* (119): 3.

Naseer, Gul Khan. 2009. Tarekh-e-Balochistan (History of Balochistan). Quetta: Kalat Publishers.

Pakistan Institute for Peace Studies. 2008. *Balochistan: Conflicts and players*. Islamabad: Pakistan Institute for Peace Studies.

PILDAT (Pakistan Institute for Legislative Development and Transparency). 2009. Aghaz-e-Huqooq-e-Balochistan Package: An analysis, background paper. Islamabad: PILDAT.

UNDP (United Nations Development Program). 2003. *Pakistan Human Development Report 2003*. Islamabad: United Nations Development Program.

Waseem, Mohammed. 2000, December 9–10. The political ethnicity and the state of Pakistan. Paper presented to the International Conference on the Nation-State and Transnational Forces in South Asia, in Kyoto.

Wirsing, Robert G. 2008. Baloch nationalism and the geopolitics of energy resources: The changing context of separatism in Pakistan. Retrieved from http://www.StrategicStudiesInstitute.army.mil/

World Bank. 2008, May 2. Balochistan economic report: From periphery to core. Report No. 40345—PK.

CHAPTER 5

Development Strategies, Religious Relations, and Communal Violence in Central Sulawesi, Indonesia: A Cautionary Tale

Lorraine V. Aragon[*]

Introduction

Indonesia's development strategies since independence after World War II have varied across the archipelago, unevenly affecting local intergroup cooperation and conflict. This chapter concerns Central Sulawesi, a province on one of the large "outer islands," where communal violence emerged after the resignation of President Suharto in 1998.[1] Although the Poso district hostilities had complex local, national, and international political dimensions that have been discussed elsewhere (Aragon 2001, 2005, 2011, 37–54; Sidel 2006; Van Klinken 2007), the focus here is how regional development policies, particularly transmigration and the intensive mono-cropping of cacao, contributed to dramatic and violence-provoking changes in Poso's demography, land tenure, and political dominance. The Central Sulawesi case provides a cautionary tale of how violence, displacement, and religious territorialization can follow as unintended side effects of regional development policies whose structural inequities intersect tragically with transregional stresses; in this case, the Southeast Asian fiscal crisis, national regime transition, global economy price shifts, and transnational Muslim-Christian distrust. This chapter begins with a chronological description of three periods of Central Sulawesi religious change and development, which are followed by an outline of Poso conflict dynamics, and results of the author's interviews with people who experienced the Poso district hostilities. Final sections include comparisons with Sulawesi regions that did not become violent despite similar development strategies, and offer some policy implications of this case study.

The communal violence in the Poso district of Central Sulawesi began in late 1998, escalated in 2000, and continued with waves of severe intervillage violence for two more years. A December 2001 government-mediated cease-fire agreement and subsequent security operations led to the formal cessation of hostilities, but periodic bombings, shootings, and other attacks continued through 2005. Some scholars have explained the Poso violence and several other post-Suharto communal conflicts as primarily local and temporal variations of an Indonesian national anxiety over religious boundaries and control (Sidel 2006). Others have privileged a studiously nonreligious narrative about elite-driven rivalries over political resources, essentially "politics by other means" (Van Klinken 2007). McRae (2007) further highlighted the judicial system's weaknesses that permitted the escalation of violence in Poso. Yet, as Van Klinken noted explicitly, his politically focused account inspired by the contentious social movements literature did not seek "to establish the 'root causes' of the wars in Poso" (2007, 87). In fact, none of the political science-oriented theorists of Poso and comparable post-Suharto communal conflicts (Bertrand 2004; McRae 2008; Sidel 2006; Van Klinken 2007) have paid much attention to specific Indonesian land use factors and their often unintended consequences.[2] By contrast, I contend that the selective impacts of changing economic development policies such as transmigration and intensive cash-cropping were critical. The fractious ethnoreligious ideologies, land alienation, and rent-seeking practices that they engaged are essential to our understanding of why grassroots support and sympathy emerged and grew for the faction leaders who sought privileges and control over increasingly valuable state and local resources (Aragon 2001, 2005, 2007, 2011).[3] Of course, once Christian or Muslim neighborhoods were burned and relatives killed, the conflict evolved to new levels, and became entangled with agents promoting international religious tensions. But, prior to the first bloodshed in 1998, the relative political and economic opportunities for Poso Muslims and Christians had shifted notably in just a few short years. Essentially, Indonesian national leaders evaded land reform and other programs to solve poverty, landlessness, and unemployment problems in heavily populated provinces such as Java and South Sulawesi by opening "empty" territories in Central Sulawesi for resettlement and labor migration. This sacrifice of the concerns of one region for others can be understood as a form of internal colonialism that externalized production costs for big businesses by appropriating resources from rural subsistence farmers and foragers of the outer islands.

Historical Background to Central Sulawesi's Religious Divisions

By the end of the Dutch colonial era in Indonesia in 1942, the two Abrahamic religions of Islam and Christianity (specifically Protestantism) each had gained followers in Central Sulawesi through the influence of foreign-migrant proselytizers. Mixed Arab and Sulawesi Muslim migrants held mercantile power from their bases at the coastline, while European Protestant missionaries had access to political power through their connections to the ruling Netherlands Indies administration, which invited Protestant missionaries to penetrate the interior mountain regions. These foreign migrants and their local religious networks influenced regional ideas about diversity, sacred land, ethnic territories, and community hierarchy.

The Netherlands Indies administration dispatched Protestant missionaries to convert highland animists in Central Sulawesi starting in the late 1800s (Aragon 2000; Schrauwers 2000). By the late 1700s, Muslim enclaves were observed near Central Sulawesi's Palu Bay. Merchants from the Muslim Bugis, Mandar, and Gorontalo ethnic groups migrating from South and North Sulawesi helped spread Islam into the coastal area of what became Central Sulawesi province after independence. In 1930, the first known Muslim scholar from the Hadramawt region of Yemen arrived in Palu and founded a *madrasa* school (Azra 1997, 1–3).

Prior to their conversion to foreign-world religions, the culturally related highland and lowland Central Sulawesi populations interacted routinely and used metaphors of siblingship to describe ties based in symbiotic trade, elite marriages, and protective alliances (Aragon 2000). The conversion of Sulawesi highlanders to Protestantism by European missionary migrants gradually distanced highlanders from coastal residents of both related and immigrant groups. Coastal natives and migrant settlers allied together as a common Muslim community, while the varied highland groups allied as fellow Protestants. Competition was introduced when the Dutch colonial government began to regulate local trade, introduce formal education for Protestant converts, and favor Protestant graduates for civil service positions, especially in the Poso region. This led Muslims to lose relative share of access to regional resources until pro-Muslim policies arose toward the end of the Suharto regime, just prior to the regional violence.

Records of migration into the Poso area during the colonial period reveal a mix of roughly the same ethnic and religious groups who reside there now, but the numbers from each immigrant group were small, in the dozens or hundreds. The Chinese, Arabs, and coastal Sulawesi Muslim traders arriving from other parts of the island resided mainly at the ports. Only some Christian Minahasa (from North Sulawesi) and Toraja (from South Sulawesi), who were introduced as civil servants or church staff by the Dutch, moved to the interior and integrated as fellow Protestants with Poso people. Among foreign migrants, only the Chinese were not oriented toward mixing religious proselytizing with their economic ventures. The Dutch employed Chinese as merchant middlemen to supply goods to themselves and the Protestant converts. Thus, the Chinese entered into an adversarial relationship with Arab Muslims, most eventually converting to Christianity and allying with indigenous Christians in the Poso violence.

Between World War II and the start of the Suharto regime in 1966, Central Sulawesi was the site of religiously polarized attacks and activities linked to the Darul Islam movement (Kahar Muzakar Rebellion) in South Sulawesi, and the Permesta Rebellion in North Sulawesi (Harvey 1974, 1977; van Dijk 1981). Some Muslim networks and Protestants prominent in the 1950–1965 regional rebellions, marking the decolonization process, regained political importance in the post-Suharto violence (Aragon 2001; International Crisis Group 2004). Yet, prior to the 1998 violence, religious sectarianism had been opposed and generally diminished by a combination of "equal opportunity" development programs such as schools and clinics, nationalist propaganda campaigns, and political suppression by military fiat during the Suharto regime from the mid-1960s to the late 1990s.

The 1980s: Religious Accommodation, Development Ethos, and Military Domination

Throughout the 1980s on the outer islands, religious affiliation was a pervasive identity distinction, but the Muslim/non-Muslim fault line was attenuated by a unifying pro-development focus. Religion, in the sense of having a state-authorized religious affiliation, was part and parcel of the Suharto regime's development ethos. Along with related aspirations to achieve a more consumerist lifestyle, it was a way for formerly "animist" peasants to be "modern Indonesians" rather than "backward" and "primitive" "pagans." In that sense, any of the five state-authorized religions of Islam, Protestantism, Catholicism, Hinduism, and Buddhism sufficed because practices were policed at the homogeneous village level rather than the heterogeneous national or provincial levels. Being a good religious citizen was an essential ingredient of Suharto-era nationalism, even among people who felt only minimally nationalistic. On the island of Sulawesi, with North Sulawesi (except for Gorontalo) being zealously Christian and South Sulawesi (except for Toraja) being zealously Muslim, the overall effort in 1980s Central Sulawesi was for the mostly coastal Muslims and mostly highland Christians to be politely tolerant toward one another, paddle hard, and simply keep their own extended households afloat.

By international and domestic standards, Central Sulawesi of the 1980s was deemed largely "undeveloped" although Community Health Centers (*Pusat Kesehatan Masyarakat* or PUSKESMAS) and primary schools were built in population centers accessible by the major vehicular roadways, many of which were still unpaved. Most rural, upland Christians and foothill Muslims grew rice, maize, and other subsistence necessities for their own households. Surpluses largely were channeled into delayed reciprocity practices that fed extended family members. Rural farmers also grew small amounts of supplementary high-value crops such as coffee, cloves, or garlic to trade for their cash needs such as clothes, soap, clinic medicines, school fees, and taxes. Peddlers and princes were few. What might look like "backward poverty" to outsiders was a nutritionally sufficient and enjoyable life to most upland farmers whom I encountered.[4]

Livelihoods differed at the coasts, the primary locations served by vehicle roads and shipping ports. There, Muslim migrants (primarily mixtures of Bugis, Gorontalo, and Arabs) and Buddhist or Christian Chinese controlled all trade, from small-scale urban kiosks to tree plantations (coconut, ebony, and other hardwoods) and cement factories. The merchants served both domestic consumer markets and burgeoning export businesses such as timber concessions.

Overall, some degree of positive peace existed in Central Sulawesi in the 1980s because there remained an old complementary division of labor between rural, upland Christian farmers cum foragers and urban, lowland Muslim or Chinese traders. In the 1980s, these groups still understood that they needed each other to succeed in life, and thus interreligious connections including marriages were valued. Regional elders and "ancestral customs" (*adat*) were honored explicitly. New migrants, still few in number, were expected to conform and comport themselves according to local behavioral norms. Many ethnic groups and extended families included both Muslims and Christians, generally the result of past migrations, intermarriage, or both. Positive peace was enacted in ritual practices, such as Muslims visiting Christians and bringing them food gifts during the Christmas week while Christians returned the identical favors to Muslims during the Idul Fitri week (Aragon 2000, 315). The gifts circulated were large glass jars of

Western-style bakery cookies, frosted layer cakes, and cases of soda pop such as Coca-Cola. These items illustrate the foreign orientation of consumer ideals in Indonesia at a time when television was new to the electrified lowland cities. Suharto's regime was being advised by the so-called Berkeley Mafia and Indonesians were being trained in economics at the University of California.

The 1980s religious accommodation and economic cooperation was also backstopped by the domination and coercion of General Suharto's military. When a night of arson against Christian churches, schools, Western missionaries, and Chinese shops in Palu followed a Protestant policeman's fight with Muslim market vendors in March 1988, Indonesian army troops carrying machine guns closed down and patrolled the affected locations, major markets, and downtown intersections for 24 hours (Aragon 2000, 316–317). That was all that was required to remind Central Sulawesi's Muslims and Christians that street violence and vigilantism were not tolerated under the Suharto regime.

It is also worth noting what kinds of development infrastructure remained absent in Central Sulawesi during the Suharto regime. First and foremost, there were no democratic governance structures in place beyond the village level, where customary councils or agricultural cooperatives often practiced free discussion and consensus-based negotiation. For the rest, both national and regional elections were cosmetic. Economic development programs were designed at the central government levels without grassroots input and, where military capacity existed, these were implemented by propaganda campaigns (such as the "Two Is Enough" birth control campaign) that were backed by the additional threat of reduced state funding or army occupation.

Villagers only envisioned what they had to gain from economic development programs such as cash for clothes, school fees, taxes, medicines, and imported commodities. Rarely did villagers imagine what they had to lose—such as land rights, fish and game habitats, cultural autonomy, and even their customary forms of subsistence. In the case of transmigration projects, Central Sulawesi highlanders generally blamed problems on the other ethnic groups relocated to their region rather than assigning culpability to government policies. The expansion of interisland transmigration sites in Central Sulawesi carved away the domains of indigenous inhabitants with efforts to establish intensive agriculture in steep and infertile areas that often were better suited ecologically to their prior swidden farming and foraging uses. As in other regions of Indonesia, many of the houses and villages set up by the Central Sulawesi transmigration program were neglected or soon abandoned because the people who moved from their

ancestral domains were asked "to change too much, too fast, in exchange
for too little" (Dove 1985, 272).

According to the 1945 Indonesian Constitution, the government has
rights to all "natural forest" and, during the Suharto era, it assigned concessions averaging 100,000 hectares in size for approximately 20 years to timber companies. In western Central Sulawesi by the late 1980s, clear-cutting
by businesses was becoming frequent despite official Indonesian regulations
that required "selective felling." Interior villagers learned too late that log-
gers removed not only "valuable trees" but also locally useful species that
timber companies define as "troublesome plants" growing in "unoccupied"
territories. One of the greatest problems faced by swidden farmers whose
territories are desired by developers is that long fallow cycles ensure that
farmers are absent from most of their customary lands at any given time.
This situation provides developers and migrants with many opportunities to
seize legally unoccupied land.

In Central Sulawesi during the 1980s, there often was a resigned acceptance of new development projects based on local peoples' certainty of their
inability to reject government proposals. Historical evidence concerning
past migrations indicates that many ethnic minorities in Indonesia adopted
their interior locales and difficult subsistence strategies precisely to avoid
overbearing state control. When government-approved enterprises built
roads to their villages and requested "hospitality" for army troops and non-
local workers, minority communities had few realistic options. Conversely,
the Indonesian government faced a difficult balancing act to meet the often
conflicting demands of foreign investors and the expectations of its own
socially heterogeneous, multiethnic populations.

Transmigration and Mono-crops: Intended and Unintended Consequences

By the mid-1990s, two nationwide New Order development policies began
making inroads (literally) in ways that changed religious and ethnic demographics. The transformed power dynamics promoted both supraethnic
religious polarization and mutual resentment. The first policy was the escalation of transmigration, the government-sponsored movement of impoverished Indonesians from the overpopulated inner islands of Java, Madura,
and Bali, to become homesteading farmers on "underpopulated" ones such
as Sumatra, Kalimantan, Sulawesi, and Papua.

The second New Order development policy that fomented inequities and
religious identity divisions was a new drive to cash-crop mono-cropping,
the government-supported replacement of food crops with smallholder

plantations of "permanent," high-value tree crops such as cacao (in Sulawesi) and oil palm (in Kalimantan). In conjunction with governance policies elevating migrant Muslims to political oversight positions, the influx of Muslim migrants in a better position to benefit from cash-cropping windfalls from clear-cut forests led to land alienation and indignation among indigenous Christian farmers and their ethnic leaders.

The unintended consequences of these policies exacerbated familiar distinctions between "natives" (*orang asli*) and "outsiders" (*pendatang*), a contrast that increasingly overlapped with "Christians" and "Muslims," respectively. Inner island regions became heavily populated in the late Dutch colonial period partly because of Java and Bali's productive volcanic soils (Geertz 1963), but the outer islands mostly lack that kind of thick, fertile topsoil and the land has a lower carrying capacity. Moreover, the "underpopulated" regions of the outer islands often are cyclically farmed or used as seasonal hunting and foraging areas by locals, who find themselves permanently displaced when this "empty" land becomes settled with migrants. Transmigration to Central Sulawesi began in 1973, and the trend toward cash-cropping swelled from the late 1980s to a late 1990s watershed of economic and political tension.

My argument here is that the "orderly" Suharto development policies reoriented religious identities away from prior complementary ecological subsistence exchanges and cooperative accommodation toward rivalry over suddenly far more valuable outer island forests, and political control over these resources.[5] The roots of those changes, including the imported Abrahamic religions, cash-cropping, and even transmigration, were planted in the Dutch period, but the exponential expansion of transmigration for nation-building purposes and the implementation of political changes that catapulted migrant Muslims into a position of political and demographic advantage in the Poso district were implemented by the Suharto government. These particular development factors, in conjunction with post-Suharto fiscal and political turmoil, world market shifts in cash crop prices, and the nation's first competitive elections since the 1950s, created the conditions for a "perfect storm" to begin in Poso city, precisely during the overlap of Christmas and Ramadan celebrations in December 1998.

Arguably, the Suharto regime program fomenting the most intergroup tensions throughout the archipelago was transmigration. Transmigration during Suharto's New Order presidency (1966–1998) took on new goals. The 1960 Basic Agrarian Law, which ceded legal control of customarily held village land (*tanah adat*) to the state for development purposes, was invoked by Suharto mainly to create transmigration projects in the outer islands (Tirtosudarmo 1995, 374). Suharto's government also altered forestry and investment laws in 1967 to allow foreign companies to finance and control new industries. By 1970, the government began to promote transmigration less as a substitute for politically threatening land reform— its original service—than as a tool for "civilizing" development in the provinces (Babcock 1986).[6]

The primary people that were moved by the state were poor and landless Muslims from the most densely populated island of Java. As the government program continued, additional volunteers were recruited from other nearby Muslim populations on the islands of Madura and Lombok. Hindus from Bali also were moved to some regions including Central Sulawesi. Besides originating from poor areas where farmland was scarce, these groups were considered by the government to be more technologically and culturally advanced than the natives living near the selected transmigration sites. Their example was expected to edify local populations.

Suharto's 1973 Presidential Decree No. 2 designated Central Sulawesi and nine other outer island provinces as new transmigration sites. The 1974 Regional Government Law and the 1979 Village Government Law then removed power from local councils of elders throughout the nation and placed it in the hands of a national bureaucracy, which increased regional governance by outsiders, usually Muslim Javanese (Kato 1989). Active and retired military officers were given control over many regions and development projects in the outer islands. Although Suharto's transmigration program was based on a highly centralized vision of a unitary nation, the program's micromanagement of diversity instead generated group tensions in many provinces. The source of these conflicts was not ethnic diversity per se, but rather the unacceptable political and economic injustices installed along with the state-imposed designs of coresidence.[7]

Between 1975 and 1980, census data indicate that migrants into Central Sulawesi totaled 83,595 individuals, or a 7.5 percent increase in the provincial population (Tirtosudarmo 1995, 376). Virtually all of these individuals would have been transmigrants because until the mid-1980s voluntary migrants were few (Tirtosudarmo 1995, 378). After that, national oil revenues declined and the transmigration program was curtailed for several years. Yet the initial transmigration projects in Central Sulawesi were planned with an eye on profitable trade markets and the construction of new roads (Hardjono 1977). Those roads then provided unprecedented access for roughly equal numbers of voluntary migrants from the neighboring province of South Sulawesi.

The ambitiously named Trans-Sulawesi Highway was constructed gradually during the 1980s, and thousands of voluntary Muslim migrants from South Sulawesi began moving north by overland routes. Documented migrants to Central Sulawesi between 1985 and 1990 numbered 70,034, then about 4.1 percent of the provincial population. Voluntary migrants settled disproportionately in urban areas, swelling the population there by 8.5 percent (Tirtosudarmo 1995, 376–377). Located at a key intersection on the Trans-Sulawesi Highway between South and North Sulawesi, Poso city grew from a sleepy fishing port and farming town to a bustling district capital of considerable ethnic and religious diversity.

Although the Poso district's population was dominated by Protestants during the colonial period, the influx of transmigrants and voluntary migrants shifted it to a slight Muslim majority by the late 1980s and produced unprecedented Muslim majorities in some subdistricts (*kecamatan*) by the late 1990s. Between 1981 and 1996, Muslims were recorded as increasing in numbers in virtually every Poso subdistrict (Sangaji 2003–2004). In the Lembo subdistrict sited for many transmigration projects, the Muslim percentage of the population went from 3 percent to 35 percent in the 15 years between 1972 and 1996. For similar reasons, the Muslim population of Pamona Selatan subdistrict climbed from 3 percent to 23 percent in the same time period. These regions' approximately inverse percentage of Christians both dropped from 97 percent, startling the native Pamona and Mori populations with their relative demographic decline. Census figures indicate that by 1998, a total of 93,961 transmigrants were moved just to sites within the Poso district. This implies that, even after statistical adjustments are made for locals who joined these transmigration villages, transmigrants from other islands comprised about 20 percent of the Poso district's almost 350,000 people by 1996 (Badan Pusat Statistik Sulteng 1998, 88; Sangaji 2003).

The two Muslim migrant groups whose arrival in the Poso district in the 1980s and 1990s became most challenging for the formerly dominant Protestants, the ethnic Pamona, were the Javanese and the Bugis. Most migrant Javanese entered either as peasant transmigrants or as high-status civil servants. The transmigrants received state-provided houses and agricultural areas on what natives considered their ancestral land. Javanese civil servants received administrative control and bureaucratic jobs withheld from local residents. By contrast, Bugis voluntary migrants came as independent merchants and entrepreneurial laborers, and they increasingly gained development jobs and access to large plots of land.

Looking comparatively at natives' resentment of Bugis and Madurese Muslim migrants in the collective violence in Sambas, Kalimantan, and Ambon, it is apparent that the Suharto administration used these groups as economic buffers or middlemen between the Javanese civil service elite and the native farming populations (Pelly 1999). The same system applied in Central Sulawesi. Migrant Muslim groups were provided with economic opportunities for development-related jobs considered beneath the Javanese bureaucrat and yet unsuited to the "backward" native subsistence farmers. One notable aspect of that backwardness was based in the Pamonas' tradition of working on family land rather than as wage laborers, unlike the Bugis. There also proved to be a significant cultural mismatch between the views of migrant Bugis and native Central Sulawesi on desirable plot size. Bugis people's interest and success in obtaining plots of land up to 20 times larger than those shared within native households produced increasing resentment as their population numbers increased, available forest land decreased, and some newly landless natives became forced to work for low wages on what they considered their own group's alienated lands.

Forests covered well over half of Central Sulawesi's surface through the 1980s. Thus New Order development there concentrated on timber industries, particularly high-value hardwoods such as ebony. Large Central Sulawesi ebony firms were controlled by the Suharto family, and they generally employed Muslim migrants rather than local people. These business activities, together with land set aside for conservation, resulted in significant portions of provincial forests being placed off-limits for local farmers, foragers, and hunters (Sangaji 2003; see also Peluso 1992). By the late 1990s, state documents claimed that 7 million hectares of Central Sulawesi land were officially sequestered for state-backed farm plantations, timber concessions, conservation areas, and mining projects (Sangaji 2007, 326). This situation legally precluded the rights of smallholder farmers from virtually all of the province's total area of 6.8 million hectares, while migrants were solicited to work at most of the government-run projects that claimed access to these resources.

There was a continued shift from subsistence to commercial agriculture throughout the 1980s and 1990s. Echoing Dutch policies, the New Order government stigmatized dry-rice subsistence farming as unproductive, even unecological, and pressured farmers to switch to wet-rice farming and new seed stock where possible. New crops such as cacao entered Central Sulawesi along with incoming migrants from South Sulawesi (Faust et al. 2003, 12). Cash crops such as copra near the coasts, and cloves, vanilla, or coffee in the interior, generated new wealth that was gained disproportionately by ambitious migrants and urban middleman merchants, primarily Muslim Bugis and Christian Chinese.

Central Sulawesi, like many outer island regions, had a long history of small farmer connections to world markets and a changing array of forest products and cash crops. During the financial crisis beginning in late 1997, cacao became the preferred crop as its sale price in rupiah, which was pegged to the US dollar, continued to rise while the fixed rupiah value of salaries and many local products fell due to inflation. The shift to growing cacao beans was a key global economy factor preceding Poso's 1998 outbreak of communal violence. Cacao's value rose in Indonesia in conjunction with the collapse of cacao industries in African nations such as Ghana, while coffee values dropped in conjunction with coffee "dumping" practices by Vietnam.

Poso district land area devoted to cacao farming reportedly increased by a factor of 22 between 1986 and 2001 (Badan Pusat Statistik Kabupaten Poso 2001; Badan Pusat Statistik Sulteng 1999; Sangaji 2003). In the province as a whole, cacao production grew one hundredfold between 1988 and 2002, by which time it amounted to nearly 90 percent of the province's foreign exchange income. Whereas successful Muslim migrants who planted and sold cacao early in the boom claimed that they worked harder than locals, local Protestants became angered by migrant successes gained from clear-cutting their former ancestral forests. Protestants saw their declining relative population and economic status in the district as a result of increasingly powerful and corrupt Muslim government officials who benefited most from the commercial industries promoted by Jakarta. Without necessarily fathoming the national-level political shifts and organizational details (Hefner 1993, 2000), many Central Sulawesi Protestants gradually began to sense that Suharto's increasingly pro-Islamist government was detrimental to their welfare.

Unlike the entrepreneurial Bugis, Protestant highlanders had few business skills and relied on localized exchange networks based on kinship obligations and feasting. Many ran up high-interest debts to immigrant merchants that required payments of future harvests or even their fields. Sometimes fallow or ancestral hunting lands were sold by highlanders who thought, mistakenly, that Central Sulawesi populations would remain as small and forests would remain as vast as they once were. As the costs and importance of education rose throughout the New Order, inherited land sometimes was sold in the expectation that its Protestant owner would no longer need it once employed in Poso district civil service. Such expectations were frustrated during the 1990s when the regional bureaucracy became more dominated by Muslims, and unofficial payments (or bribes) for entry-level positions climbed higher than most locals could ever afford (Aragon 2007). These political changes combined with transmigration, voluntary migration, and the commoditization of agricultural lands rendered many Pamona and other indigenous youth landless and jobless by the end of the Suharto regime. The lack of legal protection for settlements' communal lands was part and parcel of the local land alienation problem.

Many refugees from Poso, as well as other provincial residents, once had what they considered "good relations" with their neighbors of other faiths, and expressed disbelief when the violence began in 1998. Yet, small-scale violence occurred earlier at both transmigration and voluntary migration sites in Central Sulawesi, which became arenas for ethnic disputes over land rights and economic dominance (Acciaioli 2001, 86; Aragon 2000, 303–304). Although most problems were between locals and immigrants of different religions, some conflicts between indigenous residents and South Sulawesi migrants took place in the Bungku area where both groups were Muslim. Such data support the proposition that insider-outsider competition over the economic use of land, rather than religious strife per se, was the basal line of fracture in Sulawesi.

Prior to the 1980s, the few immigrants residing in Central Sulawesi rural communities were expected to defer to the elders and customary practices (*adat*) of the original land-clearing residents. Late New Order migrants increasingly defied these expectations. Migrants from South Sulawesi viewed themselves as equally, or even more legitimately, entitled to their island's resources and appropriations (Acciaioli 2001, 101–102; Aragon 2000, 303). In Poso, the apparently uniform yet unequally beneficial regulations of the Suharto regime aggravated the Protestants' regional nationalism and nativism as well as Muslims' willingness to listen to militant rhetoric about their unfulfilled rights to Indonesia's wealth and political supremacy. Both religious groups employed nationalist-style arguments to assert their legitimacy over the other.

Central Sulawesi mosques and Muslim organizations, such as Al-Khaira'at and Mohammadiyah, forged transethnic links among recent migrants. As ties through ancestral customs (*adat*) became weakened through New Order policies promoting only imported scriptural or "world religions," community identities and patron-client relationships reformed not through encompassing nationalism, as the Sukarno and early Suharto governments had hoped, but rather through more immediate institutions of religious solidarity (Aragon 2000). This was a failure in the Indonesian nationalist project, but not in the simple way it is generally understood, meaning only a common independence from the Dutch (Anderson 1991). Rather, the breakdown was in line with the many nationalist failures described by Kelly and Kaplan (2001), who contend that the postcolonial nation-state's frequent problems originate in the inequitable post-WWII process of decolonization.[8]

In addition, the recent and dramatic inversion between the importance of controlling land versus labor occurred not only in Central Sulawesi, but also elsewhere in Southeast Asia. Throughout Southeast Asian history until the past few decades, "the perception of forest land as infinitely available and manpower as scarce ensured that competition was fundamentally over the control of people" (Reid 1988, 122). In other words, historical politics and warfare targeted benefits from more people's labor, not gaining territory for resources. That situation and political strategy reversed itself in Central Sulawesi by the early 1990s. By that point, because of rising local and immigrant populations on fixed geographic areas, land had become scarce and labor was in surfeit. Migrants from heavily populated Indonesian provinces "overflowed" into less populated ones, at the same time when prevailing global and national economic pressures encouraged the dwindling forested regions to boost their agricultural production and extraction of natural resources for world markets.

Post-Suharto Violence, Religious Polarization, and Displacement (1998–2004)

The post-Suharto communal violence in Poso began within the national context of archipelago-wide religious attacks that damaged churches and mosques. These included the Muslim Javanese versus Christian Ambonese fight in Jakarta in late November 1998, the Christian retaliation in Kupang, Timor, and the Muslim counterretaliation in Ujung Pandang (now Makassar), Sulawesi. Often unmentioned in individual accounts of the sectarian violence, these sequential and media-fed interactions demonstrated the national public space of regional religious polarization at the end of Suharto's regime. They also implicated the ability of media reports to tap vague religious resentments and mobilize acts of sectarian revenge not directly but by remote substitution, from distances of thousands of miles. What I will term "displaced revenge at a distance" was an extreme religious form of a national "imagined community" (Anderson 1991). What shifted after 1998 was that rather than take religious revenge at a distance from the trigger event, fighters and militia aid traveled to help implement "defensive" attacks in other provinces. In Ambon and Poso, the arrival of jihad groups from other islands startled local Muslim fighters into taking the ideological aspects of their religious identity confrontation more seriously.

Starting in late 1998, and peaking in 2000, Central Sulawesi's Poso district became a site of violence between many groups of Christians and Muslims. Even in 2003, the district capital of Poso city was still a woeful site of burned and looted buildings, with all access roads under army supervision. An estimated 500–1,000 people had been killed and roughly 150,000 more had been displaced from their preconflict homes by militia attacks and arson (Aragon 2008, 176–178; BAKORNAS 2003; Human Rights Watch

2002, 38–39). That latter number, significantly, represents nearly half of the original district's population.

Poso's violence has been detailed and analyzed in both academic and policy publications (Aragon 2001, 2005, 2008; Human Rights Watch 2002; International Crisis Group 2004; McRae 2007, 2008). Therefore, the conflict will be outlined here only schematically in terms of the participation of geographically escalating religious networks, which only gradually came under state agent constraints. Following a Poso city street fight between a Protestant and a Muslim youth during the overlapping Christmas and Ramadan celebrations of 1998, defenders of the injured Muslim sought the Protestant's family for retribution. Mobs soon formed to act not in the name of the particular individuals involved, but for the injured Muslim and Protestant communities. Muslim vigilantes attacked Christian Chinese stores that sold liquor. As Protestants, Muslims, their property, and houses of worship each became damaged, allies of both longtime residents and recent migrants began to arrive in trucks from distant villages connected through kinship and religious organizations. When human casualties increased, and neither side was satisfied with the government's weak security and legal responses, vigilantism escalated to calls for outside aid. Former soldiers, local toughs, and religious militias were recruited to help their fellow Christians and Muslims, starting in 2000.

Within days of Poso city's first Muslim-Protestant brawl, there occurred not only acts of sadistic physical violence, but also the large-scale burning of neighborhoods characterized as majority Christian or majority Muslim. Ensuing flight patterns accentuated pockets of religious territorialization in the district, and the island as a whole.[9] Within the district, two religious metropoles emerged: Protestant Tentena, the highland town first missionized by the Dutch, and Muslim Poso city, the district capital where Muslim migrants first settled. This displacement pattern drew new participants into the violence as the displaced provided eyewitness accounts of injuries and attacks to fellow congregants. The flight pattern also symbolized to Muslim and Christian sides a distinct rift between church and government, a divide that scarcely existed in the colonial period when the Dutch government and Protestant missions were interdependent. Even the Poso district university (Universitas Sintuwu Maroso) was split into two campuses, one mostly Muslim and one for displaced Christians.

In urban neighborhoods, houses, vehicles, stores, police barracks, and other public buildings were burned. The motivation for such targets included personal revenge, coordinated destruction of religious targets, criminal opportunism, and even class warfare. In rural areas, cacao trees abandoned by refugees were harvested or destroyed by roving militias, gaining ground for allies and discouraging enemies from returning to religiously cleansed territory.

The burning and desecration of churches and mosques assaulted not only precious religious symbols and spaces, but also the very terms of Suharto-era admission into the Indonesian nation. As the erection of religious buildings in the late New Order showcased a marginal community's commitment to the national philosophy of *Pancasila* and modern development, these buildings' destruction represented an attack on the other side's citizenship. In a comparable manner, the gory media images of slashed Muslim or Christian bodies that emerged in various phases of the Poso conflict symbolized the potential destruction of the entire religious group (*umma* or *jema'at*) and its place not only in the nation, but also in the world (Aragon 2005). The calls for military support and assistance were relayed overseas via website reports mounted separately by Muslim and Christian religious organizations.

In 2000, Catholic migrants joined native Protestants to take revenge against Muslims who had burned their neighborhoods and churches. The horrifying excesses of these vigilante operations attracted jihad groups and supplies of automatic weapons from Java, South Sulawesi, and the Philippines to defend Poso's Muslim community. Some of these groups, such as Laskar Jihad, publicized nationalist arguments focusing on Indonesian politics and accusations that Poso Christians were planning treasonous secession (Berita Laskar Jihad 2001a, 2001b; Hasan 2002). Other more deadly paramilitary groups such as Jema'ah Islamiyah and Mujahidin KOMPAK (an acronym for Komite Penanggulangan Krisis or "Crisis Prevention Committee") had a transnational focus on expanding Muslim control in Southeast Asia and protecting the community (*umma*) from worldwide Christian conspiracies (van Bruinessen 2002; International Crisis Group 2002, 2004). Poso's religious civil war became so uncontrolled and destructive that, in the aftermath of September 11, 2001, local, national, and international pressures coalesced to urge the Indonesian government to mediate a cease-fire agreement.

The resulting Malino Accord signed on December 20, 2001, contained several unarguable points: that both sides stop violence, obey laws, expect security forces to be firm and fair, reject outside interference, stop slander, offer apologies, and promote respect for all religions and traditions. However, in terms of the proposed weapons collection, criminal prosecutions, fair aid distribution, and provision to return all property rights to their preconflict status, implementation was weak. Malino signatories and Poso district politicians were given oversight of aid funds, which often were pocketed or selectively routed to their own ethnoreligious networks. The humanitarian "development" strategies to alleviate conflict destruction often simply financed further corruption and abuse.

By the time of the Malino Accord, the vast majority of Christian and Muslim residents in Poso were utterly traumatized and weary of the violence and destruction. Little civilian violence occurred after 2001. Nevertheless, Poso's violence pattern evolved from open militia attacks to periodic "mysterious" killings, bombings, and arson, a pattern that hindered infrastructure rehabilitation, trauma recovery, religious reconciliation, and resettlement for several more years.

Lessons from Displacement: Narratives of Transmigrants and Natives

Between 2000 and 2004, I interviewed roughly one hundred people who encountered, and in most cases were displaced by, the Poso district violence to hear how they framed and justified the causes and consequences of deteriorating relations among the district's religious groups (Aragon 2008). Some transmigrants that I interviewed discussed how local primary forests initially were viewed as mere obstacles to migrants' rice agriculture plans. One Hindu Balinese transmigrant that I met came to Poso in 1979 when he was just a ten-year-old boy. His family was resettled along the coastal road near a Muslim Javanese transmigration village, and he ultimately married a Muslim woman. He said the transmigrants' initial view was that Poso had "too much forest." As recent arrivals from elsewhere, they didn't know the Sulawesi trees, including ebony, mahogany, and other hardwoods, were valuable. They just cleared the forest for wet-rice fields, which was the government's expectation. Then they burned the cut timber for cooking fires.

Starting in 1985 and 1986, cacao plants were introduced by the Indonesian government to these transmigrants. Cacao prices were low, so people didn't bother with it much. They just planted the seedlings provided in their unirrigated vegetable fields. Only when cacao prices rose tenfold (from Rp. 1,100 per kilo to a peak of Rp.13,000 per kilo in 1999), did they pick the trees, and plant many, many more. Indigenous Poso people didn't plant much cacao because, not tutored by government agents, they were unfamiliar with it. Then, during the 1998 financial crisis, as my interviewee said, "those with cacao trees had their opportunity. In six months, you could buy a car." In 2003, he said, it was easier to plant only cacao and buy rice. His family formerly sold unhusked rice from their farm to other Balinese who were merchants. Now, he said, all the remaining forest near his natal transmigration village had been cut down to plant cacao.

Most Muslim refugees that I encountered at either refugee camps in the district, or private homes outside the district, had come to Poso as voluntary economic migrants during the 1990s. Almost invariably they would tell me about several locations on Sulawesi Island where they tried to make a living before they moved to Poso. Their stories suggested that the island and district had become routine destinations for a class of highly mobile but relatively poor, landless, and uneducated laborers by the end of the Suharto regime. The narratives described widespread rural poverty, migration that followed government-backed land development schemes, and the "unexpected" religious violence.

In September 2003, I visited a Muslim refugee barracks in the Poso district where I met a young ethnic Mandar man born in South Sulawesi 20 years earlier. He had only recently migrated voluntarily to a Protestant-majority town. He said he was just a farmer, didn't know how to fish or trade, and had been given a plot of teak to harvest by a regional government agent. But, he added, because the land was part of a forest conservation area, he owned no official land title. Thus, the land that had provided his income was not legally his. In 2000, his Protestant neighbors advised him to flee. His uncle who stayed was killed. The man lost his home and everything he owned except a sack of rice. The house was destroyed as soon as he left it. The migrant's narrative illustrated how government agents oversaw the illegal logging of "conservation forests," using landless migrant farmers to accomplish the deed "off the record."

By contrast, aside from civil servants who fled Poso city, most displaced Protestants had been subsistence food farmers with only a small area of their inherited fields reserved for cash crops. In some cases, Protestants told me how they initially loaned incoming Muslim migrants fallow fields or community forest, as a way to promote good relations and trade, but then felt angry as they literally lost ground to the newcomers who viewed the land transfers as permanent. Li (2007, 103–114) also describes how many Central Sulawesi locals became tempted to sell land when migrants first offered to buy it, only to feel duped and angry when land prices continued to rise beyond their abilities to compete in the new market.

One of the key legal and policy issues involved here is that local heritage or "customary village" lands in much of Indonesia are legally untitled and shared in rotation by members of kinship groups whose ancestors first used the land for subsistence farming, foraging, or hunting. If an individual stops using the land, rights return to the community where new use-rights plans are decided by elders. Customarily, no land could be alienated by sale. Such land was increasingly privatized by government officials for "national development" although this "solution" created additional resentment among local people who blamed migrant groups drawn into the government's economic plans. Migrants' narratives that I heard corroborated reports by Indonesians working in nongovernmental organizations (NGO) arenas that increasing amounts of customary forest land, even in legally protected conservation areas, were turned over to migrants for clear-cutting. Both migrant and host communities became enmeshed in collaborative relations with powerful forest-clearing businesses and government agents.

In sum, my interviews revealed how the outcomes of broad demographic and agricultural changes were diversely perceived by Muslims and Protestants.[10] Muslim migrants said that they were "just trying to make a living" as good Muslims in a Muslim-majority nation. They told how when they arrived, the Poso district contained large parcels of "empty" forest land, which their industrious families had been able to make more productive and profitable. Local Protestants, by contrast, felt that the migrants and government did not respect their first-settler status and had unfairly displaced them from their lands. They talked about suddenly becoming the nation's "stepchildren" in their own formerly Christian region.

Displacement and Who Belongs Where

The Malino Accord tenet requiring the "return all of the displaced to their respective places of origin" was ambiguous. Some citizens and officials assumed that this meant returning displaced persons back to the home they fled between 1998 and 2002, or a new home rebuilt upon the site where an earlier one was burned. Yet, this was effectively impossible where new residents had occupied those sites. Others said that if a Protestant migrant to Poso fled to her parents' home in Tentena, or a recent migrant or militia member fled back home to Java or South Sulawesi, they already had returned to their "places of origin." Economic and political motivations for overreporting or underreporting refugees also existed. Where aid funds were prorated according to the number of refugees, figures likely were inflated by local officials. By contrast, government officials responsible for the design and implementation of the Malino Accord were motivated to ensure its reputation through claims of decreased violence and successful resettlement. In late December 2001, the Indonesian government declared that all of the more than 1 million persons displaced from the various regional conflicts would return or resettle by December 31, 2002, and state aid would be terminated (Duncan 2003, 35–36). But, the target date arrived before some areas were safe, so more aid was sought for regions such as Poso.

The resettlement of Poso's internally displaced Muslims and Christians involved the overlapping influences of religious organizations, state politicians, bureaucratic corruption, and powerful international NGOs such as the World Bank, the United Nations Development Programme, Church World Services, and Mercy Corps. In virtually all cases, however, resettlement patterns segregated Muslims and Christians from each other. Both coastal and highland communities, swelled by the addition of migrating displaced persons, became religiously "purified" through fear, threats, and attacks on property or persons. This purification campaign was assisted by the Indonesian state requirement that all citizens have a religion listed on their national identity cards, documents checked by security personnel and vigilantes alike.

It became a matter of debate, in both theoretical and practical terms, for whom Poso city or locations in the surrounding Poso district really were "places of origin" (*tempat asalnya*). The ancestors of most ethnic groups resided in Central Sulawesi before they converted to either Protestantism or Islam, but such historical nuances generally were omitted from discussion. The issue became *who belongs where* within the district, the island, or elsewhere in the nation. Some exclusivist Protestants said that Poso is historically "a Protestant region" and should remain so, with Muslims returning to their more distant "places of origin" beyond the district's territorial boundaries. By contrast, Muslims often said they have a national right to be Poso district residents, and the Malino Accord (Point 6) supported them by asserting: "Poso land is an integral part of the Republic of Indonesia. Because of this, each citizen has a right to live, immigrate, and stay in peace, respecting local customs" (Aragon 2008,179). Some exclusivist Muslims sought to up the ante by claiming that Indonesia actually is a Muslim nation (or "has a Muslim culture"), and therefore it is the Christians, vestigial lackeys of the Dutch colonial empire, who really do not belong in Poso or anywhere else in the nation. Clearly people who held these more extreme positions were in no frame of mind to advance a pluralistic reconciliation process in Poso.

In fact, the disparate viewpoints underlying these homeland disputes, and their implications for where refugees should go after the battles, were an important but rarely confronted ideological aspect of the conflict's protracted transformations. The Poso conflict thus bears in a more general way upon Indonesian migration policies, minority group inequities, and the big elephant in the room (for both Indonesia and the global economy): land reform.

Peaceful Comparisons for Poso

Although any attempt to compare the communally violent Poso district with peaceful "control groups" must be qualified by the stark impossibility of laboratory-style experiments in social history, local Indonesian comparisons from the same 1998–2007 time period are edifying. Some other districts in Central Sulawesi, such as Donggala (the district then encompassing the provincial capital of Palu) and Banggai, also received large numbers of transmigrants and voluntary migrants. Why did they not experience post-Suharto conflict? The answer, I would suggest, is that both Donggala and Banggai were overwhelmingly Muslim well prior to the rapid migration period of the last three decades of the Suharto regime. Thus, the tens of thousands of new migrants introduced no significant changes in (or challenges to) those areas' religious demography or political control. Muslims had no recent political gains to defend, and Christians had no hopes to change their status as a weak minority within their district. Protestants whom I knew in Palu said that if Muslim militias attacked their regions as an outgrowth of the Poso violence, their only option would be to flee to the mountains. Any local ethnic friction among migrant and local Muslims in these Muslim-majority areas also would not resonate with national or transnational religious conflicts. Those data suggest that demographic ratios and valences may help predict communal violence, whether or not all groups are treated with parity.

The Christian-majority regions of Sa'dan Toraja, South Sulawesi, and Minahasa, North Sulawesi (which includes the economically vibrant provincial capital of Manado) also are instructive. In Christian Toraja, the local Protestant majority worked hard to nip any interreligious problems quickly. Similar proactive measures were taken in Minahasa, which some observers called the most positively peaceful region of Sulawesi during the post-Suharto period. Regional specialists have attributed Minahasa's successful resistance against violent outbursts to a combination of several factors: disciplined and cooperative religious organizations, the resilient and fairly equitable local economy, and the local government's "more or less near-monopoly over the means of violence" through strict policing (Henley, Schouten, and Ulaen 2007, 309).

Christian-majority Minahasa presents an interesting reverse religious profile to the Muslim-majority Palu region. In both cases, the provincial capitals of North and Central Sulawesi respectively had clear and uncontested religious majorities along with a longtime religious minority presence. Both of these cities also had a more effective security apparatus than the relatively isolated district capital of Poso. In addition, I would add that Palu and Manado had more diversified economies than Poso, which may have helped absorb the impacts of rapid immigration and balance the drastic crop price and rupiah value shifts of the late 1990s.[11]

Government and religious leaders in the provincial capitals of Manado and Palu took pride in their ability to maintain calm and suppress unrest. Nevertheless, having conducted post-Suharto fieldwork interviews with government leaders, displaced persons, and ordinary citizens in both the

Palu and Manado regions, I note that religious minorities in both areas—Christians in Palu and Muslims in Manado—inevitably claimed to experience religious discrimination by their local governments, as well as feeling a palpable anxiety that the nearby communal violence in Poso, Ambon, and Maluku might spread to their cities. Thus, the early Suharto era, as well as post-Suharto Palu and Manado, although salutary comparisons, represent fewer excuses for Muslim or Protestant triumphalism about tolerance and leadership than awkward object lessons about government control and the possibilities for coercion and accommodation to coexist.

Finally, there were some efforts both within and beyond Poso to revive culturally "traditional" methods of dispute reconciliation. For example, a study of the Lindu Lake region of Central Sulawesi describes religious anxiety and recurrent ethnic tensions between Muslim Bugis migrants and indigenous Protestant Lindu people. The groups threatened each other with violence during the post-Suharto unrest but bloodshed generally was contained through tense negotiations (Acciaioli 2001). Yet, both the Lindu and Poso data reveal how attempts to revive traditional-style elders councils or ancient rituals as a means of dispute settlement were not fully respected by groups who did not share common ritual traditions, that is, locals and migrants. In Poso such attempts to revive neo-traditional forms of peacekeeping generally failed because they were empty of common meaning and substantive solutions (Aragon 2001, 70–71). In Lindu, by comparison, the councils staunched violence only when their neo-traditional approach integrated migrant representation and the more inclusive nationalist rhetoric characteristic of the early Suharto regime (Acciaioli 2001, 102–108).

Policy Implications

The medical practitioner's sage advice to "do no harm" undoubtedly is easier to repeat as a mantra than to implement. In other words, I appreciate the often inscrutable ethnographic complexities on the ground as well as the good intentions of the distantly located and humanitarian policymaker. Yet, applying large sums of money and technocratic expertise to a problem clearly is not an unadulterated good because development programs so often unthinkingly undermine prior local common practices governed by informal and constructive social norms. Development interventions inevitably benefit some individuals and groups more than others, often overfeeding the governing and merchant classes of a region, and exacerbating group resentments that succor polarization and communal violence. Too often development programs are designed to fulfill the goals of the powerful developers rather than the developed.

As an example, a 2005–2010 World Bank initiative allocated $104 million in "Support for Poor and Disadvantaged Areas" with the express goal of breaking conflict cycles by offering funds to formerly hostile groups who agreed to bank rules for former rival groups' cooperations and codevelopment (Li, 2007, 260–264). Problematically, however, the rent-grabbing potentials of local politicians and army troops were factored out as matters that the World Bank was not in a position to control. States give developers permits and are supported for their role in maintaining "peace" for development initiatives, yet state agents' rule of law violations often get a pass from discussion. World Bank reports noted the inequitable opportunities and material circumstances leading to widespread feelings of social injustice and land titling problems in regions with violence, but these factors were always set beyond the bank's technocratic mission. Development programs often seek "maximum efficiency" and productivity, relying heavily upon the very migrant laborers, ethnic middlemen, armed strong men, and self-enriching politicians who tend to promote and support conflicts.

Humbled by these political economy realizations and the widespread geographic data on which they are based (Escobar 1995), one might well concur with Li who finds "an ethnographic appreciation of the complexities of rural relations to be antithetical to the position of expert" (Li 2007, 3). Li notes that she once advised a development agency on the problems spurred by cacao programs in Central Sulawesi, and the agency responded positively and proactively to her input. However, the subsequent enlightened steps taken to grant upland farmers legal rights over their customary land quickly were blocked by Central Sulawesi's governor, who saw the development agency's political tinkering as an impediment to the success of cash-cropping and other land-based business development ventures to which he was aligned (Li 2007, 4). Li ultimately concludes that the development analyst should remain independent and refrain from contributing advice to the technocratic improvement process that he or she is endeavoring to evaluate.[12]

There is a tension between those who consider humans to have naturally feckless and violent tendencies, which must be channeled positively by "development," and those who see all forms of intervention as vestigial imperialism. Probably neither has got it right. As shown here, development in not a single kind of salve to improve humanity and eradicate "poverty." However, to seek purity through critical detachment alone seems somewhat dismissive or even cynical. It is not only critical to unpack the assumptions of prevailing technocratic development models, but also important to distinguish programs, such as timber concessions or marble mines—which are likely to benefit elites, degrade local environments, foster corruption, and service the needs of distant wealthy consumers or lenders—from targeted health or appropriate technology programs, for example, the production and distribution of fuel-efficient, inexpensive, low-smoke cooking stoves for rural residents who struggle to find fuel and become ill from smoky hearths. All too often, however, local residents' social and economic concerns—whether they want electric lines, clean water, clinics, better hearths, or cell phones—are those least investigated and addressed, even when such projects might have synergistic economic benefits for investors and locals alike.

A few specific provisos seem to follow usefully from the case presented here. First, a greater portion of budgets for antipoverty programs could be sequestered for independent, preintervention ethnographic assessments of ethnoreligious group relations, demographic and local resource use patterns, and potential rent-grabbing institutions or middlemen. This research should not be conducted solely in-house by those with technocratic expertise in supposedly universal "rational choice" models. Those who know exactly how things worked well in some other world region may not always be correct in plans for cross-cultural extrapolation. Neither should the investigation be done inexpensively by familiar in-country partners with likely agendas, conflicts of interest, and the understandable unwillingness to unsettle their sponsor's expectations. It might be useful to implement the social science equivalent of a double-blind study where an independent area specialist with a collaborative team would be asked to make an assessment of prior local relations, resource use patterns, perceived problems, and cooperative institutions well before economic intervention plans are finalized for the region. "Getting things done" to alleviate poverty or other evident social problems in "developing" nations should not take precedence over understanding the messy and complex social situation on the ground.

This leads to another policy implication of this case—the importance of considering the appropriate scale for various regional programs. Addressing problems of scale (and the linked issues of environmental and social sustainability) may be more important to the success of economic interventions and the prevention of violence than any other parameter. Solutions that work well at a small scale, such as shade-grown cash crops to supplement subsistence farming, routinely prove disastrous when promoted at a large scale with clear-cutting methods. As in Poso, the quick financial gains of cash-cropping will suddenly override concerns for sustainable food-farming, and fragile forests become too valuable for rural residents to control with their parents' normative access rules. At such points, putting more money into a program may lead to worse outcomes for land and people, such as when greater amounts of postconflict aid to Poso led first and foremost to greater amounts of corruption and militarization (Aragon 2007).

Conversely, local patterns that seem to keep the peace for one group in a particular place, such as Palu or Minahasa, may not "scale up" or transfer effectively as national solutions for Indonesia or other countries. A plan by the US Agency for International Development (USAID) to invest $10 million in Poso after 2005 sounded perilous because the capacity of local government representatives and the military to fan local violence for political and economic purposes was already well-documented in Maluku and Poso (Sangaji 2007). Moreover, the antijihadist focus of the US military-supported program seemed deaf to the complex history and social inequities on the ground.[13] At its best, though, such a large investment would include efforts for long-term monitoring of how violence becomes discouraged and symbiosis becomes encouraged among previously hostile groups. In this sense, prevention and cure should not be considered fully separate matters.

Another policy-relevant point comes from observations of the cross-cutting ties and small-scale but economically advantageous opportunities provided for diligent workers under the Sukarno and early Suharto regimes. Programs such as community health centers (PUSKESMAS) and universal primary education generally benefited all groups of all religions. The national *Pancasila* philosophy—despite the government's practices of hypocrisy, coercive propaganda, and exclusion of "isolated tribes"—did contribute generally to help members of most ethnic and religious groups feel tied to both national citizenship rights and explicit obligations for a peaceful, negotiated coexistence under state security protection. Future development interventions thus bear a responsibility to review all that has gone right to maximize the potential symbiotic or "equal access" dimensions of their programs in the context of a pluralistic society and new electoral democracy.

Finally, land development strategy is of utmost importance: to protect disadvantaged groups and minorities, land rights issues need to be addressed, including states' exploitative use of eminent domain laws. Revisions should not be done with the current knee-jerk urge to privatize and title plots everywhere according to Western legal precedent, which likely will benefit bureaucrats and migrants disproportionately, but rather with a serious effort to investigate, recognize, and creatively protect diverse and resilient forms of resource commons access (if not outright ownership) that have been governed by informal local norms for prior centuries. Addressing these four suggestions might make new regional economic strategies, incorporating diverse local ideas for tending coprosperity and sustainability, a more collaborative process that would aid a positive peace in Indonesia and elsewhere.

Notes

Acknowledgments. I gratefully acknowledge collegial discussion and invitations from James Peacock and the editors. Thanks also to Patrick Inman for provocative comments, and to Inman, Robin Miura, and the editors for helpful editing suggestions. Fieldwork support was provided by a research and writing grant from the John D. and Catherine T. MacArthur Foundation, and from the Wenner-Gren Foundation for Anthropological Research.

1. Indonesia's "inner islands" include the heavily populated Java, Madura, and Bali, which together hold nearly 70 percent of the Muslim-majority nation's 350 million citizens and the national capital of Jakarta, while the term "outer islands" refers to the more than 3,000 other populated islands.
2. It should be noted that these were necessary rather than sufficient conditions for violence because the turmoil of the post-Suharto era, as well as transnational Muslim-Christian hostilities, fed into Poso's violence (Aragon 2001, 2005, 2007, 2011).
3. These conclusions about the conflict-promoting role of Sulawesi's land development strategies generally are matched by those of Li (2007) and Indonesian NGO leaders such as Sangaji (2007).
4. Although beyond the scope of this chapter, it would be useful for policymakers to understand that lack of monetary wealth does not necessarily equal poverty, malnutrition, and misery in a rural subsistence economy, although that may be the case in an urban wage-labor context.
5. Coincidentally, ethnic differences within Christian groups (such as Pamona, Mori, Minahasan, and Toraja) and Muslim ethnic groups (such as Bugis, Mandar, Makasar, Gorontalo, and Javanese) became minimized as religion evolved as the axis of polarization.
6. The Basic Agrarian Law that gave the Indonesian government eminent domain powers was largely a continuation of Dutch law transferred to the newly independent republic. The 1967 forestry and investment laws promoting foreign capitalization were seen by economists of the time as the fastest way to spur national growth and prosperity, especially given Japanese interest in Indonesian timber for paper and pulp industries. Finally, transmigration policies formulated in Jakarta combined a sober realization about pan-archipelago economic inequities with prejudices about the "backward" and "nomadic" cultures of outer island peoples. Javanese who held power in Jakarta assumed that sending poor Javanese to other islands would contribute to the edification of the "less advanced" ethic groups.
7. High migration levels also were identified as a factor leading to conflicts in Irian Jaya (now Papua), East Timor (now independent), North Maluku, East Kalimantan, Riau, and Aceh (Tirtosudarmo 1995).
8. For Kelly and Kaplan (2001), the post–WWII decolonization process involves every former colonial unit being pegged into the United Nations nation-state format. This format suggests national sovereignty and a horizontal equality of

member states, but preexisting colonial era inequities and international rules foster further inequality between and within those states.

9. Comparable religious segregation patterns hold for refugees from the Ambon and Maluku conflicts, which produced more than 500,000 displaced persons.

10. Here I follow local use of terms indicating that someone is "native," "indigenous," or "original," rather than a "newcomer," recognizing that those categories are constructed, flexible, and political. The former terms connote a range of ideas, from "first settlers" or the colonial and chauvinistic term, "sons of the soil" to simply labeling residents who are descended from people with no known foreign origins.

11. Minahasa, especially the capital city of Manado, also received a large number of immigrants during the period under discussion, including displaced Christians and Muslims from the Ambon, Maluku, and Poso conflicts (see Duncan 2008).

12. To clarify, Li follows Ferguson to argue that policymakers' or outsider trustees' ultimate "identification of a problem is intimately linked with the availability of a solution" (Li 2007, 7; Ferguson 1994). They suggest that the paradigm of outsider or government interventions inevitably is shaped tacitly by a set of entrenched political economy factors that policymakers are unable, or unwilling, to change.

13. Further fieldwork will be required to assess postconflict development programs in Poso. On a positive note, Poso remained relatively quiet following political decentralization. As detailed in International Crisis Group reports, some key instigators of violent jihadist attacks were arrested (or killed) in 2007 and 2009. Yet, jihadist groups and camps have reappeared periodically in the Poso region (International Crisis Group 2007, 2008). Also, the significant alienation of ancestral farmlands for private development businesses continued as of 2012, exacerbating ethnic and religious community tensions in the Pamona and Lore Valley regions.

References

Acciaioli, Greg. 2001, October. Placing claims to land: The grounds of religious and ethnic conflict at Lake Lindu, Central Sulawesi. *Indonesia*, 72: 81–114.

Anderson, Benedict. 1991 [1983] *Imagined communities* (rev. ed.) London: Verso.

Aragon, Lorraine V. 2000. *Fields of the lord: Animism, Christian minorities, and state development in Indonesia*. Honolulu: University of Hawaii Press.

———. 2001, October. Communal violence in Poso, Central Sulawesi: Where people eat fish and fish eat people. *Indonesia*, 72: 45–79.

———. 2005, April. Mass media fragmentation and narratives of violent action in Sulawesi's Poso conflict. *Indonesia*, 79: 1–55.

———. 2007. Elite competition in Central Sulawesi. In *Renegotiating boundaries: Local politics in post-Suharto Indonesia*, edited by Henk Schulte Nordholt and Gerry Van Klinken, 39–66. Leiden: KITLV.

Aragon, Lorraine V. 2008. Reconsidering displacement and internally displaced persons (IDPs) from Poso. In *communal conflicts in Indonesia: Causes, dynamics, and displacement*, edited by Eva-Lotta Hedman, 173–205. Ithaca, NY: Cornell Southeast Asia Publications.

———. 2011. Distant processes: The global economy and outer island development in Indonesia. In *Life and death matters: Human rights, environment, and social justice*, second edition, edited by Barbara R. Johnston, 29–54. Walnut Creek, CA: Left Coast Press.

Azra, Azyumardi. 1997, December 8–12. Hadrami as educators: Al-Habib Sayyid Idrus Ibn Salim Al-Juffrie (1889–1969) and Al-Khairat. Paper presented at the KITLV International Workshop on Arabs in South-East Asia (1870–c.1990). Leiden, The Netherlands.

Babcock, Timothy. 1986. Transmigration: The regional impact of a miracle cure. In *Central government and local development in Indonesia*, edited by Colin MacAndrews, 157–189. Singapore: Oxford University Press.

Badan Pusat Statistik Kabupaten Poso. 2001. *Kabupaten Poso Dalam Angka* (Poso District in statistics 2001). Poso: BPS Poso.

Badan Pusat Statistik Sulteng. 1998. *Sulawesi Tengah Dalam Angka* (Central Sulawesi in statistics 1998). Palu: BPS Sulteng.

———. 1999. *Sulawesi Tengah Dalam Angka* (Central Sulawesi in statistics 1999). Palu: BPS Sulteng.

BAKORNAS-PBP and UN Office for the Coordination of Humanitarian Affairs. 2003, March 11–15. Joint BAKORNAS and OCHA Mission to Central Sulawesi. Retrieved from www.db.idpproject.org.

Berita Laskar Jihad. 2001a, September 22. Kongkolikong Para Kongkoli (Kongkoli's followers are schemers).

———. 2001b, November 3. Kongkoli is Kurang Ajar (Kongkoli is crude), (3).

Bertrand, Jacques. 2004. *Nationalism and ethnic conflict in Indonesia*. Cambridge: Cambridge University Press.

van Bruinessen, Martin. 2002. Genealogies of Islamic radicalism in post-Suharto Indonesia. *Southeast Asia Research*, 10 (2): 117–154.

van Dijk, Kees. 1981. *Rebellion under the banner of Islam: The Darul Islam in Indonesia*. The Hague: Martinus Nijhoff.

Dove, Michael R. 1985. The agroecological mythology of the Javanese and the political economy of Indonesia. *Indonesia*, 39: 1–36.

Duncan, Christopher R. 2003. Confusing deadlines: IDPs in Indonesia. *Forced Migration Review*, 17: 35–36.

———. 2008. Where do we go from here? The politics of ending displacement in post-conflict Maluku. In *Communal conflicts in Indonesia: Causes, dynamics, and displacement*, edited by Eva-Lotta Hedman, 207–230. Ithaca, NY: Cornell Southeast Asia Publications.

Escobar, Arturo. 1995. *Encountering development: The making and unmaking of the third world*. Princeton, NJ: Princeton University Press.

Faust, Heiko, Miet Maertens, Robert Weber, Nunung Nuryartono, Teunis van Rheenen, and Regina Birner. 2003, March. Does migration lead to destabilization of forest margins? Evidence from an interdisciplinary field study in Central Sulawesi. STORMA Discussion Paper Series, Sub-program A, No.11.

Ferguson, James. 1994. *The Anti-politics machine: "Development," depoliticization, and bureaucratic authority in Lesotho.* Minneapolis: University of Minnesota Press.

Geertz, Clifford. 1963. *Agricultural involution: The processes of ecological change in Indonesia.* Berkeley: University of California Press.

Hardjono, J. M. 1977. *Transmigration in Indonesia.* Kuala Lumpur: Oxford University Press.

Harvey, Barbara S. 1974. Tradition, Islam, and Rebellion: South Sulawesi 1950–1965. Unpublished dissertation, Cornell University, Ithaca, NY.

———. 1977. *Permesta: Half a rebellion.* Ithaca, NY: Cornell Modern Indonesia Project, Southeast Asia Program.

Hasan, Noorhaidi. 2002. Faith and politics: The rise of Laskar Jihad in the era of transition in Indonesia. *Indonesia,* 73: 145–169.

Hefner, Robert W. 1993. Islam, state, and civil society: ICMI and the struggle for the Indonesian middle class. *Indonesia,* 56: 1–37.

———. 2000. *Civil Islam: Muslims and democratization in Indonesia.* Princeton, NJ: Princeton University Press.

Henley, David, Maria J. C. Schouten, and Alex Ulaen. 2007. Preserving the peace in post-New Order Minahasa. In *Renegotiating boundaries: Local politics in post-Suharto Indonesia*, edited by Henk Schulte Nordholt and Gerry Van Klinken, 307–326. Leiden: KITLV Press.

Human Rights Watch. 2002, December. Breakdown: Four years of communal violence in Central Sulawesi. Indonesia Report 14, 9 (C).

International Crisis Group. 2002, August 8 (Corrected on January 10, 2003). Al-Qaeda in Southeast Asia: The case of the "Ngruki network" in Indonesia. Asia Briefing No. 20. Available at www.crisisgroup.org.

———. 2004, February 3. Indonesia Backgrounder: Jihad in Central Sulawesi. Asia Report No.74. Available at www.crisisgroup.org.

———. 2007, January 24. Jihadism in Indonesia: Poso on the Edge. Asia Report No.127. Available at www.crisisgroup.org.

———. 2008, January 22. Indonesia: Tackling Radicalism in Poso. Asia Briefing No.75. Available at www.crisisgroup.org.

Kato, Tsuyoshi. 1989. Different fields, similar locusts: Adat communities and the Village Law of 1979 in Indonesia. *Indonesia,* 47: 89–114.

Kelly, John D., and Martha Kaplan. 2001. *Represented communities: Fiji and world decolonization.* Chicago, IL: University of Chicago Press.

Li, Tania Murray. 2007. *The will to improve: Governmentality, development, and the practice of politics.* Durham, NC: Duke University Press.

McRae, Dave. 2007, April. Criminal justice and communal conflict: A case study of the trial of Fabianus Tibo, Dominggus da Silva and Marinus Riwu. *Indonesia,* 83: 79–117.

———. 2008. The escalation and decline of violent conflict in Poso, Central Sulawesi, 1998–2007. PhD dissertation, Australian National University.

Pelly, Usman. 1999. Akar Kerusuhan Etnis di Indonesia (The roots of ethnic conflict in Indonesia). *Antropologi Indonesia,* 58: 27–35.

Peluso, Nancy. 1992. *Rich forests, poor people.* Berkeley: University of California
Press.

Reid, Anthony. 1988. Southeast Asia in the age of commerce 1450–1690, Volume 1,
The lands below the winds. New Haven, CT: Yale University Press.

Sangaji, Arianto. 2003 *Rumput kering di balik anyir darah: Konteks sosial dari trajedi
kemanusian poso (The dry grass behind the bad blood: The social context of Poso's
humanitarian tragedy).* Palu: Yayasan Tanah Merdeka.

——. 2003–2004. Segregasi Masyarakat Poso. *Seputar Rakyat,* December
2003–January 2004: 13–17.

——. 2007. The masyarakat adat movement in Indonesia: A critical outsider's
view. In *The revival of tradition in Indonesian politics: The deployment of adat
from colonialism to indigenism,* edited by Jamie S. Davidson and David Henley,
319–336. London: Routledge.

Schrauwers, Albert. 2000. *Colonial "Reformation" in the Highlands of Central
Sulawesi, Indonesia, 1892–1995.* Toronto: Toronto University Press.

Sidel, John T. 2006. *Riots, pogroms, jihad.* Ithaca, NY: Cornell University Press.

Tirtosudarmo, Riwanto. 1995. The political demography of national integration
and its policy implications for a sustainable development in Indonesia. *Indonesian
Quarterly,* 23: 369–383.

Van Klinken, Gerry. 2007. *Communal violence and democratization in Indonesia:
Small town wars.* New York: Routledge.

CHAPTER 6

Exploring the Relationship between Development and Conflict: The Malaysian Experience

Ananthi Al Ramiah and Thillainathan Ramasamy

Introduction

Governments around the world struggle with how they can create and maintain prosperous and harmonious societies. There is no easy route to this goal and there are myriad approaches to achieving it. In this chapter, we explore this issue by considering the Malaysian experience of development and conflict.

Malaysia is an ethnoreligiously diverse country, with a population of 28.3 million people (DoS 2010). The three largest ethnic groups, the Malays, Chinese, and Indians, account for approximately 87 percent of the population. Numerically, the Malays are the biggest group (54 percent), followed by the Chinese (25 percent) and the Indians (8 percent) (DoS, 2006). Malaysia is one of only 13 countries in the postwar period to have grown at an average rate of 7 percent per year, and for at least 25 years. With this strong growth it was able to transition itself from a low to middle-income country in the 1990s, to produce a social transformation in terms of disidentifying particular ethnic groups with particular economic functions, and to create a large and vibrant middle class. This strong economic performance has occurred with relatively minimal violent interethnic conflict (compared to some other multiethnic countries at a similar stage of development), while maintaining full integration with the global economy.

Despite these successes, there have been economic and social areas in which Malaysia has lagged. It has not, like its neighbors—who were at a similar footing in the 1950s, for example, South Korea, Hong Kong, Taiwan, and Singapore—achieved the status of high-income country. Furthermore, there is considerable discontent among large segments of the population due to the perceived inequalities arising from the ethnicity-based distributional policy.

This chapter is organized as follows: we start by presenting results from our own empirical research, which highlight the individual-level links between relative deprivation, perceived in-group power, emotions, and various action tendencies, thereby providing a snapshot of the state of interethnic relations in Malaysia today. We then step back in time and provide an overview of the historic and sociopolitical context until independence in 1957, focusing in particular on the experience of, and outcomes from, the British colonial period and a brief discussion of how minority groups in Malaysia resisted assimilation. In the next three sections, we outline the politics, development policies, and conflict from the following periods: 1957–1970, 1970–1990, and 1990 onward. We then highlight some of the successes of the main postindependence development policy pursued by the Malaysian government, that is, ethnicity-based redistribution of wealth, in terms of meeting its goals. We conclude with a final analysis of the link between development and conflict in Malaysia, offering reasons for how interethnic relations have evolved into their present state, and suggest the path that they may take in the future.

Interethnic Relations in Malaysia Today

Interethnic relations in Malaysia today take place in the long shadow cast by Malaysia's history of troubled interethnic relations and policies by both the British colonists and postindependence governments. This history created and sharpened group identities. When success in realms as disparate as education, commerce, and public sector employment, among others, is dependent on ethnic group membership, group salience will be extraordinarily high. In the absence of opportunities for, and drivers toward, harmonious contact, such group salience can result in negative rather than positive generalized intergroup perceptions (Hewstone and Brown 1986). As former academic and opposition politician Syed Hussein Ali wrote: "The problems of ethnicity and ethnic relations are of much concern in Malaysia because they are ever present in our daily lives and are often regarded as threats to national unity and the welfare of the people" (Ali 2008, 1).

The policies pursued by the Malaysian government seem to have created great ethnic discontent among various groups, and the hardening of group identities. Our past data (Al Ramiah 2009) show that the Chinese and Indians have largely negative emotions toward the Malays—predominantly contempt—and also have a poor view of the capabilities of the Malays. Most interestingly, this research has found that the Malays share these negative views of their own group, and have, to some degree, internalized the negative stereotype about their group. Such discontent can sow the seeds for future violence, or on the flipside, can lead to political and/or economic disengagement by various segments of the population.

When considering the relationship between economic development policies and conflict, it is useful to assess the trajectory of these policies and any incidents of violent conflict that have occurred concurrently, as we will do in the subsequent sections of this chapter. However, we have scant knowledge about individual-level responses to particular policies at both an affective and a behavioral level. As Henry (2010) said, we lack knowledge of the mechanisms of institutional bias, and how these mechanisms are linked to different outcomes for members of different groups.

Al Ramiah (under review) assessed the impact of the redistribution policy adopted by the Malaysian government by creating a model that examined how people's sense of relative deprivation was linked with various interethnic action tendencies. This model was informed by social psychological theories that consider the relationship between intergroup cognitions, intergroup emotions, and action tendencies (Cuddy, Fiske, and Glick 2007; Mackie, Devos, and Smith 2000).

The study was conducted in Malaysia using a sample of minority adults from the general population. A total of 453 Chinese and Indian adults agreed to participate in the short questionnaire study. When asked which ethnic group in Malaysia holds the most political power, 94 percent of participants named the Malay group. Only these participants (N = 426; Chinese = 264, Indian = 162, mean age = 35.6 years) were used in the study. Questions tapping their sense of relative deprivation compared to the Malays, their perception of their own group's power to effect change in Malaysia, their intergroup emotions, fear of the state machinery, ethnic identification, perceived stability of the status quo, and their action tendencies toward the Malays were asked.

Relative deprivation was measured by the following question: "How satisfied/dissatisfied are you about your racial group's situation/position relative to the position of the Malays?" and *in-group power* by asking, "Do you feel that members of your racial group are powerful enough to change things in Malaysia?"

Fear of the state machinery was measured by asking participants, "Are you afraid to say anything against the policies in Malaysia?" *Anger towards the majority group* was measured by asking participants how "angry," "irritated," "resentful," and "bitter" they felt when thinking of the Malays; and *fear toward the majority group* was measured by the items "scared" and "nervous."

Ethnic identification was measured by the following question: "Does being a member of your racial group mean a lot to you?" and *perceived stability of the status quo* was measured by the following question: "Do you think that the economic policies in Malaysia which gives one racial group special rights will change?"

Finally, participants were asked questions about action tendencies when they thought about the majority Malays. *Confrontation action tendencies* were measured by asking participants how much they wanted to "argue with" and "confront" the Malays, and *withdrawal action tendencies* by asking participants how much they wanted to "avoid" and "have nothing to do with" the Malays. The *desire to emigrate* was measured by the following questions: "If you had the opportunity, would you like to move away from Malaysia to live in another country?" and "Do you spend much time thinking about living in another country?"

The frequency of participant responses across the response options for each construct were calculated. Here we report the proportion of participants who scored above the midpoint of the scale. Of all the participants 61 percent reported feeling deprived relative to the Malays, and 73 percent had a negative view of the economic policies of the government, considering them to be unfair to members of their ethnic group. Only 30 percent of participants felt that their ethnic groups were powerful enough to change things in Malaysia. In terms of intergroup emotions, participants reported feeling fear (16 percent) and anger (39 percent) when thinking of the Malays and also fear of the state machinery (34 percent). Also, 69 percent of participants felt highly ethnically identified, and 71 percent perceived that the system was stable and unlikely to change. Finally, in terms of action tendencies, 27 percent reported a desire to confront the Malays, 30 percent expressed a desire to avoid them, and 60 percent of the sample said that would like to emigrate from Malaysia if they could. In terms of mean differences between Chinese and Indian participants in their responses to these measures, we found that Chinese participants perceived the system to be more stable than Indians, and that Indian participants were more likely than the Chinese participants to say that they would like to emigrate from Malaysia, would confront Malays, and would withdraw from them. In a path model that comprised multiple regressions analyzed simultaneously, relative deprivation and perceived in-group power were treated as exogenous variables, and all other variables as endogenous. It was found that a sense of deprivation relative to the Malays was associated with increased anger toward the Malays, increased ethnic identification, and greater perceived system stability.[1] A sense of in-group power was associated with greater ethnic identification and less perceived system stability.[2]

What are the implications of experiencing negative emotions? People who felt more angry toward the Malays were more likely to confront the Malays, more likely to withdraw from them, and express a desire to emigrate from Malaysia.[3] Fear toward the Malays and fear of the state machinery, were both associated with the inclination to withdraw from Malays.[4] Ethnic identification was associated with greater inclination to confront Malays,[5] while perceived system stability was associated with greater inclination to withdraw from the Malays, and to emigrate from Malaysia.[6]

Thus a sense of relative deprivation was associated with anger that was itself associated with all three negative action tendencies—desire to confront, withdraw, and emigrate. This highlights the truism that a lack of interethnic conflict (particularly violent conflict) does not imply interethnic harmony. In this case, though minority group members may not easily confront Malays, their lack of confrontation is not, as some observers such as Muscat (2002) have argued, indicative of their contentment with the status quo. We also see that fear of the state mechanism drives withdrawal action tendencies. This finding emphasizes empirically that we cannot afford to ignore the role that such mechanisms play in determining the actions that individual actors take.

The finding that relative deprivation was associated with ethnic identification is an important one. Economic policies that make minority, or non-preferred, group members feel deprived seem to have the effect of sharpening divisive group identities and these identities are, in turn, associated with greater confrontational action tendencies. This pattern of results seems to describe perfectly the Hindraf rally organized by Hindu Indians in Malaysia in 2007, which will be discussed in a subsequent section of this chapter.

Relative deprivation was also associated with the perception that the status quo is a stable and unchanging one, which led to withdrawal from Malays and the desire to emigrate from Malaysia. As described above, such desire to emigrate was also predicted by anger. Thus, a feeling of deprivation relative to the Malays drove both greater perceived stability of the system and anger toward ordinary Malays, which culminates into a desire to emigrate. We found that the desire to move was particularly strong for those who were more educated (54 percent of participants with high school education and 64 percent of those with university education reported a desire to move away).

These findings about the desire to emigrate are in line with findings from a World Bank study on brain drain (2011), which is the first authoritative documentation of the phenomenon in the Malaysian context. This study found that the size of the Malaysian diaspora is large and has quadrupled over the last three decades, on a conservative estimate, to 1 million in 2010, and that a third of this figure represents brain drain. The authors found that ethnic Chinese account for almost 90 percent of the Malaysian diaspora in Singapore and that they are similarly overrepresented in the countries of the Organization for Economic Co-operation and Development (OECD). It further found that two out of ten Malaysians with a tertiary degree migrated in 2000 to an OECD country or Singapore. This is quadruple the world average. Of the inflow of migrants into the country, only about 10 percent had tertiary education, which is very dissimilar to the nature of migration into Singapore and Hong Kong, which tends to be of high-skilled labor.

Using a sample of Malaysians that was 81 percent Chinese, the report found that economic conditions and social injustice were considered as the top drivers of brain drain. The World Bank report included a second survey of those who left Malaysia but who were considering return, and found that 87 percent of respondents believed that Malaysia ought to shift its paradigm away from ethnically based policies, and toward needs-based, color-blind affirmative action.

We believe that these World Bank findings, coupled with those that we discussed by Al Ramiah (under review) offer some very important insights into the state of interethnic relations in Malaysia, at least from the perspective of minority group members, and suggest ways in which development policies and conflict can be powerfully related at the individual level. However, what the results do not tell us is how individual Malays may react if the affirmative action policies were dismantled or set to reduce over a certain time frame. The reaction of some far-right Malay groups such as Perkasa suggest that such an end of benefits could have deleterious consequence for interethnic relations (Kasim 2011). However, there are many Malays who support opposition parties (such as the Islamic party, Party Islam Semalaysia [PAS]) who call for, among other things, a change in affirmative action policies to become needs-based and color-blind. Future research is needed to ascertain how ordinary Malays would react to proposed changes to redistributive policies.

Historic and Sociopolitical Context until Independence in 1957

It was during British rule (from 1786 to 1942 and from 1945 to 1957) that Malaysian society was opened up to the mass immigration of Chinese and

Indian workers. Historical accounts show that the British did not regard the Malays as sufficiently industrious and diligent to succeed in their capitalist enterprise (see Brown 2005), but regarded them as obedient to Malay Sultans, generally amiable, but lazy and inept in commercial matters (Alatas 1977). The Malays were thus left to continue to cultivate the paddy fields and carry out fishing while the "harder work" of the colonial enterprise was left in the hands of imported labor.[7] Specifically, the Chinese from mainland China arrived in large numbers to work in the tin mines, mills, and docks, while the Indians (primarily from the southern Indian state of Tamil Nadu) were brought in as indentured labor to works in rubber estates and in public works. The British allowed each ethnic group to live segregated lives within particular segments of the economy, while also allowing vernacular (own language) schools for each group (Seng 2007). Of these schools, Seng (2007, 211) wrote: "The quality of Malay, Chinese, and Indian vernacular schools was generally poor and the curricula focused on their respective motherlands. Thus, the population became divided, and remained so for more than 150 years."

The Malays, who lived predominantly in rural areas, owned paddy and rubber smallholdings and operated in a low-productivity/high-cost environment, due to the more dispersed population in these areas. The few among them who lived in urban areas were in the government service. The immigrants, however, were engaged in a range of sectors: in urban areas they were petty traders and shopkeepers and thus enjoyed some economies of agglomeration; in rural areas they worked in the rubber estates and tin mines, which were more capital intensive and large scale and hence productive. A few of the Chinese immigrants also emerged as successful owners and operators of rubber estates and tin mines. The bigger estates and mines, as well as the agency houses that engaged in export-import trade, were, however, owned by British merchants. Due to low commodity prices and aging rubber trees (as a result of neglect of the Depression and war years as well as during the communist insurgency that broke out in 1948), the incidence of poverty was high and more so in the rural areas.

Several historians and commentators regard British policy toward interethnic relations as an instance of coordinated divide and rule (Abraham 1997; Ali 2008; Seng 2007). Given the length of British rule in Malaya,[8] they had many opportunities to mend the deeply rent social fabric, and their failure to do so is consistent with their policies in their other colonies across Southeast Asia (Brown 1997), and most notably in India (Prasad 1947). As argued by Abraham (1997), the British actively encouraged and coordinated the ethnic division of labor in such a way as to undermine their ability to coalesce to protest effectively against perceived injustices.

Japanese occupation in Malaya from 1942 to 1945, though brief, is an important component to understanding some of the attitudes toward the Chinese in Malaysia. Under Japanese occupation, the Chinese were treated with extreme cruelty and thousands were executed in the *sook ching*[9] "mass screening" conducted in 1942 (Cheah 2002). This cruelty was paired with a gentler treatment of the Malays, and this disparity in treatment led to resentment and distrust between the Chinese and Malays (Cheah 1981). Many Chinese who recoiled against the horror of Japanese occupation were greatly influenced by the Communist movement and some became members of the Malayan Communist Party (Ali 2008). With the defeat of the Japanese and the return of British rule, interethnic tensions were further fueled by the British, who worried about communist infiltration into Malaya, and portrayed the Chinese as *musuh dalam selimut* (enemies in the blanket)[10] (see Noor 2005; Rashid 1993, 27). The British were also alarmed at the Indians' allegiance to India and the independence struggle there (Ali 2008). They proposed the formation of a Malayan Union in which the Sultans' power would be diminished and all Malayans would enjoy equal citizenship rights (Rashid 1993).

These proposed policies touched at the heart of Malay identity and there was widespread and intense protest against the Malayan Union proposal. This massive uprising, the first by the Malays since colonial occupation, led to the formation of the United Malay National Organization (UMNO) in 1946 (Mohamad 2005; Rashid 1993) to defend Malay cultural and economic rights from attack by the British but, more importantly, to protect these rights from being usurped by the Chinese and Indians. UMNO viewed the need to defend Malay "special rights" (*Ketuanan Melayu*) as its raison d'être (Mohamad 2005; Muhammad Ikmal 1995). In response, the Indians and the Chinese formed, respectively, the Malayan Indian Congress (MIC) in 1946, and the Malayan Chinese Association (MCA) in 1949.

When the British started withdrawing from their colonies and Malayan independence was imminent, it became apparent to the elite of the various communitarian groups and to the British Colonial Office (Wade 2009), that some sort of alliance may be necessary between the communitarian groups in order to have political and economic stability. The Alliance Party was formed, made up of UMNO, MCA and MIC, that is, the Malay, Chinese, and Indian parties.[11] Thus a "consociational model" was established, with each party (in theory, and to varying degrees, in practice) tempering the demands and power of the other parties (Verma 2002).

In 1951, the British commissioned a report, *The Barnes Report on Malay Education* (Central Advisory Committee on Education 1951), which called for the establishment of national schools where pupils would be taught in

Malay and English and for the closure of vernacular schools. The Chinese rejected the recommendations of the report, seeing it as an attempt at assimilation and as a symbolic threat against their language and identity (Seng 2007). They expressed their discontent vocally through the Chinese press, which was taken seriously by the British who then commissioned the Fenn Wu Report (*Fenn Wu Report on Chinese Schools and the Education of Chinese Malayans* 1951) to represent the interests of the Chinese community. This report stressed the need to maintain a separate-but-equal model of education in which group identity and language were preserved in the form of the continuation of vernacular schools (Muhriz, Abdullah, and Wan Jan 2011). Subsequent educational policy has accepted the interests of non-Malay groups and has allowed for Chinese and Tamil primary schools to exist within the national school system, while teaching Malay as a second language, alongside Malay schools that teach English as a second language (*Report of the Education Review Committee* 1960).

Politics, Development Policies, and Conflicts, 1957–1970

In 1957, Malaya was more prosperous than most other newly independent countries and was the world's leading producer of natural rubber and tin. On attaining independence the country embarked on an ambitious program to grow and diversify the economy. It also resorted to an aggressive but prudent use of public expenditure to promote rural development (primarily to tackle Malay poverty) as well as to invest in education, health care, and infrastructure.

Though many scholars cite 1971—when the National Economic Policy was enacted—as the first instance of affirmative action in Malaysia,[12] the reality is that an affirmative action program was in place since independence to redress the economic imbalance between the Malays and non-Malays (in particular the Chinese). Article 153 of the constitution set out that the special position of Malays needed to be safeguarded; in the run up to independence, the Alliance party determined that the Chinese and the Indians would have equal citizenship rights (subject to residential qualifications) and in exchange the special status of the Malays would be protected in educational, social, and economic matters.

This program of affirmative action was carried out through a firm commitment to growth, and without undermining the extent of Malaysia's integration with the world economy. The commonly held view then was that rural poverty was caused by the small and fragmented size of farm holdings, low productivity, and exploitation by the middlemen. The traditional peasant economy of small-scale rubber production and paddy farming coexisted with the modern economy of large-scale rubber estates and tin mines, 75 percent of which were owned by foreigners (Anand 1983). The government did not nationalize or expropriate the large estates to redistribute land for boosting the size of the peasant economy (as did some countries that were taken up by the rapid rise and apparent dynamism of socialist and communist economies), but instead, restricted state land to be used for new rubber and palm oil plantations and for resettling Malay rural households to own and work on this land. State agencies (of which FELDA, the Federal Land Development Authority set up in 1956, was the best example), which were funded by the World Bank, acted as the developer and manager of these schemes to be run as "estates" (rather than small holdings).

To improve productivity in the rubber industry, the government also provided grants (from a fund mobilized from the levy of a replanting tax on rubber exports) to replant aging rubber trees with higher-yielding clones. This replanting program benefited rubber smallholders of whom two-thirds were Malay. To improve productivity among paddy farmers, who were also predominantly Malay, the government provided free irrigation facilities for the double cropping of paddy, higher-yielding seeds, fertilizers, and pesticides, as well as technical advice for the effective utilization of these inputs. Cooperatives and farmers' organizations were also set up to buy and mill the paddy into rice, as well as to provide subsidized credit (during the planting season) in competition with the private sector so as to minimize the risk of exploitation by middlemen (Cheah 2002). The government also created a range of other institutions directly and indirectly aimed at uplifting the Malay community, such as MARA (Majlis Amanah Rakyat, which is the Council of Trust for the Indigenous People, an agency set up in 1966 to facilitate and carry out economic and social development particularly in rural areas), FAMA (Federal Agricultural Marketing Authority, set up in 1965 to improve market access and pricing for rural produce), and Bank Bumiputera (incorporated in 1965 to increase Bumiputera participation in the economy). These programs were funded by the federal government through its annual budget.

The government also promoted industrialization to further diversify the economy and create jobs to absorb the rapidly expanding labor force. Initially the focus was on an import-substitution strategy, but by 1968, Malaysia extended fiscal incentives to export-oriented manufacturing with tax breaks given both on the capital invested as well as labor utilized, to encourage more employment. The government also opted to rely on private enterprise and not on public ownership so as to ensure that performance was more geared to the incentives of the marketplace. The government simultaneously invested heavily in education, health care, and infrastructure to support private investment in modern agriculture, manufacturing, and services.

Despite the government's efforts, there was an increase in interethnic income imbalances over the 1957–1970 period.[13] There was much discontent among the Malays, who seemed to be floundering economically compared to the Chinese in terms of the continued high incidence of poverty and identification of ethnicity with economic function (Jomo 1990; Salih and Yusof 1989). However, the non-Malays, particularly the Chinese, felt highly threatened by these various policies and the institutional bias in favor of the Malays. This led to the creation and strengthening of opposition parties, such as the Democratic Action Party (DAP), Gerakan (both parties with a predominantly Chinese membership, though intended to be multiracial parties), and PAS.

Campaigning against institutional bias enabled DAP and Gerakan to make significant strides in eroding popular support among the Chinese and Indian voters for the ruling Alliance Party in 1969; the Alliance returned to power, but with a considerably diminished majority. On May 13, 1969, victory celebrations by the opposition parties fueled Malay discontent and heightened the perception of Chinese-posed threat, which quickly escalated into conflict (the worst interethnic riot Malaysia has experienced) and resulted in the torching of homes and businesses and more than one hundred deaths (Kua 2007). A state of emergency was declared (which was to last two years) and the government used the Internal Security Act (a vestige of British colonialism) to detain without trial those who threatened national security (i.e., those who questioned the special position of the Malays or the status of Malay as the national language). There was also press censorship and restrictions were placed on political activity (Mohamad 2005). The shock of the riots made it expedient for the government to find a way to restore order on an ongoing basis, and served as an impetus for the formation of the New Economic Policy (NEP).

Politics, Development Policies, and Conflicts, 1971–1990

The NEP, launched in 1971, was intended to redress interethnic discontent arising from what was perceived to be an unequal distribution of resources and opportunities for advancement across the different ethnic groups. The NEP's objectives were twofold: the first objective cut across racial and ethnic distinctions and prioritized the eradication of poverty by the end of the policy period in 1990; the second objective was focused on uplifting the groups (specifically the Bumiputera) who had been disadvantaged by British colonialism (Jomo 2004). Clearly the first objective was uncontroversial. The second objective was by and large accepted by the non-Bumiputera citizens who likely saw its importance in maintaining social stability (Munro-Kua 1996) after the shock of the May 1969 riots. This is an important point to emphasize in the context of this chapter, because it suggests that the non-Bumiputera Chinese and Indians may have accepted the policy that was, on the face of it, biased against them, in order to safeguard their physical and material well-being (such as it was). Further, the Second Malaysia Plan that enunciated the NEP stated categorically that the reduction in racial imbalances was to be undertaken in an environment of an expanding economy so "that no particular group will experience any loss or feel any sense of deprivation" (*Second Malaysia Plan* 1971).

The NEP, which Muscat (2002) has described as the most comprehensive and successful set of developmental policies implemented to avoid inter-ethnic conflict, involved the setting of a 30 percent quota for the ownership of Malay corporate wealth, and employment composition in the modern sector of the economy reflective of the population composition by the end of the NEP period. In addition, the policy enforced preferential selection for Bumiputera students at institutions of higher education, such that they were given lower entry requirements to gain admission (Seng 2007).

There were key differences in affirmative action policies in the pre- and post-1971 period. Crucially, there were no explicit distributional targets in the form of clearly defined quotas in the pre-1970 period. Under the NEP, there were explicit targets set with respect to more balanced employment and wealth ownership, but not with respect to income. Quotas were imposed for the reservation of shares in Initial Public Offerings (IPOs) and for places in educational institutions. In employment, opportunities at all levels in the public sector including in government-linked companies were reserved almost wholly for the Bumiputera community. With respect to the private sector, generally no such quotas have been imposed (with the possible exception of those private sector entities that were the beneficiaries of government contracts, or in banking where the Central Bank of Malaysia has on occasion admonished banks for not hiring adequate numbers of Bumiputera employees). Under the Industrial Coordination Act, enacted in 1975, the authorities had the power to impose conditions on manufacturers applying for licenses with respect to the reservation of shares as well as jobs for the Bumiputera community.

With the country in a deep recession from 1985 to 1986 (due in varying degrees to the collapse in commodity prices following the bursting of the global inflationary bubble, the poor finances of the government and country, and the banking crisis) the government looked to the private sector as the new engine of growth. To kick start private investment, the government reduced income tax rates, reformed the labor market to make wages more flexible, and resorted to privatization on a large scale (e.g., in utilities, transport, gaming, education, and health care) to increase efficiency as well as to improve government finances. The government also substantially liberalized the Industrial Coordination Act. For example, from late 1986, foreign enterprises were exempt from reserving any shares for Bumiputera, provided they employed at least 350 full-time Malaysian workers or exported 50 percent or more of their output.

Further, Mohamad (2005; see also Coppel 1982) highlights several policies aimed at reaffirming the Malays' social and political power, such as the policy to make Malay the medium of education across all national schools in 1969, increased Islamization of school education, and the rise of UMNO as the most important of all the Barisan Nasional component parties (p. 14). She cites how the combined use of the affirmative action policy and these other changes established the Malays as the dominant group in Malaysia, thereby giving them a sense of group cohesion and strengthening their identity.

The provisions laid out in Article 153 of the Constitution were meant to be reviewed in 1972, 15 years after independence. However, the May 1969 riot and the subsequent adoption of the NEP meant that no such review was undertaken. As Wade (2009) points out, in 1970, a Malay cabinet minister vowed that Malay special privileges would remain for "hundreds of years to come" (p. 24).

Politics, Development Policies, and Conflicts, 1991 onward

The NEP transmuted into the National Development Policy (1991–2000), then into the National Vision Policy (2001–2010), and most recently into the New Economic Model (2010–2020). The Eighth Malaysia Plan, released in 2001, emphasized, among other things, continued focus on Bumiputera corporate ownership, and, in addition, stressed the need to increase Bumiputera uptake of high-income occupations, including entrepreneurship and the professions (*Eighth Malaysia Plan* 2001). The various reincarnations of the affirmative action policy illustrate the centrality of the distributional goal, and this is likely to have been due to political pressure from key stakeholders. Ariff (2011) has stated that the New Economic Model (the latest incarnation of the affirmative action policy) has been subject to vehement criticism by the Malay Consultative Council (comprising 76 Malay nongovernmental organizations [NGO]) for not being more unequivocally pro-Bumiputera. For example, many groups, such as Perkasa (an openly Malay supremacist NGO) reacted angrily in 2009 to the then new prime minister Najib Tun

Razak's plan to extend market-liberalizing policies to the services sector of the economy. Thus in the Tenth Malaysia Plan, there was no mention of this liberalization proposal.

In the post-Asian crisis period, the Malaysian economy has experienced lackluster growth and appears to have entered into a middle-income trap. This can be partly attributed to the failure of the government to continue with the liberalization program that it embarked on after the mid-1980s economic crisis. Further, due to the remaining implicit and explicit quotas on educational admission, the education system is not committed to excellence and is not producing enough knowledge workers and high-quality graduates. In addition, some of the brightest students are emigrating because of the government's lack of commitment to a meritocratic policy, and this shortfall is not being bridged by importing high-skilled labor from abroad. Despite spending double the amount on education as compared to Singapore and South Korea (as a percentage of gross domestic product [GDP]), there are too few Malaysian graduates with the required talent and the innovative capacity to move the country's manufacturing higher up the value chain.

While Malaysia's national education policy has made important strides in transforming it from its ethnically divided colonial form, it remains as yet a considerably fractured system. The switch from vernacular and English to Malay-medium instruction has had the effect of improving proficiency in Malay for all citizens and establishing it as the primary medium of inter-ethnic communication (Omar 1982), but this has not been very effective in blurring ethnic differences and in leading to the establishment of a national identity. As an indication of this, Seng (2007) reports that only 2 percent of ethnically Chinese students attend Malay-medium national schools, 98 percent preferring Chinese-medium schools instead. Ali (2008) and Mohamad (2005) report a similarly high percentage of vernacular school attendance for ethnically Indian students. This is evidence of significant segregation among the three largest ethnic groups. While Chinese and Indian parents may not openly express their discontent over the affirmative action and other policies that privilege the Malays, the low attendance of their children at national Malay-medium schools can be read as an indication of their discontent and their lack of faith in the "mainstream" educational system.

The establishment of the National Service Programme in 2004 (a three month military style camp in which young people from different ethnoreligious groups live together with the aim of, among other things, improving national integration) and the mooting of the Malaysia concept (which is intended to preserve and enhance unity in diversity) can be construed as resulting from the government's concern that Malaysians are living polarized and ethnically sensitized lives.

Development Policies from 1957 to Present:
To What Extent Were Redistributive Goals Met?

Early government policies focused on rural development and so the rate of urbanization was fairly constant between 1957 and 1970, at about 25–27 percent of the population (Leete 2007). Thereafter, it picked up dramatically due to rapid industrialization and economic growth, to reach 63 percent of the population in 2005. The share that agriculture, industry, and services contributed to total employment in the period between 1957 and 2005 can be seen in Table 6.1; it demonstrates a marked reduction in agricultural employment and shift to industry and services-based employment over that period.

The great strides that the Bumiputera and, in particular, the Malays have made is due, in large measure, to their educational attainments. In 1967–1968 a large percentage of the active population had not received any education; but whereas this applied to only 18 percent of the Chinese, it was true of a quarter of the Indians and a third of the Malays. Although members of the three ethnic groups had equivalent levels of primary education, there were marked dissimilarities in secondary and tertiary education in 1967–1968, as can be seen in Table 6.2. These interethnic gaps seem to have closed by 2004.

Table 6.1 Share that Agriculture, Industry, and Services Contributed to Malaysia's Total Employment between 1957 and 2005

	1957	2005
Employment in agriculture (as share of total employment)	57.5%	12.6%
Employment in industry (as share of total employment)	15.3%	35.2%
Employment in services (as share of total employment)	27.2%	52.3%

Sources: Leete (2007).

Table 6.2 Proportion of People from Each Ethnic Group with Secondary and Tertiary Educational Qualifications between 1967/1968 and 2004

	1967/1968		2004	
	Secondary	Tertiary	Secondary	Tertiary
Malays	7.1%	1.1%	59.5%	20.9%
Chinese	20.7%	2.2%	57.2%	21.1%
Indians	17.7%	2.2%	59.5%	16.9%

Sources: DoS (2004); Thillainathan (1976).

With respect to entry into domestic institutions of higher learning, there was an increase in the preferential admission of Bumiputera students. At the university level, for example, Bumiputera students admitted as a percentage of total admitted students increased from 39.7 percent in 1970 to 62.7 percent in 1980 and 69.9 percent in 1999 (Lee 2006). Though public education is heavily subsidized, the norm is for Bumiputera students to study on scholarship, whether they are enrolled in public or private institutions and in local or overseas institutions.

Table 6.3 presents statistics on the change in the percentage of Bumiputera urban dwellers, and the change in the percentage of Bumiputera employed in various occupations from after independence until the last decade, all of which show marked increases. Employment by occupational group for the period 2000 and beyond is now based on a new standard classification of occupations. This makes it difficult to make comparisons with prior years. But even on the new basis, the Bumiputera continue to make steady progress. The share of Bumiputera who were senior officials and managers as well as professionals increased from 11 percent in 2000 to 11.5 percent in 2005. Over the same period, those who were technicians and associate professionals increased from 13.5 percent to 14.6 percent (*Ninth Malaysia Plan* 2006).

The corporate landscape is more balanced now as compared to the pre-1969 situation (Meerman 2008). For example, in the last decade, of the top 100 companies, 22 were owned by the government and 16 were owned by Bumiputera, while 49 were owned by Chinese. However, with respect to the top ten companies, six were government-linked companies and three were Chinese. It is important to note that government-linked companies, which employ very large numbers of Bumiputera employees at all levels of the organization, dominate the corporate landscape, accounting for 40 percent of the Malaysian market capitalization.

Table 6.3 Percentage of Bumiputera Living in Urban Areas and Employed in Various Occupations Post-independence

Sector	Percentage (Year)	Percentage (Year)
Urban dwellers	11 (1957)	54 (2005)
Professional, technical, administrative, and managerial occupations	4.7 (1970)	16.6 (2000)
Registered[a] professionals	4.9 (1970)	38.8 (2005)

[a] Registered professionals refer to those registered to practises such as architects, accountants, dentists, doctors, engineers, lawyers, surveyors, and veterinarians.

Sources: Lee (2006); *Tenth Malaysia Plan* (2011); *Third Malaysia Plan* (1976).

Malaysia has also made progress in significantly reducing poverty; overall poverty, which was 49.3 percent in 1970, declined to 5.7 percent by 2004 (Leete 2007). The progress registered by the Bumiputera was particularly dramatic. Their poverty rate declined from 64.8 percent to 8.3 percent between 1970 and 2004. Interestingly, the data also show a fairly significant decline in Bumiputera poverty even between 1957 and 1970 (Leete 2007), demonstrating the effectiveness of the pre-NEP affirmative action policies.

In terms of income inequality, we present data on the ratio of mean monthly household income of non-Bumiputera to Bumiputera. This interethnic income ratio (IRR), which was 2.25 in 1970 has reduced to be within the range of 1.6 to 1.8 between 1984 and 2004 (Meerman 2008). Meerman, however, contends that the continuing discrepancy in mean income between groups may largely be due to the concentration of poverty in rural areas, and may be overestimated because it does not take into account the various subsidies that Bumiputera receive. He estimates that presently the actual disparity in income between the non-Bumiputera and Bumiputera in the modern sector ranges only between 1.15 and 1.31. Further, Meerman (2008, 107) argues that continued use of this indicator to continue redistribution efforts will perpetuate "policies that do not effectively address residual Bumiputera poverty, but do encourage emerging inequality within each major ethnic group." As further evidence of intragroup disparities, Ariff (2011) has pointed out that the within-group Gini coefficient (a measure of income inequality) is rising for all groups in Malaysia.

After the outbreak of the financial crisis, the performance of the Malaysian economy has been lackluster. The average annual GDP growth rate during the first decade of this century has been 4.6 percent. The widespread consensus is that Malaysia has been caught in a middle-income trap from the late 1990s. This feeble growth can partly be explained by the much lower rate of private investment as a share of gross national product (GNP), and a decline in foreign direct investment (FDI). Athukorala and Wagle (2011, 1) state that "outflow of FDI from Malaysia has consistently surpassed inflow of FDI, a pattern not seen in the other major Southeast Asian countries." The authors attribute the decline in Malaysia's FDI performance (and in the country's growth rate) to two factors. The first is the dualistic investment policy regime, which has freed the export-oriented light manufacturing industries (such as electrics and electronics) to foreign ownership, while several other sectors are subject to regulations on local and particularly Bumiputera ownership, which does not allow multinational companies to maximize profits (Lim 1992). The second factor is the narrow domestic human-capital base, which results in a shortage of high-skilled labor (because of the ethnicity-based admissions policies in operation at the tertiary education level), and leads to a lack of innovation.

In summary, it seems that the development policies focused on ethnicity-based redistributive goals have been successful in raising the participation of the Bumiputera in all sectors of the modern economy (crucially increasing their educational attainment) and has contributed to an increase in their absolute wealth, and their wealth relative to the Chinese and Indians. The figures presented in this section also offer clear evidence that government policies have been highly successful in dis-identifying ethnicity and economic function, a key goal of the NEP. There have, however, been economic costs to these policies, as we have shown in this section (beyond some of the social costs that we have already discussed and will discuss in the next section), though further discussion of these falls outside the scope of this chapter.

Conflict and Fear of the State Machinery

For much of Malaysian history postindependence, the Chinese and Indians have been relatively acquiescent to the affirmative action policy, despite it being disadvantageous to their own groups. Indeed, beyond the May 1969 riots, there have been few incidences of Malays attacking Chinese or vice versa (Jayasankaran 1999). Muscat (2002) attributes this acquiescence to the belief of these communities that the policies were reasonable in the context of a growing economy, and goes so far as to say that these communities may have considered it a small price to pay for interethnic harmony. However, we cannot underestimate the climate of fear that may have prevailed at the time, stoked by political figures. The Barisan Nasional, particularly its dominant party of UMNO, had spun, and continues to spin, the events of May 1969 into epic proportion, giving rise to a feeling among all citizens that Malay privileges must be respected and that dissent can lead to the recurrence of such riots (Chin 2001), as we will see below. The frequent use of such historical referents can be seen as a legitimizing myth (Jost and Banaji 1994) for the continued supremacy of one group over others. Mohamad (2005) argues that such fear-instilling discourse enabled the Malay elites to gain further advantages for their in-group through the "opportunity structures" (Munro-Kua 1996), provided by the NEP and through a range of state mechanisms that instill fear and deter dissent.

For example, the Internal Security Act was used extensively during 1987 when the government carried out an operation (Operasi Lalang) to detain without trial over one hundred opposition members who had spoken out against the government's policies, particularly with regard to the protection of the Chinese language and vernacular schools (Rashid 1993). Examples of other such state mechanisms include the University and University Colleges Act (enacted in 1971), which prevented university students and staff from engaging in any activity that might be deemed political, and the Printing Presses and Publication Act (enacted in 1984, but which evolved from the Printing Presses Act of 1948), which required that all printing presses had to have their licenses authorized by the government every year.

Fear is also stoked very openly by some Malay politicians in UMNO in their public statements. In a rally organized around the time of Operasi Lalang, and which was led by the current prime minister of Malaysia, Najib Tun Razak, then the UMNO youth chief, many supporters hoisted banners carrying phrases such as "revoke the citizenship of those who oppose the Malay rulers," "May 13 has begun," and "soak it (referring to the keris) with Chinese blood" (Lim 2000).

Such threats have continued unabated. The following statement by UMNO deputy chairperson Badruddin Amiruldin, made in the 2004 UMNO General Assembly, is an example of an open expression of threat against those who question Malay rights: "Fifty-eight years ago we had an agreement with the other races, in which we permitted them to *menumpang* (temporarily reside) on this land. In the Federal Constitution, our rights as a race have been enshrined ... Let no one from the other races ever question the rights of Malays on this land. Don't question the religion because this is my right on this land" (as cited in Noor 2005). Similar threats were made at the 2006 UMNO General Assembly by several high-profile politicians (Ioannis 2006), including the then-minister for education (now minister for home affairs) and the then-minister of agriculture (now deputy prime minister).

Muscat (2002) heralds Malaysia's development policies, primarily those based on inter-ethnic redistribution, as having been highly successful, and points to the absence of interethnic tensions as the confirmation of this success, arguing that a win-win situation was created for all Malaysians. However, he neglects to account for the role that fear of the state machinery could have played in containing interethnic discontent from spilling into open protest for most of Malaysia's post-independence history. Muscat says that even for the Indians, who have fared the worst under the redistributive policies, "there is no sign that their lagging participation in the country's income growth is causing their radicalization or any ethnic mobilization for mounting a challenge to the state" (2002, 81).

Recent events have shown that this view may have been myopic. Thousands of Indians took part in a mass antigovernment protest held in late 2007. The protest was organized by the Hindu Rights Action Force and its appeal to

Indians (the majority of whom are Hindus) was an example of members of this group coalescing around religion rather than their traditional ethnic/ racial identity. It is possible that in the face of increasing Islamization of Malaysia (Mohamad 2006), religion rather than race/ethnicity served as the most potent mobilizing force for the Indians, who defined themselves in opposition to the Malay-Muslims. This may also be attributable to the then recent destruction of Hindu temples throughout Malaysia. The protestors' principal grievance was against the affirmative action policy, which they believed had unfairly disadvantaged them, leading to their poverty and marginalization. Thus we see a real-world, large-scale enactment of the kinds of individual-level relationships that we reported from Al Ramiah (under review). There we found that minority group members who reported feeling deprived relative to the Malays, also reported feeling angry toward them, and this in turn was associated with an inclination to confront them.

Muscat (2002) himself argues that continued use of redistributive policies beyond the policy period, and beyond the objective achievement of redistributive goals, may have a perverse effect on nonrecipients. The reaction of the Indians in Malaysia in 2007 can be seen as an instance of such a perverse situation arising from the perceived immutability of redistributive policies. Al Ramiah (under review) also presents evidence supporting the role that such perceived system stability can play in driving people's actions. Sowell (1989) argued that most redistributive policies tend to outlive their sunset clauses (in the case of Malaysia, this was set to be 1990 in the first instance and then no clear cutoff date was set in subsequent versions of the policy) across the different countries in which they are instituted, due to the political pressures exerted by various stakeholders who fear the end of privilege.

The populace's discontent was most powerfully demonstrated in the poor showing of the ruling coalition of Barisan Nasional in the 2008 General Elections. Though Barisan Nasional was still able to form the subsequent government, its power was significantly curtailed by the rise of the opposition coalition made up of parties with a diverse set of interests, including, importantly, the abolition of affirmative action policies. The success of the opposition in controlling five states in Peninsular Malaysia is an expression of the openness of many Malaysians to, among other things, move beyond communitarian politics and ethnically defined special rights. The recent large-scale "Bersih" protest held in Malaysia in July 2011, calling for free and fair elections and the government's angry reaction to it, including warning people not to attend the rally, denying it official permission to be held, detaining hundreds of protest leaders and organizers, and spraying protestors with chemical gas (Gooch 2011), is a demonstration of voters' discontent with the electoral system that has kept one party in place since independence. It is also a positive sign that people feel sufficiently empowered to protest perceived injustice, even when the government uses the various instruments at its disposal to quell dissent.

Final Analysis: Development and Conflict in Malaysia

We argue that three factors have contributed to the state of interethnic relations in Malaysia today. First, as we have described, the government has pursued a range of policies with the objective of eradicating poverty, uplifting the Malays, and promoting growth and international trade. These policies have led Malaysia to be well-integrated with the global economy since independence, which has been a key driver of Malaysia's growth. The policies have also led to the disassociation of race and economic function, such that there is now a significant Malay middle class. The redistributive policies of the type that we discussed may have had the value of providing security for the Malays in that they had opportunities for advancement, and that they would not continually be less successful than their non-Malay counterparts. This may have gone some way toward containing interethnic tensions (Mohamad 2005). Second, as Ariff (2011) points out, much of the postindependence period (with the exception of some short-lived recessionary episodes) coincided with strong global growth and demand for Malaysian products and commodities. This high rate of growth, particularly from the mid-1980s, led to an increasingly large Malaysian economy, in which everyone prospered, even if at relatively different rates. Such prosperity may have dulled the relative deprivation felt by members of different ethnic groups, as their wealth was increasing in absolute terms. It could also be argued that the relative interethnic calm enhanced Malaysia's ability to grow at such high and sustained rates. It is impossible to disentangle the two, and we believe that development policies and the lack of frequent or long-term interethnic conflict are likely to have reinforced one another and boosted growth. Third, we cannot understate the power of the state machinery, threatening political rhetoric and the use of legitimizing myths, in stemming dissent. These various manifestations of state power, and their use from time to time, remind people that they take a big risk when speaking out against the government and its policies. Thus, we argue that interethnic conflict has been restricted to its more subtle forms, such as negative stereotyping and prejudice, rather than taking the form of open and violent conflicts, though, as we have shown, there have been some incidents of this nature as well. Further, as we have shown, non-Malay Malaysians (especially those who are more educated) express a desire to disengage with Malays and to migrate from the country if the opportunity should arise.

We do not believe, as Muscat (2002) has argued, that "in the case of Malaysia since the 1969 riots, the restoration and maintenance of social stability, squarely based on the extensive market-intervention preferences system, has avoided recurrence of ethnic conflict" (p. 210). As we have shown, there are many forms of state machinery and attendant public discourse that serve to remind Malaysians of the fragility of interethnic relations, and the dangers of arguing against government policies. Thus it can be argued that the relative peace that Malaysia enjoys is in part at least, of a coercive nature.

Thus, we present a tempered view of Malaysia's success in managing its development and multiethnic population. While its apparent success may be attributed to a range of factors *in addition* to its various development policies, its failures, in terms of managing interethnic tensions, seem more directly related to the continuation of its ethnicity-based affirmative action policies for the redistribution of wealth across virtually every sphere in Malaysia.

Given Malaysia's successes to date and the present state of interethnic relations in the country, we conclude this chapter with a quote from Meerman (2008, 108): "Future social cohesion and continued growth would be better served by a different non-ethnic focus: on reduced rural poverty and enhanced public sector productivity and incomes. Both growth and social cohesion would be served by a more meritocratic approach to education and public sector employment."

Notes

1. $\beta = .33, p < .001, \beta = .14, p < .001$ and $\beta = .24, p < .001$, respectively
2. $\beta = .31, p < .001$ and $\beta = -.20, p < .001$, respectively
3. $\beta = .30, p < .001, \beta = .27, p < .001$, and $\beta = .29, p < .001$, respectively
4. $\beta = .14, p < .001$ and $\beta = .08, p < .10$, respectively
5. $\beta = .10, p < .05$
6. $\beta = .12, p < .01$, and $\beta = .16, p < .001$, respectively
7. The Malays may not have opted to work as plantation laborers, as the going wage rate was below what they could have earned as farmers or even as farm hands
8. Malaysia was known as "Malaya" during British colonization.
9. *Sook ching* means "to purge".
10. That is, "enemies too close by".
11. The Alliance party is now known as the National Front (*Barisan Nasional*) and includes several other parties.
12. Malaya became known as "Malaysia" in 1963, when the northern Borneo states of Sabah and Sarawak became part of the federation. The final brushstroke in the formation of Malaysia was when Singapore left the federation in 1965. It has been argued that the inclusion of Sabah and Sarawak with their indigenous Bumiputera populations, and the exclusion of Singapore with its

predominantly Chinese population, was done with the aim of establishing a Bumiputera majority (Mohamad 2005). Both Mohamad (2005) and Muzaffar (1983, as cited in Ward and Hewstone, 1985) argue that interethnic identities have since been narrowed in terms of meaningful discourse, into the dichotomous identities of Bumiputera versus non-Bumiputera.

13. There were several reasons why policies for social restructuring and growth were slow to bear fruit. First, the rate of saving and investment was lower in the aftermath of independence, given investor uncertainties on the stance of policy. Second, the banking system did not provide project or term financing and, therefore, firms had to rely on internal sources of finance for undertaking long-dated projects which again held back the pace of investment and growth. Third, the decline in key commodity prices had adversely affected growth in real incomes despite the enormous increase in acreage and substantial boost in productivity (Anand 1983). Finally, and most importantly, the benefits of these major developments were reaped only in the post-1970 period, given the long gestation for project development or growth of the tree crops before they yielded an income stream.

References

Abraham, C. R. E. 1997. *Divide and rule: The roots of race relations in Malaysia.* Kuala Lumpur: INSAN.

Al Ramiah, A. 2009. *Intergroup relations in Malaysia: Identity, contact, and threat.* Oxford: University of Oxford.

———. under review. Fight or flight: The role of relative deprivation, emotions, identification and perceived stability in determining ethnic minorities' actions.

Alatas, S. H. 1977. *The Myth of the lazy native: A study of the image of the Malays, Filipinos and Javanese from the 16th to the 20th Century and Its Function in the Ideology of Colonial Capitalism.* New York: Routledge.

Ali, Syed Hussein. 2008. *Ethnic relations in Malaysia: Harmony and conflict.* Petaling Jaya: SIRD.

Anand, S. 1983. *Inequality and poverty in Malaysia: Measurement and decomposition.* New York: Oxford University Press.

Ariff, Mohamed. 2011. Development strategy under scrutiny. In *Malaysia's development challenges: Graduating from the Middle,* edited by H. Hill, S. Y. Tham, and R. H. M. Zin. xvii–xxiii, London, United Kingdom: Routledge.

Athukorala, P. C., and S. Wagle. 2011. Foreign direct investment in Southeast Asia: Is Malaysia falling behind? *mimeograph. The Barnes Report of Malay Education,* 1951. Central Advisory Committee on Education.

Brown, G. 2005. The formation and management of political identities: Indonesia and Malaysia compared. *Centre for Research on Inequality, Human Security and Ethnicity, CRISE, Working Paper 10.*

Brown, I. 1997. *Economic change in South-East Asia, c.1830–1980.* Kuala Lumpur: Oxford University Press.

Central Advisory Committee on Education. 1951. *The report of the Committee on Malay* Education. Kuala Lumpur: Government of Malaya.

Cheah, B. K. 1981. Sino-Malay conflicts in Malaya, 1945–1946: Communist vendetta and Islamic resistance. *Journal of Southeast Asian Studies,* 12: 108–117.

———. 2002. Japanese Army policy toward the Chinese and Malay-Chinese relations in wartime Malaya. In *Southeast Asian Minorities in the Wartime Japanese Empire,* edited by P. H. Kratoska, 97–110. London: RoutledgeCurzon.

Chin, J. 2001. Malaysian Chinese politics in the 21st Century: Fear, service and marginalisation. *Asian Journal of Political Science,* 9: 78–94.

Coppel, C. 1982. *The Chinese in Indonesia, the Philippines and Malaysia.* London: Minority Rights Group.

Cuddy, A. J. C., S. T. Fiske, and P. Glick. 2007. The BIAS map: Behaviors from intergroup affect and stereotypes. *Journal of Personality and Social Psychology,* 92: 631–648.

DoS. 2004. Labour Force Survey Report.

———. 2006. *Malaysian statistics handbook.* Malaysia: Department of Statistics.

———. 2010. *Malaysian statistics handbook.* Malaysia: Department of Statistics.

Eighth Malaysia Plan. 2001. Economic Planning Unit.

Fenn Wu report on Chinese schools and the education of Chinese Malayans. 1951.

Gooch, L. 2011, July 9. Thousands of Malaysians rally for changes to elections. *New York Times.* Retrieved from http://www.nytimes.com/2011/07/10/world/asia/10malaysia.html

Henry, P. J. 2010. Institutional bias. In *The Sage handbook of prejudice, stereotyping and discrimination,* edited by J. F. Dovidio, M. Hewstone, P. Glick, and V. M. Esses, 426–440. London: Sage.

Hewstone, M., and R. Brown. 1986. Contact is not enough: An intergroup perspective on the "contact hypothesis." In *Contact and conflict in intergroup encounters,* edited by M. Hewstone and R. Brown, 1–44. Oxford: Blackwell.

Ioannis, G. 2006. Islam Hadhari in Malaysia. In *Current trends in Islamist ideology,* Volume 3, edited by H. Fradkin, H. Haqqani, and E. Brown, 78–88. Washington, DC: Hudson Institute.

Jayasankaran, S. 1999. Easing up: Malaysia looks set to review its affirmative-action policy—which could open opportunities. *Far Eastern Economic Review,* 162: 52–53.

Jomo, K. S. 1990. Whither Malaysia's New Economic Policy. *Pacific Affairs,* 63: 469–499.

———. 2004. *The New Economic Policy and interethnic relations in Malaysia.* Geneva: United Nations Research Institute for Social Development.

Jost, J. T., and M. R. Banaji. 1994. The role of stereotyping in system-justification and the production of false consciousness. *British Journal of Social Psychology,* 33: 1–27.

Kasim, R. H. 2011. Sejauhmana kompaknya "kontrak sosial?" [Electronic Version]. Retrieved from http://www.pribumiperkasa.com/?p=3256. Accessed August 9, 2012.

Kua, K. S. 2007. *May 13: Declassified documents on the Malaysian Riots of 1969*. Petaling Jaya: Suaram.

Lee, H. G. 2006. Globalization and ethnic integration in Malaysian education. In *Malaysia, recent trends and Challenges*, edited by S. H. Saw and K. Kesavapany, 230–259. Singapore: Institute of Southeast Asian Studies.

Leete, R. 2007. *From kampung to twin towers: 50 years of economic and social development*. Kuala Lumpur, Malaysia: Oxford Fajar.

Lim, D. 1992. The dynamics of economic policy-making: A study of Malaysian trade policies and performance. In *The dynamics of economic policy reforms in South-east Asia and the South-west Pacific*, edited by A. J. MacIntyre and K. Jayasuriya, 94–114. Singapore: Oxford University Press.

Lim, K. S. 2000. GPMS' extremist demands—a prelude to escalation of ethnic tensions to justify another Operation Lalang mass crackdown to shore up Mahathir and UMNO's tottering position? [Electronic Version]. Accessed on December 21, 2005.

Mackie, D. M., T. Devos, and E. R. Smith. 2000. Intergroup emotions: Explaining offensive action tendencies in an intergroup context. *Journal of Personality and Social Psychology*, 79: 602–616.

Meerman, J. 2008. The Malaysian success story, the public sector and inter-ethnic inequality. In *Globalisation and national autonomy: The Malaysian experience*, edited by J. Nelson, J. Meerman, and E. Embong. Singapore: ISEAS.

Mohamad, M. 2005. Ethnicity and inequality in Malaysia: A retrospect and a rethinking. *Centre for Research on Inequality, Human Security and Ethnicity, CRISE, Working Paper 9*.

———. 2006, September 21. Is Malaysian an Islamic state? *The Guardian*.

Muhammad Ikmal, S. 1995. Malay nationalism and national identity. *Suomen Antropologi*, 2: 11–31.

Muhriz, T. A., A. Abdullah, and W. S. Wan Jan. 2011. *Choice, competition and the role of private providers in the Malaysian school system*. Kuala Lumpur: CfBT Education Trust.

Munro-Kua, A. 1996. *Authoritarian populism in Malaysia*. New York: St. Martin's Press.

Muscat, R. J. 2002. *Investing in peace: How development aid can prevent or promote conflict*. Armonk, New York: M. E. Sharpe.

Ninth Malaysia Plan. 2006. Economic Planning Unit.

Noor, F. 2005. *From Majapahit to Putrajaya*. Kuala Lumpur: Silverfishbooks.

Omar, A. H. 1982. *Language and society in Malaysia*. Kuala Lumpur: Dewan Bahasa and Pustaka.

Prasad, R. 1947. *India divided*. Mumbai: Hind Kitabs Limited.

Rashid, R. 1993. *A Malaysian journey*. Petaling Jaya: Rehman Rashid.

Report of the Education Review Committee. 1960. Kuala Lumpur: Government Press.

Salih, K., and Z. A. Yusof. 1989. Overview of the New Economic Policy and framework for the post-1990 Economic Policy. *Malaysian Management Review*, 24: 13–61.

Second Malaysia Plan. 1971. Economic Planning Unit.

Seng, P. L. 2007. Schooling in Malaysia. In *Going to school in East Asia,* edited by G. A. Postiglione and J. Tan, 207–232. Westport, CT: Greenwood Press.

Sowell, T. 1989. Affirmative action: A worldwide disaster. *Commentary*, 21–41.

Tenth Malaysia Plan. 2011. Economic Planning Unit.

Thillainathan, R. 1976. *An analysis of the effects of policies for the redistribution of income and wealth in West Malaysia, 1957–1975.* London School of Economics, University of London.

Third Malaysia Plan. 1976. Economic Planning Unit.

Verma, V. 2002. *Malaysia, state and civil society in transition.* Boulder, CO: Lynne Rienner Publishers Inc, US.

Wade, G. 2009. The origins and evolution of Ethnocracy in Malaysia. *Asia Research Institute Working Paper 111.*

Ward, C., and Hewstone, M. 1985. Ethnicity, language and intergroup relations in Malaysia and Singapore: A social psychological analysis. *Journal of Multilingual and Multicultural Development,* 6: 271–296.

World Bank. 2011. *Brain Drain.*

CHAPTER 7

Official Development Assistance (ODA) and Conflict: A Case Study on Japanese ODA to Vietnam

Edward M. Feasel

Introduction

Vietnam has become a model for achieving rapid economic development. In 2009, the country reached "middle income" status and joined a number of other Asian countries that have shown remarkable economic progress in a short period of time. An important element in this success has been the Official Development Assistance (ODA) that the country has received from around the world, including multilateral aid agencies such as the World Bank and the Asian Development Bank. It is Japan that has served as Vietnam's largest single donor for over a decade and has provided steady economic support during both smooth and turbulent times. This steadfast support has aided the government of Vietnam in maintaining economic stability during two international financial crises.

The robust economic progress has not meant the absence of internal conflict within the country. Peasant protests have occurred, tensions between the government and ethnic minority and religious groups have been persistent, labor unrest has happened during economic downturns and intraparty and extraparty individuals and groups seeking greater reform and fewer restrictions on freedoms have presented challenges to the Communist Party and government. Donors, including Japan, have generally steered away from these internal conflicts and focused on promoting and supporting free-market-oriented policies and actions. Multilateral aid agencies, however, have at times used their aid as leverage to require increased economic reform. And in the area of human rights, Western governments, particularly the United States, have been forceful in pointing out abuses and demanding improvements. The government of Vietnam has at times responded with positive change to these external forces. Japan, in contrast, has not tied aid to a reform agenda or timeline, nor to the easing of restrictions on intellectual and political freedoms.

This chapter attempts to look at the connection, if any, between Official Development Assistance (ODA) and conflict in Vietnam by focusing on Japanese aid. The next section provides some background on the extraordinary economic progress that has occurred in the country and the changes in government and party leadership that has accompanied the economic record. The third section then examines ODA to Vietnam over the last several decades, focusing on Japan's emergence as the top single donor and on the type of aid that has been provided. The fourth section looks at the various groups where conflict has occurred within the nation and investigates any link between ODA and other external forces on altering the government's treatment of these groups. Finally, the fifth section presents conclusions of this case study.

Background

In 1986 the government of Vietnam (GoV) embarked on a dramatic new course of economic reformation. *Doi Moi* ("renovation") was introduced after a decade of economic malaise and decades of armed conflict, with the idea of introducing market-oriented policies while maintaining the single party political structure. The Vietnam Communist Party (VCP) was well aware that a change of course was necessary, given the challenge of 600 percent inflation and the inefficient agricultural production that was at subsistence level. Under Le Duan, who headed the VCP after Ho Chih Minh died in 1969, the government continued to implement the socialist policies of central planning with collective farming, enforcing a socialist transformation on the southern part of the country after reunification in 1976. Vietnam also invaded Cambodia in 1978 to oust the Pol Pot regime and subsequently had to deal with a border war with China in 1979 and with the cessation of aid from most international donors, which only resumed in 1992. The combination of factors led to a significant deterioration in economic performance (Harvie and Hoa 1997, 40).

Le Duan died in 1986 and several of the political leaders who had led the country to victory in war left the Politburo, the top decision-making body of the government.[1] Eventually Nguyen Van Linh, a reform-minded party member from the South, was elected general secretary of the party, and he implemented the initial opening up of the economy to market forces and the gradual loosening of certain intellectual and political restrictions. The government instituted land reform, carrying out a decollectivization policy by allocating plots of land to farmers. The events three years later in Eastern Europe and Tiananmen Square, however, resulted in a retrenchment of the VCP, a rejection of multiparty democracy, and a slowdown in the reform that had been initiated under *Doi Moi*.

Do Muoi became general secretary of the VCP in 1991 and continued the economic reformation that the party had initiated. In 1993, the Land Law was instituted, furthering land reform by allowing farmers to lease land for agricultural production from the government, further increasing agricultural productivity in the country.[2,3] In 1997, General Le Kha Phieu replaced Do Muoi and while the reforms put in place were not undone, implementation slowed significantly. Nong Duc Manh was named general secretary of the VCP in 2001 after party members had become dissatisfied with the slow pace of reforms under Phieu. Mahn, of the Tay ethnic minority, was the first general secretary to come from a minority ethnic group in Vietnam. In 2006, a southerner, Nguyen Tan Dung, was named prime minister and instituted more aggressive market reforms in the country. High inflation, poor economic performance, and corruption scandals threatened Dung's position as the Party Congress approached in 2011. At the Congress, Dung was able to continue in his position, and Nguyen Phu Trong was elected general secretary as a compromise candidate.

The last two decades have seen change in the political leadership of the VCP, sometimes reflecting different views regarding the appropriate speed of economic reforms and the appropriate policies necessary to stifle dissident voices. Disagreement continues on these issues resulting in a silent power struggle within the party and government, the severity and degree of which is difficult to discern given the secretive method that policy is discussed and decided. Nonetheless, the change in leadership up to now has occurred peacefully while the government and the party have continued the program of *Doi Moi*.

The value of gross domestic product (GDP) per capita nearly quadrupled between 1990 and 1997. Growth in living standards continued at a slower rate from 1997 to 2001 and then accelerated, nearly doubling between 2001 and 2008. Having reached the $1,000 GDP per capita level, Vietnam has entered the middle-income category of countries as classified by the World Bank. This is certainly an enviable record of economic progress and is testament to the effective economic policy reform carried out by the government.

This reform included land reform, transition to a more diverse economic structure focusing on developing a "multi-sector commodity economy" (Central Department of Ideology and Culture 2007, 50), promoting the development of new private enterprises (Central Department of Ideology and Culture 2006, 25), privatization of state-owned enterprises, promotion of international trade, and openness to international aid and foreign direct investment (FDI).

One of the goals of the GoV was to achieve the United Nations Millennium Development Goals (MDG); specifically to halve poverty rates between 1990 and 2015. Vietnam has focused on achieving the goal primarily through spurring economic growth. In this area the government has achieved remarkable progress as well, as Table 7.1 depicts. Poverty rates in the country as a whole and in both urban and rural areas have declined by more than 50 percent. With the exception of the Northwest region, every major region has also experienced a reduction of more than 50 percent, in many cases significantly more than half. The government continues to revise its MDG targets in light of its poverty reduction achievements.

While growth has resulted in dramatic poverty reduction, one area of concern is the increasing inequality between rural and urban dwellers. In particular, this increasing inequality is often more severe when poverty rates are examined for ethnic minorities relative to the rest of the population. The situation is exacerbated by corruption scandals in the government, including confiscation of land and property by the government and favoritism by local officials toward Vietnamese of Kinh origin, the largest ethnic group in Vietnam, comprising 86 percent of the population. Citizens of ethnic minorities are also often members of religious minority groups that have

Table 7.1   Vietnam Poverty Rates, 1993–2010

Region	1993	1998	2002	2004	2006	2008	2010
Country	58	37	29	20	16	14	11
Urban	25	9	7	4	4	3	3
Rural	66	45	36	25	20	18	15
Red River Delta	63	29	22	12	9	8	6
North East	86	62	38	29	25	23	20
North Central Coast	75	48	44	32	29	25	21
South Central Coast	47	35	25	19	13	11	9
Central Highlands	70	52	52	33	29	25	20
South East	37	12	11	5	6	5	3
Mekong River Delta	47	37	23	20	10	9	7

Source: General Statistics Office of Vietnam, 2011 and author's calculations.

been restricted and persecuted by the government. The result has been episodes of protest and clashes with the security police over the years.

It is also true that progress in achieving robust economic growth and general poverty reduction has not been smooth in the *Doi Moi* era. The Asian financial crisis in 1997 hit the Vietnamese economy hard and resulted in lower GDP growth rates. More recently, the global financial crisis has presented significant challenges. Inflation in 2008 reached double digit levels and was at nearly 23 percent for the year. Such declines in economic fortunes can have fast and severe consequences for the most economically vulnerable segment of the population, and often result in increased criticism and protests by the affected individuals. This has been the case in Vietnam as labor unrest has been on the rise. However, in both instances of global financial crisis, the international community has supplied the much needed development assistance that has allowed the country and GoV to weather the storm and maintain stability. Leading the effort in this assistance, at least in terms of dollar amount, has been Japan.

Japan's ODA to Vietnam

ODA has played an important role in Vietnam's economic success. Japan has been Vietnam's largest single donor for over a decade now, showing the stability of the relationship that has developed between the two countries and the strong economic and commercial interests that Japan has in the country (Trinidad 2007, 113; Arase 2005, 9).[4] Figure 7.1 shows dynamics of ODA to Vietnam in gross disbursements for the period from 1990 to 2010, both for all donors, including multilateral institutions and for Japan. From the mid-1990s, Japan has continued to increase ODA to Vietnam year-over-year with the exception of the period 2000–2002 and 2009–2010. During the earlier period the economic slowdown in Japan resulted in a significant reduction of ODA given around the world; overall ODA from Japan dropped by 28 percent in real terms. Japan's ODA as a percent of total ODA by all donors to Vietnam peaked in 2000 when it reached more than 50 percent. In 2008, Japan accounted for 27 percent of total ODA to Vietnam.

When Japan resumed aid to Vietnam in 1992, it focused much of the aid on infrastructure projects. Japan's ODA disbursements around the world lies in contrast to other donors especially with regard to its emphasis on infrastructure and a reliance on significant amounts of loan aid instead of grants (Morrison 2005, 11; Trinidad 2007, 111).[5] An example of an extensive, long-term project that Japan supported through ODA in Vietnam is the Red River Delta Transport Development Program. The master plan for the project was developed in 1994 and was the first to target large-scale

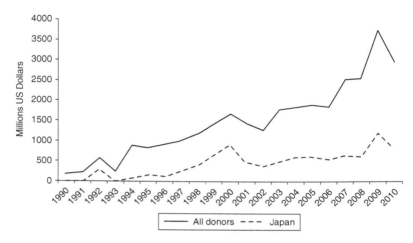

Figure 7.1 Official Development Assistance to Vietnam, 1990–2010.
Source: OECD, DAC Annual Aggregates Database.

transportation in Northern Vietnam. The primary goal was to support growth in the Northern part of the country and help the region catch up, or at least not fall further behind the South. Other donors also participated in supporting various parts of the overall plan, often building connecting roads from rural areas to the new major highways. The program lasted from 1994 to 2004 and included 25 projects on Japan's part, with nearly $2 billion in ODA, and another 27 projects by other donors totaling approximately an additional $1 billion in aid (Ministry of Planning and Investment, and Ministry of Transport 2006). A joint evaluation report by the governments of Japan and Vietnam outlines the significant scale of the projects accomplished and estimates the positive impact on travel, exports, and growth: the study also identifies some of the negative consequences that arose as a result of the project (Ministry of Planning and Investment, and Ministry of Transport 2006). The negative effects generally pertain to urban areas and include increased traffic congestion, a significant increase in accidents, and increased air and noise pollution. A 2004 migration study conducted jointly by the government of Vietnam and the United Nations also revealed that increased migration from rural to urban areas has led to insufficient housing for new migrants, water and sanitation challenges, and insufficient electricity production (General Statistics Office of Vietnam and UNFPA, 2004). Japan has been involved in projects in many of these areas as a follow-up to the original plan.

Japan's assistance to Vietnam also involved intellectual support in planning and development. One such initiative, the Ishikawa Project, exemplifies this involvement. During a visit of General Secretary do Muoi to Japan in 1995, the two governments agreed upon and launched the plan that was headed up on the Japanese side by Shigeru Ishikawa, a former academic. The project was implemented in three phases from 1995 to 2001. The long-term scope of the project allowed a focus on looking at infrastructure development as a means of generating economic growth. While the goals of the project did include macroeconomic stabilization and supporting the transition to a market economy, in practice it focused primarily on the third goal of long-term development. Based on its own development experience, Japan in its ODA policy has always emphasized development through building infrastructure and poverty reduction through generating economic growth.

Japan has been a steady donor to Vietnam despite fluctuations from other donor countries and multilateral institutions. The World Bank, International Monetary Fund (IMF), and Asian Development Bank have also provided sizeable aid to Vietnam over the years, yet this aid is often subject to meeting targets for economic reform. In the late 1990s, in a period when the Vietnamese economy struggled due to the Asian financial crisis, both the World Bank and the IMF suspended aid programs until the government made adequate progress on reforms. The World Bank withheld $500 million in loans in 1999 and the IMF $900 million in 2000 (Abuza 2001, 31). In fact, structural adjustment lending from the World Bank ceased between 1997 and 2000, as the GoV and the World Bank could not agree on appropriate goals under the latter's new lending system that required recipients to develop a detailed Comprehensive Poverty Reduction and Growth Strategy (CPRGS) (Engel 2008, 172). It was during this period that Japan ramped up ODA to help Vietnam weather the storm of the financial crisis. In March, 1998, Japanese finance minister Miyazawa announced the "Miyazawa Plan," to provide $30 billion in aid to Asian nations struggling as a result of the Asian financial crisis. In March of the next year, the prime ministers from Japan and Vietnam met in Tokyo and formalized the nearly $700 million aid package.

Following the Asian financial crisis and the criticism that many multilateral aid agencies received in its aftermath, the development discourse on ODA changed as the new millennium approached. While multilateral aid agencies began operating under the new approach much earlier, it was finally formalized by all major donors in the Paris Agenda on Aid Effectiveness in 2005. In this new strategy for aid delivery, emphasis is placed on aid being aligned with the recipient's development agenda, increased aid harmonization among donors, mutual accountability, and attention to institutional elements in enhancing the effectiveness of aid. A focus is placed on poverty reduction and a key element in implementing this strategy is the requirement that recipient countries develop a CPRGS. As mentioned earlier, disagreements on an appropriate program led to the suspension of aid from the World Bank to Vietnam in the late 1990s. One of the dilemmas for Japan in agreeing to this new vision of ODA was the country's traditional emphasis on infrastructure development. While the new ODA agenda put emphasis on poverty reduction, Japan's ODA philosophy was that poverty reduction was best achieved through infrastructure development and not necessarily by antipoverty policies targeting disadvantaged groups. Japan developed a new ODA charter in 2003 and included some of the agenda from the new ODA discourse into its charter, with a greater focus on poverty reduction, aid coordination, and attention to "human security" (Ministry of Foreign Affairs of Japan 2003). In practice, however, Japan's ODA continued to overwhelmingly emphasize infrastructure development. In 2001, the GoV completed an Interim Poverty Reduction Strategy, and the World Bank initiated a program under the new vision of ODA. The program, called "General Budget Support" (GBS), provided aid aimed at giving greater latitude to recipients in using the ODA funds as part of the general budget of the government. In exchange, the government agreed to achieve certain reforms on a specified timeline. In the case of Vietnam, there were three phases of Poverty Reduction Support credits between 2001 and 2004 and the amount in each phase depended on the pace and success of reforms achieved. Japan joined the GBS support program in the fourth phase in 2004, after influencing Vietnam to incorporate large-scale infrastructure development into the CPRGS in 2003. GBS accounts for about 10 percent of ODA to Vietnam and also sets targets for reform toward market-oriented policies, administrative reform, and reduction of corruption (Bartholomew, Leurs, and McCarty 2006, 6).

Japan has also increased coordination with other donors and multilateral agencies in Vietnam through a number of initiatives including the Transport Partnership Group, chaired by Japan until May 2004, where the GoV and donors can coordinate efforts in transportation infrastructure development and address challenges that arise (such as traffic congestion); the "5 Banks Initiative," where the World Bank, Asian Development Bank, and representation from Japan, Germany, and France all participated in attempting to improve the coordination and implementation of distributing ODA funds in Vietnam; participation in the Partnership Group for Aid Effectiveness, which in 2004 became the main forum for the GoV and donors to discuss and improve aid effectiveness; and the Comprehensive

Capacity Building Programme for ODA Management developed by Japan, the United Kingdom, and the World Bank to improve the administrative capacity in the GoV for handling ODA (Muta et al., 2007, 17–18).[6]

In 2001, major donor countries agreed to move toward untying all aid to less-developed countries. While initially slow in responding to this agreement, Japan has made significant progress. In a recent case study examining a project conducted by Japan in Vietnam, the authors found that the largest impediment to fully untying aid was the GoV's lack of capacity to handle ODA, select appropriate contractors, and the importance that Japan places on its monitoring and evaluation process of ODA projects (Clay, Geddes, and Natali 2009, 90–92). Between 2004 and 2008, 86 percent of net ODA to Vietnam was untied (McCarty, Julian, and Banerjee 2009, 23).

While Japan dabbles in the coordinated new aid approaches, it is clear that its emphasis on supporting infrastructure development has not changed. Figure 7.2 shows Japan's ODA to Vietnam in economic infrastructure compared to all other OECD Development Assistance Committee (DAC) members, and combined multilateral agency aid. The numbers show that the majority of infrastructure aid from bilateral donors is from Japan, approximately 80 percent. Since 2006, economic infrastructure has accounted for over 60 percent of total Japanese ODA to Vietnam. To get some idea of the

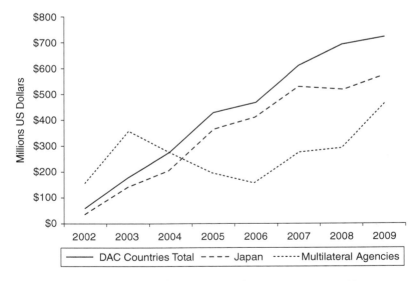

Figure 7.2   ODA to Vietnam for Economic Infrastructure, 2002–2009.
Source: OECD, DAC Annual Aggregates Database.

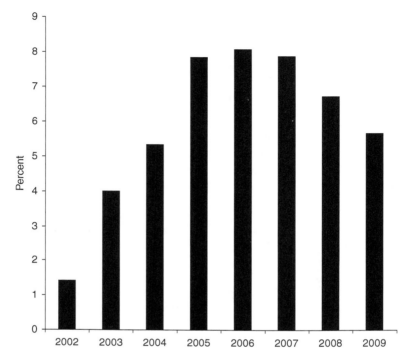

Figure 7.3 Japanese ODA for Economic Infrastructure as a Percent of Vietnam's State Capital Expenditure, 2002–2009.

Source: Author's calculations based on OECD, DAC Annual Aggregates Database and General Statistics Office of Vietnam, 2011.

significance of this amount, Figure 7.3 presents Japanese ODA in infrastructure as a percent of capital expenditures by the GoV between 2002 and 2009. Between 2005 and 2008, Japan's ODA in this area was equivalent to nearly 8 percent of what the GoV spent on capital expansion.

More recently, the global financial crisis, which has had a devastating economic impact on advanced nations, also resulted in a lower growth in Vietnam, and inflation at double digit levels. At the Consultative Group meeting held in Hanoi on December 5, 2009, a gathering that brought together both bilateral and multilateral top donors, Japan pledged $1.6 billion in ODA to support the country. The World Bank and Asian Development Bank also committed significant amounts, $2.4 and $1.4 billion respectively (Viet Nam News 2009). In large part, this is the recognition of the progress on growth and poverty reduction that Vietnam has achieved thus far. However, as Vietnam reaches the status of middle-income country, it will not be able to qualify for certain types of ODA, and several countries have already expressed their intention to scale back aid significantly in the near future. Donors also share concern that should Vietnam avoid the middle-income trap that has plagued many of its Asian neighbors including Thailand, Indonesia, Philippines, and Malaysia.[7] In these countries, Japan is also the largest single donor by far and there is no indication that Japan will change its ODA stance toward Vietnam. In fact, as assistance from multilateral agencies gradually declines with achievement of middle-income status, Japan's place as the largest donor will only become more substantial.

While economic infrastructure is the primary focus of Japanese aid, Japan is involved in other aspects as well. Many donors, including multilateral agencies, have paid significant attention to legal reform in Vietnam. Japan has been a key player in this arena as well, providing training for legal staff and participation in a Comprehensive Legal Needs Analysis conducted in 2002 (Sidel 2008, 210–214). Japan has also provided thousands of scholarships for students and professionals to study in Japan. In 2003, the prime ministers of both countries announced the launch of the Vietnam-Japan Joint Initiative to bring together members from both governments and members from the Japanese business community. The aim of the initiative was to improve the investment climate in Vietnam: toward that goal, the parties identified 125 points of concern. Now in its fourth phase, the initiative has resolved most of these points of concern. Results of the initiative have shown up in increased flow of FDI to the country. Vietnam FDI reached a high of $10 billion in 1996, when in the aftermath of the Asian financial crisis, FDI plummeted and continued to decline to $3 billion in 2002. FDI remained stifled and only gradually increased to $6 billion in 2005 (General Statistics Office of Vietnam 2009). The amount surged to over $80 billion in 2008, reflecting a dramatic increase and confidence in the stability of Vietnam. Japan is the third largest supplier of FDI, just behind Taiwan and Malaysia. The joint initiative clearly benefited Vietnam in increasing FDI and this was not restricted to investment coming from Japan.

Simultaneous with the advancement of the joint initiative, the two governments engaged in discussion on a trade partnership agreement, and after nine rounds, the Vietnam-Japan Economic Partnership Agreement was announced in 2008 (Ministry of Foreign Affairs of Japan 2009a). The agreement will gradually reduce tariffs between the two countries toward 2018. Given the sizeable aid and other assistance that is provided by Japan to Vietnam and its emphasis on the development of economic infrastructure, Japan has played an important role in assisting the GoV in reaching its targets for economic growth and poverty reduction.

Conflict in Vietnam

Despite the economic growth supported by foreign assistance, other challenges have arisen along the way from outside the economic sphere, particularly increased dissident voices, protests from ethnic minority and religious groups, and calls for the easing of restrictions on personal and group freedoms. It is not clear that the strong record of economic growth and poverty alleviation has benefited the government in avoiding tensions and conflict in these areas.

Given the restrictions on the press and the secrecy with which the government operates in Vietnam, it is difficult to discern what type of conflict is occurring in the country, including where and who is involved. To give a general picture of conflict in Vietnam, Figure 7.4 presents a conflict-cooperation scale for each year between 1990 and 2004. The scale is created using the Goldstein scale, which gives numerical values to news events, ranging from -10, the highest level of conflict, to +10, the highest level of cooperation (Goldstein 1992). Using the Kansas Events Data Set (KEDS) that contains 10 million dyadic events reported on wire services, the dataset was reduced to the 35,000 observations for Vietnam. Using events for each calendar year, the annual conflict-cooperation scale was estimated. The figure shows that 1997 and 2004 were periods of greatest conflict, as lower values indicate increased levels of conflict in the country. This is consistent with generally known events. The year 1997 saw large protests from peasant farmers in rural areas,

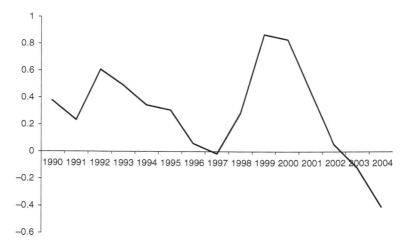

Figure 7.4   Internal Conflict-Cooperation Scale for Vietnam, 1990–2004.
Source: Authors Calculations using the Kansas Event Data Set, 2007.

centered primarily in and around the Thai Binh province. These were the largest protests experienced in the country to date, and the peasants focused their dissatisfaction on the level of corruption in the government, which often resulted in unfair confiscation of their lands and the mishandling of land grievances. This was compounded by the economic turmoil that was occurring throughout Asia. The year 2004 also saw large protests and clashes between the police and ethnic minority groups seeking greater freedoms for religious assembly and association. To better understand the episodes of increased conflict, we examine the various groups that were dissatisfied with the government's policies and actions. Generally, these groups fall into three categories: Communist members, ethnic minority and religious groups, and other domestic groups seeking economic or political change.

Intraparty Dissent

Conflicts within the Communist Party are often not transparent, but present. Since the launch of *Doi Moi*, there has been tension between hardliners skeptical of the neoliberal reforms implemented in the country, and the reformers, who vary in their views on the degree to which reform should be conducted, within both the economic and political realm. As in any case where disagreements exist within the ruling elite, there is the potential of a falling out and conflict. The military is also at the table, with a guaranteed number of seats in the powerful Politburo. However, one area on which the hardliners and the reformers generally agree on is the preservation of the party and the rejection of multiparty democracy, in order to provide greater stability in the government.

Some of the most vocal dissidents come from within the party. As such, the dissidents call for changes aimed at increasing participation and reducing corruption, but do not seek multiparty democracy (Abuza 2001, 24). Most often these intraparty voices come from members living in the South, who are more eager and willing to institute economic reform. One such notable example is the Club of Former Resistance Fighters (CFRF). The group was formed in 1986 and was comprised of former military soldiers who fought in the war supporting the North. Having strong ties to party officials, the group had influence and even outwardly supported certain party members for offices. After the democratization events in Eastern Europe, government officials were more critical of the CFRF. In typical fashion, the government created its own Vietnam Veterans Organization, which was put under the Fatherland Front, the organization where most civil society groups are located and monitored. The new veterans group was headed by one of the most famous former CFRF generals and included membership of citizens in the North. By the end of 1990, the group had over 900,000 members. Shortly thereafter the CFRF leadership was replaced and the group was no longer as vocal and critical of the government (Abuza 2001,161–183). As in the case of the CFRF, the GoV has effectively isolated dissidents over the years and prevented them from joining forces.

Japan has largely played a hands-off role when it comes to the internal decisions and workings of the government. It has suggested direction and provided aid and expertise, but has not used the potential cessation of assistance as a stick to punish lack of speed in implementing market-oriented reforms or government actions restricting certain freedoms. Instead, it has been a steady partner of the government, even increasing assistance during the most trying economic times. This has provided underlying economic support and stability and given the necessary time for the government to handle challenges and make decisions, which generally have been in the direction of increased economic reform.

Other donors and multinational institutions have played a more active role in pushing the GoV to increase the pace of reforms. As mentioned previously, the World Bank and the IMF held back funding in the wake of the Asian financial crisis. General Phieu had become general secretary in 1997, and the government and the World Bank could not agree on reform goals. As the economic situation deteriorated, the pace of reform was cautious and the government was concerned over the peasant protests that occurred in the same year. There was significant internal discussion among government leaders over this period on how to handle and respond to the peasant protests and the appropriate pace of economic reform. Ultimately, the pressure from multinational agencies combined with the economic slowdown resulted in the government embracing a more reform-oriented approach. During the National Party Congress in 2001, General Phieu intended to continue as general secretary for an additional five-year term and was supported by the Politburo. The Central Committee, however, elected Nong Duc Manh as the new general secretary. This was clear indication that the reformers who were dissatisfied with the pace of reform and the hard stance of the government had won out. Under the leadership of Manh, cooperation with donors continued despite dissatisfaction by the World Bank on certain aspects of economic reform, such as the pace of privatization of state-owned enterprises and harmonization of legal standards with international standards.

The recent global financial crisis has again resulted in significant intra-party disagreements. Nguyen Tan Dung, a reform-oriented southerner who became prime minister in 2006, initiated substantial trade and investment reforms, which supported large increases in FDI. Inflation and turbulence in the economy has increased tensions between the more conservative element within the Politburo headed by Manh, who wished to be more cautious in reform and economic expansion, and the prime minister's more aggressive policies. In mid-2008, the Central Committee gave the Politburo the responsibility of overseeing the economy for the remainder of the year, taking the responsibility away from the direct control of the prime minister, a significant move reducing his authority and role. In this instance, all donors increased their commitment of aid, pledging a record $8 billion in 2009 at the December Consultative Group meeting in Hanoi, which was attended by Dung. The move was intended to stabilize the economic situation and support the reforms that Dung had implemented. While inflation rates returned to single digits in 2009, the government continued to face economic challenges and subsequently devalued the currency four times. Despite these challenges, Dung was reelected prime minister at the Party Congress, although his hopes for becoming general secretary would not be realized (Koh 2011). The evidence here suggests that ODA can support reformers in intraparty disagreements, either indirectly in the case of Japan by contributing to robust growth and a stable economic environment, or more directly as in the case of multinational agencies moves' to limit aid based on a track record of reform.

Ethnic Minority and Religious Groups

While ODA may support reformers in intraparty disagreements, it has not been effective in addressing one of the largest sources of conflict in the country, namely conflicts with ethnic minorities and religious groups. The government has recognized 54 ethnic minority groups, many living in the rural areas of the country. For some of the minority groups, religion is also an important part of their identity. The Montagnards in the Central Highlands are Evangelical Protestants who have been persecuted by the government for their beliefs. Often criticized by the government as being influenced by external forces, namely US ties carrying over from the Vietnam War where the Montagnards fought side by side with US forces, the Highlanders have faced often brutal reprisals for protests or public gatherings. Most notable were protests in 2001 and 2004 over confiscation of churches and church members' agricultural land, forced faith renunciations, and restrictions on religious gatherings and associations (Human Rights Watch 2006). An evangelical movement has also formed in the Northern rural regions of the country, where residents there have faced similar mistreatment. In the Southern region of the country, the Ethnic Khmer who follow the beliefs of Theravada Buddhism, not Mahayana Buddhism that most Buddhists in Vietnam practice, have also protested confiscation of temple property and religious restrictions (Human Rights Watch 2009a). The Hoa Hao and Cao Dai faiths have also faced restrictions and experienced confrontation with government security forces.

Catholics in Vietnam, mostly made up of Kinh majority, have also been persecuted and have held major protests in the country. Confiscation of churches and church property, arrests of priests, restrictions on gatherings, and harassment by police have all been experienced throughout the period of *Doi Moi*. The government has also expressed concern that the Catholic Church is another external force supporting peaceful evolution, the notion that with time democracy will spread in the country. The Montagnards, Evangelical Protestants, and Catholics are most often linked to external forces and therefore face the greatest scrutiny by the government. The government has restricted the ability of the Vatican to appoint new bishops in Vietnam. The government requires all churches to be registered with the government and uses this tool to decide whether gatherings are legal or not.[8] While individual religious freedom and practice is allowed at previously unprecedented levels in the country, the ability to associate and organize is strictly monitored and restricted. The government is also involved in the appointment of church officials, another tool used to control religious groups. The government views religious organization as a privilege granted by the state, not a right of every person. Evangelical Protestant groups have faced very slow approval by the government, and all groups have faced significant government involvement in the appointment of church leaders.

The arrest of church leaders has also been a strategy of containment by the government. In 2001, Catholic priest Father Ly was arrested and sentenced to 15 years in prison for alleged antigovernment activity. Leaders of the Unified Buddhist Church of Vietnam (UBCV), which has been banned since 1981, have been arrested and sentenced to prison. Many believe that a majority of Vietnamese are secretly affiliated with the church (Abuza 2001, 187–197). In 1981, the government placed the UBCV under the Fatherland Front, but leaders of the UBCV refused to follow the government decision. Then the government created the Vietnam Buddhist Church under the Fatherland Front and banned the UBCV. Since that time, ongoing protests and arrests of church officials has ensued. Muslims were also banned since 1975, but were allowed to reopen as part of the Fatherland Front in 1992 (Abuza 2001, 205).

During tough economic periods, the government attempts to show some signs of leniency toward groups that traditionally have been monitored and restricted. This recent period has not been an exception. In 1999, although the government was responsible for appointing religious leaders in the various sanctioned religious groups, the government allowed the pope to appoint a handful of new bishops. In 2000, relations with the Vatican took a step back as the pope was denied the same ability. Beginning in 2006, the government has generally been more supportive of bishops recommended by the Vatican. In the Northern region, a number of churches have been allowed to register where Evangelical Protestants practice, although the number has been small. The government has also increased the number of prisoners given amnesty each year, usually done on Vietnamese New Year, Tet, and National Day. Ten such amnesties have been granted since 1998, increasing in number and frequency toward the current period.

In most cases, the persecuted ethnic and religious minority groups who have been at the heart of much of the tension and conflict in Vietnam live in rural poverty. With the reunification of the country the government instituted a policy of promoting growth by developing economic zones around the country, mostly as an effort to generate growth, fight poverty, and have rural minority groups incorporated into the social and economic structure of the country (Thang 2007, 12; 110–111; Human Rights Watch 2002, 31–37). As part of this strategy, Kinh were relocated to the new economic zones in rural areas. The new Land Law in 1993 increased the pace of relocations of Kinh, putting further pressure on rural areas where land was scarce. Accusations of corruption among local party officials heightened tensions as these officials allocated land in an unfair manner, discriminating against ethnic minority and religious group members in favor of the Kinh majority. In 2002, poverty rates for all minority groups, except the Chinese, were above 50 percent, significantly higher for many ethnic groups (Swinkels and Turk 2006, 2–4). The relocation polices have exacerbated conflicts over property rights and increased tensions between the minority groups with the Kinh and with the GoV. Although poverty rates have fallen, these rural areas present the most difficult challenge in achieving desired poverty reduction.

Japan has not placed any conditions on aid based on the government's treatment of ethnic minority and religious groups. This is true of multilateral aid agencies as well. Both have instead focused attention on supporting poverty reduction efforts as a means of improving the plight of minority groups as opposed to any direct call for better treatment or increased freedoms. Multilateral aid agencies have been involved in direct poverty reduction strategies. The two major programs conducted by the GoV were Program 133, from 1998 to 2000, and Program 135, started in 1998. The World Bank was involved in Program 135 that identified the poorest communes in the country. Phase Two of Program 135 was approved in 2006, with substantial aid from the World Bank. Japan has also been involved in building hundreds of schools throughout the country, many in rural poor communities.

Even in the area of poverty reduction, Japanese ODA has supported the government's efforts primarily through infrastructure development, believing this to be the best way to achieve desired results. Donors argue that additional infrastructure will aid rural minority groups by creating access to urban areas and markets. Several studies have found strong effects of infrastructure development on improving agricultural production, per capita income, and reducing poverty in poor rural communities in Vietnam (Deolalikar 2001; Larsen, Pham, and Rama 2004; Fan, Huong, and Long 2004). There is also plenty of anecdotal evidence on the effectiveness of infrastructure such as in Department for International Development's Country's Assistance Plan which states that the price of rice in the commune Can Ho fell 30 percent, once a road was constructed reducing travel time to the market town Lai Chau (Department for International Development 2008, 21). While there are benefits, unintended consequences can also occur. For the Cham Muslims who live in the rural regions of the Mekong Delta, the new infrastructure brought increased market competition and the community was forced to abandon weaving, one of its long held income-generating activities, as the decrease in demand could no longer support making a livelihood by the craft (Taylor 2007, 175). Another study found that construction of rural roads in Vietnam only benefited those who travel by bicycle and not by foot (Transport Development Strategy Institute 2004). A recent World Bank study on the impact of local market development that can be attributed to road construction in rural Vietnam found that while there were positive impacts, the results were dampened in communities that had larger ethic minority groups, lower literacy rates, and smaller population density (Mu and van de Walle 2007).

Improvements in infrastructure have also resulted in increased migration from rural areas to urban centers. Evidence from migration surveys show that up to 80 percent of household budgets in poor rural communities come from remittances from family members who have migrated to urban areas (Deshingkar 2006, 8). This is clearly an important source of income in rural areas. The surveys also show that minority migrants earn half as much as Kinh migrants (Deshingkar 2006, 11). Not surprisingly, data show remittances are lower in the poorest regions of the country, the Northwest and Central Highlands (Vietnamese Academy of Social Sciences 2007, 59). The GoV interprets this as evidence of a "weak link" with the rest of the economy (Vietnamese Academy of Social Sciences 2007, 60). Another likely contributing factor is that discrimination of minority migrants results in lower remittances due to the fact that they receive significantly lower wages.

The evidence clearly shows that Japanese ODA has had significant effect on reducing overall poverty in Vietnam, including in rural areas. However, growing inequality between minority groups and the Kinh majority has also likely been an outcome. As such, while the reduction in overall poverty helps to avoid potential conflict in the country by increasing the standard of living for the average person, the increasing inequality due to unequal benefits from economic growth, combined with discrimination and mistreatment of minority groups, can lead to increased tension and a greater likelihood that episodes of conflict will occur, such as those that occurred in 2001 and 2004.

The GoV also had a policy of encouraging ethnic minority groups to preserve cultural traits that the government regards as unique and beneficial, while removing those that are considered backward, and thereby prevent full participation in the country's political and economic system. This removal of cultural roadblocks and replacing them with ideological bridges connecting individuals to the market economy is consistent with the policy of connecting rural areas to the market economy through infrastructure development. Multilateral agencies, such as the World Bank, have actually supported these views by adopting an approach of removing physical and cultural barriers to participation in the market system (Taylor 2007, 186). This support of removing cultural impediments to economic engagement is also a source of increased resentment and conflict (Human Rights Watch 2009a; Thang 2007).

As mentioned earlier, Japan revised its ODA Charter in 2003 and placed an emphasis on human security. This addition was in recognition that conflicts in the world have increasingly become regional, based on religious, ethnic, and cultural differences, and often occurs at the substate level, therefore, requiring a more individual focus (Japan International Cooperation Agency (JICA) 2009, 1). The language used to describe this new approach is combating two major threats: threat from want (poverty) and threat from fear (conflict and disaster) (JICA 2009, 1). Two categories of spending in Japanese ODA directly address human security issues, namely Grassroots Human Security Projects and Grant Assistance for Japanese NGO Assistance (Muta et al. 2006).[9]

Between 1992 and 2009, Japan supported 382 Grassroots Human Security Projects, averaging a little over 21 projects per year (VOV News 2010). The projects are one year in duration and groups must apply directly to the Japanese government. Combined, ODA in both the Grassroots Projects and the Japanese NGO categories amounted to less than half a percent of total ODA to Vietnam (Ministry of Foreign Affairs of Japan 2008). Neither Japan nor the multilateral aid agencies have used aid as a means to challenge the treatment or policies of the government toward ethnic minority and religious groups. While possessing the means of partially addressing these human security issues by increasing ODA to minority groups through Grassroots Human Security Projects or Japanese NGO support, Japan has instead kept this funding relatively constant over time.[10]

Feigenblatt argues that by supporting an authoritarian government with a track record of human rights violations such as the GoV, it serves as a prime example where Japanese ODA practice does not match the rhetoric incorporated into its ODA Charter (Feigenblatt 2007, 9–10). Specifically, consideration of human rights issues are downplayed with an emphasis placed on economic interests (Feigenblatt 2007, 10). He also argues that Japan's "historical guilt" prevents it from taking a stronger position on human rights issues in Asia (Feigenblatt 2007, 10–11). In a rare display of criticism, an independent evaluation of ODA to Vietnam commissioned by Japan's Ministry of Foreign Affairs urges Japan to pay more attention to growing income disparities in the country and warns that improvements in growth and poverty have not been matched by similar "improvements in measures of governance," which should be a focus as well (Muta et al. 2007, 22).

In contrast to Japan's stance of avoiding issues surrounding conflict with minority groups, Western governments, especially the United States, have been very direct in confronting the GoV on their human rights abuses. In 2004, in response to the major protests and the subsequent violent crackdown on ethnic minority and religious groups, notably the arrest and imprisonment of Montagnard and UBCV church leaders, the US State Department designated Vietnam a Country of Particular Concern (CPC) under the International Religious Freedom Act. This occurred at a time when the GoV was aiming toward World Trade Organization (WTO) accession and a trade agreement with the United States. The United States removed the CPC status in 2006 and signed a bilateral agreement on Vietnam's accession to the WTO, the last agreement that was necessary, after the GoV instituted new religious laws providing a clear process and timeline of response for applications on religious group approval and a policy stating that forced renunciations of faith were not allowed. More recently, at the Consultative Group meeting in 2009, the United States and several other bilateral donors again criticized the government for restrictions on freedom of expression and called for more participation by civil society in politics. The most recent Country Assistance Plan of the United Kingdom acknowledges, "Slow but positive progress on civil and political rights in Vietnam," but that "a major human rights violation" would jeopardize ODA support (Department for International Development 2008, 24). The 2004 move by the US State Department shows the GoV responded to external actions criticizing it for human rights abuses. This is a direction that multilateral aid agencies and Japan have not pursued.

Other Domestic Groups

The peasant protests in 1997 generated the most concern for the GoV. The protest by farmers centered on the harsh economic conditions, land grievances, and corruption and abuses by local party officials. The protests sent shockwaves through the government as the peasant farmers were the heart of the socialist agenda. The government saw the issue as primarily a problem of local corruption and focused on the need to strengthen and enhance democratic centralism, where greater input from local voices would be included in the decision-making process and selection of local officials and candidates. Democratic centralism also meant, however, once a decision was made, no dissent was tolerated. Decree 29, entitled Grassroots Democracy at the Commune, was instituted in 1998 and called for greater citizen participation in decision making at the commune level. The degree to which the policy was actually instituted varied across communes and villages and depended largely on the village leader. Nevertheless, it put in place a reform that generally gained momentum at the local level over time (Jorgenson 2005, 316–345).

The government also placed greater emphasis on separating the role of the government and the party and increasing the role of the National Assembly. Improved transparency became a goal as well. While candidates for local government offices and National Assembly seats were still decided on by the People's Council at each level of administration, greater input would be garnered by local groups and citizens. Donor partners, including Japan, have assisted in facilitating this increased role of the National Assembly by providing technical and legal guidance, training, and expertise to improve the administrative efficiency of the legislative body and other government offices. In 1997, the National Assembly took unprecedented action by rejecting the prime minister's proposal to extend the term of the central bank governor and the proposed candidate for the minister of transportation. Also in 1997, the National Assembly began a televised question time with ministers, where pointed questions could be directed to government officials in a public forum.[11] This was especially important in an effort to show a strong front against fighting corruption. In many regards, 1997 marked a watershed year with changes instituted as a result of the peasant protests. In 1998, the government also gave amnesty to over 8,000 prisoners, the largest number up to that date.[12]

As mentioned earlier, it was at this critical time, when the effects of the Asian financial crisis came to a head, that the World Bank held back aid to get the GoV to adopt reform goals. Japan increased its aid and attempted to provide stability in the economic sphere, while the government addressed the economic crisis and internal dissent. While the Asian financial crisis eventuated in sweeping change in the political realm in South Korea, Indonesia, and Thailand, Vietnam avoided this outcome. Abuza argues this is largely due to the fact that there was no external group large enough to cause such change (2001, 10–15). The peasant protests were large in numbers, but participants were not part of a larger organized body that crossed local areas. While it is difficult to quantify the impact of the increased aid from Japan, it provided support in maintaining economic stability. Though there was no sweeping change, the economic crisis and the peasant dissatisfaction with the government did result in change in the political process and the role of political institutions, beyond the usual focus on economic reforms.

One of the pressing concerns of the peasant protests in 1997 was the level of corruption in the government. While the changes implemented in Decree 29 and the National Assembly were made, in large part, to address the issue, the government has continued to be plagued by corruption scandals. In 1999, 77 people were involved in the largest corruption scandal to date, including businessmen, bankers, and civil servants. In 2001, officials from the Committee for Ethnic Minorities Affairs (CEMMA) were disciplined on corruption charges. This is the agency responsible for carrying out the poverty program 135 supported by the World Bank. In 2003, Nam Cam, the major mafia godfather in the South, was sentenced to death after a televised trial that involved 154 individuals, including some major party and public officials. Several ministers and deputy ministers have had to resign over the years including in 2006 when the Project Management Unit 18 (PMU 18) scandal occurred, where charges of embezzlement, nepotism, and bribery led to the resignation of the transport minister, with many other high-ranking officials involved, including the general secretary's son-in-law (Dung 2008). PMU 18 managed funds for road construction, including ODA funds from numerous donors to Vietnam aimed at transport infrastructure development. An internal review by the World Bank of its projects to support rural road development highlights episodes of collusion and price fixing in the bidding process for contracts and the lack of capacity of the Ministry of Transportation to adequately deal with the situation. (Transport, Energy, and Mining Unit 2007, 15–16). The report recommended the need to assist the GoV in developing greater capabilities in financial and project management. In 2008, the government of Japan had to suspend aid to Vietnam as a Japanese firm was found guilty of paying bribes to Vietnamese officials in charge of the Ho Chih Minh City highway project (Kubota 2009). Aid was reinstated two months later, after new steps were put in place to monitor aid allocation. Evidence suggests that corruption has not decreased over the years despite the governments protestations to curb it. In fact the PMU 18 scandal and the temporary cessation of Japanese aid are clear indications that the large volume of aid provides another arena for corruption to occur among government officials.

One benefit of the cessation of aid was the establishment of the Vietnam-Japan Joint Committee for Preventing Japanese ODA-related corruption. The committee reached concrete agreement on changes to take place including the following (Ministry of Foreign Affairs of Japan 2009b): Ratification of the UN Convention against Corruption by June 2009; and the National Strategy for Preventing and Combating Corruption towards 2020 be implemented. While these actions were being worked on and considered by the GoV, the timing of the scandal allowed Japan to leverage its ODA to push for a concrete timeline and commitment from the GoV to deal with corruption. This is one area where Japan appears to have successfully pressed for changes in policy and action by leveraging its ODA.

Independent evaluators of Japan's ODA to Vietnam criticized the Country Assistance Plan for not mentioning corruption at all in the document (Muta et al. 2007, 13–14). They listed corruption as a "pressing issue" that Japan needed to work on and make progress. This lack of attention in official policy documents lies in contrast to other donors who have placed corruption among the top priorities to address in Vietnam. The United Kingdom for example lists corruption as a primary risk to ODA in its Country Assistance Plan and that it will directly work with GoV to tackle this issue (Department for International Development 2008, 24). Corruption will remain an issue for donors as long as large amounts of ODA are deposited in a system lacking transparency and capacity, both in terms of administrative infrastructure and human resource capability.

Similar to the Asian financial crisis, the recent recession from the global financial crisis has also presented severe challenges in Vietnam. This time, it is the factory workers who have felt the pinch with slower economic growth and escalating inflation. In 2008, over 650 labor strikes took place throughout the country. Technically, these were all illegal strikes, as strikes cannot take place without prior permission from the government. This is nearly a fivefold increase compared to 2005: 350 strikes occurred in 2006, and over 500 in 2007 (Thayer 2008b, 15). The government raised minimum wages in 2006, 2007, and in May 2009, in an attempt to combat workers' dissatisfaction, but the unrest continued. Since 2006, numerous labor activists have been arrested and imprisoned (Human Rights Watch 2009b, 3).

As strikes began to increase dramatically in 2006, another challenge emerged for the government as a new political group called "Bloc 8406" was formed. The group issued a call for greater political freedoms using the internet as a vehicle to disseminate its agenda and enlist support. It was formed by political and labor activists who had acted independently up to then. Bloc 8406 attempted to expand later in the year by uniting with the UBCV and emerge as a larger political movement in the country. The government arrested and imprisoned several leaders in 2007 and slowed down the activities of the organization. In 2011, the GoV instituted a new government decree regulating journalists and bloggers. Thayer argues that the formation and actions of Bloc 8406 is the first instance of political civil society emerging in Vietnam, a larger group that could put demands on the government for greater freedoms and respect for human rights (Thayer 2009). It was similar groups that were critical for the eventual adoption of increased freedom and multiparty democracy in Eastern Europe.

Most recently, it has been revealed that the GoV has been running Drug Rehabilitation Centers that are actually forced labor camps (Human Rights Watch 2011). Under the label "labor therapy," individuals forced to live in the Drug Rehabilitation Centers must do forced labor. The number of such centers has doubled between 2000 and 2010, and the maximum detention length has increased from one to four years. ODA funds designated for drug rehabilitation or HIV/AIDS relief from the United States, World Bank, UN, and other donors support the centers. This is a clear intersection between ODA and abusive treatment of citizens and may be an opportunity for Western governments to leverage their ODA to affect change in the actions of the government.

Furuoka, in a study on Japanese aid sanctions, finds that Japan implemented only positive aid sanctions, an increase in foreign aid, in the case of Thailand and Indonesia, and did not use negative aid sanctions, a decrease in foreign aid, even though there were opportunities (2007). Evidence here shows that this is indeed the case in Vietnam as well. The Japanese policy has been to generate growth through the development of economic infrastructure, and generating an appropriate investment climate has been the focus of Japanese ODA, and to a large degree, the policy of multilateral agencies as well. The GoV has focused on providing a stable environment and also instituting economic reforms to improve the investment climate. As former Japanese Ambassador to Vietnam Norio Hattori has stated, "The important point here is that Japan does not force Vietnam to reform, but that Vietnam recognizes this as its own problem and addresses it with a sense of ownership" (Hattori 2009, 3). While this statement refers to economic reforms, it is just as applicable to Japan's stance in facilitating political reform and addressing the removal of restrictions on freedoms in Vietnam. The policy not only enhances economic stability and thus the avoidance of conflict under current conditions, but also potentially undermines the change that could arise from further economic deterioration and citizen dissatisfaction with government policies. Such change, however, could come at a very high price in terms of conflict. In a country that has been ravaged by war for decades, perhaps it is the desire to avoid this that has led to the current scenario, one where there is no external group large enough to foment sweeping political change as in other countries in Asia during the Asian financial crisis or Eastern Europe in 1989–1990. There is no guarantee, however, that a large enough economic downturn would not change the situation. Based on its track record, though, Japan would be there supporting with ODA all along to prevent such an outcome.

Conclusion

The program of *Doi Moi* has achieved remarkable economic progress in a short period. Japan's partnership through ODA and other technical support has been instrumental in helping Vietnam achieve its growth and poverty-reduction goals. Evidence suggests that ODA can play an important role in supporting reform-minded government leaders in intraparty disputes over the need for and pace of economic reforms. Japan's strategy has been to provide aid without demands, supporting a stable economic and investment climate for the country. Multilateral aid agencies have been more forceful in demanding a particular reform agenda and timeline. Both have been successful in achieving the ultimate goal of continuing and increasing the pace of economic reform. Both, however, have stayed away from interfering in the government's handling of conflict with ethnic minority and religious groups and other external groups calling for change. While donors, including Japan to a much lesser degree, have supported the direct poverty alleviation projects carried out by the government often targeting ethnic minority groups, they have not tied their aid to improving human rights conditions. Western governments led by the United States, however, have been more direct in condemning human rights abuses and calling international attention to the matter. The GoV has responded with positive change to such external pressure.

Japan's ODA policy in Vietnam is consistent with its general policy carried out around the world: a strong belief in the importance of economic infrastructure in the early stages of development for generating economic growth and poverty reduction. The government generally does not engage in social engineering in the recipient country, attempting to target certain groups for special aid or treatment. Instead, the philosophy is more akin to "a rising tide lifting all boats," providing a more stable economic and social environment in the country. In the case of Vietnam, the rising tide has been very powerful and the benefits have been great. However, there have been groups left behind, namely ethnic minority groups that often have a religious dimension to their identity. Their plight has resulted in increased discontent and episodes of protest and violence. While the emphasis on infrastructure has generated significant returns, there is indication that the benefits have not been shared equally. The Kinh majority have fared significantly better than minority groups. This disparity has been one source of tension between ethnic minorities and the government. ODA, from Japan and elsewhere, has also been an indirect source of disenchantment as corruption scandals emerge, one after another. While ODA appears to have reduced conflict within the Communist Party and supported social stability through positive economic performance, its effects on inequality and corruption has contributed to polarization between the party and both nonparty members and ethnic minorities.

In addition, while the economic conditions of the average citizen have improved greatly, there are other groups, religious and political, that remain frustrated by the lack of freedom of association and assembly and whose vehemence periodically is displayed in public protest. Past behavior by the GoV suggests that Japan could leverage its aid and influence the government's actions and treatment of these groups. There is no indication, however, that there is any willingness on the part of Japan to alter its ODA agenda in this direction. Instead, Japanese aid continues to pursue a commercially oriented foreign assistance approach that ignores any potential leverage for reducing conflict. This is in contradiction to the language incorporated in Japan's revised ODA Charter. While the new charter placed an emphasis on human security, ODA policy in Vietnam has not changed despite episodes of conflict. Japanese ODA policy in Vietnam has focused on effectively dealing with the "threat from want," or poverty, while mostly ignoring the "threat from fear," at least with respect to human rights violations. One avenue to address this deficiency is to increase aid in the form of Grassroots Human Security Projects and support for Japanese NGO's, a category where funding to Vietnam has remained low and unchanged. External evaluators of Japanese ODA to Vietnam also recommended that the Japanese government work more collaboratively with other donors to address difficult areas of concern such as rising inequality and corruption as opposed to adhering to a stand-alone approach (Muta et al. 2007, 22–28).

Japan's ODA policy has gained it great favor in Vietnam and the relationship between the two countries has advanced steadily over the period of *Doi Moi*. According to a recent Gallup poll, 56 percent of Vietnamese polled approved of Japan's leadership (Gallup 2008). This is significantly higher than approval ratings of the Japanese government in its own country.

The strong relationship is further exhibited in the compulsory education that Vietnamese children receive. In the eleventh-grade citizenship book that students are required to study, Japan is discussed as the desirable economic model to emulate for the country of Vietnam, having replaced the Soviet model that used to hold the place in the text (Lucius 2009, 38–39). Given Japan's history in the region, there is no doubt that ODA is also used as a vehicle to improve its image. In this regard, it appears to have been successful in Vietnam, but this is also true due to the high regard that the citizens of Vietnam feel for their government; in other words, within Vietnam, Japan is not viewed as supporting a repressive regime. The World Values Survey indicates that in 2000 and 2005, 76 and 80 percent of respondents from Vietnam, respectively, stated that they had a great deal of confidence in their government (World Values Survey 1981–2008). Gallup numbers for 2008 show that 87 percent of the respondents in Vietnam have confidence in their government (Gallup 2008). In all three cases, Vietnam ranked highest among all countries included in the worldwide poll. These numbers suggest that Japan has been supporting a popular government, providing stability during turbulent times. In the end, this may be the greatest contribution to conflict avoidance that Japan could make. Although evidence suggests it could also make gains in more sensitive areas that its own ODA Charter calls for, namely, in the area of human security.

Notes

1. The main power center in the government is contained in a triumvirate of the party general secretary, the prime minister, who is responsible for the daily affairs of the government, and the president, whose role is mostly ceremonial. All three are members of the powerful Politburo, a body whose numbers has ranged from 13 to 19 members over the years and is the main decision-making body in the government. The Central Committee, consisting of 170 members, is responsible to appoint members of the Politburo. The National Assembly is the representative body where constitutional and legislative powers exist.
2. In the government's land reform scheme, the government, as a representative of the people, owns all land but leases it to private farmers. These farmers are able to sell the land to other farmers or the government can pay the farmers for the land if it is confiscated.
3. Vietnam went from being a net importer of rice before *Doi Moi* to becoming one of the largest exporters of rice in the world.
4. The three main institutions administering ODA in the Japanese government are the Ministry of Foreign Affairs, which administers grant aid and is responsible for overall ODA oversight; the Japanese Bank for International Cooperation (JBIC), which is responsible for the loan aid program; and the Japanese International Cooperation Agency (JICA), which provides technical assistance.

5. While the largest percentage of international aid from Japan is directed at infrastructure, spending on human development, which includes spending on education and health, holds the top rank for the World Bank.
6. Japan has also used its increased involvement with donors in the international arena to influence ODA policy norms and generate a focus toward more emphasis on infrastructure. A joint study by Japan, the World Bank, and the Asian Development Bank entitled, *Connecting East Asia: A New Framework for Infrastructure* (2005), is one result of such efforts.
7. The "middle-income trap" is the fact that many countries achieve middle-income status, but then find it difficult to become a high-income country.
8. Churches, once registered, are placed under the Fatherland Front organization.
9. ODA from Japan prior to 2003 included both areas of spending, however, the category Grassroots Projects added the term "human security" to its title, and part of the original Grassroots Projects that included Japanese NGO's were moved to a new category that separately identified these NGO projects.
10. Japan has increased spending in these areas in other countries such as Afghanistan and Iraq, but the amount has not changed significantly in Vietnam.
11. Many attributed Nong Duc Manh, who was later appointed general secretary of the party in 2001, with instituting the changes in the National Assembly and creating a more consultative body.
12. The GoV would use the granting of amnesty to prisoners time and time again in an attempt to improve its image.

References

Abuza, Zachary. 2001. *Renovating politics in contemporary Vietnam.* Boulder, CO: Lynne Rienner Publishers.

Arase, David. 2005. Introduction. In *Japan's foreign aid: old continuities and new directions*, edited by David Arase, pp. 1–20. London: Routledge.

Asian Development Bank, Japan Bank for International Cooperation, and the World Bank. 2005. *Connecting East Asia: A new framework for infrastructure.* Washington, DC: World Bank.

Bartholomew, Ann, Robert Leurs, and Adam McCarty. 2006. *Joint evaluation of general budget support: Vietnam country report.* International Development Center, School of Public Policy, University of Birmingham.

British Broadcasting Corporation. 2006. *Vietnam ministry hit by scandal*, London, Englad.

Central Department of Ideology and Culture. 2006. *Vietnam: Vision 2020.* The Gioi Publishers.

———. 2007. *Vietnam: Twenty years of renewal.* The Gioi Publishers.

Clay, Edward J., Matthew Geddes, and Luisa Natali. 2009. *Untying aid: Is it working?* Aarhus: Danish Institute for International Studies.

Deolalikar, Anil B. 2001. *The spatial distribution of public spending on roads in Vietnam and its implications*, Manila, Phillippines: Asian Development Bank.

Deshingkar, Priya. 2006. *Internal migration, poverty, and development in Asia: Including the excluded*. Brighton: Institute of Development Studies and Oversees Development Institute.

Department for International Development. 2008. *Vietnam: Country assistance plan 2007–2011*. London: Government of the United Kingdom.

Dung, Thuy. 2008, October 14. Church victimized and scapegoated for PMU18 scandal. *VietCatholic News*.

Engel, Susan. 2008. Hegemony and the World Bank in Vietnam. In *Hegemony: Studies in consensus and coercion*, edited by Richard Howson and Kylie Smith, pp 159–183: Routledge Press.

Fan, Shenggen, Pham Huong Lan, and Trinh Quang Long. 2004. *Government spending and poverty reduction in Vietnam*. Washington, DC: International Food Policy Research Institute.

Feigenblatt, Otto von. 2007. *Japan and human security: 21st century official development policy apologetics and discursive co-optation*. Bangkok: Chulalongkorn Univeristy. Furuoka, Fumitaka. 2007. *Japan's positive and negative aid sanctions policy toward Asian countries: Case studies of Thailand and Indonesia*, Munich, Germany. Munich Personal RePEc Archive.

Gallup. 2008. Gallup world poll. Retrieved from http://worldview.gallup.com. Accessed June 27, 2009.

General Statistics Office of Vietnam. 2009. *Foreign direct investment projects licensed in period 1998–2008*. Hanoi: Government of Vietnam.

———. 2011. Statistical Data. Retrieved from http://www.gso.gov.vn. Hanoi: Government of Vietnam

General Statistics Office of Vietnam and United Nations Population Fund. 2004. *The 2004 Vietnam migration survey*. Vietnam: Hanoi.

Goldstein, Joshua S. 1992. A conflict-cooperation scale for WEIS events data. *The Journal of Conflict Resolution*, 36 (2): 369–385.

Government of Vietnam. 2001. *Interim poverty reduction strategy paper (I-PRSP)*. Vietnam: Hanoi.

———. 2003. *The comprehensive poverty reduction and growth strategy (CPRGS)*. Vietnam: Hanoi.

Harvie, Charles, and Tran Van Hoa. 1997. *Vietnam's reforms and economic growth*. New York: St. Martin's Press.

Hattori, Norio. 2009. Experiences of Japan-Vietnam joint initiative: Towards dramatic changes in the investment climate in Vietnam. Speech given at 2nd OECD Southeast Regional Forum, in Bangkok, Thailand.

Human Rights Watch. 2002. *Repression of Montagnards: Conflicts over land and religion in Vietnam's Central Highlands*. New York: Human Rights Watch.

———. 2006. *No sanctuary: Ongoing threats to indigenous Montagnards in Vietnam's Central Highlands*. New York: Human Rights Watch.

———. 2009a. *On the margins: Rights abuses of ethnic Khmer in Vietnam's Mekong Delta*. New York: Human Rights Watch.

———. 2009b. *Not yet a worker's paradise: Vietnam's suppression of the independent worker's movement*. New York: Human Rights Watch.

Human Rights Watch. 2011. *The Rehab Archipalego: Forced labor and other abuses in drug detention centers in Southern Vietnam.* New York: Human Rights Watch.

Japan International Cooperation Agency. 2009. *Annual Report.* Tokyo, Japan.

Jeffries, Ian. 2006. *Vietnam: A guide to economic and political developments.* New York: Routledge.

Jorgenson, Bent. 2005. Democracy among the Grassroots: Local responses to democratic reforms in Vietnam. In *Southeast Asian responses to globalization: Restructuring governance and deepening democracy,* edited by Francis Loh Lok Wah and Jaokim Ojendal, pp. 316–344. Copenhagen: Nordic Institute of Asian Studies.

Kansas Event Data System (KEDS). 2007. Philip A. Schrodt (Distributor). Retrieved from http://web.ku.edu/~keds/

Koh, David. 2011. *Unexciting changes in Vietnam at the 11th Party National Congress.* Singapore: Viewpoints, Institute of Southeast Asian Studies.

Kubota, Yoko. 2009, February 23. Japan to resume Vietnam aid after bribery scandal. *Reuters.*

Larsen, Theon Ib, Pham Huong Lan, and Martin Rama. 2004. *The impact of infrastructure development on rural poverty reduction in Vietnam.* Unpublished. Washington, DC: World Bank Lucius, Casey. 2009. *Vietnam's political process: How education shapes political decision-making.* New York: Routledge.

McCarty, Adam, Alexander Julian, and Daisy Banerjee. 2009. *The developmental effectiveness of untied aid: Evaluation of the implementation of the Paris Declaration and of the 2001 DAC recommendation on untying ODA to the LDCs: Vietnam country study.* Vietnam: Mekong Economics Ltd.

Ministry of Foreign Affairs of Japan. 2003. *Japan's official development assistance charter.* Tokyo: Government of Japan.

———. 2008. *Japan's ODA by Country.* Tokyo: Government of Japan.

———. 2009a. *Japan-Vietnam Economic Partnership Agreement.* Tokyo: Government of Japan.

———. 2009b. *Japan-Vietnam Joint Committee for Preventing Japanese ODA-related Corruption.* Tokyo: Government of Japan.

Ministry of Planning and Investment, and Ministry of Transport, Government of the Socialist Republic of Vietnam, and Ministry of Foreign Affairs, Government of Japan. 2006. *Vietnam-Japan joint evaluation on the Japanese ODA program for the transport infrastructure development in the Red River Delta area of the Socialist Republic of Vietnam.* Tokyo: Government of Japan.

Morrison, Kevin. 2005. The World Bank, Japan, and aid effectiveness. In *Japan's foreign aid: Old continuities and new directions,* edited by David Arase, pp. 23–40. London: Routledge.

Mu, Ren, and Dominique van de Walle. 2007. Rural roads and local market development in Vietnam. *Impact Evaluation Series No. 18.* Washington, DC: The World Bank.

Muta, Hiromitsu, Koichiro Agata, Kiyoko Ikegami, Yoshikaza Imazato, Teruo Kawakami, Yasunaga Takachiho, Yayoi Tanaka, Hiroko Hashimoto, and Tatsuya

Watanabe. 2006. *Evaluation of Japan's Grant Assistance for Grassroots Human Security Projects.* Tokyo: Ministry of Foreign Affairs of Japan.

Muta, Hiromitsu, Kiyoko Ikegami, Yoshikazu Imazato, Izumi Ohno, Yayoi Tanaka, Mari Noda, Jiroko Hashimoto, Katsuya Michizuki, and Tatsufumi Yamagata. 2007. *Country assistance evaluation of Vietnam.* Tokyo: Ministry of Foreign Affairs of Japan.

Sidel, Mark. 2008. *Law and society in Vietnam: The transition from socialism in comparative perspective.* Cambridge: Cambridge University Press.

Swinkels, Rob, and Carrie Turk. 2006. Explaining ethnic minority poverty in Vietnam: A summary of recent trends and current challenges. Paper for CEM/MPI meeting on Ethnic Minority Poverty, September 28, in Hanoi, Vietnam.

Taylor, Philip. 2007. *Cham Muslims of the Mekong Delta: Place and mobility in the cosmopolitan periphery.* Honolulu: University of Hawaii Press.

Thang, Nguyen Van. 2007. *Ambiguity of identity: The Mieu in North Vietnam.* Chiang Ma, Thailand: Silkworm Books.

Thayer, Carlyle, A. 2008, November 6–7. Political update: Vietnam overview. Paper presented at The Australian National University, in Australia.

———. 2009. Vietnam and the challenge of political civil society. *Contemporary Southeast Asia,* 31 (1): 1–27.

Transport Development Strategy Institute. 2004. *Study on road network impacts on the poor.* Hanoi: Government of Vietnam.

Transport, Energy, and Mining Unit. 2007. *Implementation, completion, and results report on a credit in the amount of SDR 74.7 million to the Socialist Republic of Vietnam for the Second Rural Transport Project.* Washington, DC: World Bank.

Trinidad, Dennis D. 2007. Japan's ODA at the crossroads: Disbursement patterns of Japan's development assistance to Southeast Asia. *Asian Perspective,* 31 (2): 95–125.

Viet Nam News. 2009, May 12. VN earns record $8b in aid. *Viet Nam News.*

Vietnamese Academy of Social Sciences. 2007. *Vietnam poverty update report 2006: Poverty and poverty reduction in Vietnam 1993–2004.* Hanoi: The National Political Publisher.

VOV News. 2010, April 11. *Japan praises efficiency of ODA funded projects in Vietnam:* VOVNEWS.

World Values Survey, 1981–2008. Official Aggregate v.20090901. 2009. World Values Association. Retrieved from http://www.worldvaluessurvey.org. Aggregate File Producer: ASEP/JDS, Madrid.

CHAPTER 8

Socioeconomic Change, Intraethnic Competition, and Political Salience of Ethnic Identities: The Cases of Turkey and Uzbekistan

Ebru Erdem-Akcay

Introduction

Developmental strategies will inevitably have impacts on the society, and subsequent changes in social networks and authority structures may result in higher political salience of ethnic identity, political mobilization, and eventually identity-based conflict. This chapter employs a comparative case study of the relationship between developmental policies, socioeconomic change, and ethnic politics. Through a juxtaposition of Kurds in Turkey and Tajiks in Uzbekistan, the causal links between regional development policies and the different levels of politicization of Kurdish and Tajik ethnic identities are explored.

Kurds in Turkey and Tajiks in Uzbekistan are comparable on many dimensions. They are Persian minorities in countries with a clear majority of Turkic peoples and both minority populations have been concentrated in specific regions (southeastern Turkey and Samarkand-Bukhara respectively). They both have a common religion with the majority groups, Sunni Islam. Despite the similarities, the political salience of ethnic identity of the two groups differs. While Kurdish identity has been the basis of an armed struggle led by the Kurdistan Workers' Party (PKK) as well as electoral competition through pro-Kurdish political parties, Tajiks in Uzbekistan have not engaged in politics on the basis of their ethnic identity.

I have elsewhere argued that intraethnic competition between the existing traditional elites and the emerging new elites leads to the politicization of ethnic identity, and possibly to conflict (Erdem 2006). That study explained the role that local socioeconomic organizations and the authority structures embedded in these organizations play in social and political identifications of ethnic group members. It discussed how socioeconomic change led to changes in the local socioeconomic organizations and authority structures. When the existing authority structures begin to fail in answering the needs of the people in newer socioeconomic contexts, a new set of elites emerge and challenge the existing elites, to replace them as the political leaders of the ethnic group members. The new elites use the ethnic card to unite the group members, which politicizes the "ethnic" identity as opposed to subethnic or supraethnic identities.

This chapter focuses on one part of this causal story: what exactly is the effect of socioeconomic change on the society? What are the different dimensions of this effect? How much of the structural change is attributable to the regional development policies of the state, or how much of the lack of change is due to the state's disregard for the region in which the ethnic group resides? In answering these questions, the emphasis will be on the ground level, societal changes rather than politics and discourse at the elite level.

First, I give a brief background of the two groups providing information about their regional dispersion, economic interdependence, and co-ethnics in the neighboring states. Then, in two separate sections, I discuss the developmental strategies and their effects on the two ethnic groups. In each section, I pursue a common set of questions: What were the socioeconomic conditions like before? What is the nature of the "development?" What are the respective roles of the state and the private sector in the development process? How do the people react to development? Does the development and its intended or unintended consequences provide resources, opportunities, or detriments to ethnic elites' mobilization efforts?

Background

As mentioned above, Kurds and Tajiks share many common traits. Although they have lived in relative peace with the Turks and Uzbeks respectively, their ethnic identities have been socially salient; the "us and them" distinctions were maintained.[1,2] Another important commonality between the two groups, geographical concentration, probably helped the maintenance of ethnic group characteristics and boundaries.[3] Although the exact boundaries of the ethnic regions within the two countries are not well-defined, Kurds consider southeast Anatolia as "northern Kurdistan," Kurdistan being the historical homeland that encompasses northern Iraq, southeastern Turkey, and parts of Iran and Syria that neighbor these areas. Likewise, Tajiks consider the Samarkand-Bukhara region as part of their historical homeland, which extends into most of today's Tajikistan and northern Afghanistan. Originally, regional concentration of the Kurds was higher compared to that of Tajiks, who also live in foothill pockets in the Fergana Valley, in addition to the Samarkand-Bukhara region. However, Kurdish emigration that has been continuing since the 1960s has changed the dispersion of Kurds in Turkey. While most Kurds still live in the region, a sizable part of the group members in Turkey lives outside the southeast (Mutlu 1996).[4] Tajiks' pattern of migration is different: the small-scale internal population movements have mostly been from the countryside to the provincial city center (Erdem 2006, 116).

The discussion on the historical homelands inevitably raises the issue of the co-ethnics across the border. Kurds do not have an independent state, although Kurds of northern Iraq have achieved autonomy and are officially governed by Kurdish Regional Government since 2005.[5] Tajiks, however, had a republic of their own under the Soviet Union; and this republic became an independent state in 1991—the same year Uzbekistan did. Interestingly, the politics of both ethnic groups are primarily oriented toward the political center of the country they live within rather than their brethren across the border.

The PKK, for example, had the primary goal of gaining independence *from* Turkey; uniting Kurds in Iraq, Iran and Syria was an ideal rather than a goal. Achieving a united Kurdistan would involve negotiations (and power struggles) with northern Iraq–based Kurdish groups, Patriotic Union of Kurdistan (PUK) of Jalal Talabani, and the Kurdistan Democratic Party (KDP) of Massoud Barzani, and the PKK, which has preferred to concentrate its efforts within Turkey. This does not mean that the Kurds on the two sides of the Turkey-Iraq border were indifferent to each other. Kurds of northern Iraq have aided PKKs armed struggle, most importantly by providing safe havens for PKK camps in the region. However, it is uncertain whether either Kurdish party of Iraq has supported PKK toward the goal of independent, united Kurdistan or toward having some negotiation power against Turkey in regional politics. Both KDP and PUK have at times collaborated with the Turkish government and military against the PKK, which hints that the latter might be the case.[6]

The Tajiks in Uzbekistan have found themselves in a difficult position when the Soviet Union dissolved and Tajikistan succumbed into a civil war soon after. According to my personal correspondences in 2003 in Samarkand, Tajiks felt strongly about their ethnic identity and they would not be happy about being politically dominated by the titular nation, Uzbeks. However, they preferred to be citizens of a country aspiring to be the regional leader rather than a country suffering from conflict and poverty. Their identification with Samarkand was so strong that they could not think of immigrating to Tajikistan to be with their ethnic brethren. Samarkandi respondents in my research talked of Tajikistan with fondness and longing but made it very clear that they could never leave this city and they were planning to establish a future for their children in Samarkand despite the challenges of being a minority in Uzbekistan. For Tajiks in Namangan, Tajikistan does not come up as an ethnic or cultural reference in conversations, it is mentioned only in the context of employment opportunities in cities such as Khojent.

Connections between Tajiks living in Uzbekistan and Tajikistan are weak and to a large extent limited to the Tajiks of Samarkand (Roy 2000, 70). The nationalists in Tajikistan may have irredentist aspirations such as making Samarkand and Bukhara part of Tajikistan, but the lack of connections makes any mobilization in Uzbekistan difficult. Moreover, Tajikistan is simply not powerful enough, politically and economically, to lay an official claim on these Tajik-populated cities, and such a claim would only result with Uzbekistan claiming in turn Khojent (formerly Leninabad), the predominantly Uzbek-populated province in northern Tajikistan, which is the economic locomotive of the country. If Tajikistan achieves political cohesion and becomes an economic success that can rival Uzbekistan, Tajiks on either side of the border may dare open the "can of worms," that is, border change.[7] However, this still remains an unlikely scenario.

Post-1999 Kurdish politics in Turkey and Tajiks in independent Uzbekistan have both focused on the terms of their citizenship within their respective countries. The choice of abandoning the idea of secessionism, after having fought for it in the case of the Kurds and only entertaining the idea in teahouse conversations in the case of the Tajiks, is very much related to the economic (inter)dependence between the two ethnic groups and the majority groups in the two countries. As will be elaborated below, the patronage system established in the Soviet period and continued in the independence era ties Tajik regions strongly to Tashkent. The failure of a private economic sector independent from the state and wealth associated with such economic activity only exacerbates regions' dependence on the state allocations. This is true for not only for the Tajik areas but also for all other regions in Uzbekistan. In the Kurdish case, the level and the nature of economic interdependence between the southeast and the rest of Turkey have changed over time, as will be elaborated in detail in the next section.

Interestingly, the socioeconomic changes that led to increasing interdependence also led to decreasing regional autonomy and increasing salience of the Kurdish ethnic identity.

Developmental Strategies, the GAP, and Kurdish Identity in Turkey

Ethnic identity has not always been the *politically* salient identity for Kurds in Turkey. For most Kurds, until 1980s, their tribal identity was the basis of social organization, political action, and their connections to the state (Beşikçi 1969; Bruinessen 1992, 103). A "tacit contract" between tribal leaders (*ağas*) and the Ottoman government ensured the administrative autonomy of the Kurds in return for their loyalty to the Ottoman state (Bozarslan 2003; Özoğlu 2004). Despite interruptions due to Ottoman and republican centralization attempts, renewed versions of this "tacit contract" dominated the state-Kurdish society relationships even after the establishment of the republic in 1923.[8] In the republican era, the political parties in Ankara sought the cooperation of the tribal leaders. They provided political power and patronage to the tribal leaders, and the tribal leaders delivered the vote of the tribe for the respective party. This arrangement not only kept the tribal socioeconomic organization in place and in effect, but also made the tribal identities politically salient, because individual Kurds engaged in political activity such as voting and patronage seeking based on them.

One intriguing question about the incorporation of the Kurdish society into the political and economic structure of the new state of Turkey is why the state did not exert its centralizing policies in the southeast but rather continued providing the tribes their administrative autonomy. The modernist, progressive ideology of the republic would contradict the idea of connecting with the Kurdish individuals through the feudal tribal leaders rather than through the ties of citizenship. In addition, the modernization and nation-building policies, which were vigorously carried out in the rest of the country in the Atatürk era (1923–1938), were administered in the southeast only partially. The reason for the discrepancy is simply that the new Turkish state did not have the capacity to challenge the tribal structure and could apply its policies only to the extent that it could penetrate the society. Failing to eliminate or overcome the authority of the tribe and its hierarchy, the state relied on the tribal organization for many aspects of administration, which inevitably resulted in the continuation of the "tacit contract" between the tribes and the state.[9]

Until the 1980s, when PKK's armed insurgency started, the administration in the southeast was both centralized and decentralized at the same time. As in the rest of the country, the southeast was divided into administrative units such as provinces, districts, and municipalities. Each unit had centrally appointed or in some cases elected authorities and their associated bureaucracies, including the courts, the police, and the military. The difference between the southeast and the rest of Turkey was twofold. First, in the southeast, the tribal system challenged the authority of the state, and bureaucracy's enforcement could not infiltrate the cultural barriers. Second, the region was geographically remote, largely rural, and to a large extent inaccessible due to terrain and climatic conditions.[10] Take the issue of mandatory primary schooling: since the early years of the republic, the rates of schooling have increased and the gap between girls' and boys' rate of schooling has narrowed although it has not disappeared.[11] The same educational policies did not succeed in the southeast, because the traditions did not favor schooling, especially for girls, and because the state could neither establish schools in the dispersed rural settlements nor get the kids into classrooms where facilities existed. As a result, the region has the lowest schooling rates and the largest gender gap in education.[12]

The discrepancy between the southeast and the rest of the country regarding the state's ability to enforce its modernization policies and to bring services inevitably caused a divergence in terms of economic performance and human development.[13] The southeast came to be defined by both Kurds and Turks as "backwards." The "backwardness" has engendered prejudiced, and sometimes derogatory, perceptions of the natives of these regions in the rest of the country as well as resentment toward the "neglectful" state in the region itself. Was the state indeed "neglectful?" What was the place of the Kurdish regions in the national development plans throughout the decades? What were the consequences of development policies in the region? An account of three different eras of Turkish economic development—the *étatist* era (1931–1960), the import-substitution industrialization (ISI) era (1963–1980), and the liberalization era (1980–present)—helps answer these questions.

Étatisme of the 1930s was a response to the failure of laissez faire policies of the earlier years of the republic to build enough capital for industrialization and to the failure in the Great Depression. The economic policies of the single-party regime of the Republican People's Party (RPP) in this period relied on state *dirigisme*, which called for heavy involvement of the state in investing for state-owned industries as well as creating and nurturing a private sector.[14] The five-year industrial plans, which were the blueprints of state development policies, specifically emphasized an even distribution of industrial centers and developing industries based on local resources; the second plan in 1938 singled out the East as a priority (Hershlag 1964,

194–195). At least in theory, the state development plans did not discriminate against the Kurdish-populated areas. In practice, though, the regional disparities grew as a result of state-led industrialization.

In the southeast, the state invested in a few industrial facilities and railroads connecting the east of the country to its west. However, the areas around Istanbul and Izmir dwarfed other regions in terms of the investment they received and the development they achieved. This was partly due to the convenient geographical location of these coastal regions and, in a related vein, because of private sector's strict preference for investment in these regions. Knowledge of and political connections with Ankara and its bureaucracies determined which private investors had access to the patronage distributed through the industrialization programs. In the southeast, these private investors were the tribal leaders; the "tacit contract" described above ensured that these traditional authorities got the state patronage. They used these resources to bolster their economic status, and thus increased social authority over the tribe. State developmental policies indirectly strengthened the tribal order.

The end of the *étatist* era was a period of hardship, stagnation, and turmoil due to World War II and the transition to multiparty politics. The entrance of the Democrat Party (DP) into the political arena as a challenger to the RPP and its eventual electoral victory in 1950 did not substantially change the way the Kurdish population was connected to the state. DP was a splinter party off of RPP, and it continued the tradition of working through the tribes. Now, the two rival political parties affiliated themselves with rival tribes, and party politics and electoral competition became new arenas where local tribal rivalries played out (Beşikçi 1969, 218–222; Bruinessen 1992, 75).[15] The role of tribal authorities as local allies for the Ankara-based political parties also implied the continuation of channeling the state patronage to and through them (McDowall 2000, 398–399). Postwar Marshall Plan aid could have been a big boost to the Turkish economy in the early 1950s, but the funds were distributed as patronage to gain an advantage in the new competitive electoral arena. In the southeast the tribal leaders, as the deliverers of votes, got their share; however, they did not invest the funds as productively as the patronage recipients in the west.[16] By 1970s, investment in the region by local capitalists still had not increased: Beşikçi compares the landlords in the west and the *ağa* in the east, and notes that the capital accumulation in the east flowed to the west (1969, 107–109).

The year 1960 was an important turning point for Turkey, both politically and economically. The new constitution after the 1960 military coup expanded the political space, which eventually led to ideological fragmentation and polarization in the Parliament as well as within the newly politically active population. Although the governments shifted between center, right, and left parties or mixed-ideology coalitions until 1980, the overall economic development plan remained as import-substitution industrialization (ISI). ISI policies and their results in Turkey were very similar to those in Latin America. State-led heavy industrialization initiatives went hand in hand with investments in big public works projects. The State Planning Organization (DPT), established in 1961, drafted five year development plans to determine targets and methods for development.[17] One of DPT's major initiatives was what later became the Southeastern Anatolia Project (GAP), a long-term, major irrigation and hydroelectricity production project involving the Tigris and Euphrates rivers. The planning for the project began in the 1960s, but the project was slow to materialize. The first major component completed, the Keban Dam on the Euphrates, started operation in 1975.

The east and the southeast of Turkey did not benefit much from the earlier attempts of industrialization and development plans, although the latter emphasized even, balanced regional development. In addition to the aforementioned access problems, these regions did not have the resources to put to industrial use, and given the distance to the ports and markets it did not make economic sense to build industries there. There were some mineral resources, which received investment, but the major economic activity of the southeast—agriculture—needed irrigation to become a large-scale, wealth-producing sector.

GAP recognizes the significant resource the region has been blessed with: water. Since its inception, various components of the project that were actualized throughout the decades, put this increasingly valuable resource to multiple uses. The dams, tunnels, and canals have allowed for new opportunities in rural areas, making possible irrigated, industrial agriculture. The dams can be used for producing clean energy as well as regulating water flow. The latter is both a drought control mechanism and a new negotiation card that Turkey has in regional politics with Syria and Iraq.

GAP is one of the largest water management projects in the world. The Southeastern Anatolia Project Regional Development Administration describes GAP as

> a multi-sector and integrated regional development effort approached in the context of sustainable development. Its basic objectives include the improvement of living standards and income levels of people so as to eliminate regional development disparities and contributing to such national goals as social stability and economic growth by enhancing productivity and employment opportunities in the rural sector. The project

area covers 9 administrative provinces (Adiyaman, Batman, Diyarbakir, Gaziantep, Kilis, Mardin, Siirt, Sanliurfa, and Sirnak) in the basins of the Euphrates and Tigris and in Upper Mesopotamia.

The GAP had originally been planned in the [19]70s consisting of projects for irrigation and hydraulic energy production on the Euphrates and Tigris, but transformed into a multi-sector social and economic development program for the region in the [19]80s. The development program encompasses such sectors as irrigation, hydraulic energy, agriculture, rural and urban infrastructure, forestry, education and health. The water resources development component of the program envisages the construction of 22 dams and 19 hydraulic power plants and irrigation of 1.82 million hectares of land. The total cost of the project is estimated as US$32 billion. The total installed capacity of power plants is 7476 MW and projected annual energy production reaches 27 billion kWh.

The project rests upon the philosophy [of] sustainable human development, which aims to create an environment in which future generations can benefit and develop. The basic strategies of the project include fairness in development, participation, environmental protection, employment generation, spatial planning and infrastructure development (GAP 2009 see also Ünver 1997).

The lengthy quote is a good illustration of the state's many and multidimensional expectations from the project. However, the project, the infrastructural aspects of which are far from being completed, is already too late to shape the fate of the region. The society and the politics in the region had already changed considerably before the water reached the Harran plains through the Şanliurfa tunnels in 1995, the most significant achievement of the project up to date.

In the 1960s, the level of private sector industrial output and employment surpassed that of the public sector in Turkey (Mutlu 2001, 111). Although state-owned enterprises were still the locomotives of the industrial production and although state involvement through subventions or initiatives were lifelines for the private sector in industry or agriculture, private industry increasingly set the tone and direction of development in the following decades. For example, private industry did not have social goals and based their investment decisions on pure logic of efficiency and economy. This resulted in an ever-increasing concentration of private investment in Marmara and Aegean regions, making these regions a magnet for the unemployed across the country.

As development took off in the west, the GAP was still very far from delivering the promised opportunities. Irrigation was not the only problem with agriculture in the region; land ownership and associated inefficiencies and lack of initiative were as serious. Largely due to the tribal organization and political connections of the *ağa*s, distribution of land ownership was highly unequal. Morvaridi reports that 231 families and 96 extended families in the region owned whole villages, while 38 percent of households, including nomads, were landless (1990, 309).[18] With large land concentration in the hands of a few, most agricultural workers are employed as sharecroppers or wage laborers, which in turn results in low productivity. Substantial land reform is necessary to change these unfavorable employment and land ownership situations; however, it has been politically infeasible. The few who own the land tend to be the tribal leaders who are the local allies of the political parties. Although GAP master plans or action plans include social development goals, they have not mentioned land reform or redistribution in the region; only limited land consolidation is undertaken.

An official land reform policy does not exist; but have the economic changes in the region and associated immigration within and out of the region changed land ownership patterns? Based on a survey in 180 southeastern villages, Akşit and Akçay (1997) report that land ownership trends are changing toward more equality. However, Karapınar provides evidence from national agricultural survey data showing that this is not the case.[19] He argues that "the level of inequality in terms of income generating assets (land and water combined) has increased, not decreased" (2005, 192).

Although GAP did not involve policies that could drastically transform the socioeconomic structure in the region, the overall development in Turkey and the changing economic realities in the region started to upset the traditional system. Beşikçi had argued in 1969 that machination of agriculture coupled with rapid population growth could be the sole dynamic that could lead to the destruction of the feudal structure in the east (p. 107). As he predicted, traditional relationships governing land and labor have been transforming into capitalist forms of socioeconomic relationships, especially in the plains where economic activity is gradually getting integrated with the rest of the country (Akşit and Akçay 1997, 525). However, this integration is filtered through preexisting "politically embedded inequality" within the region (Karapınar 2005, 166). Social feudal relationship between the *ağa* and tribesmen are being transformed into capitalist-labor relationships, but the inequality remains. As elaborated below, interviews in Harran show that this inequality between the haves and the have-nots are shaping the political discourse and GAP (Harris 2006).

Rural-urban migration is another factor contributing to the weakening of the tribal system both in the mountainous regions and in the plains. Employment opportunities in the industrialized areas around İstanbul or

İzmir attracted those who were left unemployed, by increasing machination of agriculture in the region, and who were looking for alternatives to sharecropping arrangements, agricultural work, rural life, submission to the rule of the tribe, and the authority of the tribal leader.[20] Migration increased toward destinations in the industrial centers in the west and the regional city centers, such as Diyarbakır, Gaziantep, and Adana. Migration is important not only because it depletes the population base of the tribes, but also, more significantly, because the people who move away become "free agents." The patronage network of the tribes does not cover these individuals due to the distance and because of the different nature of patronage they need in the urban areas. I have argued elsewhere that emerging ethnic elites have chosen the ethnic identity to unite these "free agents" to build a constituency base, and that the union of these new Kurdish elites and the new Kurdish constituency made ethnic identity politically salient (Erdem 2006). This process of ethnic mobilization finally culminated in the PKK-led insurgency in the 1980s; with a Marxist-Leninist discourse, PKK mobilized the disenfranchised Kurds against the exploitative state as well as its local allies, the exploitative *ağa*s.

The period after 1980 was defined by the coup, which introduced a new, politically more restrictive constitutional framework, and by the liberalizing economic reforms, which gradually diminished state's involvement in economic activity. The armed insurgence of the PKK, which developed into a protracted civil war in the southeast, is another political development that dominated the political agenda starting in 1984.

Both political and economic policies toward the southeast were determined by the state's desire and need to bring an end to the insurgency. The state first resorted to the old strategy of utilizing the tribes and contracted state-friendly tribes as "village guards." It soon became obvious that this move only exacerbated the violence, because the rivalry between the state and the PKK became redefined in terms of local rivalries. Simultaneously, the state attempted to increase state control over the area through establishing the OHAL (state of emergency) regional government, initiating forced migrations to eliminate remote settlements and increasing military presence in the region. These policies increased people's resentment, and mostly backfired. Nonmilitary responses to the insurgency were developed only after the conflict caused thousands of casualties, humanitarian and material damage. This is when GAP became more than a comprehensive infrastructural project.

With the realization that a solely military solution to the violence in the region is not feasible, GAP was transformed from an irrigation and hydroelectricity project to a comprehensive plan for regional development with significant sociopolitical components and goals. Many societal level programs, such as vocational education, sponsoring women's crafts, and development of agricultural and irrigation technology, were included in the GAP Master Plan; however, certain aspects of the master plan have been inadequate in meeting the demands or misguided in its methods. Çarkoğlu and Eder (2005) draw attention to the difficulty of administrating participatory programs when the mistrust of the Turkish state persists. A report by the think-tank TESEV heavily criticizes the plan for its state-guided approach and disregard for practical details (Ensaroğlu and Kurban 2008, 20–22). Both studies have qualms about programs' success given the fact that their design and implementation have not involved local civic organizations. Successive governments have presented GAP as a solution to the "Kurdish question;" however, it is difficult for a plan that does not acknowledge the ethnic dimension of the problems to address it.

How do the people react to GAP and its larger developmental goals? Some Kurdish nationalists see it as exploitation of the Kurdish region and its resources, based on the fact that hydroelectricity produced in the region is used by the consumers and industries elsewhere. Some object to the presentation of the project as an undertaking by the benevolent state for the people of the southeast, arguing that it is not aimed at developing the region but benefiting the nation as a whole (Mutlu 2001, note 80). There are serious objections to the environmental and cultural costs of the project, most notably to the inundation of Kurdish settlements and cultural heritage sites by the dams' reservoirs. Hasankeyf is one such site, which civil organizations are campaigning to save. Kurdish politicians portray it as an example of the Turkish state's assault on the local culture.[21]

However, those who are able to benefit from the project, especially from its irrigation and credit programs, have positive attitudes toward the project.[22] That said, not all are able to benefit from the irrigation.[23] The welfare gap between the landed and the landless has reportedly grown and those who engage in animal husbandry have felt a strong negative impact (Harris 2006; Harris 2009: para. 21–27). Existing wealth, social status, and land size create inequalities in the management of water sharing. Kurds who live in nonirrigated areas express their resentment, using ethnic discourse, that it was predominantly Arab areas that received the water (Harris 2006).[24] The benefits of GAP are not distributed evenly; for example, GAP does not at all benefit areas with rugged terrain, such as Hakkari province.

A final note on interdependence between Kurds and Turks after GAP: the changing demographics as a result of decades of Kurdish migration to the west has made secession impractical, as the common joke that Istanbul is now the largest Kurdish city hints. The GAP has also increased the level of interdependence between the Kurdish and Turkish areas. Although the water, hydroelectricity, mineral resources, or revenues from the region are not absolutely essential to the rest of the country, Turks feel a stronger attachment to the region because of the investment diverted to the region over the decades.[25] In this sense, GAP has anchored the region to the rest of the country. At the same time, the economic dependence of the region upon the rest of the country grows as the economy of the region, albeit very gradually, gets integrated into the national economy. Beyond the necessity of continued investment to foster the region's development, the ties between Turkish and Kurdish regions, including the networks of transportation, communication, and finance, would be difficult to sever, as would Turkey's European Union connections.

Interestingly, PKK's separatist violence took place as the region was getting closely integrated to the rest of the country. The developmental transition upset social and economic equilibria in the region and gave the Kurdish nationalists, who were products of this transition themselves, the opportunity and the constituency for ethnic mobilization. The objectives of Kurdish politics were reoriented from secession/independence toward cultural rights and autonomy in 1999, the year in which PKK leader Abdullah Öcalan was caught and Şanlıurfa tunnels became fully operational. As of 2010, PKK still engages in terrorist attacks, the militarized conflict still continues, although it is not as intense as it was in the 1990s. Pro-Kurdish Peace and Democracy Party (PDP) does not relinquish all ties with the militants but it states its goal as "democratic autonomy" and not secession.[26]

Nowhere in the official documents on GAP can one find a reference to ethnic conflict or PKK, it is as if the project does not have any objectives related to this violent conflict. However, a closer examination of the development of the project over time shows that the project evolved in a way that responds to the conflict. While it was only a hydroelectricity and irrigation project in the 1970s, it became an economic development project in the 1980s, and social and cultural programs were added after the 1990s. The initial stages addressed only economic grievances and unemployment of the people in the region. Later policies reveal an understanding that the region needs social and cultural investment as much as economic development. These policies are state's answers to the question, "How can we stop the people from supporting the PKK?"

PKK violence is not as intense as it was before the 2000s, and Kurdish politics has taken a more peaceful route through the Kurdish parliamentarians and municipal level administrators. It is difficult to assess how much of these developments can be ascribed to the GAP and its social and economic outcomes. However, if the colossal regional development project GAP gives us any lessons about how to engineer developmental strategies toward conflict avoidance, it should be that dumping money and building infrastructure do not prevent conflict. Inclusion of local social programs such as vocational training, increasing activism of municipalities, many of whom are governed by pro-Kurdish mayors, and NGO involvement in issues such as women's rights and cultural services seem to have positive effects, starting in the 1990s. If these local level governmental and nongovernmental initiatives did, in fact, contribute to the positive developments toward peace in the region, it would be a testament that governments should administer projects toward peace locally. Governments cannot efficiently manage all aspects of development centrally, without involving private actors.[27] In the next section, in the case of Uzbekistan, we shall see an example of total government control and management and how it can minimize the risk of ethnic conflict at the cost of economic stagnation.

Regional Balance and Tajik Identity in Uzbekistan

Tajik ethnic identity in Uzbekistan is socially salient, and both Tajiks and Uzbeks routinely use ethnic identifications to define themselves or other individuals in social settings. However, Tajik identity has not been the basis of political activity; the political arena is to a large extent devoid of ethnic references. Glasnost policies of late 1980s had created an environment where Tajik cultural associations were established in Bukhara and Samarkand, and as a response to their campaigns the authorities had allowed some improvements on cultural rights. After independence, two Samarkandi groups joined to establish Samarkand Tajik Cultural Movement whose demands ranged from more cultural rights to integration of Tajik-populated areas of Uzbekistan with Tajikistan. In 1992, the Uzbek government closed the association and reversed all policies favoring Tajik cultural rights, such as Tajik-language broadcasts and publications.[28] In the following years, Tajik schools, newspapers, local radio and TV broadcasts, and a National Association of Tajik Culture have been allowed; however, Tajik ethnic-identity-based political action and mobilization have not been triggered (Yalçın 2002, 112–113).[29]

I will argue here that there are two main reasons why Tajik identity has not become politically salient. First, the careful management of identities under the Soviet Union, which was continued by the Karimov regime, emphasized regional identities as the basis of politics. Second, local authority structures have remained intact even through the considerable changes brought about by the Soviet transformation of society, economics, and politics, and co-optation of these local structures enable the continuation of state control over the society today.

When Uzbekistan became independent in 1991, it inherited a Soviet infrastructure and legacy that it largely put to use toward its goals as an independent state. The region-based political and economic administrative system, infrastructures for economic production, and services such as education, nationalities, and nativization policies that neither destroyed nor fully empowered region's ethnic identities were continued with some modifications. These policies were responsible for 70 years of relative ethnic peace under the Soviet Union, their continuity contributes to the relatively low political salience of ethnicity in Uzbekistan. I will briefly elaborate on the Soviet legacy before I expand on the independence period.[30]

Soviet administrative structure in Central Asia was solidified at the grassroots level through collectivization.[31] In this brutally revolutionary period, which started with the first Five Year Plan in 1928, the social structure of Central Asia was Sovietized. Kazakh, Kyrgyz, and Turkmen nomadic tribes were subjected to forced settlement. Lands cultivated by sedentary Uzbek and Tajiks were taken under state ownership and agricultural production was brought under state control. Throughout the collectivization process, all social units such as tribes or villages became territorial politico-economic units within the Soviet system of collective and state farms, under the name of *kolkhoz* and *sovkhoz* respectively. After collectivization, these socioeconomic units became integral parts of the communist system of economic production, Soviet administrative hierarchy, and the Communist Party, resulting in institutional integration of the people and the state (Jones Luong 2002, 64–66; Roy 2000, 85–91).

A critical fact throughout the process of collectivization was that the preexisting social groupings were not (or could not be) disrupted drastically (Jones Luong 2002, 65; Simon 1991, 98). For Uzbeks and Tajiks, local authority structures, social networks, and economic activity were based on place of residence. With collectivization, the *mahalla* (neighborhood), which is the basic social organization in the urban areas, became the basis of *rayon* (districts) and the *kishloq* (village), which is the rural counterpart, just became *kolkhoz* (collective farm) or *sovkhoz* (state-owned farm). This meant that the authority structures that already existed in these local communities were able to survive and continue as constituent parts of a new administrative structure.[32]

The Soviet administrative structure was based on vertical hierarchical integration of regional units. Moscow had control over all regions and could exert it if necessary; however, different levels of the hierarchy—republic, region, district/village—enjoyed autonomy in day-to-day administration and answered to the authorities in one higher level in the hierarchy. Local administrations remained loyal to the system because of the structured nature of the administrative system, the centralized patronage provision, and the lack of feasible alternatives.[33] At the very local level, the Soviet state and the Communist Party co-opted the leadership of the *kolkhoz*es and the *mahalla*s, who became local *apparatchiki*.[34] Once the loyalty of the *kolkhoz* administration was ensured, administration of individual citizens was left to these local administrations. *Kolkhoz*es and *mahalla*s became the links between individuals and the state.

Since the Soviet system made local social units the basis of political and economic administration, these residence-based social networks continued to be the basis of individuals' identification. In this sense, the political identities that people of Uzbekistan ascribe to today are Soviet constructs on traditional pre-Soviet foundations. For example, Tajiks' salient residential identities such as being *Samarkandi* or *Namangani* or being urban versus rural, date back to pre-Tsarist era; these identities developed based on the way Tajiks were integrated to the Emirate of Bukhara and the multiethnic empires before it. The Soviet state reconstructed the preexisting state-society relationships within its own federal system and communist ideology.

Developmental policies of the Soviet period focused on extracting the resources to develop industries at the center and providing at least a minimum-investment across different territorial-administrative units at different levels.[35] The former designated Uzbekistan as a cotton-producing republic, which eventually led Uzbekistan to have a cotton monoculture at the cost of environmental disasters. The latter ensured that basic state services, such as education, health, and utility infrastructure reached all regions.[36] These policies integrated the units to the Soviet state and economy, increased interdependency between the various levels of the hierarchy, and in addition, generated competition between units at the same level (e.g., between the *kolkhoz* of the same region or between regions of the same republic).[37] Development of irrigation infrastructure and education policies illustrates the point.

Irrigation is crucial to cotton production, and two major river networks of Central Asia, Amudarya and Syrdarya, were utilized for irrigation toward cotton cultivation. After World War II, especially starting in 1960s, irrigated areas were extended drastically in order to maximize cotton production.[38] Increasing irrigation had numerous negative environmental externalities, such as the shrinkage of the Aral Sea, soil salinization, erosion, and water pollution, which continue their effects today (Bucknall et al. 2003; Saiko and Zonn 2000; Strickman and Porkka 2008). However, it made Central Asia the main supplier of Soviet textiles industry. Regional administrators claimed centrally distributed funds citing their cotton contribution, but the cotton prices set by Moscow determined republican revenues.

Similar to irrigation projects and agricultural policies, education policies served the dual purpose of service provision to Central Asians, which benefited the Soviet state in return.[39] The Soviet state has had phenomenal success in educating the people. Literacy rates increased substantially; while it ranged from 2 percent to 7 percent in 1926, it was around 99 percent in the 1970s (Fierman 1991, 30–32; Glenn 1999, 82). High school attendance increased accordingly.[40] While widespread education provided the positive externalities such as high human capital and qualified labor, it also enabled indoctrination of local people with Soviet ideology and identity.[41] Individuals benefited from the opportunities brought by education, but education made them increasingly "Soviet."

In time, education became integral to the nativization policies, which were applied in various stages.[42] In its initial era between 1921 and 1934, the Soviets tried to get the local population into the positions of governance. As long as they showed their allegiance to the Soviet state, members of the titular nation could be brought to prominent positions, no matter what their familial affiliations, education levels, and professions were, or where they came from.[43] These policies were suspended during the purges (1936–1938), where Russians took over administrative positions left vacant by the purged locals. Policy of bringing natives to administrative positions resumed in a different form after World War II. Then, instead of the pre-purge preferential treatment for the natives, upward mobility was restricted to those who were not only loyal but were also able to "operate in a Russian environment" (Fierman 1991, 23).[44] The Soviet state drew talented and loyal people to its cadres, especially to the party organization, from deep within the society, including the remotest villages. These cadres, in turn, promoted the idea of "nation" through the administrative systems of their respective republics.[45] Education was crucial in the development of these loyal local cadres.

Did the inclusion of natives in administration make any difference in terms of economic development or ethnic relationships during the Soviet period? Economic and developmental policies were drafted centrally by Moscow, but they were administered locally. The widespread corruption and subversion allowed members of the *nomenklatura* to favor their own; however, within the republic, competition for economic and political resources and their distribution were on regional basis, not ethnic. Recruitment did favor Russians and the titulars, but political networks mattered more than ethnicity in recruitment.[46] In this regard, inclusion of natives did not drastically alter ethnic relationships.

Independent Uzbekistan: Stagnation Means Continuity

A quick analysis of region-level development data in the United Nations Development Programme's 2008 Uzbekistan Report shows three patterns: First, 11 of the provinces are quite similar in their performance in various social and economic categories; second, province of Navoi is performing better in many categories; third, contrary to Navoi, the Karakalpakastan autonomous region is performing badly (UNDP Uzbekistan 2008, 166–179).[47] Navoi is enjoying the mining industry built around the gold reserves it has, and Karakalpakstan's economy is suffering the consequences of the Aral Sea disaster. Other regions are similar in terms of economic profile thanks to availability of irrigation, which enables agricultural production even in originally desert areas. In addition to similar natural resource endowments and the Soviet developmental legacy, The Uzbek government's emphasis on regional balance is responsible for this picture.

Despite the attempts to bolster Uzbek nationalism, regionalism continues to be the basis of political power and competition, resource distribution, economic production, and selection of political cadres in independent Uzbekistan. Regionalism and equality of regions are promoted through discourse and through political and economic practice; however, it is common knowledge that Tashkent has a *primus inter pares* status (Liu 2005). For example, central leaders emphasized creating "a parliament that would strike a 'better [regional] balance of power' by allocating resources 'more evenly' among regions," while discussing the new electoral system (Jones Luong 2002, 193). Regions and cultural distinctions between them are emphasized even in the state-organized *Nevroz* and independence celebrations.[48]

The need to establish a "regional balance" comes up even in the most mundane issues, such as intercollegiate competitions or the determination of how many weeks the primary soccer league should continue. The students whom I trained for English-language competitions (*olimpiada*) said that a college from Tashkent always gets the first place, and the second place is alternated between Samarkand and Fergana Valley colleges. On a program on the Uzbek national channel, the Uzbek Soccer Federation representative argued that the reasonable duration of the primary soccer league was 30 days. He insisted that there should be at least one team from each province, arguing that it does not matter if the teams are not good enough to be in the *Oliy Lig*. It should not be surprising that there are 13 stars on the Uzbek flag, one for each 12 provinces and another for Karakalpakstan.

This sensitivity for regional balance applies to new investments as well. It was reiterated by many Samarkandi individuals that the government had the Koreans build the automobile factory (Uzdaewoo) in Andijan of Fergana

Valley, but it also had the Turks build the midi-bus factory (Samkocauto) in Samarkand.[49] Morgan Liu's focus group studies also show that regionalism, interregional competition, and Tashkent's special status are common themes in people's discourse on economic conditions in their region or in the country (Liu 2005).[50]

Interestingly, part of Liu's study is conducted with Bukharan focus groups. She identifies the ethnicities of focus group participants; however, Tajik and Uzbek responses do not differ much in their reactions. Members of both ethnic groups respond as *Bukharis*, along regional lines, and they do not raise the issue of ethnicity or make claims of ethnic discrimination. This is probably why the government is sensitive about maintaining a regional balance in economic development. Economic grievances are not expressed along ethnic lines, and the government probably wants to keep it that way.

One might ask if the ethnic dimension is totally sidelined as a result of the government's economic balancing act. Socioeconomic indicators show the existence of a rough balance across regions, and existing economic grievances are framed in regional terms. Nevertheless, such a balance does not exist in recruitment to positions of political power at the national level. This is important, because in the state-controlled economy of Uzbekistan, political power translates into economic power. Being Uzbek and being from Karimov's home, Samarkand province, are advantageous in achieving political power. This advantage eventually leads to economic advantages.

In the later decades of the Soviet Union, Uzbeks asserted their titular status in different arenas. Although Soviet state policy provided opportunities to all ethnic groups, Uzbeks got some preferential treatment in Uzbek Soviet Socialist Republic. This preferential treatment only got more prominent after independence, because it is now supported by the state's nationalist ideology. I have observed that on many occasions Tajiks complain that they have to register themselves as Uzbeks in their national identification cards in order to enjoy the advantage of being Uzbek in employment or university admission. However, Uzbeks —especially those in Fergana Valley— complain that Karimov government favors Samarkand and Jizzak. Although Karimov's ethnicity is not known,[51] based on his hometown people hint that he must be Tajik, which brings in an ethnic dimension to the government's regional favoritism.

In short, regional development policies are not a threat to the relationships between the state and the Tajiks, because regional development policies do not really exist, and existing economic investment is managed with regional concerns in mind.[52] However, such cautious regional management does not exist for access to political power and recruitment. Grievances on this issue are still expressed in regional terms; however, they could easily be expressed in ethnic terms if ethnic entrepreneurs had the opportunity to raise the issue. Uzbek government's national economic policies do not make the emergence of such entrepreneurs possible, because, as we shall see below, the state dominates the economy and suppresses the private sector. In this environment, possible ethnic entrepreneurs are probably either being incarcerated by the state or seeking patronage from it.

At the national level, Uzbekistan's economic policies have shown very slow and gradual development after independence. In the first few years, the efforts were directed at establishing stabilization during the transition from a communist economy. However, the transition from communism was not to a market economy as was the case in many postcommunist countries. The Uzbek government's preferred method of stabilization seemed to be inaction, or keeping the system as it was. Property regime started to change with privatization of real estate, small companies, and with conversion of state and collective farms to private ownership under individual farms (*dehkan*).[53] However, the state maintained its tight control of economic activity, especially in cotton production. State's stakes in important industries such as mining (gold and oil among others) and telecommunications were retained. State has also used exchange rate restrictions and foreign trade controls, which cripple economic activity.

Although Uzbekistan is a case of postcommunist transition, the trajectories and the outcomes are akin to fast-forwarding the economic histories of Latin American countries and Turkey since the 1930s. Since Uzbekistan's economy was channeled toward meeting the cotton need of the Soviet textiles industry, industrial production was negligible.[54] Uzbekistan initially relied on primary products exports and was lucky that the international prices for cotton and gold were favorable. By late 1990s Uzbekistan had moved toward ISI, although this developmental model had long become outdated and discredited since 1980. Like Turkey in 1960s, Uzbekistan was trying to develop industries in consumption goods such as textiles and cars; however, it did not have the necessary domestic capital base and foreign direct investment (FDI) was limited. ISI policies led to predictable results: Low quality goods, high inefficiency, and low returns due to small domestic markets and limited export success (Pomfret 2006, 29–30; 31–32). The failure of the ISI experiment was exacerbated when cotton prices fell in October 1996 and with the adverse affects of the 1998 Russian economic crisis. To thwart balance of payment pressures, the government resorted to strict exchange rate policies and closed borders to stop goods imports (Pomfret 2006, 31).[55] Although exchange rate convertibility was restored and border trade controls were somewhat relaxed in early 2000s, the economy remains largely stagnant and dependent on cotton, gold, and oil/gas exports.[56]

Interestingly, the Uzbek government has been overly cautious, if not discouraging about FDI. Corruption, lack of transparency, and lack of clarity about property rights have prevented FDI in Central Asian countries, in general.[57] In Uzbekistan, FDI in strategic industries is not possible.[58] FDI has been directed to construction and agricultural-goods-processing industries—including tobacco, automotive, and textile industries.

Uzbek government is not very trusting of its domestic private sector either. Early privatization benefited the former Soviet cadres and Karimov's close circle, and these individuals became economic tycoons loyal to the government, causing resentment among the citizens who increasingly faced poverty.[59,60] Through the years, a new group of private entrepreneurs, who are primarily traders, emerged. While cross-border trade is an economic activity that even simple housewives engage in, these "businessmen" performed larger scale trade activities with partners in different countries. The government has generally been suspicious of these businessmen, because their loyalty cannot be guaranteed. They do not owe their business or their wealth to the government; quite the contrary, they are hurt by the government's restrictive trade policies and protectionism. The government either co-opts them into state-controlled economic sphere or it suppresses them. Pomfret reports that authorities, who see bazaars as "hotbeds of illicit activities," harassed them and argues that the riots in March (Bukhara and Tashkent) and November (Tashkent and Fergana Valley) 2004 were associated with the closure of bazaars (2006, 36; see also Azamatova 2004; Cooke 2004; Salimov 2004). Another example is the imprisonment of 23 businessmen for alleged Islamist fundamentalism, which eventually led to the Andijan uprisings of May 2005. Note that these episodes of suppression were not intended and were not perceived along ethnic lines, even in the Bukhara case.[61]

In short, developmental and economic policies show a lot of continuity from the Soviet period and the result has been a stagnant, state-controlled economy with limited room for private entrepreneurship or FDI. The economy remains largely agricultural, and agriculture remains largely labor-intensive.[62] The country is 63 percent rural and this rate has remained relatively stable throughout the independence period.[63] The urban modernized sectors of the society are either co-opted into the bureaucracy, or are employed in private retail and service sector.

Socioeconomic development since 1930s has undoubtedly modernized and transformed Uzbekistan, especially in the urban centers. However, these changes have not disrupted the traditional society, with the partial exception of Tashkent. The lives of ordinary people revolve around their place of residence; lives are very local. I have met youngsters who have not left their neighborhood to visit Samarkand's city center, which was just a 10-minute walk away. The connections with the locality and the social networks associated with it continue because there is very little migration, and those who migrate keep their ties with their original towns because they do not move too far away and they visit back often (Erdem 2006).

In the minds of most people, Tashkent, the capital, is very far away and the source of patronage is not Tashkent but their local governments. If an individual needs some form of patronage, they first go to their neighbors, relatives, or the neighborhood government. The neighborhood government is the only extension of administration with which most people ever have contact. Despite introduction of limited private land ownership, cotton production is still under state control, regional governments are the sole buyers of *shirkat* cotton, and they pressure them about meeting the targets, not much different from the pressure on the *kolkhoz*s to meet the quota. Although they realize that the ultimate power lies in Tashkent and the regional government depends on it, the highest level of government they consider relevant to them as individuals is that of governor's office (*hokimiyat*). Even if they face some injustice from the local government, they do not appeal at the higher levels of the administration. In this setting, it is not surprising for this reality to be the basis of people's identities.

Life, social relationships, economic opportunities, and political patronage are all local for a majority of Uzbekistanis, and the Karimov government's praise of the *mahalla* hints at their intention to keep the localism alive (Sievers 2002).[64] Leaving "home" comes with a cost of losing the relationships, opportunities, and patronage one has. As long as there is a dearth of private opportunities independent of Tashkent or alternative sources of wealth, this system will not be challenged. The Uzbek government has managed to prevent development outside its control by not developing some sectors and by co-opting or suppressing private entrepreneurs. The peace in the country and the quiescence in ethnic relationships come with a cost of economic stagnation, inefficiency, and poverty.

Conclusion

Economic development cannot be envisioned independent from its sociopolitical context, because economic development changes the balance of social and political relationships. When traditional authority structures are subjected to change, the patron-client relationships may be disrupted. If those who are disenfranchised from their traditional patronage networks have a common ethnicity, political entrepreneurs may try to establish a new patronage network that unites these individuals under the banner of that ethnic identity. Critical questions to ask are as follows: what do governments do to prevent the emergence of new patronage networks and how can governments be sure that the new patronage networks do not become violent organizations?

This chapter suggests that lack of development may be a way of keeping the stability and preventing challenges to the state. However, as the case of Uzbekistan shows, this is by no means the optimal method, and it takes an authoritarian government to co-opt any political entrepreneur. The alternative is to encourage peaceful incorporation of the new entrepreneurs into the political system. In Turkey, the 1980 coup drove the new Kurdish leaders out of the political arena. When these new Kurdish leaders finally had access to the political system and entered the Parliament, politics based on Kurdish identity took a more peaceful turn; however, Kurdish identity, rather than tribal identities have become the politically salient identity for many Kurds living in southeastern Turkey.

Since economic development projects inevitably have effects on the society, such projects should be comprehensive projects with society level components. Top-down projects that do not involve the societal level actors and organizations are may be interpreted as center's imposition on the periphery despite the best intentions. Especially, if the development project is introduced as a response to an identity-based political challenge, the strategy needs to address the identity-related concerns

Notes

1. A caveat on "passing" should be mentioned for the Kurds. Many Kurds have assimilated into the Turkish culture and consider themselves Turkish. Most of them are Kurds who have migrated out of their traditional towns and found assimilation to be a fairly low-cost strategy of adapting to their new Turkish-dominated environments. This assimilation makes determining the exact number of ethnic Kurds (as opposed to Kurdish speakers) in Turkey impossible. Kurdish identity has remained socially salient in the traditionally Kurdish regions. Such passing is not observed in Tajiks because they mostly still live in their ethnic communities (see the discussion about migration below).

2. The distinction between social and political salience is important. An identity is politically salient if individuals choose that identity among their multiple identities in the political context, and if they engage in political action based on that identity. An identity is socially salient if this identity category is the basis of personal social relationships and in- and out-group dynamics. The two types of salience are associated with different types of violence: a politically salient identity is more likely to be the basis of insurgency and civil war, whereas socially salient identity is more likely to be the basis of communal violence such as pogroms and riots. This chapter focuses on political salience and is

primarily interested in state-ethnic group relationships rather than intergroup relationships.

3. The size of the population for either group is not exactly known because the states in question avoid ethnic population statistics, and because there are problems with definitions of the groups. Estimates of Kurdish population in Turkey range from 5 to 23 percent (see Table 2.1 in Erdem (2006)). Numbers for Tajiks in Uzbekistan range from 4 to 10 percent depending on the source (Roy 2000). Uzbek government has not conducted a census, which makes the last Soviet census (1989) the most recent official data (Ferrando 2008, 489). The year 1996's estimate of Tajik population reported on the website of the Embassy of Uzbekistan in the United States is 5 percent.

4. According to Mutlu's estimates 7.046 million Kurds lived in Turkey in 1990, and most of them still live in the east and southeastern regions. He concludes, "81.80 percent of the Kurds were in these two regions in 1965. After twenty-five years of massive movement out of these places, 65.22 percent still lived in the two regions in 1990" (1996, 532).

5. Iraqi Kurds' autonomy dates back to the first Gulf War, after which north of 36th parallel was maintained as a no-fly zone by the United States. Kurdish regional government was established by KDP and PUK in 1992 and became constitutional in 2005, after the fall of Saddam's regime. Currently, the regional government is a federal unit with its own elected parliament and president and its armed forces. For details see Kurdish regional government website at: http://www.krg.org.

6. Until the American occupation of Iraq that ended Hussein's regime, KDP and PUK had been rivals, fighting with each other for the control over Northern Iraq as much as they fought with the Iraqi regime. The strategic framework of this rivalry has shaped their approach to the PKK and Turkey. Currently, the two parties are at peace as a result of an arrangement whereby Talabani is the president of Iraq and Barzani is the president of the autonomous region of Iraqi Kurdistan.

7. Olivier Roy has an enlightening discussion of the history of the creation of the Soviet republics and "nations" of Central Asia, and how the borders reflect Stalin's divide-and-rule strategy (Roy 2000, 56–74). As in postcolonial Africa, new countries accepted the Soviet borders upon independence, even if all had irredentist claims, because it was understood that no border realignment can be *pareto optimal*.

8. Imperial order of 1846 that led to an administrative restructuring and Land Code of 1858 were aimed at centralization of Ottoman Kurdistan. Republican Turkey has emphasized centralized government since its inception in 1923.

9. The new republic was indeed far from being able to eliminate tribal authority structures in the name of modernity and progress. Quite the contrary, Ankara had to face the challenge of tribally organized Kurdish uprisings and found the solution in co-opting along the very tribal lines. The legacy of these uprisings remains today: state's heavy-handed approach in suppressing these uprisings feeds into Kurds' suspicion of the Turkish state as much as

the shock of the uprisings feeds into Turks' obsession about separatism and distrust of Kurds.

10. A comparison of the southeast and the Eastern Black Sea region would be illustrative in isolating the effect of the tribal culture and authority. Eastern Black Sea region, home to the Laz ethnic group, is also remote, largely rural, and mountainous; however, there is no tribalism in the region. The state has had similar problems of access to the region, but the societal access has not been a serious problem. This region's performance in socioeconomic criteria is worse than many regions in the country except the East and the Southeast; however, Laz ethnic identity has not been politically salient.

11. See TÜİK (2006, 2–3). for schooling ratios and gender ratios since 1993.

12. Author's calculations based on 2009 Statistics Institute of Turkey data on number of students by region and province—TÜİK (2009a); and schooling rates by province—TÜİK (2009b).

13. According to the latest UNDP Human Development Report on Turkey, in 2004, among 81 provinces, East and Southeastern provinces occupied the bottom 17 positions in human development (UNDP Turkey 2004, 64–65).

14. Various industries were targeted in this period but the most important was probably the steel and coal industry in the Zonguldak-Ereğli-Karabük region. Numerous facilities in textiles, glassworks, sugar, paper, cement, and ceramics industries were established throughout the country. For more details on this period, see Boratav (1982).

15. Party competition did not give the tribes too much bargaining power, because just like a tribe could threaten to vote for the rival party, the party could threaten to affiliate and provide patronage to the rival tribe.

16. One of the major impacts of the Marshall Plan aid was the mechanization of agriculture. Morvaridi reports that the "number of tractors in use increased from 1658 in 1948 to 40 282 in 1955, reaching 637 449 in 1987" (1990, 305). There were regional disparities in the mechanization of agriculture. Based on 1988 figures, Morvaridi reports that although the southeast accounts for 13.3 percent of the total cultivated land, only 3.9 percent of Turkey's tractors are in this region. Corresponding figures for the Aegean region are 9.8 and 19.9 percent (1990, 308).

17. It is noteworthy that the post-1960 five year plans were not named "industrial" plans but "development" plans.

18. See fn. 19 for not using the most recent 2001 data. On land distribution see also Ünver (1997). Karapınar (2005) studies a case in rural Diyarbakir province where an absentee landlord owns the whole village. This landlord has acquired the land registries, which were to be distributed to the villagers who worked the lands, in his own name. The case shows how connections with, and knowledge of, central bureaucracy brings economic and social power.

19. Based on statistics from national agricultural surveys, Karapınar shows that the size of area owned by households owning more than 50 hectares increased between 1980 and 1991, as the share of land owned by households owning less than 5 hectares decreased. He reports that "by 1991, approximately 70 percent

of the total arable land rested with the wealthiest 15 percent of the rural population, while almost half of the population owned 6 percent of the land" (2005,
168). For some curious reason, more than 2 million hectares have disappeared
in the more recent 2001 agricultural survey, yielding a picture of improvement
in equitable land ownership. Karapınar argues that this is mistaken because
"67 percent of the missing data were in the categories of large landownership
(i.e., over 50 hectares)" and there was not a significant change in the middle-
and small-size holdings categories since 1991 (2005, 170).

20. These migrations are different from the seasonal migrations for seasonal work
in cotton fields. Higher education opportunities also attracted young people
from the Southeast to Istanbul and Ankara. Young Kurdish university students
later became active within the leftist movement in the 1970s and established
the PKK after the 1980 coup.

21. For example, Osman Baydemir of pro-Kurdish Peace and Democracy Party,
mayor of Diyarbakır, said: "As is clear in the cases of dam projects included in
the GAP project [sic], positive effects of the dams on the economic and social
life are not expected. On the other hand, the energy produced is not utilized for
the development of the region but to a large extent for the western regions where
the country's economy has been centered. Turkey's energy deficit is attempted
to be met through unsustainable projects that will leave historical and cultural
ruins in the region" (Diyarbakir Güneş Evi 2008).

22. Akşit and Akçay (1997) have evaluated households' practices and attitudes
regarding irrigation based on the mother tongue of the household, and have
found that Turkish, Kurdish, and Arab households do not display statistically
significant differences (528). This is evidence that land-owning households
from all ethnic groups in the region enjoy the benefits of the project in similar
ways.

23. Karapınar shows that GAP has actually created an intraregional inequality
between the provinces that benefit from GAP irrigation and those that do not.
Only 13 percent of the agricultural component of the project is completed and
only provinces of Harran Plain benefit the increasing agricultural output value
(2005, 176–177).

24. Harris (2006, 194) discusses how Arab and Kurdish identities are being redefined along landowner-landless worker lines in the irrigated areas of Harran.
Kurds resent that landowners, who tend to be non-Kurds in this particular
area, have benefited disproportionately from irrigation and this has caused
new intraregion tensions. However, the real resentment is directed toward the
state, because it was the state's decision to start irrigation in the Arab-populated
pocket rather than other Kurdish-populated areas, and because the state over-
looked Kurds' interests yet again (Harris 2006, 193; 194).

25. According to Mutlu's calculations, the southeast has received more public
investment than its contribution to public revenues, the ratio of these two
quantities is higher for the southeast than other regions. In some years during
the 1963–1995 period, the southeast received public investments amounting
more than ten times its contribution to public revenues (2001, 115).

26. For PDP's statement on their plan on democratic autonomy, see http://www
.bdp.org.tr/english/documents/democratic-authonomy.html

27. Central administration could make the projects reflect political considerations
at the center rather than the needs of the region in question, even to the point
of generating negative social outcomes as the increasing inequalities in the irrigated areas. Çarkoğlu and Eder (2005) criticize GAP for the level of corruption
and unaccountable budgetary allocations that emanate from patronage relationships and short-term electoral considerations.

28. See Fierman (1997, 377). It is uncertain why the government policies concerning Tajiks and Tajik culture took a repressive turn. Probably, Tajik identity
became a sensitive issue and politicization of Tajik identity became too threatening when the Tajik civil war started. However, note that the government also
suppressed the nonethnic opposition, such as Erk and Birlik parties. For Tajik
organizations established in 1989 see (Babak, Vaisman, and Wasserman 2004,
388–390 and 400–403).

29. This is not to say that Tajik identity is not a politically sensitive issue. Ethnic
challenges to the regime are politically sensitive enough to ban political parties based on national principles constitutionally (Article 57 of the Uzbek
Constitution). An "Uzbek party," Party of the People's Accord and Unity
exists in Kyrgyzstan, a similar political organization does not exist for Tajiks.
Karimov government has been monitoring and managing possible threats that
Tajik mobilization could pose for its regime, which is probably the reason why
no census has been undertaken since the 1989 Soviet census, and previous census data is difficult to access (Ferrando 2008, 492–493). The argument here
is that, concerns about Tajik mobilization have not borne out despite predictions that Tajik irredentism and separatism could lead to conflict (Foltz 1996;
Haghayeghi 1995).

30. The focus will be on the nativization policies rather than nationalities policies.
For studies that elaborate on how the nationalities policies simultaneously built
and undermined national identities see Adams 1999; Brubaker 1994; Martin
2001, 2–23; and Slezkine 1994.

31. Although the region has a complex and interesting history and interethnic traditions, it is impossible to do them justice given the space limitations. I will
focus on the contemporary period, referring to Soviet policies that shaped current institutions and policies. Note that many Soviet policies such as territory-
based administration or indirect rule based on indigenous political structures
were continuation of colonial policies of the Russian Empire. Colonial policies of the Russian Empire were, in turn, shaped by the existing precolonial
administrative structures. For example, the Emirate of Bukhara, which encom-
passed much of the Tajik-populated areas, was incorporated as a vassal state and
given autonomy in local administration. For an ethnic history of the region see
Porkhomovsky (1994).

32. During the period of dekulakization that accompanied collectivization, local
notables and leaders were exiled or killed. However, the local communities and
their socioeconomic networks remained intact, and produced new leaders to

replace the removed ones in most cases (Roy 2000, 102). As we shall see below, this is also true for the period of purges, which removed the "ex-kulaks."

33. This system of indirect rule ensured enforcement of Soviet policies as well as strengthening the position of the local authorities, because they were representatives of, and had the backing of, Moscow. Of course, this system is also open to subversion and corruption at different levels of local administration. Fierman writes for the late Brezhnev era that "the Central Asian political elites withheld information from the center and avoided meeting many of its demands. As their power at the republic level increased, they packed republic political, economic, and cultural institutions with their relatives, friends, political allies, and other colleagues from their home regions. Their collective 'conspiracies' also contributed to maintaining silence on the increasingly serious economic problems" (1991, 25).

34. Or replaced them with loyal locals or Russians as in the period of purges.

35. It is not possible to get reliable information about republics' contributions to the all-union funds or regional spending of central government from official statistics (Gleason 1991, 3). As Bahry and Nechemias (1981) have shown, claims about interregional inequality in the USSR depend on the statistics and methods used. I am not claiming that regions were equal as the official "merging of national units" rhetoric that continued through the Brezhnev era claimed. Based on my observations on what remains of the services brought in the Soviet period in urban and rural Uzbekistan, I am seeing the "glass full." Although Soviet administration in Central Asia was exploitative and although these republics were seen as "backwards," they were not left alone to struggle the "backwardness." The Soviet state had motives and considerations other than the well-being of the locals, but the outcome benefited the locals nonetheless. We cannot say the same for Turkish investments in the "backwards" southeast.

36. Urban areas and easily accessible regions had an advantage; however, remote and rural areas did receive services even if it was inferior in quantity and quality.

37. Gleason (1991) argues that the relationship between the Central Asian republics and Moscow conforms with characteristics of dependency relationships, despite the fact that the Soviet system was socialist, not capitalist.

38. Small-scale irrigation existed along the riverbanks before the Tsarist period. Irrigation systems were initially developed by the Tsarist administrations, mainly in the Ferghana valley. Soviet irrigation projects were more ambitious in terms of the area coverage and production goals, as can be exemplified by the Virgin Lands program that started in 1954 and aimed at grain production in the steppes of northern Kazakhstan. According to Pomfret, irrigated area expanded from over 3 million to 5 million and 8 million hectares between 1900, 1960, and 1980s respectively (1995, 29). Also see Craumer (2005 [1992]) for agriculture in Soviet Central Asia, and Saiko and Zonn (2000, 350–355) on environmental impact.

39. Education was also part of a larger project of homogenization and modernization of the local cultures. The Soviet state aimed at standardizing the national language by emphasizing one dialect, enhancing its written literary aspect, and

disseminating this standard literary language across the communities in the republics. Besides the "national" language, Russian was taught in the schools in order to promote inter-republican communication within the Union. Aside from language, the Soviet authorities also attempted to alter or destroy certain local customs. Campaigns for unveiling the women (or "emancipation" of women in general), criticizing excessive expenditures during traditional community events such as weddings or funerals, and abolishing the "bride-price" are but a few of such attempts. These were part of the strategy of eradicating the subnational identities, such as clan or religion and eventually making Central Asians Soviet peoples.

40. According to 2005 Uzbekistani figures, literacy remains universal, schooling rate is 78 percent and 84 percent of secondary-school-age population is attending school (UNDP Uzbekistan 2008, 158; 162).

41. On this point, see, for example, Guboglo 1990 [1982].

42. See Martin (2001, 2–22) for details on this early period, especially the connection between the nationalities and nativization/indigenization policies.

43. Rashid writes of these early local administrations: "Uzbeks who rose through the ranks of the Communist Party of Uzbekistan (CPU) after 1920 maintained an ambivalent relationship with Moscow. Obedient Communists, they also constantly resisted Moscow's domination—to which Stalin responded by instigating several ruthless purges" (2002, 80).

44. However, this is also the period when Uzbekistan became "quasi-feudal" under Rashidov, and the infamous "cotton affair" played out (Pomfret 1995, 66).

45. Brezhnev employed a policy similar to the Kurdish "tacit bargain." "He offered a 'political contract' to local officials. Acceptance of the goals of the regime and suppression of local dissidence was repaid with the confident expectation of long job tenure. Brezhnev's 'cadres stability compromise' produced remarkably long tenures for regional officials in Soviet Asia" (Gleason 1991, 350).

46. See Jones Luong (2002, 82–90). In the case of Uzbekistan, we cannot talk about "clans" (defined as a form of kinship group) in cadre recruitment, see (Tunçer-Kılavuz 2009) for an accurate description of the role of different identities and affiliations in politics.

47. Tashkent city is, of course, a special case with an economic life of its own.

48. Personal observation, also confirmed by Adams (1999, 364–365).

49. Since then, Samkocauto and Korean Daewoo went bankrupt; however, both plants continue operating under different names and ownerships.

50. With the exception of *Tashkentlik*s, because of Tashkent's widely acknowledged special status, Tashkent is not a part of interregional competition or rivalries.

51. Islam Karimov was an orphan from Samarkand, who got educated and made a political career through the Soviet system. He was primarily a "Soviet" man, his ethnicity is still not known, which is convenient in avoiding the use of ethnic discourse in evaluations of his policies.

52. Uzbekistan is trying to develop tourism industry, which would benefit Samarkand and Bukhara; however, there are many obstacles before the development of tourism (Akhiaev 2001; Najibullah 2009).

53. According to Yalçın, between 1992 and 1993 "over 1.2 million state owned dwellings, comprising 95 percent of the state housing stock, were privatized" (2002, 192–193). Most of collective farms stayed state controlled, under the name of *shirkat*. See Yalçın (2002, 190–193) and Pomfret (2006, 27) on privatization and Pomfret (2006, 33–34) on *dehkan* and *shirkat*s.

54. Industrial sector constituted 30 percent of the country's net material product (NMP) in 1991, but this sector includes the metallurgy industry, that is, gold mining, oil and gas production.

55. Although border closings did not have any ethnic motivations, it has disproportionately negatively affected two groups. Kazakh Uzbekistanis along the border who worked for better wages in Kazakhstan had difficulties in crossing the border after the closings. Similarly, the cross-border trade between Kyrgyz towns of Osh and Karasuu was dominated by Uzbeks, who traded with their co-ethnics across the border, and border closings reduced the volume of trade and increased the risk and corruption (bribes) associated with this trade. The complaints about the border closings were not expressed in ethnic terms in my various personal correspondences in 2003.

56. See ICG (2003) and ICG (2004, 14–21) for an overview of the economic landscape in the early 2000s.

57. See (Bukharbaeva 2000) for a snapshot of difficulties foreign investors face in Uzbekistan.

58. See (Jones Luong and Weinthal 2001) for Uzbek government's approach to FDI in oil and gas industry and a comparison to Kazakhstan and Turkmenistan.

59. The country's 30 large enterprises, except for a cement company, were not privatized until 1999 (Pomfret 2006, 31).

60. According to recent reports, Karimov government has started targeting these tycoons. Speculated reasons include ensuring Karimov's businesswoman and politician daughter Gulnara Karimova's succession after her father, and eliminating the ex-Soviet cadres in order to make way to new younger and loyal allies (Najibullah 2010; Pannier 2010). See ICG (2007, 5–6) for an evaluation of Ms. Karimova's businesses.

61. In Bukhara and Samarkand, Tajiks' frustrations are not channeled into Islamist fundamentalism as is the case in Fergana valley either (Balfour 2000).

62. Due to lack of mechanization of cotton harvesting, students are forced to skip school and pick cotton. According to one report, 80 percent of Uzbek cotton is picked by hand. (Khaidarov 2000).

63. Urban population in Uzbekistan has dropped from 40.1 percent In 1990 to 36.9 percent in 2010 according to UNDP Human Development Report (UNDP 2009, 193). The drop in urban population rate is probably due to the emigration of urban Russians.

64. Continuity of local social networks is probably responsible for people's ability to survive increasing poverty (Kasymov 2001).

References

Adams, Laura L. 1999. Invention, institutionalization and renewal in Uzbekistan's national culture. *European Journal of Cultural Studies*, 2: 355–373.

Akhiaev, Solekh. 2001, February 5. Uzbek Tourist Drive. *RCA* Issue 39. Retrieved from http://www.iwpr.net/report-news/uzbek-tourist-drive. Accessed June 11, 2010.

Akşit, Bahattin, and A. Adnan Akçay. 1997. Sociocultural aspects of irrigation practices in south-eastern Turkey. *International Journal of Water Resources Development*, 13: 523–540.

Azamatova, Matlyuba. 2004, November 5. Uzbekistan: Furious traders riot. *RCA* Issue 324. Retrieved from http://www.iwpr.net/report-news/uzbekistan-furious-traders-riot. Accessed June 11, 2010.

Babak, Vladimir, Demian Vaisman, and Aryeh Wasserman. 2004. *Political organization in Central Asia and Azerbaijan: Sources and documents*. London and Portland, OR: Frank Cass.

Bahry, Donna, and Carol Nechemias. 1981. Half full or half empty?: The debate over Soviet regional equality. *Slavic Review*, 40: 366–383.

Balfour, Jennifer. 2000, November 16. Bukharans shun radical Islam. *RCA* Issue 30. Retrieved from http://www.iwpr.net/report-news/bukharans-shun-radical-islam. Accessed June 11, 2010.

Beşikçi, İsmail. 1969. *Doğu Anadolu'nun Düzeni: Sosyo-ekonomik ve Etnik Temeller [The order of eastern Anatolia: Socio-economic and ethnic foundations]*. Istanbul: E. Yayinlari.

Boratav, Korkut. 1982. *Turkiye'de devletçilik [Etatism in Turkey]*. Ankara: Savaş Yayınevi.

Bozarslan, Hamit. 2003. Kurdish nationalism in Turkey: From tacit contract to rebellion (1919–1925). In *Essays on the Origins of Kurdish Nationalism*, edited by A. Vali, 163–190. Costa Mesa, CA: Mazda Publications.

Brubaker, Rogers. 1994. Nationhood and the national question in the Soviet Union and post-Soviet Eurasia: An institutionalist account. *Theory and Society*, 23: 47–78.

Bruinessen, Martin van. 1992. *Agha, shaikh, and state: The social and political structures of Kurdistan*. London and Atlantic Highlands, NJ: Zed Books.

Bucknall, Julia, Irina Klytchnikova, Julian Lampietti, Mark Lundell, Monica Scatasta, and Mike Thurman. 2003. *Irrigation in Central Asia: Social, economic and environmental considerations*. Washington, DC: The World Bank.

Bukharbaeva, Galima. 2000, May 24. Investors Shun Uzbekistan. *RCA* Issue 4. Retrieved from http://www.iwpr.net/report-news/investors-shun-uzbekistan. Accessed June 11, 2010.

Çarkoğlu, Ali, and Mine Eder. 2005. Developmentalism alla Turca: The Southeastern Anatolia Development Project (GAP). In *Environmentalism in Turkey: Between democracy and development?* edited by F. Adaman and M. Arsel, 167–184. Hants, England: Ashgate.

Cooke, Kieran. 2004, December 13. Uzbekistan's angry street traders. *BBC News (Business)*. Retrieved from http://news.bbc.co.uk/2/hi/business/4080221.stm. Accessed June 10, 2010.

Craumer, Peter R. 2005 [1992]. Agricultural change, labor supply, and rural out-migration in Soviet Central Asia. In *Geographic Perspectives on Soviet Central Asia*, edited by R. A. Lewis, 132–180. London: Taylor and Francis.

Ensaroğlu, Yılmaz, and Dilek Kurban. 2008. *A roadmap for a solution to the Kurdish question: Policy proposals from the region for the government*. Istanbul: Turkish Economic and Social Studies Foundation.

Erdem, Ebru. 2006. *Political salience of ethnic identities: A comparative study of Tajiks in Uzbekistan and Kurds in Turkey*. Stanford, CA: Stanford University.

Diyarbakır Güneş Evi. 2008. Hasankeyf'te baraj değil Güneş Evi Yapalım [Let's build Sun House in Hasankeyf, not a dam]. Retrieved from http://www.gunesevi.org/newsviewer.aspx?id=12. Accessed June 3, 2010.

Ferrando, Olivier. 2008. Manipulating the census: Ethnic minorities in the nation-alizing states of Central Asia. *Nationalities Papers: The Journal of Nationalism and Ethnicity*, 36: 489–520.

Fierman, William. 1991. The Soviet 'transformation' of Central Asia. In *Soviet Central Asia: The failed transformation*, edited by W. Fierman, 11–35. Boulder, CO: Westview.

———. 1997. Political Development in Uzbekistan: Democratization? In *Conflict, Cleavage, and Change in Central Asia and the Caucasus*, edited by K. D. a. B. Parrott, 360–408. Cambridge and New York: Cambridge University Press.

Foltz, R. 1996. The Tajiks of Uzbekistan. *Central Asian Survey*, 15: 213–216.

GAP Regional Development Administration. 2009. What is GAP? Retrieved from http://www.gap.gov.tr/gap_eng.php?sayfa=English/Ggbilgi/gnedir.html. Accessed Nov. 12, 2009.

Gleason, Gregory. 1991. The political economy of dependency under socialism: The Asia Republics in the USSR. *Studies in Comparative Communism*, 24: 335–353.

Glenn, John. 1999. *The Soviet legacy in Central Asia*. New York: St. Martin's Press.

Guboglo, M. N. 1990 [1982]. The general and the particular in the development of the linguistic life of soviet society. In *The Soviet Multinational State: Readings and Documents*, edited by M. B. Olcott, 246–257. London: M. E. Sharpe, Inc.

Haghayeghi, M. 1995. *Islam and politics in Central Asia*. New York: St. Martin's Press.

Harris, Leila M. 2006. Irrigation, gender and social geographies of the changing waterscapes of southeastern Anatolia. *Environment and Planning D: Society and Space*, 24: 187–213.

———. 2009. States at the limit: Tracing contemporary state-society relations in the borderlands of southeastern Turkey. *European Journal of Turkish Studies [Online]*, 10.

Hershlag, Z. Y. 1964. *Introduction to the modern economic history of the Middle East*. Netherlands: E. J. Brill.

ICG (International Crisis Group). 2003. *Uzbekistan's reform program: Illusion or reality?* Osh and Brussels: International Crisis Group.

————. 2004. *The failure of reform in Uzbekistan: Ways forward for the international community*. Osh and Brussels: International Crisis Group.

————. 2007. *Uzbekistan: Stagnation and uncertainty*. Bishkek and Brussels: International Crisis Group.

Jones Luong, Pauline. 2002. *Institutional change and political continuity in post-Soviet Central Asia: Power, perceptions, and pacts*. Cambridge: Cambridge University Press.

Jones Luong, Pauline, and Erika Weinthal. 2001. Prelude to the resource curse: Explaining oil and gas development strategies in the Soviet successor states and beyond. *Comparative Political Studies*, 34: 367–399.

Karapınar, Barış. 2005. Land inequality in rural southeastern Turkey: Rethinking agricultural development. *New Perspectives on Turkey*, 32: 165–197.

Kasymov, Arslan. 2001, May 17. Uzbekistan in denial over poverty. *RCA* Issue 52. Retrieved from http://www.iwpr.net/report-news/uzbekistan-denial-over-poverty. Accessed June 11, 2010.

Khaidarov, Ulugbek. 2000, October 26. Uzbek child labor scandal. *RCA* Issue 27. Retrieved from http://www.iwpr.net/report-news/uzbek-child-labour-scandal. Accessed June 11, 2010.

Liu, Morgan Y. 2005. Hierarchies of place, hierarchies of empowerment: Geographies of talk about postsocialist change in Uzbekistan. *Nationalities Papers: The Journal of Nationalism and Ethnicity*, 33: 423–438.

Martin, Terry. 2001. *The affirmative action empire : Nations and nationalism in the Soviet Union, 1923–1939*. Ithaca, NY; London: Cornell University Press.

McDowall, David. 2000. *A Modern history of the Kurds*. London; New York: I. B. Tauris (Distributed by St. Martin's Press).

Morvaridi, Behrooz. 1990. Agrarian reform and land use policy in Turkey: Implications for the Southeast Anatolia Project. *Land Use Policy*, 7: 303–313.

Mutlu, Servet. 1996. Ethnic Kurds in Turkey: A demographic study. *International Journal of Middle East Studies*, 28: 517–541.

————. 2001. Economic bases of ethnic separatism in Turkey: An evaluation of claims and counterclaims. *Middle Eastern Studies*, 37: 101–135.

Najibullah, Farangis. 2009. *Uzbekistan promoting itself to tourists, but maintains exhausting visa regime*. RFE/RL, 25 October 2009. Retrieved from http://www.rferl.org/content/Uzbekistan_Promoting_Itself_To_Tourists_But_Maintains_Exhausting_Visa_Regime/1860459.html. Accessed June 10, 2010.

————. 2010. *The demise of Uzbekistan's cash cow Zeromax*. RFE/RL. Retrieved from http://www.rferl.org/content/Zeroing_In_On_The_Demise_Of_Uzbekistans_Cash_Cow/2073867.html. Accessed June 10, 2010.

Özoğlu, Hakan. 2004. *Kurdish notables and the Ottoman state: Evolving identities, competing loyalties, and shifting boundaries*. Albany: State University of New York Press.

Pannier, Bruce. 2010. *Big business in Uzbekistan targeted in wave of arrests*. RFE/RL March 12, 2010. Retrieved from http://www.rferl.org/content/Big_Business_In_Uzbekistan_Targeted_In_Wave_Of_Arrests/1981882.html. Accessed June 10, 2010.

Pomfret, Richard W. T. 1995. *The economies of Central Asia*. Princeton, NJ: Princeton University Press.

———. 2006. *The Central Asian economies Since independence*. Princeton, NJ: Princeton University Press.

Porkhomovsky, Victor Ya. 1994. Historical origins of interethnic conflicts in Central Asia and Transcaucasia. In *Central Asia and Transcaucasia: Ethnicity and Conflict*, edited by V. V. Naumkin, 1–30. Westport, CT and London.

Rashid, Ahmed. 2002. *Jihad: The rise of militant Islam in Central Asia*. New Haven, CT: Yale University Press.

Roy, Olivier. 2000. *The new Central Asia : The creation of nations*. New York: New York University Press.

Saiko, Tatyana A., and Igor S. Zonn. 2000. Irrigation expansion and dynamics of desertification in the Circum-Aral region of Central Asia. *Applied Geography*, 20: 349–367.

Salimov, Timur. 2004, November 25. Uzbek City baulks at government controls. *RCA* Issue 328. Retrieved from http://www.iwpr.net/report-news/uzbek-city-baulks-government-controls. Accessed June 11, 2010.

Sievers, Eric W. 2002. Uzbekistan's Mahalla: From Soviet to absolutist residential community associations. *The Journal of International and Comparative Law at Chicago-Kent*, 2: 91–155.

Simon, Gerhard. 1991. *Nationalism and policy toward the nationalities in the soviet union: from Totalitarian Dictatorship to post-Stalinist society*. Boulder, CO: Westview Press.

Slezkine, Yuri. 1994. The USSR as a communal apartment, or how a socialist state promoted ethnic particularism. *Slavic Review*, 53: 414–452.

Strickman, Rachel, and Miina Porkka. 2008. Water and social changes in Central Asia: Problems related to cotton production in Uzbekistan. In *Central Asian Waters: Social, Economic, Environmental and Governance Puzzle*, edited by M. M. Rahaman and O. Varis, 105–115. Helsinki: Water & Development Publications, Helsinki University of Technology.

Tunçer-Kılavuz, İdil. 2009. Political and social networks in Tajikistan and Uzbekistan: "Clan," region and beyond. *Central Asian Survey*, 28: 323–334.

TÜİK (Statistics Institute of Turkey). 2009a. IBBS 1., 2., Ve 3. Düzeye ve Eğitim Seviyesine Göre Okul, Şube, Öğrenci, Öğretmen, Usta Öğretici ve Derslik Sayısı. Retrieved from http://www.tuik.gov.tr/PreIstatistikTablo.do?istab_id=140. Accessed June 2, 2010.

———. 2009b. IBBS 3. Düzeye ve Eğitim Seviyesine Göre Okullaşma Oranı. Retrieved from http://www.tuik.gov.tr/PreIstatistikTablo.do?istab_id=990. Accessed June 2, 2010.

———. 2006. *National education statistics: Formal education 2003/'04*. Ankara: Türkiye İstatistik Kurumu Matbaasi.

UNDP. 2009. *Human development report 2009 overcoming barriers: Human mobility and development*. New York: United Nations Development Programme.

UNDP Turkey. 2004. *Human development report: Turkey 2004*. Ankara: UNDP Turkey.

UNDP Uzbekistan (National Human Development Report Team). 2008. *Education in Uzbekistan: Matching supply and demand.* Tashkent: UNDP Uzbekistan.

Ünver, I. H. Olcay. 1997. South-eastern Anatolia Integrated Development Project (GAP), Turkey: An overview of issues of sustainability. *International Journal of Water Resources Development,* 13:187–208.

Yalçın, Resul. 2002. *The rebirth of Uzbekistan: Politics, economy and society in the post-Soviet era.* Reading, UK: Ithaca Press.

CHAPTER 9

Local versus Transcendent Insurgencies: Why Economic Aid Helps Lower Violence in Dagestan, but not in Kabardino-Balkaria

Mikhail Alexseev

Introduction

A decade after two wars over Chechnya's independence (1994–2002) claimed dozens of thousands of casualties and hundreds of thousands of refugees,[1] significant violent insurgency in the region has persisted. Though on a smaller scale, insurgent attacks on Russian government forces and civilians continue at the time of writing at the rate that is common in low-level civil wars—a familiar phenomenon in weak, developing states. Systemic violence has changed in two principal ways since the early 2000s. First, the conflict is no longer confined to Chechnya, but has spread to the neighboring ethnic provinces, especially Ingushetia, Dagestan, and Kabardino-Balkaria (KBR). From April 2008 through April 2010, operations by government and rebel forces in these four North Caucasus republics claimed approximately 1,500 deaths (Center for Strategic and International Studies 2010). Second, the dominant motivations for insurgency have changed, as secular nationalist separatism gave way to a combination of militant Islamism, profound grievances arising from government abuse of power, and competition for economic resources among local elites (Kavkazskii Uzel 2009; Latynina 2009).

Since the end of large-scale fighting in Chechnya, Moscow pursued a two-pronged strategy against armed insurgency in the region—the use of military force against the militants and their suspected accomplices, and large-scale economic development assistance. Speaking in July 2010, at a special working meeting of Russia's dominant political party, United Russia, Prime Minister Vladimir Putin emphasized the importance of economic development in defeating armed opposition. The willingness of young people to take up arms, he said, stemmed from their *nesostoyatel'nost'*—a Russian term for economic unsustainability or bankruptcy. Successful economic development, Putin intimated, was vital for prevailing in "the fight for people's minds—a fight we cannot afford to lose." Putin announced Moscow's monumental program of government-guaranteed economic investment in the North Caucasus, with plans for the gross regional product to grow by 10 percent every year and for the massive job creation in oil-refining, hydropower generation, recreation industry, tourism, and agriculture (RIA-Novosti 2010).

Investing in economic development as a bulwark against violent insurgency in the North Caucasus, however, has had a mixed record over the first decade of the 2000s. On the one hand, the Russian government provided close to $30 billion (800 billion rubles) of developmental assistance without repayment requirements to the North Caucasus region from 2000 to 2010—a significant sum for the population of just over 9 million people. This type of aid—most of it in the form of unconditional supplemental appropriations (*dotatsii*) to local budgets—increased tenfold over the same decade—from about 18 billion rubles at the start of 2000 to 180 billion at the start of 2010 (Rosbalt 2010). By 2010, Moscow was spending over 30,000 federal tax rubles ($1,000) per capita, in the North Caucasus ethnic republics—about six times more on average than for all of Russia (Biriukov 2010). Schools, hospitals, roads, airports, housing complexes, and recreation facilities have been built anew or repaired. Unemployment rates dropped significantly. Chechnya's capital Grozny—which looked worse than the Nazi-ravaged Stalingrad in wartime pictures of the 1990s—has been rebuilt with downtown high-rise residential complexes, repaved avenues, a reconstructed airport, Europe's largest mosque, and marble fountains. By about 2006, the organized violent insurgency seemed to be on the brink of being eradicated, along with suicide-bomb attacks that claimed hundreds of lives in three preceding years across Russia.

On the other hand, this economic development strategy has been less than successful in at least two important respects. First, the insurgency reorganized under new leaders with new organizational patterns, and gained new bases of support in other North Caucasus republics. Second, the rebels stepped up their attacks, managing to retaliate in kind whenever government forces intensified counterinsurgency measures. From 2008 to 2011, the insurgency has been progressively more lethal, defying the official lifting of the State of Counter-Terrorist Emergency in Chechnya in April 2009 and subsequent government claims of imminent eradication of all armed rebels. By comprehensive—though still incomplete—counts of the Center for Strategic and International Studies, the North Caucasus saw 1,100 incidents of violence related to the antigovernment armed rebellion in 2009, compared to 795 such incidents in 2008. The number of fatalities in these incidents increased from fewer than 600 in 2008 to more than 900 in 2009. The number of suicide bombings—most of which took place in Chechnya—nearly quadrupled. Most violence in 2009 happened from May to October—after the state of counterterrorist emergency was lifted in Chechnya in a symbolic recognition of putative normalization in the region. Violence increased in all four affected provinces year-on-year—from about 350 to 420 incidents in Ingushetia, 210 to 285 in Chechnya, 150 to 375 in Dagestan, and 45 to 50 in KBR.[2]

In important respects, the resurgence of violence from 2009 to the time of writing in late 2010 challenges the Russian government's determination that economic development will wipe out social support for the armed rebellion.

Most strikingly, violence increased in Chechnya—the largest recipient of federal economic aid in the region since 2001. Moscow's transfers of unconditional aid into Chechnya flowed apace despite the 2008–2009 financial crisis, reaching eight times the Russian per capita average by early 2010. At over $1,600 per person, these transfers amount to the annual GDP per capita of the Philippines and exceed the GDP per capita of 59 out of 192 nation-states (Biriukov 2010; Central Intelligence Agency 2010). The Russian government's decision to lift the counterterrorist status in the republic in April 2009 was partly justified by the success of economic reconstruction in diminishing the armed rebellion. Yet, 12 months since the lifting of the counterterrorist operation status, the situation has become significantly bloodier than the 12 months before. The number of police, military, and FSB servicemen killed by the rebels increased from 52 to 97, and the wounded from 150 to 185. The number of armed rebels failed to decrease. Government police, military, and security forces in Chechnya killed 189 and arrested 186 alleged rebels from April 2009 to April 2010—compared to 136 and 90, respectively, from April 2008 to April 2009. This is also more than five times the 70 rebels the Chechen president claimed to be in existence throughout 2009.[3]

Budget revenues also increased significantly, approximately doubling from 2006 to 2008 in the three republics where violence spread outside of

Chechnya and spiked in 2009 (Table 9.1). These revenue increases occurred for the most part as the result of the Russian central government transfers, or economic assistance. If anything, the slowest growing budget revenues and the smallest share of federal assistance was in KBR—the least violent of the four republics covered in Table 9.1.

The logic of comparative political analysis suggests two approaches to understanding why the central government economic assistance has failed to prevent the armed insurgency in the North Caucasus from spreading across the region and getting more violent after 2008. The first one is to examine the noneconomic motivations for rebellion—particularly those related to ethnic, clan, religious, and other group identities. The second is to "unpack" economic motivations and investigate specific aspects of economic aid and the socioeconomic context at lower levels of aggregation than at state or province level, so that their linkages to militant insurgency are less likely to be compounded by other factors.[4]

This study has pursued both approaches. Both are needed because the implications of mainstream theories fall short of explaining variation in violence across the North Caucasus systematically, as the next section demonstrates. The following analysis is based on newly available socioeconomic and

Table 9.1 Federal Aid in Budget Revenues of the North Caucasus Republics (million rubles)

	2006	2007	2008	2006–2008	2006–08 percent change
Dagestan					
Revenues	27,124	38,782	52,614	118,520	94.0
Federal contribution	20,773	30,409	38,332	89,514	84.5
percent federal	76.6	78.4	72.9	75.5	
Ingushetia					
Revenues	6,439	9,245	12,709	28,393	97.4
Federal contribution	5,739	8,331	11,622	25,692	102.5
percent federal	89.1	90.1	91.4	90.5	
Chechnya					
Revenues	31,625	63,566	64,684	159,875	104.5
Federal contribution	28,089	58,880	59,652	146,621	112.4
percent federal	88.8	92.63	92.22	91.7	
Kabardino-Balkaria					
Revenues	11,089	15,001	18,937	45,027	70.8
Federal contribution	6,390	9,015	10,865	26,270	70.0
percent federal	57.6	60.1	57.4	58.3	

violent-events data by county, city, and town in two republics where violence spread from the core conflict zone in Chechnya and Ingushetia—KBR to the West and Dagestan in the East. The examination of insurgency-related violence in these republics is methodologically justified because it enables one to compare and contrast sociological, political, and agency (ideology/leadership) explanations both at the republic (province) and at the county/city/town level. The central focus on the plausible theoretical interpretation and policy implications of the principal empirical finding—that is, that central government aid in 2006–2008 had a statistically significant relationship with lower rates of violence by county in Dagestan in 2009–2010, but with higher levels of violence in KBR within the same time frame (although in the latter the overall relationship was statistically weaker). A particular attention is given to assessing if and how these two republics and some of their counties differ vis-à-vis the interaction between insurgency organization/leadership and social bases of support for the insurgency.

Comparative Political Theories of Ethnic Conflict and the Spread of North Caucasus Insurgency after 2008

Greed Explanations

One prominent theory of civil wars and insurgencies in political science—supported with extensive country-level multivariate analyses—identifies "opportunity structures" leading to violence in any given year. Its key elements are material—poverty (low level of GDP per capita), government weakness (lack of police and military power), rough terrain (particularly mountains), availability of tradable natural resources, and large populations (Fearon and Laitin 2003). Other studies emphasized the role of economic growth and employment of young males in the worst-performing economies, as well as the location of "lootable resources" within a state (Collier et al. 2003; LeBillon 2008).

Key elements of this "opportunity structure"—notably rough terrain—go a long way in explaining the onset of separatist wars in Chechnya in the early 1990s as well as the nonemergence of similar wars in the then restive republics of Tatarstan and Bashkortostan. It may also explain why civil war broke out in Tajikistan, but not in the neighboring Uzbekistan after the collapse of communism in 1991. However, this framework has serious problems in explaining the rise and spread of violence across the North Caucasus after 2008—particularly comparing Dagestan and KBR. First, the insurgency became more violent where the economy performed better. As the earlier cited CSIS data shows, from 2008 to 2009 violence increased about ten times faster in Dagestan than in KBR. But by 2008, Dagestan had an about 10 percent higher gross regional product per capita ($2,051). In 2008, consumer spending in Dagestan grew 25 percent compared to 14 percent in KBR. Over the same year, Dagestan's unemployment rate dropped from 20.2 percent to 13.4 percent, whereas KBR's unemployment rate rose from 17.6 percent to 18.3 percent. The percentage of the unemployed who failed to find a job for more than 12 months was higher in KBR (58 percent) than in Dagestan (50 percent). Dagestan's budget revenues from 2006 to 2008 almost doubled—a nearly 25 percent faster growth than in KBR (Rosstat 2009).

Second, the government weakness factor—unlike in the chaotic, transitional 1990s—no longer applies in the region. Across the board, Russia's government on Putin's orders increased its coercive powers, deploying tens of thousands of well-equipped military, police, and intelligence officers. They continued to police the region, man roadblocks, and conduct dragnet counterinsurgency sweeps well into remote mountainous areas. These operations were not affected by the economic slowdown in 2009, as Moscow tapped into the massive stabilization fund accumulated over the previous decade, when the oil prices rose to historically unparalleled levels. Violence continued to increase even in Chechnya, which built up the most formidable counterterrorist force that recruited thousands of former rebels. Moscow also strengthened direct political control over regional governments through the institution of presidential envoys, the abolition of gubernatorial elections, and tight state control over national television channels.

Third, the rough terrain explanation is problematic. For example, Dagestan and KBR both sit on the northern slopes of the Great Caucasus Mountain Range. If anything, the significantly higher, forest-blanketed, water-source rich mountains of KBR provide a better shelter for would-be rebels than the lower, more arid, and more flattop ranges of Dagestan. A more careful look at violence patterns in the two republics by county also shows that in KBR several areas with excellent rebel-friendly terrain were significantly less violent than exposed flatland areas, while in Dagestan more violence took place in the flatter northern counties such as Kizlyar, farther from the mountains than the counties adjacent to the mountain ranges. The effect of road availability is also indeterminate. On the one hand, Fearon and Laitin and other scholars who emphasize material incentives for insurgency have interpreted roads as an indicator of government capacity to project power (Fearon and Laitin 2003, 80; Buhaug and Rod 2006; Kilcullen 2008). On the other hand, comprehensive statistical analysis of geospatial distribution of about 38,000 violent incidents across more than 4,000 villages in the North Caucasus from 2000 through 2008 showed that the roads facilitated the spread of violence in the region (Zhukov 2012).

Fourth, access to natural resources easily tradable on global markets no longer plays the same role as it did in the 1990s during the Chechen wars for independence. Indigenous oil sources, mostly in Chechnya, had been depleted. The Russian military and security forces improved pipeline protection and cracked down on illicit oil drilling, refining, and gasoline distillation. This raised the cost of this source of funding to the insurgents, while the benefits to them decreased as the number of fighters declined significantly since the early 2000s. Corruption, embezzlement, extortion, and foreign contributions have been noted as funding the insurgency—further complicating the job of teasing out the role of natural resource access (*Novaya Gazeta* 2009).

Creed explanations

Ethnicity, religion, region, clan, family, corporate, and other types of group identity play a significant part in social interactions and the politics of the North Caucasus—one of the world's most demographically diverse regions. Local legends tell visitors that the Caucasus is known as "The Language Mountain" where God at the last minute settled various peoples who were left over from other places after the Earth was created. But disentangling how these identities may contribute to violent insurgency remains elusive.

The per capita incidence of violent incidents from mid-2008 to mid-2010 was the highest and rose most significantly during that time period in the almost ethnically homogeneous republic of Ingushetia, rather than in the most ethnically heterogeneous republic of Dagestan (with the largest group comprising 27 percent of the population and 14 main groups in all) or in the three-way divided KBR (with Kabardinians making up 55 percent, the Russians—25 percent, and the Balkars—12 percent).[5] Despite latent tensions and sporadic social protest, only a handful of insurgency-related violent incidents in 2009 are traceable to the enduring interethnic grievances and hostility—particularly between the Ingush and the Ossetians over the rights to settle in North Ossetia's Prigorodnyi County, between the Balkars and the Kabardins over pasture and agricultural land use, between the Akkin Chechens and the Avars and between the Avars and the Kumyks over land use in Dagestan.

The ethnic composition in the North Caucasus republics remained largely unchanged between the censuses of 1989 and 2002—except for the outflow of ethnic Russians, especially from Chechnya, Ingushetia, and Dagestan. Due to higher birth rates and lower death rates than the Russian average, these republics remained among Russia's top out-migration areas. In my field observations on migration effects across Russia, I found one striking contrast between the North Caucasus and central or Far Eastern Russian cities. In the latter, street markets and most noninternational chain outlets featured large numbers of migrant traders—prominent among them ethnic Central Asians, Chinese, Koreans, Turks, Armenians, and Azeris. In the former, however, the local traders dominated the markets—this author, for instance, observed only locals trading in central markets and in the streets of Nalchik (KBR) and Grozny (Chechnya) in 2009 and 2010. Higher ethnic homogeneity has not been associated in sociological and political science research with propensity for interethnic violence. At the country level, statistical analysis of the Minorities at Risk data has found that ethnic fractualization has little relationship with civil wars and violent insurgencies when controlling for resource access, economic development, and terrain.[6]

Islam and religious cleavages are also hard to relate to regional differentiation in violence dynamics in the North Caucasus. On the one hand, the republics in the eastern part of the region where Islam has been more widespread and practiced—Ingushetia, Chechnya, and Dagestan—have seen most violence from 2008 to 2010. On the other hand, most targets of rebel attacks were local police, security, and government officials—mostly recruited from the ethnic and religious kin groups. This is very revealing, because the insurgents also had ample opportunity to attack any of the several dozen thousand federal police, military, and security forces stationed in the region and comprised predominantly of ethnic Russians and non-Muslims. Attacks on those forces, however, have been almost eight times less frequent in 2009 than attacks on ethnoreligious kin.[7] This dynamic would be consistent with the Fearon and Laitin "opportunity structure" argument, but the latter falters on other grounds discussed above.

The nonemergence of systemic violent insurgency in North Ossetia—barring episodic mass terrorist attacks—is another problem for the Islamic extremism explanation, given the combination of a territorial dispute in the southeastern part of the republic (Prigorodnyi County) divided between predominantly Russian Orthodox ethnic Ossetians, and the predominantly Muslim Ingush. Overlaying this cleavage is the division between the Muslim and Christian Ossetians in the neighboring southern counties. Yet Islamic identity has not engendered alliances between the Ingush and Muslim Ossetians. Furthermore, Muslim Ossetians have not been reported as contributors to the antigovernment insurgency the way Muslims have been in Ingushetia, Dagestan, and Chechnya. Large non-Muslim, ethnic Slav populations in KBR—accounting all in all for more than a quarter of the republic's population—have not been systematically targeted in violent attacks predominantly claimed by Islamist radicals.

Perhaps most importantly, the "creed" explanations of intergroup violence falter on broader theoretical grounds that control for interactions among identity types. One of the powerful insights from the micro-level empirical analyses of ethnic strife is that crosscutting group cleavages or identities—particularly religious, ethnic, and linguistic—mitigate conflict, while cumulative cleavages reinforce it (Varshney 2002). From this perspective, one would expect more violence against the Russian government forces and their local supporters over 2009 to occur in practically monoethnic Ingushetia and Chechnya than in the ethnically tripolar KBR, and in KBR more so than in heterogeneously multiethnic Dagestan. This was hardly the case. From 2008 to 2009, Dagestan was the place where the number of violent incidents representing insurgent activity increased most rapidly, by 250 percent. This was a significantly sharper rise than KBR's 11 percent, Ingushetia's 20 percent, and Chechnya's 40 percent (Center for Strategic and International Studies 2010). The twofold discrepancy between Chechnya and Ingushetia also confounds the cumulative cleavages explanation.

Finally, explanations based on ideas, ideologies, and faith have significant problems of their own. Principally, the argument that the post-Soviet Islamic revival became fertile ground for ideological proliferation of global jihadism in the region is hard to sustain, despite some well-documented accounts of the linkages that emerged between the North Caucasus insurgents and jihadists worldwide, including Al-Qaida. The principal problem with this argument is that it overpredicts violence generally and fails to specify the temporal and spatial patterns of violence. The model is underspecified, making jihadism appear as a "force of nature" that is destined to spread across Russia's Muslim regions and to pose formidable security threats to the Russian state. Gordon Hahn's extensive scholarly research on this issue illustrates the problem. In summarizing his findings on the spread of militant jihadist networks in the North Caucasus, Hahn concludes that their emergence "has the potential to spread war and terror to other parts of Russia. Its ideological influence and network of combat jamaats may spread to Tatarstan, Bashkortostan, and Moscow itself." The terms "potential" and "may" raise methodological red flags, because they don't specify the timing and the likely geographic patterns. Will this "spreading" occur at once in all regions? If it's likely to happen in some regions before others, why would that happen? Will the "spreading" take one, two, or twenty years? Meanwhile, five years since Hahn drew this conclusion, none of these regions have seen an escalation of jihadist-related violence along the lines of the most turbulent North Caucasus republics. A significant part of the problem is that the "jihadist network" argument assumes that social support for the militants takes place uniformly—even though Hahn's own well-researched discussion of specific social context in different republics suggests that such uniformity is unlikely (Hahn 2007, 93).

Alternative Considerations

Several important considerations based on the impact of public policies, particularly resource allocation, can also be controlled for, if not ruled out, in the context of the North Caucasus. First, with the insurgency perpetrated by a widely dispersed network of loosely related or unrelated cells with the overall force of no more than a few hundred by the best available estimates, it has not sought to channel resentment against government into resentment toward other social groups. Rather, the insurgents tapped into antigovernment sentiments, especially with regard to local police forces, to recruit fighters and supporters from as diverse a social and ethnic base as possible. In fact, the chief ideologist of the Islamist antigovernment coalition of insurgents in 2008–2009 was an ethnic Russian, Alexandr Tikhomirov (known under his jihadist alies as Said Buryatskiy). In KBR, the militant Jamaat Yarmuk that was behind the October 2005 mass attack on police and government offices in the republic's capital Nalchik, has been led by ethnic Kabardins, but recruited both Kabardins and Balkars—lending a poignant double entendre to the statement by a Balkar imam from Elbrus county at the focus group session conducted by this author in April 2010 in Nalchik that "the Kabardins and the Balkars are like two edges of the same dagger." In Dagestan, the Shariat Jamaat has been led from 2002 to 2009 by a succession of an ethnic Avar (Rasul Makasharipov), ethnic Lak (Rappani Khalilov), and an ethnic Avar from Azerbaijan (Ilgas Malachiyev) (Sazayev-Guriev 2009).

Second, because the regions remained primarily out-migration areas, the rapid inflow of outsiders into ethnically homogeneous areas—known to have engendered spikes in hate crime in US metropolitan areas—was not a factor. Even though the Russian government invested disproportionately in the North Caucasus compared to the national averages, inexpensive local labor remained widely available, while continued instability, reputation for violence, and wariness of outsiders deterred prospective migrants. While some migration into the more rapidly developing provincial capitals such as Grozny occurred, it was mostly local and has not played a galvanizing role in the insurgency.

Third, in terms of resource allocation, all North Caucasus republics gained a share of national income, making differentiation between relative intergroup gains and absolute in-group gains mostly a nonfactor in mobilization for violence.

Fourth, the Russian government continued to categorize the insurgency as terrorism and banditry akin to common crime, and thus has not changed the principal discourse on economic and political issues. It did not announce changes in development aid or redistributive strategies. The leaders of the North Caucasus republics generally made allowances for the fact that Chechnya has special development needs, given the two devastating wars from 1994 to 2001. Therefore, they acquiesced to the Chechen president's special personal relationship with Russia's leader Putin that translates into disproportionately higher levels of federal funding for Chechnya. Any residual grievances against this preferential treatment of Chechnya are not plausible explanations for violent insurgency, galvanized mostly by either Islamist ideology or very specific local political and economic issues. For this reason, it is hard to find clear connections between any particular development strategy at the level of the North Caucasus republics and the salience of self-perceived identities based on language, religion, class, region, or ethnicity. Similarly, this makes it hard to pinpoint how inclusion of different groups in the process of development at the level of the republics may have affected support for militant insurgency.

Fifth, no major new social groups—such as settled migrant laborers—were created in the region and no major ethnoterritorial dispersals or redistricting has occurred since the separation of the Checheno-Ingush Soviet Autonomous Republic into the republics of Chechnya and Ingushetia in 1991. An indicator that such redistribution has been largely unimportant in accounting for the violent insurgency in the region is the lack of aggressive mobilization over the unsettled administrative border between Chechnya and Ingushetia—although uncertainty about jurisdiction along this line has likely helped the rebels to circulate from one republic to the other and use the area for staging attacks on government forces elsewhere.

Finally, rent-seeking institutions of favoritism and collusion between government officials and private actors—particularly of the informal, patrimonial kind—have persisted in the region from the Soviet days where they thrived in defiance of Communist rule. The role of these networks are hard to gauge, but they are likely to contribute to social support for the insurgency as they operate below the radar screen of official statistics even at the lowest (county, city, and town) level of socioeconomic data aggregation. Because these networks control the real distribution of resources and taxation, they most likely override formal indicators across groups that could, in theory, be used to identify particularly aggrieved populations in the region.

Beyond Systemic Theoretical Challenges

This overview highlights a fundamental agency-structure challenge in explaining insurgencies and violence extremism. On the one hand, it is widely recognized that certain social, political, and economic environments are likely to increase the likelihood that the insurgents would emerge from them and not from somewhere else. On the other hand, it is also generally understood that the number of violent extremists is so small relative to the rest of the adversely affected populations that these social, political, and economic environments are not what sets them apart from those who do not become violent extremists (particularly when the findings come from research at the country level) (Denoeux and Carter 2009). Some leading experts on terrorism have emphasized the role of individual-level cognitive and psychological factors as a way out of this conundrum. For example, Jessica Stern (2004, 281) concluded from her interviews with terrorists from diverse religious backgrounds that their distinctive characteristic was emotional intensity: "All of them describe themselves as responding to a spiritual calling and many report a kind of spiritual high or addiction related to its fulfillment." Yet, this ideational explanation has at least two fundamental problems. First, it does not specify where these spiritual callings come from in the first place. Second, because Stern's and similar analyses were based on interviews with or on the examination of backgrounds of terrorists, they cannot establish how many individuals with similar callings did not become violent extremists. In short, just as it is unclear why only few individuals become violent extremists in response to the structural "push" factors such as poverty that affect large populations, it is also unclear why only few individuals become violent extremists in response to ideational "pull" factors such as jihadist recruitment messages disseminated to even larger populations via the internet.

These agency-structure problems are serious. They challenge the very notion that economic development assistance may have any effect at all on insurgency-related violence. If the contextual/structural "greed" factors are decisive, economic development will have to reach a level when practically all members of the population are satisfied (devoid of grievances) with respect to their economic well-being and social status—so that no one would be left out to be "pushed" into violent extremism. Yet, it is hard to imagine how this is possible in practice, given that communities suffering from hardship can be found even in the most economically developed and socially equitable countries. If the ideational, individual-level "pull" factors are paramount, however, then economic assistance would be epiphenomenal by default, given that spiritual callings may inspire individuals to violence regardless of their socioeconomic conditions.

While not claiming to attempt resolving these challenges, this study offers two ways to deal with them—one methodological, and one theoretical. The methodological approach is to reduce the level of aggregation and thus to mitigate the "ecological inference" problem (King 2007). This is done by using socioeconomic data and violence data for counties and cities within the North Caucasus republics (provinces)—the lowest level of aggregation publicly available from the Russian government statistical agencies. The underlying rationale for this approach is to follow the money, but to do so in more ways than tracking the amounts flowing into the republics. First, it is important to differentiate among different types of federal development assistance. The analysis also assesses how this money is categorized in meaningful, context-specific ways. Second, the funds are tracked down to the county, city or town level where specific projects are financed and payments to specific entities and individuals are disbursed. Third, because these federal developmental transfers make up most of the local budgets, it is important to track budget spending as an indicator of what sectors are targeted.

Another aspect of this approach is that empirical analysis is done first. This is partly consistent with the conclusions of the sweeping literature review on violent extremism undertaken under the auspices of the US Agency for International Development (USAID) in 2009. The "single most important point," according to the review, is that "VE [violent extremism—M.A.] must be seen in context" and that "there can be no general theory about why and how much the turn to VE occurs, because the answer to that question will vary from one setting to another" (Denoeux and Carter 2009, x).

The theoretical approach is to focus not so much on the "pull" and "push" factors but on the insurgency's organization and especially on the relationships and patterns of interaction between the insurgents and the communities where they emerge and/or operate. This is informed by the Weberian analysis of political authority and institutions—specifically the way it has been developed to explain the successful institutionalization of revolutionary and reformist parties in Russia, France, and Germany (Hanson 1996; Hanson 2010). The first key insight from this analysis is that charismatic (ideational) leadership—typically appealing to universal, timeless values—is crucial to engendering what Stern describes as "spiritual calling" among the recruits to the cause. The second key insight is that such leadership and the movements behind it will be short-lived, unless the charismatic leaders can also successfully appeal to the self-interest (instrumental rationality) of the movement participants. This means that Islamist insurgency leaders will be the most successful in contexts where they can appeal *both* to the religiosity of the prospective converts and to their material interests. One form of the successful institutionalization of suicide terrorism, in Weberian terms, is the practice in the Palestinian territories when the terrorist organizations provided significant financial support to the families of suicide bombers—initially inspired by the charismatic appeal of timeless happiness in paradise. Both motivations are critical. Without charisma the movement would become corrupt and decline. Without catering to material interests the movement will become extinct or marginalized once the true-believer initiators perish. The interaction between charisma and self-interest will vary by context, but the theory calls for watching out for this interaction and, hence, for the insurgency's organization in local (county, community) contexts.

Development Aid and Insurgency: A Micro-Level Plausibility Probe in Two Regions

Quasi-Experimental Design

To probe into these complexities, the following analysis focuses on two republics—Dagestan and KBR—where violence spread from the core insurgency strongholds of Chechnya and Ingushetia. It begins with an empirical assessment of the relationship between various forms of federal economic (development) assistance to the counties and cities, as well as key government spending areas, and the patterns and nature of systemic insurgency-related violence.

To investigate this relationship, the study uses the before-and-after cross-sectional quasi-experimental design. It was picked to maximize inference given the data limitations. The dependent variable in the analysis is the number of insurgency-related violent incidents per 10,000 people by county and major city in Dagestan and KBR from January 2009 through June 2010. The independent variable is the amount of federal economic assistance per capita to the same counties and cities from 2007 through the end of 2008. This analysis takes advantage of the county- and city-level data made available by the Russian government statistical agency, *Rosstat,* online in 2010. It uses all the data posted by *Rosstat* for these republics.

While it may be tempting to think that the data for more years would enable an analyst to generate better insights, it is important to understand that no general theoretical or methodological prescription warrants the selection of data for any particular number of time units for the independent and dependent variable or for aggregating or parsing out these time units in any given way. The key point is whether any socioeconomic data—for one day, one month, one year, or one hundred years—is representative of the general pattern of spending for whatever period of time policymakers or analysts may see as substantively meaningful in a given context. The present study demonstrates how one or two years of economic assistance might affect insurgency-related violence in the subsequent one-and-a-half years.[8] While this setup has its limitations, data aggregated for a larger number of years would have limitations of its own. For example, it could be argued that economic assistance has an impact no sooner than in 3 years, or in 4 years, or in 15 years. Or, it can be argued, that only assistance given in the previous year matters. Any amount of years may be deemed insufficient and any accumulation of data is, essentially, arbitrary. Thus, the data limitation in this study is not that it makes the findings less valid or reliable, but that it reduces the number of empirical tests one can apply to the relationship between different time segmentation and violence, and restricts opportunities to test for cumulative effects of economic assistance beyond two years. The same considerations apply to data aggregation for the outcome variable in this quasi-experimental probe.

The Data

Principal forms of federal economic aid to the North Caucasus. The term "development aid" in this study refers to the federal government transfers to provincial and, from there, local budgets that are collectively called *bezvozmezdnye postupleniia*—meaning allocations that do not have to be repaid. These nonrepayable allocations, in turn, have three categories:

- *Dotatsii*—verbatim meaning "donations" and sometimes translated as "grants" or "subsidies"—these transfers are not required to be repaid, they can be spent on what the local government deems necessary, and they do not require co-sharing contributions from the local budget. This is the closest one gets to free money.
- *Subventsii*—translated as "subventions"—these transfers, while they do not have to be repaid and do not require co-sharing from the local budgets, have to be spent in specific, predetermined areas.
- *Subsidii*—verbatim meaning "subsidies" and sometimes also translated as "grants-in-aid"—these transfers require co-sharing from local budgets. However, they can be spent in any area of local government's choosing and they do not have to be repaid.

The principal distinction is between *dotatsii* and the other two types of nonrepayable allocations. The former comes with no strings attached. The latter come with conditionalities. However, spending objectives are more flexible and local governments have room to stretch the definition of spending categories to accommodate their needs—including paying off patronage networks, kin, discontents, and private security providers (who may collude with the insurgents). The Russian government data indicates what is intuitive—that most nonrepayable transfers to counties in Dagestan and KBR in 2006–2008 came in the form of *dotatsii* and *subventsii*—the types of aid that do not require co-sharing from local budgets. Data analysis revealed that the way these federal aid transfers vary by county, city, and town in Dagestan and KBR relates nonrandomly to incidence of insurgency-related violence.

However, aid disbursements are not the whole story, even though they provided, on average, 92 percent of county and municipal budget revenues in Dagestan (with a standard deviation of about 8 percent) from 2006–2008 and 63 percent of county and municipal budget revenues in KBR (with a standard deviation of about 23 percent).[9] Spending—or failure to spend—in specific sectors is what ultimately matters with respect to support for insurgency. First, spending in specific sectors may improve economic conditions and thus reduce grievances among the general public that serve, eventually, as a source of support for the insurgency. Second, though this may be unfortunate on ethical grounds, budget allocations generate "embezzlable" funds that could be diverted to appease at least some insurgents or their support groups. This study reports on data that this author collected on spending categories that most likely relate to both of these considerations:

- *National security and law enforcement*—supplementary, marginal local funding for police, courts, and other security or military services and operations (spending on these functions is typically restricted to the federal budget; local budgets may fund "local organizations for public order maintenance" such as public order volunteers and, jointly with the federal budget in special agreed-upon circumstances, the "law enforcement activities") (*VUZLIB* 2010).
- *Housing*—funding for maintenance of municipal housing (comprising most housing in Russia, particularly in urban areas); maintenance services, equipment, and transportation; and public utilities, including water, sewage, public saunas, laundry, and dry-cleaning facilities, public transportation (bus, trolley, streetcar services), energy companies (water-heating plants, electric power plants, etc.), infrastructure (roads, bridges), hotels, and "communal space maintenance equipment" (*kommunal'nye mashiny*) (street cleaning machinery, garbage trucks, snow-clearing machines).
- *Education*—funding for preschools, secondary schools, secondary-level vocational-technical training, retraining and skills improvement,

postsecondary vocational-technical training, and related administrative costs

- *Culture*—funding for "agencies and organizations that promote the enrichment of people's cultural values and science" through the arts (*iskusstvo*—i.e., literature, architecture, sculpture, graphics, applied decorative arts, music, theater, cinematography, painting, and related art forms) and mass media ("systematic dissemination through press, radio, television, and cinema the society's cultural values and educating attitudes, opinions and behavior of the public, as well as the spread of culture and advertizing").
- *Health care, physical fitness, and sports*—funding for free public health care through municipal health-care institutions, as well as for the "encouragement of promoting physical fitness and sports."
- *Social services (social policy)*—funding for welfare programs and job search services; assisted living facilities for elderly and the disabled; schools for people with special needs; payments to those disabled as a result of the Chernobyl nuclear accident and other radiation catastrophes; compensations for work in emergency situations; payment of military pensions; unemployment benefits to women with children under three years old who lost their jobs due to the liquidation of the employer companies, agencies, or organizations; campaigns and events to promote fitness of children and the adolescents; contributions to the base pension payments; pensions of military servicemen and their families; transportation for the disabled; sanatorium and vacation center vouchers for war veterans and the disabled; installation of home telephones for war veterans and the disabled; and related services (Smolyaninova 2010).

National security and law enforcement expenses comprised a miniscule portion of local budgets—just over 1.5 percent in Dagestan in 2006–2008 and less than 0.15 percent in KBR in 2008 (Rosstat 2010). However, they are a proxy of local government support for broader counterinsurgency operations conducted by the federal government forces that may significantly affect violence rate in a county regardless of how local governments spend development money.

The remaining spending categories fall into three groups. The first one is housing and utilities. This represents economic activities that gainfully employ younger males with lower education levels and blue-collar job skills who may otherwise join or help the insurgents. Provision of housing also improves general well-being among all population strata. These expenditures amounted to about 9 percent of county budget spending in

Dagestan in 2006–2008 and 12 percent of county budget spending in KBR in 2008.

The second group includes education, culture, and health care/sports. Successful spending on these activities is likely to reduce support for violence because these activities—particularly education—are likely to promote more cognitively sophisticated behavior. Cultural and sporting activities also offer an additional outlet for self-expression and testosterone-driven impulsive behavior that may dampen the likelihood of one's engagement with militant groups. This is also the largest group of spending items. Education spending accounted for about 57 percent of all local budget spending in Dagestan from 2006 to 2008 and about 60 percent in KBR in 2008. Health-care and sports/fitness spending was, respectively, 12 percent and 9 percent, and culture—about 3 percent and 4 percent.

The third group, social services, is tracked to control for residual public spending effects, given its low share in overall local budget spending. Its share of local budget spending was about 9 percent from 2006 to 2008 in Dagestan and about 3 percent in KBR.

Local budget spending, however, may fuel social support for the insurgency if money is diverted. Funds in all of these spending categories may be channeled, as it is well-known among the locals, to kin or useful private networks. The embezzled funds from any of these spending categories may thus indirectly fund the insurgency. Which specific category may be most "embezzlable" depends on specific context and therefore is treated here as an empirical question. What follows is the exploration of how violence relates to total local budget spending, as well as spending in each of the specific categories above.

Data on violent insurgency

The study tracked the same type of violent incidents related to the antigovernment insurgency by county as the Center for Strategic and International Studies tracked by republic, using reports by Russia's main wire services (RIA-Novosti, Itar-Tass, and Interfax, and local media sources, *Kavkazskii Uzel* and *Voinenet.ru*).[10] The analysis uses the data for all such incidents—even though a substantial number of them are action by government security forces. One could arguably look exclusively at rebel attacks only—but two problems then arise, suggesting the totality of incidents is likely to be a more reliable indicator. First, a large number of reports make it hard to determine who initiated violent action. The typical story is of police officers stopping a car to check the drivers' identity and the people in the car refusing to comply and firing at the police. This typically is followed by a shootout.

Information in most cases is insufficient to disaggregate police action from the action of the attackers and determining who initiated the incidents (the police checkup or the passengers' response) and whether the police fired first but later reported that the passengers fired first. Second, a considerable number of actions undertaken by the security forces is in itself evidence of rebel activity—particularly the discovery of planted bombs, arms caches, rebel hideouts, and arrests of alleged rebels.

To control for population size (given that more incidents may happen in any area simply because more people mean more potential recruits and more targets), the analysis was based on the number of violent incidents per 10,000 residents.

The Empirical Findings

Many Counties, Two Tales: Patterns of Developmental Aid and Violent Insurgency

The statistical probe with county-level data shows that development aid in Dagestan and KBR relates differently to insurgency-driven violence. Two distinct patterns emerge. In Dagestan, on average, counties and cities that received more federal development aid (*dotatsii, subsidii,* and *subventsii*) per capita in 2008 saw less violence in 2009–2010. In KBR, on average, counties and cities that received more federal development aid in 2008 saw more violence in 2009–2010 (Figures 9.1 and 9.2). As regression coefficients show, federal aid may explain about 27 percent of variation in violence at the county level in Dagestan and about 23 percent in KBR. Because in reality a perfect linear relationship is unlikely, correlation coefficients are not necessarily informative substantively. They do, however, offer an important first probe—given the amount of noise in the real-world data, a significant bivariate correlation is a good indicator that a potential important relationship exists and is worth investigating further so that other factors can be controlled.

A visual examination of broader patterns in Figures 9.1 and 9.2 shows that this relationship is particularly plausible in Dagestan's 43 counties and cities. Entities that received more than the average amount of development aid per capita (22,000 rubles) from 2006 to 2008 had at most just one violent incident related to the insurgency from January 2009 to June 2010—just over half the average violence rate. At the same time, cities, towns, and counties that received a less-than-average amount of federal aid per capita were significantly more likely to see more-than-the-average number of insurgency-driven violent events. All 12 county-level entities in

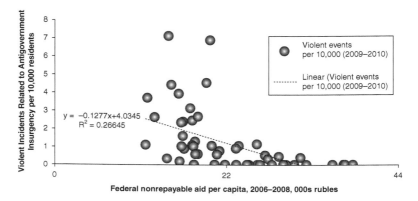

Figure 9.1 Insurgency and Federal Developmental Aid by County and City in Dagestan.

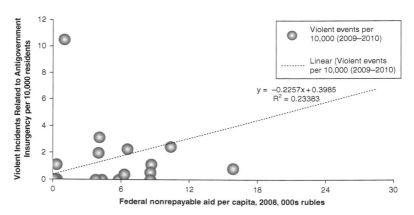

Figure 9.2 Insurgency and Federal Developmental Aid by County and City in Kabardino-Balkaria.

Dagestan where violence was twice or more frequent than the average are the ones that received less than the average amount of federal development assistance.

In KBR, however, the visual distribution pattern indicates a weaker relationship—even if the data for Elbrus county and the town of Tyrnyauz is merged, thus eliminating the outlier in the top left corner (This would be justifiable since the *Rosstat* data for these particular entities suggests that revenues and expenses for Tyrnyauz were included, to a large extent, in county expenses in 2008). A significant portion of the correlation is explained by the Elbrus County and its main town of Tyrnyauz, if the data for the two are merged.

It is also notable that the amount of completely unconditional aid—*dotatsii*—correlated with violence levels about as strongly as the total amount of aid in both Dagestan and KBR.

The patterns are the same when it comes to budget spending (Figures 9.3 and 9.4). Three spending categories from the same group (education, culture, health care/sports) showed the strongest correlation with violence.[11] Overall, the more money spent in these categories, the less likely one would see violence in any given county in Dagestan, and the more likely one would see violence in KBR. Spending on education at the county level explained approximately 30 percent of the variation in insurgency-related violence in Dagestan and 28 percent in KBR.

Spending on national security related to violence rates no more than chance, although in KBR, the suggested relationship was negative. This general nonresult is unsurprising given that most law enforcement and security operations are financed directly from Moscow and are not included in county-level data. In both KBR and Dagestan, social policy spending had no significant relationship with violence rates by county. This finding is intuitively plausible given both the small scale of spending in this category and the large list of items it is supposed to finance. In methodological terms, this kind of allocation creates too much "noise" in the data. Finally, spending on housing and utilities also had no systematic association with violence levels by county. Again, this is hardly surprising given that most of

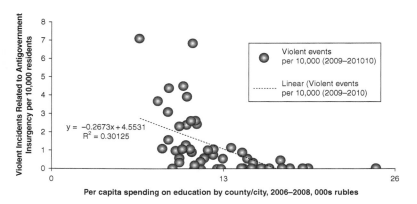

Figure 9.3 Insurgency and Local Government Spending on Education in Dagestan.

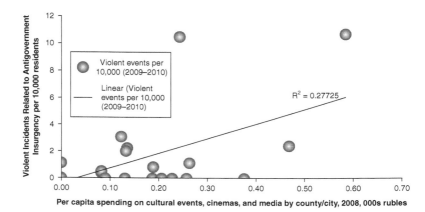

Figure 9.4 Insurgency and Local Government Spending on Culture, Kabardino-Balkaria.

these—rather limited—funds support the already existing municipal housing and a long list of services. Most likely, this form of spending contributes to neither significant change in socioeconomic circumstances that might reduce antigovernment grievances, nor to the availability of the "embezzlable" funds that might support the insurgency.

These are preliminary findings using direct one-way measures of association. But they suggest an important and counterintuitive conclusion with significant policy implications warranting more careful and systematic future examination. Specifically, they show that developmental aid at the local level may help reduce or increase violence, depending on the type of insurgency in a region.

The Tale of Two Insurgencies: Exploring the Nexus between Social Context and Insurgency Organization

An interesting analytical puzzle emerges if one puts the statistical findings in a broader historical and social context by county in Dagestan and KBR. On the one hand, in both republics, the most violent counties appear to represent the dynamics of Islamist radicalization in the context of ethnic group divisions that have been embedded in socioeconomic grievances, the legacies of Moscow's governance in the region (particularly, the administrative-territorial division, property rights, and political appointments), and the associated emotional narratives of victimization and discrimination.

Thus, in Dagestan, the most violent counties relative to population size were the ones with a significant proportion of ethnic Kumyks in the local population. One of Russia's leading North Caucasus experts, Sergey Markedonov, pointed out that the Kumyks experienced a systemic demotion in their social status in Dagestan since the arrival of Soviet power in 1917. Until then the Kumyks were considered the first among equals among Dagestan's dozens of ethnic groups, to a large extent because the Kumyks had the highest proportion of literate population in the area, which meant that they occupied a disproportionate number of government posts and the Kumyk language served as Dagestan's interethnic lingua franca. With the arrival of Soviet power, Kumyk lost this status as Moscow pushed universal education and established a system of interethnic rotation in government. The redrawing of administrative boundaries in the interests of Soviet planners and politicians also sparked off local conflicts over land rights and use with other groups (Markedonov 2007). As it turns out, the Karabudakhkent county—the scene of intense conflicts over land use between the Dargins and the Kumyks in the early 2000s—saw most per capita incidents of violent insurgency in Dagestan in 2009–2010 (6.9 per 10,000 population). In four of the remaining five most violent counties in Dagestan—Makhachkala (4.4 incidents per 10,000 people), Khasavyurt (3.9 incidents), Kizil-Yurt (3.7 incidents), and Buynaksk (2.4 incidents)—Kumyks comprise from about 10 to 30 percent of the population. Higher-than-average levels of violence were also recorded in Novolak county (2.6 per 10,000) and Kazbek county (2.4 per 10,000)—the site of protracted territorial disputes and grievances between the Chechen-Akkin ethnics who were deported into exile to Central Asia from 1944 to 1957 and the Laks and Avars who moved into the areas vacated by the deportees.

Similarly, in KBR, higher incidence of violent insurgency appeared to be associated with areas that had a significant proportion of the republic-level ethnic minority group, the Balkars. Developments in KBR suggest that the Balkars have substantial grounds for grievances and protest mobilization. Like Chechens, they were deported by Stalin to Central Asia in 1944 and when they returned in 1957 they found their traditional land reapportioned and partially settled by other local ethnics, notably the Kabardinians (who also constitute the majority of KBR's population at approximately 55 percent). These grievances were reignited after the passing of the Russian federal law number 131 ("On the general principals of local governance in the Russian Federation") designed to further centralize executive authority in Russia. The KBR government derived two local laws from this federal law, which resulted in the transfer of large tracts of agricultural and pasture lands, traditionally considered as the property of the predominantly

Balkar settlements, into the incongruously called "inter-settled areas"—a bureaucratic euphemism meaning that these lands could now be developed by representatives of other, predominantly Kabardinian, settlements. And as it happens, most violent incidents per capita in 2009–2010 happened in the counties where these land disputes became the most intense and where ethnic Balkars—while a minority in KBR as a whole—comprised the majority of the county population. Elbrus county, with approximately 65-percent population ethnic Balkars saw 10.7 incidents per 10,000 inhabitants. Cherek county, the only other one in KBR where Balkars account for the majority of the population (61 percent), also witnessed per capita violence levels that were among the highest in the republic with 2.4 incidents per 10,000 inhabitants.

However, the relationship between violent insurgency incidence and federal economic assistance in two previous years was diametrically opposite in the two republics. In Dagestan, the counties with the highest levels of violent insurgency in 2009–2010 *and* pronounced ethnoterritorial and ethnopolitical conflicts all received below-average amount of federal economic assistance per capita in the previous two years—that is, 19,870 rubles in Karabudakhkent, 14,920 rubles in Makhachkala, 15,860 rubles in Khasavyurt, 11,800 rubles in Kizil-Yurt, and 16,430 rubles in Buynaksk. In KBR, the two counties with the strongest Balkar ethnoterritorial grievances and Balkar-Kabardinian tensions and the highest levels of violence in 2009–2010 received several times the average amount of per capita federal economic assistance by county in 2008—that is, 28,380 rubles in Elbrus and 10,350 rubles in Cherek.[12]

This is a serious puzzle. It seemed at first glance that the county-level analysis illuminated a cluster of significant "push" and "pull" factors explaining violent insurgency in the North Caucasus—to wit, ethnic fractionalization, socioeconomic, and political disputes rooted in the history of governance, and receptivity to Islamic faith and recruitment efforts of the Islamist ideological entrepreneurs. But this does not mean that economic assistance would work the same way in these counties. Since assistance had diametrically opposite effects in counties with the similar profiles of underlying conditions reviewed here, it suggests that some other characteristics or drivers of the insurgency have not been taken into account. It means that this cluster of factors is not enough to explain how economic assistance may affect violence.

It is beyond the scope of this chapter to examine all the combinations of alternative factors, but one important missing dimension—offering a plausible non-ad hoc explanation of the puzzle—is the relationship between the organizational mode of the insurgency and its social base. What if money may dampen or fuel violence depending not on how much is spent and on what, but on how the insurgency's leaders and their supporters relate to local communities?

Community-Centered versus Itinerant Insurgencies

In fact, one may visualize two ideal types of relationship between insurgent organization and local communities that would enable one to explain the difference between the effects of economic assistance on the insurgency-related violence in Dagestan from those in KBR.

If, due to the societal makeup and traditions, the insurgency has strong and widespread roots in the political and economic competition within local communities, the availability of funding at the county level reduces scarcity—and, hence, the intensity of competition that is ultimately about power and resources. Because the insurgents in this situation have stakes in the outcome of competition for resources, the availability of funds helps appease or buy off the conflicting parties and thus reduce the intensity of the struggle. This type of insurgency organization may be viewed as community-centered.

If, however, the insurgency organization has little stake in the outcomes of local competition for power and resources, while the key community figures have little incentive to engage the insurgents' support, the availability of more funding in any given locale will motivate the insurgents to divert these funds to the broader insurgent network so that they can sustain operations across a wider area. This pattern would emerge, for example, if the insurgency is highly mobile and is organized around a network of small bases outside populated areas. Consequently, it would have weaker roots in the local community, would move around more from one small base to another, and would have greater stakes in funding the network. Thus, the money the insurgents manage to divert from the public is more likely to go toward funding their antigovernment operations in pursuit of larger organizational goals across wider regions than toward appeasing the feuding clans or other local groups in a community or across communities. Hence, the availability of more federal economic aid to the region would signal greater opportunities to extract rent and attract more insurgent activity. This type of insurgency organization may be described as itinerant or mobile-dispersed.[13]

It is important to note that this distinction, while consistent with the divergent effects of federal economic assistance in Dagestan and KBR, is drawn in theory. In practice, every insurgency is likely to combine the community-concentrated and the itinerant organizational capacity. The crucial distinction is likely to be of the degree, rather than of a kind. With this caveat, one still may be served well by examining whether the insurgent organization in Dagestan has been more community-concentrated and the one in KBR more mobile-dispersed. The existing typologies of insurgency preclude the very possibility of making this substantively meaningful distinctions between Dagestan and KBR.[14]

Dagestan and KBR: Urban Jungles and Forested Mountains

In both the republics, the leading insurgent organizations in 2009 and 2010—the Shariat Jamaat in Dagestan and the Yarmuk Jamaat in KBR—identified with the same Islamist (Salafist or Wahhabi) conglomerate, *Imarat Kavkaz,* and its Chechen war veteran leader Dokku Umarov, and designated Russian government security forces and local officials serving the Russian state as its principal targets. Both groups have framed these targets in international jihadist terms, respectively, as *kafir,* or the infidels, and *murtad,* or the apostates. The key figures of both organizations have had combat experience in the Chechen wars of the 1990s and early 2000s and/or in large-scale antigovernment operations conducted by the Chechen separatist and jihadist terrorist leaders such as Shamil Basayev and Amir Khattab.[15]

However, to operate successfully in Dagestan and KBR these—and other insurgent groups—have to adapt to different geographic, demographic, and sociocultural realities. Regarding those realities, Dagestan and KBR differ in three fundamental ways that, in turn, underlie the different foundations for the insurgency-society interaction in the two republics.

First, climate and terrain differ significantly. KBR is set amidst lusciously forested foothills and mountain ranges—the tallest in Europe—generously endowed with long, deep, winding valleys and ubiquitous water supply from freshwater springs, rivers, and waterfalls and mineral water minifountains dispersed through these wooded mountains. Whereas, Dagestan is set in the arid Eastern part of the Great Caucasus Mountain range. Its mountains look almost for habitation, with dramatically rising vertical walls and vast exposed plateaus. Due to the development of resorts around Europe's tallest mountain—the twin-peak dormant volcano, Elbrus—KBR has a better developed road network linking the mountain areas with the major population centers. This makes it significantly easier for insurgents in KBR than in Dagestan to establish and maintain a dispersed network of small mountain bases and to strike targets of opportunity.

Second, the demographics differ in important respects. Dagestan's population is more than 2.5 times larger than KBRs. This translates into more people outside Dagestan's capital of Makhachkala (population 466,000 in 2009) settling in mid- and small-size cities and clusters of villages. In KBR, outside the capital Nalchik (295,000 in 2009) population is concentrated in small towns and villages. County population distributions illustrate this succinctly. In Dagestan, five counties outside of Makhachkala form significant urban-rural clusters with more than 100,000 residents, two of which (Derbent and Khasavyurt) have more than 225,000 residents. The Karabudakhkent county with about 70,000 inhabitants abuts Makhachkala, forming an urban-rural cluster with the capital. All of these rural-urban con-glomerations had higher-than-average levels of insurgency-related violence per capita in 2009–2010. In KBR, only two counties outside Nalchik had populations exceeding 100,000 (Baksan with about 117,000 residents and Prokhladnyi with 106,000). The highest rates of violence per capita were in Elbrus county (population about 35,000 including the county center of Tyrnyauz). Other than in Nalchik and Baksan, all other counties where more-than-median levels of violence were registered were at the bottom of the population ladder in KBR (Cherek with 21,000 residents; Prokhladnyi county with 45,600; Chegem settlement with 18,000; Mayskiy county with 12,600; Urvan county with 41,700; and Lesken county with 29,000—listed in descending order on the scale of reported violence).

Third, the social-cultural context differs in two important ways. One of them is the difference in elemental social organization historically rooted, in part, in the geographic and demographic distinctions discussed above. Clan and family liaisons in Dagestan traditionally form around territorially concentrated *jamaats* (traditional communities called this way long before the word came to be used to designate radical Islamist groups). These may be groups of villages or interlinked neighborhoods within an urban area or an intersection of neighborhoods in the rural-urban cluster. In contrast, in KBR—and, for the most part, elsewhere in the North Caucasus—clan relations link more geographically dispersed families and individuals. One extreme form of the latter type of relationship is the Chechen *teip* in which the unwritten law is that their members must visit at least one other remote *teip* member once a month.[16] The second difference is that Islamic faith took root earlier in Dagestan than in KBR and became a stronger part of the social fabric. In part, this integration into local societies is demonstrated by the predominance of Sufism—a form of practicing Islam in which believers link up with the deity through intermediaries, the enlightened Sufi sheikhs. Yet, this societal and communal integration meant that Dagestanis came to associate themselves more strongly with the local, "ethnic" Islam than with universal Islamic values. In a 1997 poll in Dagestan, only 56 percent of Avars, 50 percent of Dargins, and 48 percent of Lezghin considered them-selves "simply Muslims." The rest classified themselves first and foremost as the "Caucasus Muslims." In the same poll, however, 86 percent of ethnic

Kabardinians—as well as 88 percent of closely related ethnic Adygeans and 94 percent of ethnic Cherkess, considered themselves "simply Muslims" rather than the "Caucasus Muslim."[17]

Taken together, these three factors mean that in Dagestan militant insurgents have fewer opportunities to base their operations in the mountains, but more opportunities to get integrated in urban and urban-rural clusters with local communities where they need to combine clandestine operations with relatively open day-to-day life. Their operational base is akin to the urban jungle. The reverse applies to KBR where more insurgent activities rely on dispersed bases in forested mountains.

To what extent are these differences notable in studies of the insurgency in these republics?

Dagestan

Russia's experts on the North Caucasus point out that the most distinctive feature of violent insurgency or terrorism in Dagestan is that it is deeply rooted in local issues and isolated from jihadist movements elsewhere in the region. Three factors make these parochial roots particularly tenacious. First, Islam—recall that in Sufism, religious luminaries (*prosvetlennye*) have special authority in local communities as intermediaries between the believers and God—has been practiced longer than anywhere else in the North Caucasus. A religious-based insurgency would thus not only have a larger social base of sympathizers and supporters, but would also spawn local rivalries linked to religious leaders and their secular allies, including those in government institutions and business. Second, this fragmentation and competition among radical Islamist insurgent networks is most likely exacerbated through ethnic and clan cleavages that are the most numerous and complex than elsewhere in the region, given Dagestan's ethnic heterogeneity. Third, institutionalization of ethnic and clan power-sharing in formal and informal political institutions in the Soviet and post-Soviet periods makes collusion among politicians, law enforcers, and business elites more likely along mutually reinforcing ethnic and clan lines. This means, in turn, that competition for economic resources would require additional enforcement, raising the incentives for the insurgents to get involved in these ethnoclan interest-group struggles and for the interest-groups elites to pay insurgents protection money.

Investigating the situation in Dagestan, the Russian government daily, *Rossiiskaia Gazeta,* concluded that "inter-clan conflicts drag in criminal, terrorist, and extremist groups as well as law-enforcement agencies. The law in these circumstances is only the means of turf wars." (Borisov 2005a).

Ultimately, the reports said, "[violent] events in Dagestan result from the internecine struggle among local elites. The struggle for power here is gravely mixed in with terrorism. Terrorism is the camouflage for this struggle." (Borisov 2005b).

A journalist who has covered the region for years wrote a series of exposés on insurgency in Dagestan in *Novaya Gazeta,* Russia's only serious independent newspaper that frequently criticizes federal authorities' policies in the North Caucasus.[18] The author of the exposés, Yulia Latynina, traced what on the surface appears to be Islamist-driven violence—due, indeed, to widespread adherence to radical Islam particularly among the younger people—to cutthroat competition among insurgents for the monopolistic privilege to extort "Allah protection money" from government contractors and government officials distributing resources, as well as to vicious infighting among the insurgents for access to their illicit "Wahhabi gang banks" (*vahhabistskiy obshchak*) (Latynina 2009).

Russia's leading expert on Dagestan, sociologist Enver Kisriev, who chairs the Center for Regional (formerly, Civilizational) Studies at the Russian Academy of Sciences' Institute of Asia and Africa and conducts surveys in the region, explained the worsening security situation on the basis of his observations in Dagestan in September 2010: "At some point, there were ideological rebels, bandits, law-breakers. But now they have already been integrated into the economic system ... they now send ultimatums on flash memory sticks and control not only the small and medium-size businesses, but also big business in the North Caucasus."[19]

According to Abdul-Nasir Dibirov, president of Dagestan's Institute of Economics and Politics, "an important distinctive characteristic of Dagestan's terrorism is that the anti-Russian motivations [such as the drive to set up an independent Islamic emirate in the region] are weak. If you discount a few ready-made slogans borrowed from the Chechen terrorists, the Russian theme is nowhere near to being dominant. This is because Dagestan's terrorism has first and foremost purely Dagestani roots. The economic, social, political, and cultural state of Dagestan's society, past and present, is the principal driving force and the source of objectives for Dagestan's terrorists."[20]

Kabardino Balkaria

The county-level pattern of insurgent violence and, in particular, the role of Baksan county best exemplify the itinerant or mobile-dispersed nature of the insurgency-society interaction in KBR. Baksan county is a telling outlier with respect to the pattern of ethnic divisions, governance grievances, and intergroup protest that characterizes the most violence counties in Dagestan and KBR. And it is also a county that lies outside the dominant relationship pattern between federal economic assistance and insurgent violence in KBR. From January 2009 to mid-2010, Baksan county (population 57,800) saw 2.25 and Baksan town (population 58,300) saw 3.1 violent incidents per 10,000. The Baksan county level of violence was about 50 percent above the KBR mean of 1.7 incidents and more than five times the median level of 0.4 incidents. The Baksan town level of violence was close to double the mean and eight times the median. Yet, less than 2 percent of the local population are ethnic Balkars and the lands that became the focus of intense Balkar-Kabardinian disputes since the 2003 law on local government were outside the county. The amount of federal economic assistance in nonrepayable funds (*bezvozmezdnye postupleniia*) was, however, about average for KBR in 2008, at 6,560 rubles per capita for Baksan county and 4,110 rubles per capita for Baksan town.[21]

Baksan's location and its role as the hub of insurgent operations are significant, illustrating the mobile-dispersed, or itinerant, nature of KBR's insurgency. The city sits at the juncture of major highways going through North Ossetia to Ingushetia and from there to Chechnya (Kavkaz Highway), as well as directly to Chechnya except for a short stretch across the northern tip of North Ossetia. It is also within striking distance—about an hour's drive—of the capital Nalchik. At the same time, the county stretches southwest along the best road into the highest reaches of the Great Caucasus Mountain Range around Mt. Elbrus, Europe's tallest peak lying at the juncture with Asia. This location offers an ideal connection to the core insurgent groups in Chechnya and Ingushetia; to high-publicity value targets in the capital Nalchik and in the resort areas of Chegem and Elbrus; and to the recruitment base in mountainous areas around the city of Tyrnyauz—an incongruous cluster of Soviet-era five-storied concrete apartment complexes, built to support the once-thriving tungsten mining and processing. This author has traveled with his local colleagues extensively along these roads in 2009 and 2010 and noted their good quality and the availability of side roads, some paved, leading deep into the mountain valleys.

It was, in fact, in Baksan county where the Chechen militant Islamist leader, Shamil Basayev set up camp in preparation for a daring raid on the capital Nalchik in October 2005 and established an operational hub with the local Yarmuk Jamaat. In that raid approximately two hundred militants from different parts of KBR and elsewhere in the North Caucasus, organized in ten mobile groups and attacked the city and district police headquarters and a gun store. The Russian government forces repelled the attack after two days of fighting. Officials reported 142 dead and about 100 wounded.[22]

Notably, directing the attacks by radio from the highest point in the hills surrounding Nalchik, near the 40-feet-tall stone head of the Caucasus Prometheus, was Shamil Basayev's local supporter, Anzor Astemirov, an ethnic Kabardinian who was born and spent his childhood in the Ukrainian city of Kremenchug. Following the attacks, Astemirov remained the central figure and one of the principal organizers of KBR insurgents. He rose through the hierarchy of the Chechen-dominated anti-Russian insurgency. After the latter transitioned from a predominantly separatist to an Islamist movement under Dokku Umarov in the fall of 2007, Astemirov came to be regarded as its chief ideologist.

Regional patterns of violence in KBR in 2009–2010 showed significant path-dependency with the 2005 raid—centering around Baksan county where Basayev reportedly had temporary headquarters for nearly a year during that time and spreading along the major road leading into the mountainous areas in Elbrus County. Practically all incidents happened along the artery of roads converging in Baksan—particularly along the Baksan-Chegem-Tyrnyauz-Elbrus corridor. It is also the area where government security forces discovered most weapons caches and rebel hideouts.

Reports of local government activities provide circumstantial indications of the dispersed nature of the insurgency's social base. An investigation by a *Versiia* online magazine and an independent analysis by one of Russia's top academic experts on the North Caucasus demonstrate how social support for insurgency in KBR materialized. In the late 1990s and early 2000s, police and law enforcement agencies in KBR responded to Moscow's alarm over the rise of militant "Wahhabi" Islam in the region by identifying all local "Islamic extremists." Journalist Orkhan Jemal notes, however, that KBR's authorities encountered a serious problem: "Unlike in Chechnya and Dagestan, they faced a shortage of actual Wahhabis... They heard that the Wahhabis donned long beards and short moustaches and wore pants reaching down to about mid-ankle with no underwear. Yet those kind of people were practically absent here."[23]

Having failed to identify serious Wahhabi suspects, the local government gave this task to the leader of KBR's Islamic Spiritual Directorate—the government-approved leader of local Muslims. His subordinates compiled the list of about 50 names. Jemal reports that having seen the list, KBR's police chief got incensed and demanded that more people should be identified, since otherwise local police budgets would not be increased as much as he anticipated. Precinct police officers then started listing everyone attending the early morning–prayer ritual (*namaz*) at local mosques. They reasoned that if someone got up before dawn to pray, they were more likely than other

Muslims to be violent Islamist extremists.[24] Later, Jemal recounts, whenever a violent act happened anywhere in Russia, police would detain and interrogate people on this list—resulting, according to Jemal, in maltreatment of suspects, including beatings and torture.[25]

Moscow Carnegie Center's Aleksey Malashenko tells a similar story of how police mischaracterization of mainstream Muslim scholars and activists as radicals directly contributed to local mobilization for the 2005 raid on Nalchik Malashenko (2008). An insurgency of marginalized radicals emerged pursuing broader, universalist goals of the Imarat Kavkaz movement. Local targets were attacked because they symbolized those goals, in contrast to Dagestan where local targets often related to local issues and disputes. Yet, at the same time, both insurgencies retained outward Islamist rhetoric and stated motivations.

Conclusion and Implications for Policy

At the level of comparative theory, the principal contribution of this study is that economic incentives are moderated by community orientation of the insurgents. In this sense, the results bring to mind the notion of "value rationality" based on the fusion of Weberian "ideal types" of authority and political behavior. The same socioeconomic inputs may produce diametrically opposite results depending on how local contexts enable the integration of charismatic, universalist goals with specific organizational needs of the insurgents and interests of their community supporters. Movements exclusively based on charisma are likely to be short-lived, while movements based exclusively on self-interest are likely to lose sight of their initial ideological objectives.[26] The results are consistent with the Weberian logic in that reduction of scarcity would reduce competition among instrumentally motivated actors, but not among charismatically motivated actors.

The important practical implication of the analysis concerns government policies for reducing social support for armed insurgencies. While such support may be motivated economically—as has been the case in both Dagestan and KBR—the effectiveness of government intervention depends not only, and perhaps not so much, on the source of grievances that generate the social support base, but on how insurgents tap into this popular support. If these goals are instrumental, in the Weberian sense, and relate predominantly to resource allocation at the local level, government aid may reduce violence. If, however, the insurgents tap into dispersed communities that they need to mobilize with appeals transcending specific community interests and they would be more likely to emphasize universalist, then development assistance is less likely to be effective even though it may be targeting a similar economically aggrieved population. Predominant religious practices in a society are also likely to contribute to this difference.

Even in a relatively small region like the central-east part of the North Caucasus, development assistance may produce diametrically opposite results depending on local context. Moreover, it is notable in this study that developmental aid came almost entirely from the federal government and with few strings attached. The more the insurgent organization is integrated in local communities, the more the outside aid is likely to help.

As for the itinerant insurgencies, perhaps the lesson from this comparison of Dagestan and KBR is that although it might be tempting to spend on large local economic projects, it would be more effective to spend on improving the quality of law enforcement, security, and government institutions more broadly. For example, replacing heavily manned ubiquitous traffic police stations along KBR roads—frequently targets for insurgent attacks that also put ordinary drivers through time-wasting checks and encourage bribery—with a significantly smaller and well-paid highway patrol force in fast vehicles capable of going up rugged mountainous roads, would be a viable policy option. Yet it has not come up on the agenda of policy debates in Russia about reducing insurgency-driven violence in the region.

In the end, both economic assistance and the quality of government institutions are vital, but this study indicates in what regions to spend scarce aid resources first and for what purposes. Most importantly, this study finds that the idea that economic assistance could work, if designated for sectors likely to reduce economic grievances of the local population, has limited implications. It is important, before adopting development aid policy, to study the local insurgency's goals and orientation to the local communities. If this is ignored, the developmental aid may just as well pave the road to greater violence with good intentions.

Notes

1. Exact data are unavailable, but reports of the Russian human rights group Memorial, the US Holocaust Museum, and Russian government statistics indicate this was the order of magnitude of violence in the Chechen wars.
2. The study defined violent incidents as "abductions of military personnel and civilians, bombings, assassinations of key civilian and military leaders, rebel attacks, police or military operations against suspected militants, destruction of property by militants, and the discovery of weapons." Those incidents were tracked in the North Caucasus republics of Chechnya, Ingushetia, KBR, North Ossetia, and Dagestan (Center for Strategic and International Studies 2009). The estimate of the number of events by republic is approximate, based on the charts.
3. http://georgia.kavkaz-uzel.ru/articles/164059/

4. In methodological terms, the first approach reduces the omitted variables' bias and the second increases the number of observations and improves the specification of causal variables.

5. According to the Center for Strategic and International Studies (2010, 14), from April 1, 2008, to March 31, 2010, Ingushetia, with a population of approximately 0.47 million had 491 deaths due to violent incidents, whereas Dagestan, with a population of about 2.6 million had 511 deaths due to violent incidents.

6. For the review of the models see Green, Strolovitch, and Wong 1998; Fearon and Laitin 2003.

7. Based on the author's data compiled from reports on violence in the region at www.voinenet.ru, *Kavkazskiy Uzel,* Interfax, Itar-Tass, RIA-Novosti, and human rights and rebel websites.

8. *Rosstat* aggregated the data for KBR differently by county and several constituent cities in different years, making a comparison with the Dagestan data possible for only 2008. However, because the regional-level data patterns are consistent between the republics over the 2007–2008 period, as shown in Table 9.1, the data for KBR for 2008 was used as a reasonable proxy for the two-year federal economic assistance pattern.

9. The standard deviation values indicate that this is a substantively meaningful variation for exploring how it may relate to variation in violence rates. Based on Rosstat 2010.

10. See note 2.

11. Correlation coefficients for all three were respectable and had the same signs in each republic, but since this was the empirical question, it was important to identify which categories related to violence more strongly and compare those stronger factors across the two republics.

12. The average amount of per-capita federal economic assistance (*bezvozmezdnye postupleniya*) by county in Dagestan in 2007–2008 was approximately 22,000 rubles and in KBR for 2008—approximately 5,900 rubles.

13. These insurgency types are also likely to represent different predominant motivations. The crucial distinction is whether the principal goal of a violent act is substantively local (village, town, county, city) or universalist in going beyond the local context and relates to issues such as nationalism or promotion of universal religions (e.g., Islam, Catholicism) or political ideologies (e.g., Marxism, Trotskyism). For example, insurgents often attack local policemen or officials, and they often claim to espouse radical religious or ideological views. In a community-centered insurgency, the actors would try to eliminate a policeman or an official to get members of another local kin or corporate group to take that position or to signal nonacceptance of specific acts of the victims and to deter their successors from doing the same (e.g., granting construction contracts to rival business interests). By contrast, in an itinerant insurgency that is focused beyond local issues, the militants would eliminate officials indiscriminately to send a message that the prevailing state doctrine (including the form of

government, national borders, or the role of religion) is unacceptable, and eventually to allow the broader movement/organization—which may have no stakes in a specific county, town, or city—to seize power and impose new institutions or boundaries. However, determining motivation *ex ante* is prohibitively hard in most cases for those who are not insurgency insiders.

14. The Pentagon defines an insurgency as "an organized movement aimed at the overthrow of a constituted government through the use of subversion and armed conflict"—but it does not specify whether only individual members of the government are targeted for replacement or the entire system is targeted for replacement; it also does not specify whether the overthrow refers to a local, provincial, or national government (www.dtic.mil/doctrine/jel/new_pubs/jp1_02 .pdf). The Sociology Index distinguishes six types of insurgency—"secessionist, revolutionary, restorational, reactionary, conservative, and reformist"—but does not separate them on the basis of their relationship to local communities (http://sociologyindex.com/insurgent_and_insurgency.htm). It is noteworthy also that the distinction between the *community-centered* and *itinerant* insurgency is made on terms of Weberian "ideal types" and that in reality the motives are more mixed and complex.

15. Based on mainstream international media sources cited on http://en.wikipedia .org/wiki/Yarmuk_Jamaat; and http://en.wikipedia.org/wiki/Shariat_Jamaat.

16. Enver Kisriev, personal communication, Makhachkala, about October 3, 1997. See also Kisriev 2003.

17. See Krivitsky 1997, 42. These identifications could have changed, however, the survey data goes back to the formative years of Islamist radical groups and still remains a significant indicator of the insurgency-relevant social preferences of local populations.

18. Its main correspondent on the region, an international prize-winning nonfiction author and journalist, Anna Politkovskaya, was assassinated in Moscow in late 2006 after preparing a series of investigative reports on Chechnya.

19. http://www.svobodanews.ru/content/transcript/2118149.html

20. http://president.e-dag.ru/aktualnye-temy/borba-s-terrorizmom-i-ehkstremiz mom/dibirov-a-n-terrorizm-kto-vinovat-i-chto-delat/ (June 6, 2007), accessed September 7, 2010.

21. The average amount was 5,900 rubles and the median was 4,200 rubles per capita in 2008 according to Rosstat 2010.

22. http://en.wikipedia.org/wiki/2005_Nalchik_raid

23. http://www.islam.ru/pressclub/smi/radik

24. Sufyan Zhemukhov, former editor of KBR's main newspaper, *Kabardino-Balkarskaia Pravda,* independently told the author about this practice by local police.

25. http://www.islam.ru/pressclub/smi/radik

26. Students of political theory and comparative politics such as Hanson (1996) have provided rigorous qualitative definitions of these motivations based on specific conceptualizations of time.

References

Biriukov, Andrei. 2010. Na odnogo zhitelia Kavkaza biudzhet tratit v shest' raz bol'she, chem na odnogo srednestatisticheskogo rossiianina [Budget spending per one resident of the Caucasus is six times higher than per one average Russian], *Marker,* August 26. Retrieved from http://www.marker.ru/news/717. Accessed August 30, 2010.

Borisov, T. 2005a, April 16. Prokuratura vzletela na vozdukh [Procuracy blown to smithereens]. *Rossiiskaia Gazeta,* no. 3748.

———. 2005b, June 28. Klandayk Clandike. *Rossiiskaia Gazeta* no. 3806.

Buhaug, Halvard, and Jan Ketil Rod 2006. Local determinants of African civil wars, 1970–2001. *Political Geography,* 25 (3).

Center for Strategic and International Studies. 2009. *Violence in the North Caucasus 2009: A Bloody Year* Washington, DC, 3–8. Retrieved from http://www.csis.org /hrs.

———. 2010. *Violence in the North Caucasus: Spring 2010: On the rise, again?* Washington, DC. Retrieved from http://www.csis.org/hrs

Central Intelligence Agency. 2010. *CIA world factbook.* Retrieved from http:// en.wikipedia.org/wiki/List_of_countries_by_GDP_percent28nominal percent29 _per_capita. Accessed September 2, 2010.

Collier, Paul, V. L. Elliott, Havard Hegre, Anke Hoeffler, Marta Reynal-Querol, and Nicholas Sambanis. 2003. *Breaking the conflict trap: Civil war and development policy.* Washington, DC: World Bank.

Denoeux, Guilain, and Lynn Carter. 2009. Guide to the drivers of violent extremism, United States Agency for International Development February 2009. Retrieved from http://www.usaid.gov/locations/sub-saharan_africa/publications /docs/guide_to_drivers_of_ve.pdf.

Fearon, James D., and David D. Laitin. 2003. Ethnicity, insurgency and civil war. *American Political Science Review,* 97: 75–90.

Green, Donald P., Dara Z. Strolovitch, and Janelle S. Wong. 1998. Defended neighborhoods, integration, and racially motivated crime. *American Journal of Sociology,* 104 (2): 372–403.

Hahn, Gordon M. 2007. *Russia's Islamic threat.* New Haven, CT: Yale University Press.

Hanson, Stephen E. 1996. *Time and revolution: Marxism and the design of Soviet institutions* Chapel Hill: North Carolina University Press.

———. 2010. *Post-Imperial democracies.* Cambridge: Cambridge University Press, 2010.

Kavkazskii Uzel. 2009. Posle provozglasheniia Umarovym Imarata Kavkaz obstanovka na Severnom Kavkaze obostrilas [After Umarov's proclamation of Imarat Kavkaz the situation in the North Caucasus has worsened], September 1. Retrieved from http://www.kavkaz-uzel.ru/articles/158739. Accessed September 1, 2010.

Kilcullen, David. 2008, April. Political maneuver in counterinsurgency: Road-building in Afghanistan. *Small Wars Journal,* 24.

King, Gary. 2007. *A solution to the ecological inference problem: Reconstructing individual behavior from aggregate data.* Princeton, NJ: Princeton University Press.

Kisriev, Enver. 2003. Why is there stability in Dagestan but not in Chechnya? In *Potentials of disorder,* edited by Jan Zurcher and Christoph Koehler, 103–126. Manchester: Manchester University Press.

Krivitsky, K.V. 1997. Religioznyi factor v etnopoliticheskoi situatsii na Severnom Kavkaze. [Religious factor in the ethnopolitical situation in the North Caucasus] In *Religiia i politika v sovremennoy Rossii* [Religion and politics in modern Russia] Rossiiskaia akademiia gosudarstvennoy sluzhbu [Russian Academy of Government Service]: Moscow, Russia.

Latynina, Yulia. 2009. Pochemu Rossiia teriaet Dagestan. Dagestanskie dnevniki [Why Russia is losing Dagestan? Dagestan diaries] *Novaya Gazeta,* April 22, 2009. Retrieved from http://uisrussia.msu.ru/docs/nov/2009/42/nov_2009_42_16.htm. Accessed September 1, 2010.

LeBillon, Philippe. 2008. Diamond Wars? Conflict diamonds and geographies of resource wars. *Annals, Association of American Geographers,* 98: 345–372.

Malashenko, Aleksey. 2008. *Islam dlia Rossii* [Islam for Russia] Moscow: Carnegie Center, 2008.

Markedonov, Sergey. 2007. Byla li opravdana reforma vlasti v Dagestane? [Was political reform in Dagestan justified?] *Zolotoy Lev* No. 111–112 April. Retrieved from http://www.zlev.ru/111/111_18.htm.

Novaya Gazeta. 2009. Investigation series.

RIA-Novosti. 2010. SKFO po-putinski: bor'ba s ideologicheskoi ekspansiey i 10 protsent rosta VVP [Southern Federal District Putin-style: Fighting ideological expansion and 10 percent GDP growth], July 7. Retrieved from http://www.rian.ru/economy/20100706/252645108.html. Accessed September 1, 2010

Rosbalt. 2010. Putin: Za 10 let biudzhet vlozhil v Severnyi Kavkaz 800 mlrd. rublei [Putin: In 10 years the budget allocated 800 billion rubles to the North Caucasus], July. Retrieved from http://www.rosbalt.ru/2010/07/06/751270.html. Accessed September 1, 2010.

Rosstat. 2009. *Regiony Rossii 2009,* online edition.

———. 2010. Baza dannykh pokazatelei munitsipal'nykh obrazovanii [Database of municipal entities' indicators] for the Republic of Kabardino-Balkaria in 2005–2009. Retrieved from http://www.gks.ru/dbscripts/munst/munst83/DBInet.cgi#1. Accessed September 3, 2010.

Sozayev-Guriev, Yegor. 2010. Zemlya—osnova napryazhennosti v Kabardino-Balkarii [Land is the source of instability in Kabardino-Balkaria]. Retrieved from http://www.infox.ru/authority/state/2010/03/05/balkarcyy___PND__8_m.phtml. Accessed September 10, 2010.

Smolyaninova, Ye. N. 2010. Biudzhetnaia sistema RF [Budget system of the Russian Federation] Sayt uchebno-metodicheskikh materialov VGUES [Site of educational and methodological materials of the Vladivostok State University of Economics and Service] 2010, 10–12. Retrieved from http://abc.vvsu.ru/Books/budget_sist_rf/page0010.asp; http://abc.vvsu.ru/Books/budget_sist_rf/page0011.asp; and http://abc.vvsu.ru/Books/budget_sist_rf/page0012.asp. Accessed September 8, 2010

Stern, Jessica. 2004. *Terror in the name of God: Why religious militants kill.* New York: HarperCollins. 281.

Varshney, Ashutosh. 2002. *Ethnic conflict and civic life: Hindus and Muslims in India*. New Haven, CT: Yale University Press.

VUZLIB Ekonomiko-pravovaya biblioteka [Economic and legal library]. 2010. Retrieved from http://www.vuzlib.net/beta3/html/1/14383/14408/. Accessed September 9, 2010.

Zhukov, Yuri. 2012. Roads and the diffusion of insurgent violence. *Political Geography*, 31 (3): 144–156.

CHAPTER 10

The Conflict-Development Nexus in Asia: Policy Approaches

William Ascher and Natalia Mirovitskaya

The motivation behind this effort is to sensitize policymakers, activists, and development practitioners to the challenges of conflict-sensitive development in Asia. An epicenter of new economic growth and the current destination of "shifting wealth," Asia faces major challenges associated with such rapid socioeconomic transformation: demographic shifts and new societal aspirations, new technologies, environmental stresses, and drastic changes in economic structure and societal institutions. Higher incomes and even better human development indicators—traditional goals of economic development—do not necessarily translate into more stable and peaceful societies, as was demonstrated by the Arab Spring, the 2010 unrest in Thailand, or the rapid growth of Naxalism in India. The sharp reversal of growth in Arab countries following the pro-democracy revolts is another reminder of the complexity of structural transformation. How the governments of Asian countries are able to handle the ongoing structural changes will eventually define whether Asia indeed becomes a solid center of economic gravity of the new millennium or its "boiling pot." Under these circumstances, considerations of conflict-sensitive development become critical for the region.

We must emphasize that these considerations are about the interaction of diverse contexts and dynamics, rather than a set of one-size-fits-all "best practices" or universal rules. The variety of patterns we have seen as development initiatives play out is a crucial reminder to eschew the fool's errand of searching for universal principles governing development and conflict, and instead to take into account the full range of potential risks and opportunities for each development strategy in each context. Of course, strategies also must be assessed for their potential to bring prosperity, with its promise to reduce resentment and desperation, or at least—as Al Ramiah and Ramasmay's assessment of Malaysia indicates—to deter aggressive actions when all are prospering. Yet even economically successful strategies can trigger violence if they are not formulated with regard to the sociopolitical conditions of affected groups.

If context is crucial, can any general lessons about the development-conflict nexus be useful? The answer is yes, because some patterns, revealed in both this volume's case studies and the overview chapters, have been common enough *to warrant consideration* in formulating development policies. Some patterns are straightforward: resentment against perceived economic discrimination stokes antagonism. Social exclusion and inability to voice dissent solidify perceptions of unjust treatment. Threats to livelihood can provoke highly aggressive actions. Clearly, governments must be concerned about large gaps between the wealthy and the poor, about restricted social mobility, and about circumstances of economic desperation triggering aggressive confrontations over jobs, natural resources, or other assets and opportunities. We have seen economic hardship leading to insurrections, provoking government reaction and high levels of violence in India, Pakistan, and Sri Lanka in South Asia; in Indonesia, the Philippines, and Thailand in Southeast Asia; and in Syria currently. It is not difficult to connect a group's perceived discrimination, exclusion, or asset expropriation to its animosity toward government, and in turn to clashes with officials (especially "uniforms") or other state workers (e.g., forest guards or dam builders).

Yet beyond the obvious is the point that development strategies also affect group-to-group relations. Connecting economic policy impacts to animosity toward other ethnic, religious, or linguistic groups is more complicated, and the fact that economic hardship attributed to government policy often spills over onto other groups regarded as allied with the government is often beyond the analytic framework of policymakers in the capital, far from the socioeconomic realities on the ground. Our cases reveal several patterns worth bearing in mind.

Contrary to the point that economic development and the emergence of a market economy mold narrower group identities into a larger national identity, this process is not guaranteed and is often painful. Moreover, some cases demonstrate that many development policies trigger the emergence of new economic actors, who assert claims to resources and opportunities previously enjoyed by others.

Similarly, many policies alter economic roles of people in particular groups, putting them in harm's way because these roles are viewed as exploitative. These role differentiations across groups also often reinforce stereotyping the entire group and therefore collective culpability. For example, agricultural promotion prompts transitions from subsistence to surplus-trading agriculture, creating middleman roles that are also widely viewed as exploitative, as is the case throughout Southeast Asia. Yet governments can mitigate resentments due to role differentiation. For example, Landa (1999) recommends government actions, ranging from education to contract enforcement, to facilitate non-Chinese Southeast Asians' entry into the merchant class. The rationale is that this would reduce the stereotyping of the Chinese by demonstrating that non-Chinese middlemen also charge prices and make profits that producers or consumers view as exploitive. Similarly, policies promoting natural resource extraction in India, Pakistan, Vietnam, and many other countries paint those exploiting the resources in a negative light. Yet governments can create mechanisms for broader sharing of resource revenues.

Also, disadvantaged groups are not necessarily simply passive. Preexisting social identifications may become prominent political identifications as groups are confronted with economic policies or conditions that their leaders (or aspiring leaders) believe can be improved by mobilizing around these identifications. Thus Ebru Erdem-Akcay's analysis explains the mobilization of Kurds in Turkey in contrast to Uzbekistan's Tajiks. Whereas Kurdish leaders committed to the struggle for independence have both economic grievances and the expectation of eventual success, the vacuum of development initiatives in Uzbekistan has limited the economic issues available to potential Tajik provocateurs to invoke. The affirmative action programs in India and Malaysia have kept caste or ethnic identifications highly prominent in contentious politics, undermining early postindependence hopes that these distinctions would fade away in the process of nation-building.

Our cases also demonstrate that, if development strategies promote population movements (whether voluntary or forced), the original residents feeling a threat from newcomers are unlikely to make fine distinctions as to who is responsible for encroachments, often reinforced by the government's tendency to side with the newcomers (Fearon and Laitin 2011, 199).

Another subjective aspect is that while rapid economic transformation (currently ongoing in Asia) sometimes amplifies income inequalities, the *perceptions* of income discrepancies among groups also shape beliefs of both exploitation and influence over government economic policies. Many Syrian Sunnis probably believe, incorrectly, that the bulk of Alawites have become wealthy through their influence on Bashar Assad's "Alawite regime."

These considerations speak to the relevance of specific contexts and subjectivities. Although much of the debate over development strategies is cast in broad, ideological terms, our cases demonstrate the crucial importance of the practical implementation of development strategies, and the role of auxiliary policies and institutions that flesh out how a strategy is enacted and how it is perceived. Edward Feasel's assessment of infrastructure-oriented foreign assistance highlights that it was implemented to the disadvantage of Vietnam's minorities; the assessments of the resettlement program in Central Sulawesi and regional development initiatives in northeast India did not plan for the newcomers to exceed the rights that the plans foresaw.

In this regard, the Malaysian success in maintaining peace despite explicit redistribution holds an important lesson: although the Chinese faced a gradual transfer of their national income share to the Malays, the level of certainty regarding the limits of the transfer was high. The New Economic Model circa 1970 satisfied the Malays; the Chinese and Indians did not feel sufficiently threatened (and were keenly aware of their own vulnerability) to go to the barricades. Contrasting this with the situations in Indonesia, northeast India, Balochistan, and many other cases, we see the potential for violence when development initiatives create open-ended uncertainty for particular groups, including losing important economic roles to other contenders, the possibility of catastrophic loss of property rights, losing majority status in the subnational jurisdiction, and so on. Although all development initiatives entail risk for all actors, the key is to bound the risk faced by stakeholders, particularly those who are not specifically targeted for benefits.

These lessons are especially important for the design of three categories of strategies that prove to be particularly challenging. First, the initiatives requiring the most restraint, planning, and institutional development are those involving population movements. Regional development and resettlement strategies bringing people of different ethnicity, religion, or language into proximity have strong but often unpredictable potential to trigger aggressive confrontations. The Ganguly-Oetken analysis indicts India's regional development strategy that attracts outsiders to relatively undeveloped areas where clashes over resources, political power, and culture have been acute, and where state authorities are widely regarded as corrupt and unwilling to respect the property rights of the indigenous *adivasi*. This has provided ample opportunity for provocateurs to co-opt many of these people into the Naxalite rebellion. Lorraine Aragon's narrative of conflicts in Central Sulawesi recounts parallel confrontations resulting from Indonesia's explicit resettlement strategy. The Balochistan insurrection reviewed in the Cheema chapter on Pakistan was aggravated by the government's stillborn megaproject at the Gwandar port, seen as a threat to the Baloch majority status in the area, paralleling the fears of Arabs in the Iranian area of Khuzistan. These examples demonstrate that the conflict-inducing potential of spatially unequal development is amplified when geographical disparities in public and private resources combine with ethnic identities and unequal access to socioeconomic opportunities. Such cases do not imply a blanket indictment against policies that induce population movements, but rather an admonition that policymakers must carefully assess the likelihood and nature of potential clashes, and try to build in mitigating measures. These may include direct or indirect policies to limit the number of people moving into an area, so as not to exceed its "socioeconomic carrying capacity." And before resettlement-inducing initiatives are launched, policymakers must consider the need for social and governance institutions to preempt potential conflict.

Second, the oscillation between liberalization reforms and retrenchments creates numerous opportunities for violent confrontations. The reimposition of price controls often sets up the need for drastic future price increases and leads to subsequent protests; the cycle of privatizations and nationalizations frequently incites anger over perceptions of unfair confiscation and corruption; the opponents of liberalization are mobilized more than once, as are the opponents of state intervention. We see, however, that the pain of economic policy reform can be ameliorated by social-safety-net programs that have been effective in Indonesia, Turkey, and other countries.

Third, several cases speak to the care required in the design of external assistance, which has the potential to mitigate or aggravate intergroup conflict, depending on both context and specific means. Mikhail Alexseev's demonstrates how the transfers from the central government of the Russian Federation aggravated violence in Dagestan by raising the stakes of locally oriented competition over resources, in contrast to the transfers to Kabardino-Balkaria, where insurgents had a lower priority with respect to the local communities. Edward Feasel argues that Japanese foreign assistance may have reduced overall conflict in Vietnam by raising the level of economic development, but its emphasis on infrastructure projects selected by the Kinh-dominated, authoritarian government increased income disparities and minorities' resentments. As noted in Chapter 2, even disaster assistance can fund insurrections, as in the case of Sri Lanka.

While these development strategies are particularly strongly associated with incidents of intergroup violence, other development policy initiatives have potential either to increase intergroup tension or to ensure stronger social cohesion. The design and implementation of labor market reforms, fiscal policies, education and social protection policies have substantial impact on societal stability.

In conclusion, it is clear that although development strategies can exacerbate conflict, thoughtful design of development initiatives and their implementation through a context-specific combination of policies and institutional changes can reduce the risks, so that long-term development can fulfill its potential to bring more Asian countries into the set of prosperous and peaceful nations.

References

Fearon, James, and David Laitin. 2011. Sons of the soil, migrants, and civil war. *World Development,* 39 (2): 199–211.

Landa, Janet. 1999. The law and bioeconomics of ethnic cooperation and conflict in plural societies of Southeast Asia: A theory of Chinese merchant success. *Journal of Bioeconomics,* 1: 269–284.

Index

Korea, South, 127; liberalization
reforms, 51
Krantikari Adivasi Mahila Sanghatan
(KAMS) (India), 107
Kurdish homeland, 83–84
Kurdish Regional Government
(Iraq), 243
Kurdistan Democratic Party (KDP)
(Turkey), 243
Kurdistan Workers' Party (PKK)
(Turkey), 241, 243, 251, 253
Kuwait, 5, 8, 9; Bidun stateless people,
8, 87; clan and tribal divisions,
9; dependence on oil and gas, 19;
economic growth, 69; education, 76;
foreign aid, 21; health care, 76, 79;
hydrocarbon exploitation, 86–87;
liberalization reforms, 52; natural
resource strategy, 19; state
enterprise, 57
Kyrgyzstan, 5, 7, 13; contested
borders, 14; economic growth,
69; education, 74, 76; healthcare,
76; income distribution, 17;
liberalization reforms, 52, 55;
natural resource strategy, 19;
state enterprise, 57

Labor, 316; British encouragement
of ethnic division, 189; Central
Sulawesi Poso region, 155; India,
121; Indonesia, 163; Malaysia, 184,
189, 192, 195, 197; market reforms
of, 319; North Caucasus (Russia),
282, 286; Pakistan, 139; Russia,
278; Tajik, 244; Turkey, 250, 251;
Vietnam, 209, 213, 231
"Labor therapy" (Vietnam), 48
Laitin, David D., 9, 85, 282, 284
Land development strategy, 317; land
rights issues, 177
Land Law (Vietnam), 211, 225
Land reform, 212; Turkey, 250;
Vietnam, 212
Landa, Janet, 317

Language policy, 63–64; and
colonialism, 64
Laos, 5; climate change, 27;
desertification, 28; economic
growth, 70; education and health
care, 76; income distribution,
17; liberalization reforms, 53;
transboundary cooperation, 84
Latin America, 7, 10, 260;
import-substitution industrialization,
248; withering of extreme leftist and
rightist movements, 9
Latynina, Yulia, 305
Le Duan, 210
Lebanon, 5, 8; economic growth, 69;
education, 74, 76; health care, 76,
79; income distribution, 17
Leekpai, Prime Minister Chuan, 83
Li, Tania Murray, 170, 175
Liberalization reform, 50–54, 57,
66–68, 319; Asia, 4; Bahrain, 54;
China, 54; disruption in Latin
America and Africa, 4; "Economic
Freedom" assessment, 54; foreign
direct investment (FDI), 54;
harmonization with other economies
within trade pacts, 55; Hong Kong,
54; India, 59, 73, 105; Indonesia,
54; Iran, 54; Japan, 54; Kuwait,
54; macroeconomic state sector
restructuring, 71; Malaysia, 54,
196; Industrial Coordination Act,
195; Northeast Asia, 54; Oman, 54;
Pakistan, 54; Pan-Arab Free Trade
Area, 55; Papua New Guinea, 54;
price controls, 319; privatization
and nationalization, 319; Qatar, 54;
Saudi Arabia, 54; Singapore, 54;
South Asia, 54; South Korea, 54;
Sri Lanka, 54; Syria, 54; Taiwan,
54; Thailand, 54; trade openness,
50, 54–55; Turkey, 246, 251; United
Arab Emirates (UAE), 54
Lindgren, Mathilda, 10
Liu, Morgan, 259